THE U.S.–JAPANESE ECONOMIC RELATIONSHIP: CAN IT BE IMPROVED?

Grateful acknowledgment is made to
The U.S.–Japan Foundation
whose grant made possible this research and
its publication as one of the first books in a series by
the School of International Politics, Economics and Business,
Aoyama Gakuin University

THE U.S.–JAPANESE ECONOMIC RELATIONSHIP: CAN IT BE IMPROVED?

Edited by
KICHIRO HAYASHI

NEW YORK UNIVERSITY PRESS
New York and London

Library of Congress Cataloging-in-Publication Data

The U.S.–Japanese economic relationship: can it be improved? / edited
    by Kichiro Hayashi.
        p.   cm.
    Bibliography: p.
    Includes index.
    ISBN 0-8147-3458-8
        1. United States—Foreign economic-relations—Japan.   2. Japan—
Foreign economic relations—United States.   3. United States—
Economic policy—1981–   4. Japan—Economic policy—1945–
I. Hayashi, Kichiro, 1936–   . II. Title: US–Japanese economic
relationship.
HF1456 . 5 . J3U5545   1989
337 . 73052—dc19   88-28722
                                                                        CIP

New York University Press books are Smyth-sewn and
printed on permanent and durable acid-free paper.

CONTENTS

v

PREFACE

The primary purpose of this book is to contribute to pragmatic knowledge for the reduction of existing as well as latent economic conflict between the United States and Japan, and for the better management of our interdependent economic systems. More specifically, we wish to produce practical implications and recommendations for business and public policy leaders through identification of similarities and differences in the behavior and process of formulating and implementing policy on three different levels in Japan and the United States. These levels are national, industrial, and corporate.

The problem—the original motivation behind our research endeavor—is that Japan and the United States have not sufficiently understood one another, particularly in the processes and behavior of objective formulation and implementation. There have been many actual instances in which a lack of mutual understanding aggravated the problem on various levels between the two countries. The result has almost always been further frustration characterized by the United States "pushing harder" and Japan "pulling wrong."

We have identified many sources of such a lack of understanding, misunderstanding, and miscommunication between the two countries on the national, industrial, and corporate levels. We feel we have explained comparatively to American businessmen and public administrators why Japan has developed her characteristic institutions and processes, how they are rational and efficient in the Japanese context, and how their malfunctions and problems are solved. This intention has been motivated by our observation of general dissatisfaction resulting from such "explanations" that take the form "Japanese phenomena occur because they are Japanese." Likewise, we have explained some American institutions and processes by contrasting them to the Japanese.

There is a considerable amount of literature relating to United States–Japan relations. However, little of it systematically considers the differences between the United States and Japan in the basic concepts involved in viewing micro- and macroeconomic systems such as the firm and the economy. For instance, not enough has been done about the comparative concept of *relations,* e.g., how the two countries differ in answer to such questions as what relations basically mean, which is central in analyzing United States–Japan relations. Let us look at it a bit more here.

It has been found in our research that the two countries' managers hold a common concept of the future—that the future is to be created. The difference is that U.S. managers think that the future is to be created essentially by individuals, while Japanese managers think that the future is to be created by mutual relations. Similar research I conducted in the mid-seventies revealed that the dominant Japanese view was that the future emerges out of the unknown, beyond our control or creation. This indicates that the Japanese view has changed drastically during recent years, coming somewhere near the U.S. view. However, the difference still is clear.

Attempts to create the future involve planning. Therefore, the concept of planning implies the concept of how the future is created. We have found that there is a great deal of difference in the concept of planning between the two countries. U.S. managers understand planning in terms of informational exchange and the formulation of the skeleton, and they wish to take part in the process, while Japanese managers deem planning to be the process of formulating a blueprint of collaboration and thus a detailed program of concerted action. Half of the Japanese managers surveyed, unlike their U.S. counterparts, were willing to leave the planning of the overall framework to top management.

The individualistic view does not favor detailed programs of action in fear that they might not allow individual freedom within the overall framework. For similar reasons, this orientation prefers participation in creating the overall framework. However, the Japanese concept that the future is shared through mutual collaboration presumes that the frame is created with all members of the organization taken into account, making it unnecessary for every member to participate in creating the framework.

Collaboration holds the possibility of conflict. The concept of conflict is almost diametrically opposite in the two countries. U.S. managers seem to feel that conflict is inevitable, and to some extent natural, and that when it does occur it is best to face it and argue for a fair solution. In contrast, Japanese managers feel that conflict is unnecessary and undesirable and that it is best to solve problems without contention or confrontation.

What differences in the concept of relations do these differences in the basic concepts create between the two countries? The U.S. view tends to conceive relations as competitive and instrumental and liable to produce zero-sum games (a gain for one party is a loss for the other), while the Japanese view sees relations as interdependent and liable to produce positive-sum games (it is possible for both parties to gain). In the latter view, relations are deemed conducive to mutual benefits, while in the former, there is no natural tendency to mutual benefit. As a result, Japanese tend to create organic organizations, while Americans tend to create mechanistic organizations.

A critical implication of the difference in the concept of relations is that the two countries diverge in their basic understanding of which international relations serve their common interests—for example, Japanese emphasize mutual spirit while Americans require mechanistic rules.

This difference in the concept of relations is more deep-rooted and significant than we might think. In fact, one of the findings from our collaborative research is that the major differences between the United States and Japan in the process of managing economic systems, from the firm level to the level of industrial policy for the economy, have roots in the different concepts of relations.

For instance, I compared intracorporate relations between American and Japanese managers among twenty-five Japanese subsidiaries in the United States and fifteen U.S. subsidiaries in Japan. Three out of every four American managers in the Japanese subsidiaries in the United States were frustrated, ultimately because of the conceptual differences that lie behind Japanese decision making and interpersonal relations. Aside from some subtle changes currently underway in Japan, the Japanese firm is communally owned by the employees, sociopsychologically speaking. This concept of the firm is connected with the concept of employee relations as the complementary and lasting relations of co-owners.

In contrast, U.S. executives deem intracorporate relations to be instrumental for attaining objectives centering on profit making and manage them as mechanistic relations based on job descriptions.

With these differences undiscussed but subconsciously rooted in their minds, Americans who work for a Japanese organization cannot truly become part of it. As a result, they cannot participate effectively in the decision-making process. This causes frustration. The main subject for discussion in mixed organizations should be how to hybridize their differing concepts of the firm, i.e., which is it, individuals or their mutual relations that make decisions to create the future. Such discussions should lead the way to finding a common ground or context on which Americans and Japanese can collaborate better.

Minato and Roehl compared Japanese interfirm relations with those of the United States within the context of the subcontracting structure. The Japanese subcontracting structure is pyramidal with the core assembler on top. Interfirm relations in Japanese subcontracting arrangements are long-term, interdependent, and non-contractual. In contrast, the issue for the assembler in the United States is "make or buy" parts needed for assembly. If you decide to buy them, the relations between suppliers and the assembler are short-term, contractual, and arm's-length. Clearly, different concepts of relations are working in the two countries.

In the analyses, Roehl emphasized economic analysis such as technology transfer costs in Japanese subcontracting, while Minato advocated the advantage of organic interfirm relations seen in the Japanese structure. This implied that the difference in the concept of relations existed not only in economic realities but also in the mind of the researchers.

Sakurai and Haley compared intragovernmental relations between the two countries, centering on the formative processes of industrial and economic policy. In Japan, critical in the processes of policy formation are long-lasting relations, both within the ministries and between the bureaucrats and industry, based on little personnel turnover, and the resultant effectiveness in information collection. In the United States, personalities in Congress play a major role, and since personnel turnover is always high, policy making fluctuates greatly. The underlying legal culture in Japan may be highlighted by an emphasis on societal harmony, while its counterpart in the United States may be the right of the individual. The premise behind the culture is complementary relations in Japan, while it is universal rights on the basis of zero-sum competition in the United States. Thus, the differences in the process of policy formation between the two countries cannot be separated from the differing concepts of relations.

Ishiyama and Pugel analyzed government-people relations, centering on the process of industrial-policy implementation. Americans believe in free enterprise, with competition at the base of all economic relations, and insist on small government. As a result, they are skeptical about industrial policy that is formulated largely by government. An associated thought is that industrial policy tends to be a source of inefficient allocation of resources and market-distorting.

In contrast, Japanese government, industry, and academia have collaborated to dream up the future Japanese industrial structure characterized by knowledge-intensive industries. Tax reform, considered as a form of industrial policy, has been characterized by confrontation-evading behavior in Japan, while it has created many scenes of outright confrontation in the United States, in the observation of Pugel.

Thus, the concept of relations has penetrated every level of economic systems, and its substantive differences baffled mutual understanding sometimes subtly and other times drastically. Having valued relations, Japan seeks for them seemingly almost at any cost. Without knowing of the "hidden" internal relations but knowing Japanese values through experience, the United States has tried to solve its problems with Japan by exerting pressure on Japan. This truncated version of United States–Japan relations is indicative of the superficial mutual understanding of the other country's concept of relations. In this book we are trying to suggest certain policies to overcome these problems.

Our methods of research have essentially involved crossbreeding within a binational eight-person team consisting of four pairs of Japanese and American researchers. Under a research grant from the United States–Japan Foundation and administrative support from Aoyama Gakuin University, the four pairs conducted independent, comparative research on their respective problem areas in the first year. In the second year, the eight researchers engaged in intrateam discussions of their findings in order to draw common implications and recommendations, as well as to develop a new paradigm of United States–Japan relations into the twenty-first century.

We looked for scientific explanations through comparative-pattern models of process and behavior. Explanation may be contrasted with description as telling us not merely what happens, but why particular occurrences develop. Our main approach has not been quantitatively analytical, but data handling has been numerical in part.

In the processes of information collection and analyses through interviews and questionnaires, we used some interactive methods between the Japanese and American researchers as well as between the researchers and selected practicing interviewees developed most recently under a genre of new paradigm research. This approach was made possible by our backgrounds and experiences.

For instance, Sakurai has constantly served on numerous committees and subcommittees of the Ministry of International Trade and Industry for seventeen years and has lived three years overseas. His partner, Haley, has been involved in research and other professional tasks in Japan six times for a total of six years, besides his experience in West Germany and Australia. Ishiyama had been an official in the Japanese Ministry of Finance for sixteen years and lived overseas for six years. His partner, Pugel, was Associate Director of the Center for Japanese Business and Economics at New York University, and invested a year in Japan to do this research in close association with Ishiyama. Minato was an Economist for the Osaka Prefectural Institute of Economic Research, primarily for small business, for eight years. Roehl is known as a Japanologist with much direct involvement in Japan. Both Roehl and Haley speak Japanese fluently. Hayashi worked for a Japan-based multinational firm for four years, and has been engaged in empirical research involving numerous multinationals in Japan and overseas for the last sixteen years, including fourteen years living overseas. Hayashi's American partner withdrew from the project because of insurmountable circumstances. Cole contributed his chapter in his place.

We are fully aware, however, that familiarity does not necessarily grant an explanation, particularly a scientific explanation, though it helps us to see one. Furthermore, a scientific explanation is not necessarily a semantic explanation: if the person across the cultural divide to whom an explanation is addressed in this type of pragmatic comparative research does not "get it," the meaning has not been conveyed. As you have seen, our binational team is well qualified in this respect.

ACKNOWLEDGMENT

We first wish to express our deepest gratitude to those managers of the Japanese and U.S. firms, government officials, and other professionals in Japan and the United States who kindly received us for interviews and shared their experiences with us; to those managers and professionals who kindly responded to our questionnaires; and to others who collaborated with us in one way or another—all of whom together made this book possible.

Our deepest appreciation must go also to the U.S.–Japan Foundation that funded the research and the conference which resulted in this book. Particularly, Chairman William D. Eberle, former President Richard W. Petree, and Program Director Ronald Aqua of the Foundation provided us with effective moral support, for which we are grateful.

Since this research project was conceived of as a school project of the School of International Politics, Economics and Business, Aoyama Gakuin University, the whole process consisted of a number of contributions of varied form from several parties in the university. Among others, we wish to thank Chancellor and former Dean Kinjiro Ohki, former President Masakazu Uzawa, and Dean Fumio Ito for their positive support of the project. We also wish to thank Professor Shigeru Ishikawa and Professor Shinkichi Eto, former Directors of the school's Institute of Research and the other members of the Institute's Steering Committees for their administrative contributions; and the members of the school's Research Advisory Committee for their academic comments.

We also wish to express our gratitude to Professor Keiichiro Nakagawa, current Director of the Institute of Research and Professor Hiroshi Ohta of the current Steering Committee who made painstaking preparations for the successful international conference in 1987 from which this book has been developed. We must note here that the conference would not have been as successful without the support by Keidanren (Federation of Economic Organizations).

Another note of deep appreciation must go to Professor Shizuo Saito for his unique contribution throughout this project. Administrative assistance was provided by Ms. Nanako Shinagawa and her colleagues, deserving gratitude. There are many others whose names have not been included to avoid having the list become too long. In a way, the book is an example of "Japanese management and teamwork, also participated in by Americans" when it works. My hearty thanks are in order.

Kichiro Hayashi, editor

CONTRIBUTORS

CHAPTER AUTHORS

Robert E. Cole is Professor of Sociology and Business Administration at the University of Michigan. He has been an active researcher on Japan for over twenty years focusing primarily on Japanese work organization. He recently completed a book on the diffusion of small group activities in Japan, Sweden, and the United States. His current research focuses on the use of Japanese approaches to quality improvement in the United States.

John O. Haley is Director of the Henry M. Jackson School of International Studies and Professor of Law and East Asian Studies at the University of Washington in Seattle. A graduate of Princeton (A.B. 1964), the Yale Law School (L.L.B. 1969) and the University of Washington (L.L.M. 1971), he has also studied in Japan (Kyoto 1971–1972) and the Federal Republic of Germany (Freiburg 1980–1981). He has published widely on Japan's legal and administrative process and has taught at the University of Washington since 1974, as well as in Japan (Kobe 1983), Australia (March 1980), and most recently at the Harvard Law School (1986–1987).

Kichiro Hayashi is Professor of International and Comparative Management, School of International Politics, Economics and Business, Aoyama Gakuin University. He received his B.A. from Kobe and his M.B.A. and Ph.D. in Business and Economics from Indiana University. He taught at California State (Hayward), McMaster (Canada), and UCLA. His current interest is model building in human decision making with a human communication perspective. He received the Ohira (late Prime Minister) Memorial Prize for his book, *Crosscultural Interface Management,* 1985.

Yoshihide Ishiyama is Director of Economic Research at IBM Japan (since 1986). He had his career in the Japanese Ministry of Finance for 1969–1983 during which period he served in the IMF for three years and completed his Ph.D. in economics at Stanford University. He was Associate Professor, Aoyama Gakuin University for 1983–1986. His books include *The New World Economic Affairs* (Japanese).

Tetsuo Minato is Professor of Business Systems at Aoyama Gakuin University. He was graduated from Osaka Prefectural University and served as Industrial Analyst, Institute of Economic Research, Osaka Prefecture for 1973–1981. His fields of interest are small business and subcontracting, particularly comparative analyses with reference to Asian countries. He is currently a Visiting Scholar at Yale University.

Thomas A. Pugel is Associate Professor of Economics and International Business at the Graduate School of Business Administration, New York University. He received his B.A. in economics from Michigan State University and his Ph.D. in economics from Harvard University. He was the co-editor of *Fragile Interdependence: Economic Issues in U.S.–Japanese Trade and Investment* (Lexington Books, 1986). He has served as research consultant for government, business, and international organizations.

Thomas Roehl is Assistant Professor of International Business at the Graduate School of Business Administration, University of Washington, Seattle. He teaches on the Japanese business system and is the director of the school's Pacific Rim Project. He received his M.A. in political science from the University of Oregon, his M.A. and Ph.D. in economics from the University of Washington. He has published many articles, including "Industrial Policy and Trade: Three Myths of Japan" in the *Journal of Contemporary Business.*

Masao Sakurai is Professor of Law, School of International Politics, Economics and Business, Aoyama Gakuin University. He received his L.L.B., B.A., and S.J.D. from Keio University. He is a member of the American Society of International Law, International Law Association, Japanese Association of International Law, and Japanese Association of Private International Law. He has gained wide experience in the legal problems of international joint ventures and private foreign investment through his consultation. His books include *Country Risk: How to Cope with International Business Risks* (Japanese).

COMMENTARY AUTHORS

Martin Bronfenbrenner is Professor of International Economics, Aoyama Gakuin University and Kenan Professor of Economics Emeritus, Duke University (since 1984). He received his B.A. from Washington University (St. Louis) and his Ph.D. from the University of Chicago. His fields of interest are macroeconomics and the Japanese economy. He taught at Duke (1971–1984), Kyoto (1980), Carnegie Mellon (1962–1971), Minnesota (1958–1962), Michigan State (1957–1958), and Wisconsin (1947–1957). His other experience includes U.S. Treasury and Federal Reserve System (1940–1947), tax economist, SCAP (Tokyo, 1949–1950). He is listed in *Who's Who in America,* in the World and in Economics, and in *American Men of Science.*

Kenneth D. Butler has been an international business consultant in Tokyo since 1977, specializing in cross-cultural interactions between foreign and Japanese firms. He received his Ph.D. from Harvard University and was an assistant professor at Yale University for 1963–1967. He directed the Inter-University Center for Japanese Studies in Tokyo (administered by Stanford University) for 1967–1977.

Mikio Kawamura is General Manager, Semiconductor Department, Mitsubishi Corporation, Tokyo Head Office. He was employed by Mitsubishi Corporation in 1958 upon his graduation from Hitotsubashi University with a B.A. in Economics. He has been stationed in New York (1964–1967), Montreal (1967–1971), and London (1981–1986). While in London, he was Chairman and CEO, Triland Metals Ltd., a ring-dealing company of London Metal Exchange. He is an Individual Subscriber, LME; Adviser, Arthur Andersen, Tokyo and Kankeiren on futures trading; and a Member of the British and Japanese Associations for Canadian Studies.

Robert McIlroy is Professor at the School of International Politics, Economics and Business, Aoyama Gakuin University (since 1988). He was graduated from Phillips Academy, Princeton University, and Harvard Law School and worked for a few years each as a lawyer, CPA, and diplomat before becoming a teacher. He is also an adjunct lecturer in the Faculty of Law of Sophia University (since 1983). He was Associate Professor in the Department of International Relations, the University of Tokyo for 1986–1988.

Yoshio Sato is Vice President, Keio University and Professor of Economics at its Faculty of Business and Commerce. He received his M.A. and Ph.D. in Economics at Keio University and was Visiting Research Fellow, University of California, Berkeley for 1966–1967. He is Director of the Japan Economic Policy Association; Secretary General, Japan Association for Small Business Studies; member, Study Commission of Industrial Structure—Small and Medium-sized Business under the Japan Society for the Promotion of Science. His books include *Small Industries in the Giant City Tokyo*.

John P. Stern is the Executive Director of the U.S. Electronics Industry Japan Office and the representative in Japan of the Office's three industry sponsors, the American Electronics Association, the Electronic Industries Association, and the Scientific Apparatus Makers Association. He was the first foreigner to be elected a director of a Japanese telecommunications standardization association, the Telecommunication Technology Committee. He is a graduate of Princeton University and of the Harvard Law School.

Masato Yashiro is President, Esso Sekiyu KK, Director, Toa Nenryo Kogyo KK; Member, Board of Directors, Keidanren; Executive Member, Board of Directors, Petroleum Association of Japan; and Member, Trilateral Commission (Japan, N. America, and Europe). He was graduated from the Law Department, Kyoto University and completed post-graduate courses in International Relations at Tokyo University in 1958.

1

ECONOMY AND CULTURE: THE CASE OF U.S.–JAPAN ECONOMIC RELATIONS

ROBERT E. COLE
University of Michigan

INTRODUCTION

THE BROAD issue addressed by this chapter—the social and cultural aspects of economic relations—was suggested by a remark made recently by Lester Thurow on the subject of United States–Japan relations. What needs to be done is very clear, Thurow argued. The problem is simply that the will to act is lacking on both sides. This raises some provocative questions, and the purpose of this chapter will be to focus on the extent to which this lack of will involves social, cultural and political factors.

Before tackling that issue, however, certain assumptions that underlie my perspective on the current crisis in United States–Japan economic relations need to be clarified.

First, both countries, by pursuing divergent fiscal policies, are responsible for the rapid buildup of trade and current-account surpluses in Japan and deficits in the United States. It follows, then, that policies aimed at correcting the situation must involve both countries. Yet politicians and commentators in both nations are all too quick to point fingers as they blame the other country's political and industrial leadership for the current crisis. If, in the first half of the 1980s, Japan had followed a more expansionary policy and the United States had followed a less expansionary one, the problems we are facing today would be far smaller. In other words, it is the divergence, or lack of complementarity, of U.S. and Japanese policies that have contributed greatly to the current state of affairs. That in turn suggests that there are ample opportunities for both countries to take actions now that would mitigate the problem.

Secondly, the framing of the current crisis in terms of trade barriers and trade imbalances is simply incorrect. The worsening of the U.S. current-account deficit cannot be attributed to increased trade barriers on the part of the Japanese. While the Japanese may have been slow in reducing these barriers, they have certainly dismantled more old ones than erected new ones since 1980. Moreover, we cannot expect an accelerated reduction of these barriers to make a major contribution toward eliminating the trade imbalance. While U.S. politicians in particular find it easy to address the issue in terms of trade barriers and to seek solutions in that area, they are bound to be disappointed.

Trade barriers are a perfectly legitimate area of concern for affected industries and government policy makers. However, there appears to be a consensus among economists of many different persuasions that steps taken to reduce such barriers will have only a modest impact on trade imbalances. A major implication of this view is that we must look at the macroeconomic problems of the U.S. budget deficit and the Japanese current-account surplus, along with the issue of trade barriers, in terms of the underlying social, cultural, and political conditions.

1. WHAT IS TO BE DONE?

But here we are in 1988 with the question Lenin asked in 1902: What is to be done? The answer seems pretty clear. While we debate the precise fashion in which to proceed, economists from a variety of different perspectives seem to agree on the overall outlines. We need macroeconomic policy coordination. The United States must get its federal budget under control, trimming the growth in both defense expenditures and entitlement programs while raising taxes (a strong case can be made for a tax on gasoline). Japan and West Germany must cut taxes and foster more growth. As Martin Feldstein argues, in the absence of such a package, we will see either large-scale protectionism or the collapse of the dollar in the next few years. And either (or both) of these outcomes will almost certainly push us into a worldwide recession.

If all this is so clear to the experts, why aren't the respective parties rushing to take action? "Lack of communication," comes back one response. At the recent seventh Shimoda Conference, the periodic Japan–United States Forum, both Japanese and American participants are quoted as saying that the current trade tensions mostly stem from poor communication and misunderstanding.[1] In a separate interview, Clyde Prestowitz, a former high-ranking U.S. Commerce Department official, argues that a communication gap arises from a failure to agree even on a mutually acceptable definition of the word *dumping*. Prestowitz further argues that each country lacks an understanding of the motivations behind the other's action, presumably both at the governmental level as well as at the firm level.[2] The Japanese are said not to have much understanding of why the Americans are so upset. Similarly, the Americans, according to Nathaniel Thayer of Johns Hopkins University, are oblivious to what Japan actually considers its greatest problem, yen appreciation.

1.1. Cultural Implications

Implicit in these perspectives is the understanding that cultural differences shape our respective views and obscure our perception of the other's. Prestowitz argues that if we could give the authority to make decisions in United States–Japan negotiations to Americans who really understood Japan and Japanese who really understood America, we could bridge this communications gap. It follows that once we were rid of this communications problem we could settle our economic problems because we would know who was causing them and what constraints on decisions were operating, etc. This notion that communications lies at the heart of our bilateral problems has adherents on both sides of the Pacific, but it seems to have a particularly strong hold in Japan.

There are serious problems with this perspective. One problem is that the reasoning is often fuzzy. The definition of dumping, to use the earlier example, is not necessarily a matter of cultural differences between Japan and the United States. It is an issue that has plagued GATT since its inception. Secondly, these arguments about communication typically lack empirical support. Once people get past their communications problems, they may find either a basis for common action or conflict based on divergent interest. There is no reason *a priori* to assume that the gateway to common interest lies just on the other side of the communications door. To be sure, in the very broad sense that Japan and the United States are increasingly interdependent economies with a strong national-security relationship, there is common interest in not doing anything to destroy that basic relationship. But this does not guarantee agreement on which policies best serve the mutual interest, let alone on whose interest is better served by any particular policy. Thus, Americans are no less understanding of the problems created by yen appreciation in Japan than the Japanese were of the problems created by dollar appreciation earlier in the decade. Just as we found out how many American firms could compete at 240 yen to the dollar, we are now finding out how many Japanese firms can compete at 125 yen to the dollar. This has nothing to do with understanding; it has to do with whose interests are being served! We sometimes choose "not to understand" our trading partner's problems when our interests are being served by continuing current arrangements.

Ideally, mutual understanding would eliminate the focus on peripheral issues and help the parties concentrate on the core issues. But the fact of the matter is that it is sometimes better to focus on peripheral issues when they can distract the parties from intractable core areas of dispute. I am not suggesting that the core areas are always intractable but only that increased communication is not the panacea it is often held up to be.

One other observation about communication is in order. We must not overlook internal communication problems in each nation, which are often more serious than the cross-national communication problems. That is to say, both American and Japanese economists have a great deal of difficulty agreeing among themselves, they have difficulty in communicating with their respective political leaders, and the politicians in both countries have a great deal of difficulty in communicating with their constituencies. We can see this clearly in the attempts to convince Americans to cut their budget deficit and to get Japan to stimulate its economy and restructure its industry. These are, after all, complicated and sensitive issues, and it is easier for American politicians, for example, to convince voters that they are doing something about the trade problem and unemployment by voting for a protectionist trade bill than by taking away an entitlement program. Similarly, Prime Minister Nakasone had been much better at promising Americans that he would implement the Maekawa Report recommendations for restructuring the Japanese economy toward internal growth industries than he had been at convincing the Japanese public and the bureaucracy of the urgent need for action on these programs.

1.2. Political Factors

This brings us to a second reason why our politicians are not rushing to enact the solutions that we say are so obvious. "Politics," it is often claimed, are at the root of the failure to coordinate macroeconomic policy. In Lester Thurow's analysis of the situation, he implied that it was a lack of *political* will that stood in the way of action. But what is political will? Some say that we have moved toward economic internationalization and interdependence, but our political system lags behind. Others say that it is the constraints on the domestic political process that limit our ability to coordinate economic action. But, again, it is not politics per se that these people are talking about. What often underlies references to politics are explanations of an economic, sociological, or psychological nature. The point here is not the earlier one regarding the much overused explanation of poor communication. It is not that politics is an overused explanation, but that political factors must be understood as intervening variables whose constituent elements are composed of economic interest and social and cultural factors.

When we speak of a lack of political will to take coordinated international action, we imply, first, that there is some sacrifice of short- and even long-term domestic goals associated with some political action. Sacrifices involve costs and the notion that there are value preferences among sections of the electorate that are not being met. These value preferences are rooted in social, cultural, and economic conditions. The U.S. Congress has trouble cutting back on entitlements because over time constituents have come to regard these entitlements as social rights. Likewise, it is difficult for congressional representatives, regardless of political coloration, to vote for slowdowns in the defense budget because of the powerful constituencies (including some unions) that have been built up around the country in support of these allocations. In addition, a strong anti-Soviet ideology animates the current American political leadership, making it even more difficult to cut military expenditures. President Reagan has trouble raising taxes because he and his closest advisors are prisoners of a market ideology that has deep cultural roots in American history. In no other industrial nation has there evolved such a celebration of Adam Smith and the market; surely this is not accidental. By contrast, while the Japanese have effectively used the market mechanism to promote economic growth, they have a very pragmatic view of the role of market. And these attitudes are not burdened with heavy ideological weight. Historically, the Japanese have not viewed government intervention as inevitably producing ineffective decisions, nor have they seen the market as a panacea. That very pragmatism has evolved as part of their cultural heritage.

1.3. Japanese Traditions

When we talk about necessary changes in Japanese macroeconomic policy, one of the factors to be reckoned with is Japan's high savings rate. There are a variety of factors responsible for this, and economic incentives are not trivial factors. Still, there can be little doubt that the historic drive to catch up with the West over the last hundred years, combined with some traditional ascetic traditions, has instilled a strong anti-consumption mentality among the Japanese. The Japanese still think of themselves as inhabiting a poor country. These facts must be faced in trying to raise consumption. But even policy makers have trouble accepting the need for such a change—after all, a high savings rate was one of the things that made the United States succeed in the past.

The reason these constraints on decision making are so potentially disruptive to international policy coordination has to do with who votes in whose elections. The Japanese don't vote in U.S. elections, and vice versa. To be sure, lobbyists for foreign countries provide a weak proxy for such direct participation, but nationalism insures that they do not overstep "proper boundaries." Social and cultural constraints arising from each country's unique historical experience restrict any international policy coordination that is seen by domestic constituencies as hostile to their interests. Legislators and government bureaucrats in both countries know how to horse-trade around conflicting domestic issues to arrive at policies minimally acceptable to their constituents. But little has been developed in the way of mechanisms that allow such compromise solutions at the international level.

The Japanese are, in fact, more inclined to recognize the importance of culture in explaining their behavior. In a world dominated as they see it by Western culture, they have often been tempted to interpret their circumstances in terms of their presumed cultural uniqueness. Thus, the Japanese often cite cultural differences as a justification for restricting Western imports (e.g., "We can't let Western rice be imported because rice culture is part of our national heritage."). The continuing strength and recent resurgence of *nihonjinron* literature (which concentrates on identifying and analyzing the shared set of core characteristics that make up Japanese society) underlies this perspective. Carried to its logical extreme, *nihonjinron* literature requires a fabrication of history that provides the basis of nationalism.

2. CULTURE AND HISTORY

It is precisely because culture has been used for such purposes in the past that many social scientists are inclined to dismiss it as an explanatory variable unless they are explicitly studying nationalism. Economists are extremely uneasy in the presence of the culture variable. They tend to see culture as reflecting irrational or nonrational behavior. And it can't easily be isolated and measured. Along with most behavioral scientists, economists tend to treat culture as a residual black box—to be invoked as an explanation only after all others have been exhausted. More significant is their fundamental error in believing that if they have shown behavior to be compatible with economic rationality, they have therefore disqualified culture as an explanation. This view probably comes from the norms of parsimony, which require that we look for the simplest explanation (in the sense of the fewest possible variables). In an over-determined model, where we do have more than one explanation, we naturally tend to favor those interpretations that fit within our own discipline. There are indeed economists who speak of culture as a consumption good or activity, but there are relatively few who have gone beyond that to explore its implications and systematically incorporate culture into their models.

Yet, if *culture is the sum total of historical experiences as reflected in current value preferences*—and that is the definition of culture we are using—then there is no reason why it should not sometimes be quite consistent with economic rationality. We need to rescue the concept of culture from the nationalists and see to it that we use it as a social science tool to understand the different value preferences that affect behavior. Social science use of the concept should not be limited to anthropologists researching primitive societies.

2.1. American Cultural Pluralism

If the Japanese have overemphasized culture as an explanation, Americans have tended to underestimate it. We may speculate that in a multi-ethnic immigrant nation, it was easier to evolve a sense of national identity based on social change and progress. Therefore, tradition came to be seen as a barrier to national success. In this context, we sometimes act as if we think only the Japanese have culture—an empirical impossibility given the definition of culture used here. Interestingly, even the Japanese have been inclined to dismiss culture as an explanation for American behavior. Clearly, the culture of pluralism was quite beyond Prime Minister Nakasone's ability to grasp. While the Japanese have been all too adept at understanding the cultural aspects of nineteenth-century Western imperialism, they have been less understanding of the concept of American culture. Upon learning that the Japanese were defending their restriction of foreign rice by claiming that rice was part of their culture, Senator Levin of Michigan was quoted as saying, "Well then automobiles are part of our culture." Many Japanese would probably dismiss such an equivalence. "How can one compare seventy years of history," they would say, "with 2,000 years of rice cultivation in Japan—where the very word for cooked rice is the word for meal?"

In the world of U.S. autoworkers in Michigan, however, one can also find a rich heritage and a distinctive world view that has been shaped by their employment. This includes the employees' very standard of living, their sense of work, their dreams and aspirations, the tradition of union democracy, and hard-won rights. Indeed, the very notion that the development of the American automobile industry made the car available for the mass market is at the core of the American way of life. These are not trivial matters. One craftsman I recently interviewed described how everything he had been taught about what constitutes a good union man over the last fifty years had been turned upside down when he was ordered to do the work of another craftsman. Now we may say that this is an inevitable consequence of international competition and that it is more efficient to have multiskilled workers. But it should certainly come as no surprise that when people find their lives and values turned upside down, they will resort to political action to try to protect themselves.

2.2. Culture as Ideology

One more word about rice is in order. Culture can often be used as a smokescreen to avoid opening markets. Here we are dealing with culture as ideology. The Japanese say that their rice tastes different from American rice and other varieties (and they make the same argument for meat). Who is going to be the arbiter of what constitutes domestic culture? Unless we are dealing with a simple smokescreen, the easy answer is to let the consumer decide how much more he or she is willing to pay for the luxury of eating domestic rice. In other words, if there really is a cultural element here, then we ought to be willing to eliminate any formal trade barriers, since culture will be more effective in restricting imports in any case. As indicated, however, I think culture is often used as a smokescreen by government bureaucrats far more concerned with protecting domestic constituencies than with the preservation of culture. How would the Japanese have felt if the U.S. government in the 1970s had said, "Americans have an innate cultural commitment to large cars, therefore we are going to impose high tariffs on small cars to preserve American culture"? It is not my intent to trivialize the rice issue. Self-sufficiency in food has a powerful hold in any nation. Nonetheless, agriculture does not deserve the unique status that it tends to receive in trade matters—at least not on any logical grounds.

3. CULTURE AND POLICY

It is clear that one of the more significant barriers to improving U.S. economic performance lies in the quality of the country's educational system. Yet this social infrastructure has been allowed to decay without strong action being taken. Why is this the case? Again, the economic rationale for action is clear but none has been forthcoming. Why aren't the hours of schooling being lengthened to accommodate the increased information needs of a modern industrial society? Why is nothing done to replace the loss of competent female teachers as this once captive high-quality labor force seeks new opportunities in the private sector? In short, why isn't the investment being made in better salaries to attract more competent teachers? And why do we allow a level of illiteracy that is more befitting a developing nation than a world leader? How is it that racism continues to stain our educational system, depriving the nation of much needed talent? My reason for listing these problems is to highlight the fact that the policy issues enumerated here are rooted in social and cultural factors. Thus, when we talk about coordinating economic policy, we need to have an understanding of the distinctive social and cultural factors that are operative. These factors reflect and provide the value preferences serving as constraints on our policy decision.

It is not my intention to suggest that culture is an irremovable obstacle to economic policy. Such a statement would be absurd, and, as already stated, culture can provide strong support for rational economic policy. When culture is an obstacle, however, it is important to note that not every cultural change represents a threat to the entire cultural system. Not long ago, a high-level U.S. official was quoted as saying that Japan's closed market would not be opened unless changes were made in the very cultural fabric of Japanese society. The Japanese were properly quite upset at the remark. Apart from its lack of diplomacy, it seemed to attack the entire way of life of the Japanese by suggesting that it is inappropriate in the light of Western culture. While we may sympathize with the Japanese reaction, we should also understand what underlay and motivated that comment.

3.1. The Import-Substitution Mentality

In my own research on market barriers to penetration of the Japanese auto market by foreign firms, I concluded that we were faced today with a cultural legacy of an "import-substitution mentality." That is to say, during the Japanese effort to catch up with Western industrialization, foreign advisors and products were tolerated only as long as it took to replace them with indigenous personnel and products. If a Western country had a product or process technology desired by the Japanese, reverse engineering, intelligence from the West, and the start-up of indigenous production were the preferred alternatives to imports (even if local production was more costly in the short run). If all else failed, joint ventures and licensing were short-term strategies adopted as necessary expedients to acquire and digest foreign technology.

These kinds of sentiments and motivations come through powerfully as one reads the company histories of Japanese auto manufacturers and suppliers. A powerful nationalism drove Japanese manufacturers to be as self-sufficient as possible. Toyota Motor Company, with its reluctance to even accept foreign licensing of technology, most typified this sentiment in its extreme form.

Throughout a good deal of the history of the Japanese auto industry, these sentiments were implicitly and often explicitly encouraged by government policy. When official controls ended with Japan's assumption of full status as a member of GATT, the import-substitution mentality was so strongly imbued among middle-level bureaucrats in the public and private sector that it continued to hold sway.

It will take time for a new generation of corporate decision makers to learn to look abroad for suppliers and for middle-level government bureaucrats not to instinctively sabotage efforts to make access to the Japanese market easier for foreign producers. Clearly, proper economic incentives can facilitate the process. What we now have is a cultural legacy that was economically rational in terms of Japanese efforts to industrialize rapidly. Under the changed circumstances resulting from Japan's rise to the role of economic leader and defender of free trade, the import-substitution mentality has become a liability. This cultural legacy must change, and it can change without tearing apart the entire cultural fabric of Japan. Contrary to the nationalist interpretation, culture is not an organic system—an integrated whole—that can be destroyed by any successful challenge to it. On the contrary, the historical evidence is that culture shows remarkably elastic properties in responding to historical challenges.

In that connection, there is one area where the cultural legacy of the import-substitution mentality potentially has an important continuing role to play. For part of that legacy involved the development of extremely close relationships between Japanese manufacturers and their suppliers. By extending extensive technological, managerial, and financial support to their suppliers, Japanese manufacturers tried to bring both manufacturers and suppliers up to worldwide competitive standards. This reservoir of skills and experiences can now be put to good use in minimizing emerging trade tensions. As Japanese manufacturers increasingly locate facilities in the United States, their initial tendency has been to minimize local content and to bring their Japanese suppliers with them when necessary. Unfortunately, this has the added effect of further aggravating trade tensions by further displacing local industry. If they had used their accumulated expertise in upgrading suppliers in approaching American suppliers, trade tensions would have eased. At the same time, they would be contributing to a technology transfer and rejuvenating American industry in the same way they had earlier benefited from the transfer of American technology to Japan.

4. CONCLUSION

We have seen here that culture and social conditions act on both the efforts to resolve the macroeconomic coordination of policy and the specific trade issues that face the two countries. Thus, understanding the root of United States—Japan economic relations requires an understanding not only of economic and political factors but also of social and cultural ones. Lack of communication is often used as a substitute for meaningful understanding of these relationships. Social scientists have a significant role in educating both policy makers and the general public on the nature of these relationships. But they too need a little more education about each other's contributions before they can achieve that goal.

NOTES

1. *Japan Economic Journal,* May 2, 1987.
2. *Japan Economic Journal,* April 25, 1987.

COMMENTARY
ON CHAPTER 1

MARTIN BRONFENBRENNER
Professor, Aoyama Gakuin University

INTRODUCTION

I WOULD like to address Professor Cole's chapter not as an international economist but as an economic historian, a political scientist, and a free-floating pessimist. (I have more experience in pessimism than in any specialized academic field.)

My "economic history" point I owe largely to Professor Komiya Ryūtarō of Tokyo University. It is a comparison between Japan's international economic position today and Great Britain's position a century ago. Victorian Britain, like contemporary Japan, was running large current-account surpluses with the rest of the world, and recycling these surpluses, on a commercial basis, to developing countries both in and out of the British Empire—including the United States. This state of affairs continued for two generations or more, ending in 1914. So obviously there is nothing *economically* improper or anomalous about large current-account surpluses. On the contrary, they are economically viable over a long term.

There are, however, at least four differences between Victorian Britain and contemporary Japan, which we should not forget entirely. One such difference is that Japan's rise to prominence has been faster than Britain's, and therefore more difficult for the rest of the world to adjust to. A second difference is that Victorian Britain was a free-trade country whose markets were open to "distress goods" from abroad; it was less "adversarial" in its trading practices than its successors have been. A third difference is that such pre-Victorian rivals as France, Holland, and Belgium, even when losing out to Britain in world-market competition, were much less seriously threatened by British competition in their home markets than is the United States today by the Japanese. And a fourth difference is that, in Britain itself, the jobs lost by free trade were mainly low-paid farm-labor jobs, while the jobs gained were largely better-paid industrial ones. The United States is much less fortunate in this respect; hence the call for "industrial policy."

Even allowing for these differences, I think that Professor Komiya's (and my) basic conclusion still holds: there is nothing economically pathological about the present Japanese-American economic "imbalance," and no reason why it cannot continue in its "unbalanced" state.

JAPAN-BASHING

Now I want to talk politics, or at least political economy. Here my main point, in which Professor Komiya is not implicated, is that "Japan-bashing" is a more dangerous pastime than most American politicians realize, and that a Japan-bashing trade bill, in particular, may have disastrous consequences for the Japanese-American alliance quite apart from its economic fallacies.

Let me be blunt: I think U.S. economic policy toward Japan is being set by fools, whose major foolishness is to forget that the Occupation ended thirty-five years ago, and that Japan can no longer be ordered about like a puppet government of an occupied country. Fortunately for the Americans, Soviet economic policy toward Japan seems also to have been set by fools—but Mr. Gorbachev is no fool. Moreover, he seems positively to enjoy fishing in such troubled waters as the Persian Gulf. The Japanese-American alliance is already a caldron of somewhat troubled waters, and promises to be a better target for Mr. Gorbachev next year or the year after than it is today.

The Political Consequences

Here is my pessimistic scenario of the situation that may face U.S.–Japanese political-economic relations even before the turn of the present decade.

The United States will pass, either over President Reagan's signature or over his veto, a Japan-bashing trade bill. Then the presidential campaign of 1988 will be waged largely on the issue of which candidates of which party have bashed or will bash the Japanese most effectively. Various Japanese export industries will have been badly hurt by all this bashing, while the American economy will not have gained much by bashing them—beyond higher inflation, a still-cheaper dollar, and/or higher money wages.

Then, rather than now, Mr. Gorbachev will make his move. He will offer the Japanese the return of one or more of the four islands off the coast of Hokkaido, and the demilitarization of those he proposes to retain. He will offer the Japanese bigger and better fishing rights in Soviet waters, reversing the trend of postwar Soviet fisheries policy. He will offer Japanese manufacturing and financial firms profitable export and lending roles in the economic development of Soviet Siberia and Central Asia. And what will he ask in return? Very little. Just nonalignment, meaning the dismantling of the entire American network of naval and air bases from Hokkaido to the Ryukyus, all of which the Japanese left has itself been demanding since 1952. And also perhaps, along with the unilateral Japanese denunciation of the 1960 Security Treaty, the reversal of Japan's recent increases in defense expenditures, something else the Japanese left has been demanding right along.

Will the Japanese yield to any such siren song? It depends when the song is sung, and which Japanese we are talking about.

Surely the Japanese would not yield today, but after Japan-bashing shifts into high gear, after the trade bill is passed, and after the 1988 elections? That may be quite another matter.

And surely Mr. Nakasone would say no to the siren song, but he will surely be out of power by the time we are talking about. As for his successors, whatever their party and factional affiliations, it seems seriously unlikely that their rapport with the American administration will equal the "Ron-Yasu" rapport of 1986. And furthermore, lest we forget, the new Japanese administration too may have come to power on a wave of "America-bashing" inspired by the earlier rampages of the American protectionists.

MY PESSIMISM

I am assuming that acceptance of this putative Gorbachev offer would be a dangerous risk if not a disaster for both America and Japan, but this is not the place to argue these fundamentals with my neutralist and pacifist friends in either country. And what frightens me particularly, as an American, is the way the American side has avoided concern with the possible consequences of Japan-bashing. This is a major error, leaving the alliance in much greater danger, both long term and short, than the authorities seem to realize. Which is more important, the labor vote in half a dozen key states in 1988 or the future of the Mutual Security Treaty?

To repeat: Mr. Gorbachev is no fool, he enjoys the fishing in troubled waters, the United States is engaged in troubling the waters of the Eastern Pacific and the Sea of Japan for his benefit, and an increasing element of Japanese opinion is ready to be inveigled by a "Gorbachev plan" along some such lines as I have outlined. Those are the grounds for my pessimism.

POSTSCRIPT—SPRING 1988

Professor Hayashi has permitted me the opportunity to make the above remarks less obsolete than they would otherwise be.

Mr. Nakasone is now out of power as I anticipated. His successor, Mr. Takeshita, has not transformed the Ron-Yasu relationship into a Ron-Noboru one, while Ron has himself turned lame duck and will retire from the scene after January 1989 at the latest. The Japan-bashing (and consumer-bashing) trade bill has passed Congress, but its fate remains uncertain. Mr. Gorbachev is biding his time about the "Northern Territories" issue—the four islands off Hokkaido. It may be significant that Mr. Muto, the Japanese Ambassador in Moscow, has made bold to stress the issue with him, and also that Japanese public opinion polls seem to be becoming less anti-Soviet and more anti-American. . . . And so my pessimism of 1986 remains in limbo, neither confirmed nor unconfirmed.

COMMENTARY
ON CHAPTER 1

MASAMOTO YASHIRO
President, Esso Sekiyu K.K.

INTRODUCTION

A S PROFESSOR Cole remarked in Chapter 1, some people attribute the trade conflict between Japan and the United States to their cultural differences. As a business executive, I notice a striking difference between Japanese and U.S. businesses in their perception of the fundamental objective of business corporations.

In the eyes of American management, the ultimate objective of business corporations in the United States is to maximize earnings. On the other hand, Japanese corporations usually have diverse objectives, and maximizing earnings is just one of them. Individual corporations conduct their business in accordance with the priority of those objectives, and, therefore, profit maximization may be relegated to an objective of secondary importance, if that is deemed necessary.

CORPORATE STANDARDS

Why are these approaches different? In the United States, firms are expected to earn a maximum return on shareholders' investment. Success or failure of corporate management generally is judged by whether the business corporation earns an adequate profit or not. However, Japanese business corporations do not necessarily attach the same degree of importance to the interests of their shareholders. Japanese management does not always give their shareholders the top seat. Frequently, financial institutions that lend money, suppliers of raw materials, distributors of their products, employees and various other related parties are considered to be of similar importance.

One hears in Japan that American top management tends to be excessively concerned with short-term profitability, and that less attention is given to long-term interest of the company. I do not agree with this. For a company like Exxon, involved in the energy business, it takes about eight to ten years to start commercial production of oil after exploration, discovery, and development of oil reserves. If commercial production is to continue for ten years, the total time span involved would be twenty years. The company must make a judgment on what kind of return the proposed investment would eventually generate in that twenty years. So not all American businesses are dictated to by short-term profitability considerations.

Historically, Japanese businesses have relied on outside capital, mainly borrowings from city banks. Their net-worth ratio is very low compared with their U.S. counterparts. In Japan, corporations take little account of a return on the current market value of their shares. Their yardstick for dividends is a certain ratio, say 10 percent, of par value (Y50, etc.) of a share, and an earnings-payout ratio is generally not used. Thus, the combination of the low level of net-worth ratio and the extremely low dividend level means that Japanese businesses need to earn a return only slightly better than their bank borrowing cost.

In the United States, business firms are expected to pay dividends, which should compare reasonably well with bank interest rates on *current market value of their shares*. Thus, U.S. businesses generally are required to earn an after-tax net profit of around 10 to 15 percent on their total capital employed versus a 5 to 7 percent return in Japan.

Among Japanese corporations, future growth and diversification into new fields are sometimes considered more important than good current performance. At present, the market value of shares in

Japan is about seventy times net profit per share, compared with around fifteen times in the United States and the United Kingdom. The principal reason why Japanese shareholders are satisfied with very low returns on their investment is their expectation of stock-price appreciation, since capital gains are rarely taxable.

The lower profit requirements of Japanese businesses enabled them in the past to make preinvestment in manufacturing facilities and permitted them to export at marginal cost. Such a strategy worked well when the world market was expanding. But today, production capacity worldwide is in surplus and Japan's export-oriented policy is creating conflicts in many markets.

INTERNATIONALIZATION

In such an environment, it is no longer possible for Japanese corporations to seek volume expansion of their businesses on the strength of low-profitability requirements. Rapid changes in the international environment compel Japanese businesses to place greater emphasis on high-value-added products. And in the process of shifting the emphasis from quantitative expansion to high-value-added products and higher unit profit Japanese business corporations will have to adjust their management philosophy to new realities.

We often talk about the "internationalization" of the Japanese economy. I personally believe that this "internationalization" should lead Japan to accept goods and investments from abroad, rather than advancing into foreign countries. Being a mono-ethic society, the Japanese can get along well among themselves but much less so with foreigners. This could be a serious impediment to the "internationalization" of Japan. What is urgently required of us is a good means of assimilating things and people from abroad into our society. I think that Japan, which is a homogeneous society, needs external stimuli to maintain Japan's vitality and energy in the new environment.

2

A COMPARATIVE ANALYSIS OF CROSS-CULTURAL-INTERFACE MANAGEMENT: THE UNITED STATES AND JAPAN

KICHIRO HAYASHI
Aoyama Gakuin University

INTRODUCTION

THE PRIMARY objective of this chapter is to propose three new pragmatic concepts to explain the nature of strategic problems in culturally mixed organizations and to suggest corporate policies to alleviate them. The three concepts are the concept of *cross-cultural-interface administration,* the concept of *hybridization* and the concept of *third culture.* The concept of third culture came from cultural anthropology and was first discussed by John Fayerweather (1969) in the field of international business. In this sense, it is not a new concept of my own coinage. The term was not taken up, however, by later researchers in international business. In this chapter, the concept is enlarged and substantiated.

Emphasis has not been placed upon integration with the existing literature in this research, primarily because little has been done on the subject. Part of the existing literature that comes closest to the subject matter is presented at the end.

Problems relating to cross-cultural interface within mixed organizations—e.g., foreign subsidiaries—are serious and profound for Japan-based multinationals. The single reason why little research has been done in this area in Japan is because Japan-based multinationals have a short history. Little has been done in the United

States because problems of U.S.-based multinationals are substantially different from those of Japan-based multinationals. These differences are fully illustrated by the case discussions in this chapter.

After the concepts are defined and explained, various cases are discussed to illustrate dimensions of the concepts. This approach has been taken because the concepts are new and would not be fully understood unless they are illustrated in action. Policy suggestions centering around these three concepts are presented toward the end of the chapter.

Cross-cultural interface refers to points of contact between cultures. Cross-cultural organization likewise refers to any organization that includes cross-cultural interface within it. This chapter deals with cross-cultural interface and its administrative attributes in the United States and Japan.

The underlying objective is to identify the sources of mutual misunderstanding and miscommunication between the two countries on the organizational level of analysis. From this we hope to develop practical policy implications to alleviate some of the future economic and cultural conflict between the two countries.

In this chapter, we take the foreign subsidiaries of some U.S. and Japanese firms as examples of cross-cultural organizations. This has three salient implications. First, it attempts to anticipate the problems of a future internationalized society, in that what is happening cross-culturally today in foreign subsidiaries is a precursor of the future. Second, it examines the major factors that will determine the future of the internationalization process of the firm; and third, it clarifies an important dimension of international control in the multinational enterprise. All of these pertain to the management of the internationalization processes of a country.

The nature and control of cross-cultural interface greatly depend upon the concept of the subsidiary and the strategy and objectives that the head office holds for the subsidiary in question. The strategy of the head office must be reflected in the pattern of the intraorganizational division of labor between local managers and parent-sent expatriate managers. This pattern in turn determines the administration of cross-cultural interface. It would not make much sense if the control of cross-cultural interface were examined while the pattern of local-expatriate division of labor was ignored.

Thus, we need to clarify the typology of the local-expatriate division of labor and compare the dominant types of U.S. subsidiaries with Japanese subsidiaries.

Here one comes to realize the importance of the role of third-culture facilitators who understand both cultures and span them as cross-cultural-interface administrators. Thus, we need to examine current situations regarding the role, behavior, attributes, problems, etc., of such intercultural spanners covered in this chapter.

All in all, the central problems of cross-cultural interface involve cross-cultural communication. Prior research revealed that the greatest problem pertains to intercultural differences in the basic assumptions, concepts, habits, etc., surrounding the decision-making processes. A questionnaire was distributed to shed some light on these problems, and the results are discussed in Chapter 9 of this book.

At the end of this chapter, a summary comparison is made between the United States and Japan in regard to the administration of cross-cultural interface in their respective subsidiaries, and the implications for international business and diplomacy.

1. CONCEPTUAL FRAMEWORK

1.1. The Concept of Cross-Cultural-Interface Administration

In general, cross-cultural interface emerges when two or more people belonging to different cultures come in contact with one another. It is where dissimilar concepts, thoughts, meanings, and values come into contact and collide. This could happen anywhere, in the organization or out of the organization, temporarily, periodically, or permanently.

Cross-cultural interface may be classified into functional and nonfunctional interface. Nonfunctional interface may be found in one's relations with neighbors and with colleagues outside of work, etc., where the nature of the contact is not specifically designed to achieve predetermined objectives. Functional interface involves collaborative relations for specific objectives. The cross-cultural interface within the foreign subsidiary we propose to examine in this chapter is an example of functional interface. Inter-governmental negotiations, and other interfaces in and out of international organizations, are also functional interfaces.

In a functional interface, cultural differences get mixed in while functional interworking goes on. As a result, unlike the case of neighborhood conversation or friendly contact, cultural differences are inflected, twisted and controlled for individual and organizational objectives in the functional interface. Thus, we need to consider functional attributes and arrangements as well as personality and culture.

The foreign subsidiary necessarily develops cross-cultural interface between parent-sent expatriates and local managers. This is true even with completely "nativized" subsidiaries, since the interface appears on the board level. In every subsidiary, cross-cultural interface becomes a crucial point of control when (1) the performance of the subsidiary is critical for the parent firm; (2) the strategic domain of the subsidiary business depends upon certain know-how of the parent firm; (3) the subsidiary is integrated with other subsidiaries in other countries under the control of the same parent firm; and (4) the head office is interested in controlling the subsidiary in more than numerical dimensions such as profit, sales, costs, etc. The head office's concept of the subsidiary in question is thus the first determinant of the cross-cultural interface of the subsidiary.

This concept is in turn reflected in the policy regarding the intraorganizational division of labor between parent-sent expatriates and local managers. The policy includes both the choice of typology and the direction of transition toward the future. This involves choosing between autonomous, heteronomous, and combinational types on the policy level and independent, dependent, and mixed types on the administrative level. These will be discussed in detail under a separate section. For the moment, it suffices to say that the pattern of intercultural division of labor is the second determinant of the interface.

The third determinant of the interface is the attitude of the subsidiary management toward management styles such as Japanization, localization or hybridization. For instance, you need to design and control the interface in a certain way to hybridize the style of subsidiary management.

Prior research by this author has identified the greatest problem of interface administration as the intercultural dissimilarities in the concepts and processes of decision making. More specifically, the problem entailed the differences in underlying assumptions, attributions and styles in searching for the true cause of a problem rather than apparent managerial institutions and systems. These present a major challenge to the task of the interface administrator. So far, however, very little has been done to provide these administrators with conceptual and practical guides. This chapter provides several useful case studies in this regard.

1.2. Typology of Expatriate-Local Division of Labor

Let us examine the types of intercultural organizational structure in the Japanese and American subsidiaries included in the study.

To begin with, we need to set the prototypical structure, as seen in Figure 2.1, divided into three hierarchical units of strategic, administrative, and operating units. The top strategic unit consists of three levels of president, senior (or executive) vice presidents and vice presidents who are responsible for policy and strategy. The middle administrative unit consists of vice presidents, directors, and managers who have functional responsibilities (such as sales, finance, personnel, etc.). Managers and those below constitute the operating unit. Thus, vice presidents and managers belong to two units, bridging the upper and lower units.

Figure 2.1 Prototypical Organization of the Foreign Subsidiary.

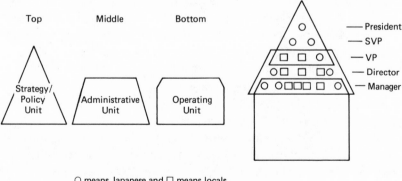

O means Japanese and ☐ means locals.
T = Technology, P = Production, S = Sales,
H = Human Resources Management, F = Finance

The head office can control, first, the strategy and policy of the foreign subsidiary through president, senior or executive vice presidents, and vice presidents of the subsidiary. Second, it can control functional administration through vice presidents, directors, and managers. Third, it can control local operations at the operating level. Note that reference is being made here to the human side of control where the targets of control are concept and corporate culture. The other side of control is through management methods and institutions. These are two sides of the same coin.

The first level of strategy and policy control falls into three categories. The autonomous type is one in which the top strategic unit is dominated by parent-sent expatriate executives. In the heteronomous type, dominance goes to local executives. When parent-sent expatriates and local executives are in balance, we call it the combinational type. The first of these is autonomous in the sense that the parent firm manages the local subsidiary autonomously through the executives it sends to the local scene. The second is heteronomous in that strategic management is left to the judgment and initiative of the local executives.

The second level of administrative control is also classified into three categories depending upon which culture is embodied by the dominant group of the administrative unit, mainly directors. Directors are the center of the unit with real functional responsibilities.

When directors are predominantly parent-sent expatriates in Japanese subsidiaries, it is very likely in the present stage of the game that the administrative orientation is Japanese. This is true even if the "directional policy" (illustrated in Figures 2.7 to 2.9) is to localize or hybridize administrative styles and methods, since the point of view must be that of the head office. This is called the independent type because, viewed from the parent firm, the administrative functions of the subsidiary are independent of local initiatives. For similar but reverse reasons, the dependent type is one in which local directors dominate the administrative unit. Japanese subsidiaries in the United States are seldom oriented to Japanize their administrative concepts and methods under the dependent type, but examples abound in ASEAN (Association of South-East Asian Nations).

If the division of labor falls somewhere between the independent and dependent types, we call it mixed. This type is based on the balance between Japanese and local concepts. The independent, dependent and mixed types represent the concepts and the resulting patterns of control that the parent company(ies) has for the subsidiary. The concept may be any one or a combination of the following:

- Nominal control: budget-centered control
- Limited managerial control: managerial freedom bestowed within a set of policies or norms
- Tight managerial control: all major actions under the direction of the parent firm

Many U.S. subsidiaries in Japan are of the dependent type under nominal control, while many Japanese subsidiaries in the United States are of the independent or mixed type under limited or tight managerial control.

The independent, dependent and mixed types for the administrative unit may be depicted in Figure 2.2.

Actual divisional structures show variations departing from but centering on these prototypes. One typical variation of the independent type is a transitional type from independent to mixed, which has many of the manager-level positions filled by locals whom they wish to train. We specifically call this variation the instructing type, or the limited independent type, shown by Figure 2.3. Even the Japanese subsidiaries of the independent type usually have the position of personnel manager filled by a local, and even those of the instructing type often have the positions of financial

Figure 2.2   Independent, Dependent, and Mixed Types.

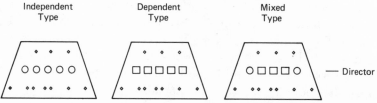

Only the administrative unit has been taken out of the prototypical organization (see Figure 2.1) to show the salient features.

Figure 2.3   Independent and Instructing Types.

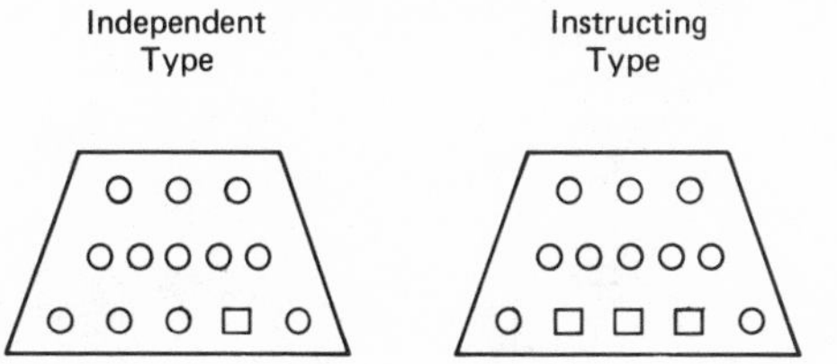

Independent
Type

Instructing
Type

and R&D managers filled by expatriates, which led us to draw the chart as shown.

A typical variation of the dependent type is one in which one or more of the functions dealing with manpower (personnel), money (finance and accounting), product (production and sales), and information (technology and legal matters) are left to locals. In fact, sales is frequently one of the functions left to locals. This variation is called the partially dependent type. A further variation of the partially dependent type is the learning type, in which parent-sent expatriates are placed in lower positions within the administrative unit so that they learn local administrative concepts under local administrative leadership. In actual cases, these expatriates frequently take charge of technology. These are depicted by Figure 2.4 and are contrasted with the mixed type.

1.3. The Concept of Hybridization

To administer a cross-cultural interface is to administer the process of internationalization. In the broad sense, internationalization refers to changes relating to the international transfer of resources such as products, capital, manpower, and/or information. Change involves not only the transfer itself but some preceding change that caused the transfer as well as any end result of the transfer.

Cross-cultural interface takes place at one of the critical points of intercultural contact—where negotiations and transactions are conducted for the international transfer of resources. The interface administrator is expected to facilitate cross-cultural communications for effective transfers of resources. While such transfers are effected, however, changes also take place within the systems involved in the interface transactions. These systems include

Figure 2.4   Partially Dependent and Dependent (Learning) Types.

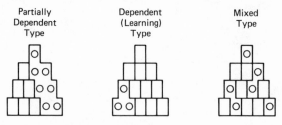

Partially Dependent Type   Dependent (Learning) Type   Mixed Type

○ represents personnel embodying Japanese culture,
while ☐ is personnel embodying local culture.

interface administrators and others who are regularly in touch with them, and all management systems directly or indirectly involved in the interface transactions.

The resulting changes necessarily influence the transactions that take place at the interface itself. For this reason, among others, it is important to control the resulting changes. Some of the most important changes are Japanization, Americanization, localization, hybridization, and internationalization (in the narrow sense).

Japanization (Americanization) means that the state of the system, human or managerial, approaches the average or typical state of its approximate counterpart in Japan (America). Likewise, localization means that system states approach the average or typical states of their approximate counterpart in the host country. The critical aspect of these changes is that Japanization and localization occur simultaneously and in the reverse direction, as depicted in Figure 2.5.

Since Japanization (Americanization) and localization are linked in reverse order on this axis, any change in one direction that does not involve simultaneous change in the other direction cannot be represented—e.g., universal states common to both countries. This representation can be used for any managerial concepts, systems, practices, and organizational cultures of Japan or the United States. When Japanese (American) firms go international, they move from right to left on the axis. Related to this movement—and a common source of problems—is the corollary counter-Japanization (counter-Americanization). It is important to understand how this process differs from the one represented by two separate axes, one being Japanization (Americanization) and the other localization.

Figure 2.5   Localization/Japanization of Human Beings.

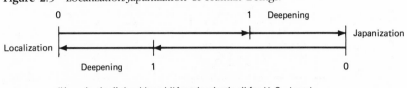

"Japanization" should read "Americanization" for U. S. -based
multinationals, i.e., U. S. firms located in Japan.

The Japanization (Americanization) and localization of persons
follows the same pattern, except that the speed of change, particularly the accompanying counter-change, varies among individuals.
These variations may be depicted by Figure 2.6.

In Figures 2.5 and 2.6, 1 denotes the level of localization (or
Japanization/Americanization) consistent with the average or typical
states of the host society in the eyes of local people. The area
beyond 1 represents the deepening process. Counter-deepening
movement within the deepening area is not objectively observable
because the behavior still satisfies the typical norm of the society.
For instance, being stationed for a short period in a foreign post
would not change a person's behavior substantially enough to be
noticed.

Mr. A in Figure 2.6 would not become localized without being
considerably counter-Japanized, relative to Mr. B and Mr. C. Mr. C
could become equipped with the two cultures relatively easily. The
same can be said about Japanization (Americanization) of foreigners and returnees when the directions are reversed. If Mr. A became
like Mr. C, the coordinates of his view would have changed. This
would allow Mr. A to move more freely between different cultural
points of view.

On the axis of Japanization, those persons located to the right of 1
are defined as the embodiment (representatives, composers) of
Japanese culture, while, similarly, persons located to the left of 1 on
the localization axis are the embodiment (representatives, composers) of local culture. Anyone simultaneously located to the right of 1
on the Japanization axis and to the left of 1 on the localization axis
would be within the "third culture space."

Hybridization represents a movement from a point combining
Japanization (Americanization) and localization on the Japanization
(Americanization)-localization axis to a third position on a new axis,

Figure 2.6 Difference Among Individuals in Ease of Enculturation.

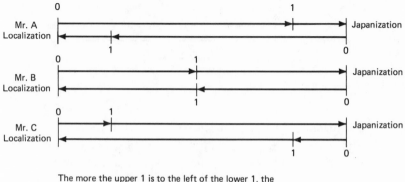

The more the upper 1 is to the left of the lower 1, the
greater the person's capacity to accommodate both cultures.

as depicted by Figure 2.7. It is important to note when Japanese
(American) systems are hybridized with local environment and the
results are innovative and functional in ways not seen in either the
base country or the host country. Here we are talking about outcome, not intention. Note that hybridization may accompany a low
or high level of localization. This point is generally misunderstood.

Suppose that the state of the managerial system of a firm is
denoted by s_1 in Figure 2.8, and those of another firm by s_2. Figure
2.8 shows that the first firm is behind the second firm in localization
and hybridization. The hybridization of the second firm also involves more local components than that of the first firm. It is
hypothesized that hybridization progresses in an L-curve, as drawn
in Figure 2.8, since it is considered a function of time and experience (moving from right to left).

Lastly, system states that represent any combination of the levels
of Japanization (Americanization), localization, and hybridization
may be chosen and used as international standards in foreign
subsidiaries in a number of host countries. In other words, we
define internationalization as the same system states prevailing in
many foreign constituents of the system. Note the important point
here that this third direction of change (after localization and
hybridization) may start at either an early or advanced point of
localization—and likewise at an early or advanced point of
hybridization.

For instance, a departure from an early point of localization may
be seen in the regular morning ceremony (exercises and a speech

Figure 2.7   Hybridization.

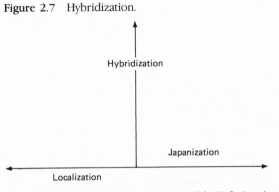

"Japanization" should read "Americanization" for U. S. -based
multinationals, i.e., U. S. firms located in Japan.

by management) of Matsushita Electric in many of its foreign factories, while the Contention System practiced by IBM in many of its
overseas subsidiaries represents a beginning from an advanced
point of hybridization. These are both cases of internationalization,
which is often confused with localization. Internationalization is
depicted by Figure 2.9.

1.4. The Concept of Third Culture

Usually we assume that the Japanese embody Japanese culture
and Americans American culture, but the Japanese can become
Americanized and Americans Japanized. If we denote the base-

Figure 2.8   Hybridization Curve.

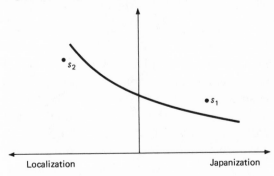

"Japanization" should read "Americanization" for U. S. -based
multinationals, i.e., U. S. firms located in Japan.

Figure 2.9 Internationalization.

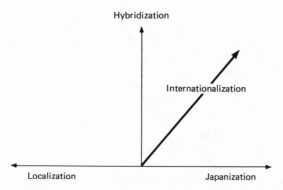

"Japanization" should read "Americanization" for U. S. -based
multinationals, i.e., U. S. firms in Japan.

country culture by *first culture* and the host-country culture by
second culture (without connoting first to be ahead of or above
second), we can define a person of *third culture* in terms of the
following necessary conditions.

1. He or she commands the languages of first and second cultures well enough to be able to translate linguistically from one
culture to the other.

2. He or she is acquainted with the knowledge, values, and
meanings of first and second cultures well enough to be able to
translate culturally from one culture to the other.

3. He or she is deemed a legitimate member of at least one of the
two relevant cultural groups. If he or she is recognized as a legitimate member of both groups, he or she is considered a person of
super third culture.

Third culture usually develops out of first or second culture.
Someone who embodies first (second) culture must be proficient
in the language, knowledge, values, and meanings of that culture as
well as hopefully possessing legitimate membership in it.

The three necessary conditions would facilitate the intercultural
spanning done by the cross-cultural-interface administrator. A wide
range of third-culture accomplishments, from a low to a high level
of achievement, is conceivable, with a resulting range of low to high
levels of intercultural spanning.

Figure 2.10   Third Culture or Third-Culture Persons.

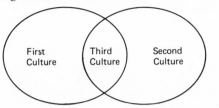

There are also other factors that influence intercultural spanning. For instance, the knowledge of and experience in specific business functions (such as marketing, accounting, finance, technology) is important, since intercultural spanning rarely takes place without involving these functions in international business.

2. CROSS-CULTURAL ORGANIZATIONAL STRUCTURE IN UNITED STATES AND JAPANESE OVERSEAS SUBSIDIARIES

Under our earlier conceptual framework, we defined and discussed the autonomous, heteronomous, and combinational types of top management, and the independent, dependent, and mixed types at the administrative level. Variations at the manager's level within the administrative unit further produced the instructing and partially dependent types, etc. In total, we count twenty-seven types, as depicted in Figure 2.11.

Of the twenty-five Japanese subsidiaries visited by the author in the United States and the fifteen U.S. subsidiaries in Japan, twenty-one offered enough data to develop the distribution shown in Figure 2.11. Salient tendencies to be detected in this distribution are as follows.

First, the dominant top-level type for Japanese subsidiaries in the United States is autonomous, followed, after a considerable distance, by combinational and heteronomous. This is about the same as U.S. subsidiaries in Japan, except that the autonomous type is slightly less dominant.

Second, the distributions of firms by type at the administrative level are also shown by Figure 2.11. Three things stand out here. First, the mixed type is a conspicuous attribute of Japanese sub-

Figure 2.11 Distribution of Organizational Typologies: Japan and the United States Compared

Typology	Top Level	Director Level	Manager Level	Middle Level	Number of Japanese Subs.	Number of U.S. Subs.
		◯ Ind.	◯	Independent	1	0
			◯□	Indep./Instruct.	0	1
			□	Instructing	0	1
	◯ Auton.	◯□Mix.	◯	Inconveivable	0	0
			◯□	Mixed	7	0
			□	Part. Dep.	3	2
		□ Dep.	◯	Inconceivable	0	0
			◯□	Dependent	3	0
			□	Dependent	2	2
		◯ Ind.	◯	Inconceivable	0	0
			◯□	Instructing	0	0
			□	Instructing	0	0
	◯□Comb.	◯□Mix.	◯	Inconceivable	0	0
			◯□	Mixed/★	2	1
			□	Mixed	0	0
		□ Dep.	◯	Inconceivable	0	0
			◯□	Dependent	2	0
			□	Dependent	0	1
		◯ Ind.	◯	Inconceivable	0	0
			◯□	Inconceivable	0	0
			□	Inconceivable	0	0
	□ Heter.	◯□Mix.	◯	Inconceivable	0	0
			◯□	Mixed/★	0	1
			□	Part. Dep.	0	0
		□ Dep.	◯	Inconceivable	0	0
			◯□	Dep./★	0	0
			□	Dependent	1	3
				Total	21	12

◯ = _Personnel embodying Japanese culture._
□ = _Personnel embodying local culture._
/★ = _Typologies that are expected to increase in the future._
Inconceivable = Highly unlikely, given the current conditions of Japanese firms.

sidiaries in the United States. Second, use of the dependent type represents a leading organizational approach in both U.S. and Japanese firms. Third, the instructing type, which is the dominant type for Japanese subsidiaries in ASEAN, is conspicuously lacking for Japanese subsidiaries in the United States.

The dominance of the mixed type at the administrative level for Japanese subsidiaries is also noteworthy for its deep roots in Japanese management. This point is discussed at length in my book *Cross-Cultural Interface Management* (1985) and will not be repeated here. In brief, however, it is related to a relatively low propensity to standardize, which in turn has to do with the importance attached to the dynamic balance of fairness and balance among stakeholders. To secure this balance, more people need to be at the local scene to administer the relations between employees, between the subsidiary and the head office, between the subsidiary and external business partners, etc.

3. CROSS-CULTURAL-INTERFACE CONTROL: CASE STUDIES

Unless complete nativization has been achieved in a foreign subsidiary, some kind of cross-cultural interface will emerge. And even under complete nativization, a cross-cultural interface will emerge on the board level, as mentioned earlier.

Different cultural groups come into contact at the interface in the process of administrative collaboration within the subsidiary. One of the greatest sources of problems in the operation of the interface is the difference in the concept of the firm. This tends to be a blind spot in that the different conceptions tend to be either overlooked or assumed away and are seldom taken up for open discussion.

In the United States, the firm is a frame in which the manager allocates and deploys resources (including human) to maximize profits for the owners of the firm. This means that employees are part of the means the manager uses to achieve the organizational objectives, so that the employees are not different from other management resources. The concept of the adversarial system on the basis of which U.S. labor unions operate stems from this U.S. concept of the firm.

In contrast, Japanese employees are seen as special resources who collectively own the firm—not legally, but at least behaviorally. Collective ownership, distinguished from individual ownership, does not allow what is owned to be divided up by individual owners. The only way to benefit from ownership is to receive a stream of benefits, pecuniary or nonpecuniary, by retaining one's status as an owner. This explains Japanese priorities on growth over profits.

This basic difference in the concept of the firm translates into numerous misunderstandings and problems for the effective control of the interface. From the U.S. employee's point of view, the firm should be a place for fair exchange between the total benefit package and what he/she can contribute to the organizational objective. The latter must be translated into the employee's job. Thus, the actual content of one's contribution (i.e., job description and qualifications) needs to be clear, and the pay needs to match the job. In contrast, a Japanese joins the firm as if he were an adopted son of the family. (This is changing a little among young people.) Japanese expatriates claim that Americans do not love their firm, while Americans claim that they live up to the standards of their profession and that love for the firm is not measured only by how many evenings one stayed in the office until 9 p.m. We will get down to more concrete examples in the following material.

3.1. The Lack of Third Culture

Gamma Electronics Corporation—a Japanese subsidiary in the United States of the combinational, mixed type

Mr. Peter Banting, Director of Administration of Gamma Electronics, a Japanese electronic machinery manufacturing subsidiary located on the east coast of the United States, told this author of his first-year experience with this Japanese firm.

In the U.S., the professional experience and academic background are specified as required qualifications for each job. In addition to such qualifications required of my job for this scale of firm, I have brought with me a good expertise for organizational development as an extra souvenir. It is common sense in the U.S. that one works hard in the first year to produce evidence for which the management is very glad to have hired the person.

In other words, an employee could develop a favorable prospect for the future with a firm if management came to believe that he/she contributed more than what was expected from the job and its matched pay.

> I worked very hard during the first several months to develop a plan for better organizational structure in addition to my daily work, and presented it to the boss, a Japanese VP in charge. I waited for a few weeks, but I got no response from him. I needed some initial feedback for me to pursue further, so I went to ask for his comment on my plan. But he did not give any clear indication. Meanwhile, I worked on some other ideas I had developed and presented them to him, but no response came back. I began to feel that what I was doing was perhaps not too meaningful for him or for the firm. After a few more ineffective interactions, I formed a feeling that my efforts were superfluous at best. Later, I concluded that I was being rejected and would not have a bright future with this firm.

He added that the turnover rate of the U.S. managers on the administrative level in this firm was more than 30 percent and that those who left the firm were competent, leaving behind those who did not seem to have opportunities elsewhere.

Mr. Kenji Yamaguchi, one of the top Japanese executives of the firm, commented, when interviewed separately,

> The first year is the time for settling in and adjustments. It never occurred to me that the first year was so critical in setting one's career with the firm. In fact, I would not know what to do with it if you brought an innovative plan without careful ground work to prepare the way to implement the innovation.

When this author told Mr. Banting what Mr. Yamaguchi said, he reacted by saying,

> They could have told me what to do then. The Japanese way is different and not easy for non-Japanese managers to understand, but almost no Japanese has a high propensity to explain. From a U.S. point of view, there are only two possible reasons why no explanation is provided. One is that the Japanese believe that the Americans would not be intelligent enough to understand them even if they tried to explain. The other is that the Japanese would not trust the Americans.

This is an example of a communication gap because the Japanese were not even aware of what needed to be explained.

Cross-cultural organizations are full of these communication gaps that help misunderstandings develop and expand before anyone is even aware. Particularly abundant are the communication gaps that originate in the different concepts of the firm. Foreign subsidiaries require intercultural spanners who detect these gaps quickly and bridge them through linguistic as well as cultural translations. The subsidiary in question lacked intercultural spanning, which resulted in very expensive losses of competent U.S. managers.

Oklahoma Chemicals Japan—a U.S. subsidiary in Japan of the heteronomous, dependent type

The most serious problem in Oklahoma Chemicals Japan was mutual distrust, which existed at all levels. A considerable degree of distrust existed even between the head office in the United States and its expatriate executives in Japan. Monthly financial statements as well as monthly reports from each department did not help. Several times a year the head office sent inspectors to Japan to examine the local activity in detail.

Such inspections were directed at every detail of expenditures. At one time, the financial statements had to be completely redone because a component that had just been delivered and was still unpaid was included as part of inventory.

Distrust was mutual. The president of the local subsidiary was fed up with being controlled by the ignorant head-office staff who had no experience in Japan. This frustration was manifest in the tendency of the president to hide from the head office any information not convenient for him. For instance, various excuses were made when frequent requests from the head office to translate the labor agreement into English were not complied with. Another frequent cover-up involved hiding the red ink of the bottom line in the fiscal statements by assessing the value of inventory higher than it actually was.

The firm in this example has been in operation in Japan for nearly two decades as a wholly owned manufacturing subsidiary with several hundred employees. In the top management team, the president and vice president for production are Americans and the vice president of sales and director of R&D are Japanese. The two American executive officers have been in Japan for nearly fifteen years. Everyone else is Japanese.

Poor interpersonal relations prevailed between the American executives and Japanese administrators. The president and vice president for production did not like discussions and preferred giving orders. Confronted with arguments from below, the president often said, "This is my order. Do it." Because most Japanese administrators did not speak English, the American executives spoke Japanese, but their command of the Japanese language was far below polite Japanese. This made things worse. Many Japanese could not but feel looked down upon.

Some Japanese managers also criticized the American executives for their "unusually high" expense accounts, "unusually long" Christmas and summer vacations, or not showing up on Saturdays—when everyone else was supposed to work. One of the common points of disagreement was pricing. The (American) vice president for production insisted on cost plus, while Japanese sales personnel insisted on competitive market prices.

Particularly critical was the antagonism between management and workers. In the business downturn some years ago, many employees did not have enough production work to do. In disappointment, they were cleaning and painting the factory, when the president appeared in an expensive new company car. He did not seem to notice their reproaching eyes. Then management told the union to fire ten workers. The union rejected it on the ground that management bonuses for that year were not at all reduced from the previous level. When management was about to enforce the decision, the union threatened a strike.

The president and vice president for production never wore the uniforms, caps, and shoes of the firm. They never ate at the canteen. When employees had informal parties, they solicited the Japanese executives and administrators for donations, but they never came to the American executives. In sum, there appeared to be no sharing of corporate culture.

The obvious fact to be noticed in this example is that there is simply no third culture within the firm to bridge the two cultural groups. The responsibility for this lies with management.

3.2. The Specialist for Cross-Cultural Interface

Beta Electronics, Inc.—a Japanese subsidiary in the
United States of the autonomous, mixed type

The local point of view.   Mr. Ronald McGee, Vice President of
Personnel, Beta Electronics, electronics manufacturers of a Japanese
parent with 1000 employees, commented,

> We understand well that the head office needs to control its subsidiaries,
> particularly P/L and capital equipment, but the authorities and responsibili-
> ties of the American executives currently are severely limited. We share a
> feeling that there is hardly any delegation of decision authority to Americans.
> Three or four American executives left the company out of frustration within
> the past year or two.

There apparently is some communication gap in the company.
According to Mr. McGee,

> Japanese firms have no concept of authority. For instance, our formal report-
> ing channels are 70 percent by function, so that our operational divisions
> report to the same divisions of the head office, etc. But in actuality, we do not
> really understand what is going on because informal contacts and exchange
> are so widespread all over the organization. Consensus-forming also takes so
> long that it is detrimental to our industry, where quick decisions are vital. We
> propose something to the head office, and three months later they respond.
> This is too late. They need to develop the concept of authority and de-
> termine how much can be decided locally.

Mr. Mark Johnson, Vice President of Sales, also said,

> The Japanese told me that I was the top person in sales, but they added in a
> hurry that I would need to discuss my decisions with those who would be
> influenced by my sales decisions. It turned out that I would not be able to
> decide pricing or anything by myself. In the U.S., someone four levels below
> me would be given the right to appeal on pricing to incease sales.

These remarks are related to the difference in the concept of
future between the United States and Japan as discussed in the last
chapter. Japanese believe the future is to be created together by
collaboration. The resulting difference in the concept of organization is also quite evident. These ideas apparently have not been
discussed in this firm.

Mr. McGee also made the following comment:

What is most frustrating is the difference in the concept of personnel. My firm has a notion that personnel is police audit. In my mind, personnel is administrative services. Also, they emphasize the concept of life-long employment, which is fine, if they also emphasize the concept of career path. But they do not.

We need more information before we decide whether Mr. McGee's claim is appropriate, but his comment certainly points to the problems of cross-cultural communication and to the likelihood that he is not a third-culture person. For the moment, let us go ahead to what a Japanese is trying to achieve in the same subsidiary.

No-win situations for intercultural spanners. Mr. Hiro Yagami, Director, Corporate Planning, is responsible for intercultural spanning within the subsidiary. He (j in Figure 2.12) reports to SVP Finance (Japanese, or J) and the President (J). Intercultural spanning refers to bridging between individuals or groups that belong to different cultures, or what is called in this chapter cross-cultural-interface administration. Cross-cultural communications critically influence this bridging. Let us examine the organizational structure of Beta Electronics before we look into Mr. Yagami's functions.

The current President was an SVP Operations/Technology prior to promotion, and he promoted VP Sales (A) to SVP and created a good rapport. The SVP Finance (J) had lived in the United States for

Figure 2.12 Organizational Structure.

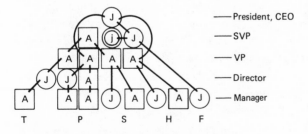

A = American, J = Japanese, T = Technology,
P = Production, S = Sales, H = Human Resources,
F = Finance, j = Mr. Hiro Yagami, the interface
spanning specialist.

eight years and was comparable to the divisional manager in the head office. These three executives comprise the management council and are also intercultural spanners between the head office and the subsidiary.

Given the organizational structure, the leadership and personality of the SVP Sales and Technology are critical in organizational efficiency and intercultural relationships, as he is in the highest position to interpret the Japanese top managers.

It takes great skills and experience of head-office executives to identify truly capable locals for promotion. Some critics have commented that many Americans who work for Japanese subsidiaries lack good perspective and depth of knowledge—merely reiterating what they read in the newspapers, and only worried about defending their jobs. One capable American who understood Beta's situation commented, "The Japanese were trying very hard to understand what some untalented Americans who I would fire insisted upon. The problem in Japanese subsidiaries is not Japanese management, as some insist, but the lack of balance in judgment on personnel." The American view presented by Mr. McGee could be interpreted as an expression of frustration against judgment on personnel.

Besides poor judgment, other reasons cited in interviews for the relative lack of first-rate local talent include the lack of attractive employment packages, the lack of an internal environment including the quality of subordinates for supporting first-rate talent. The lack of attractive packages stemmed from the objection of the head office to offering superior remuneration and benefits in one subsidiary relative to others. Equal reward to everyone is the consideration that always weighs heavily among head office priorities.

Under such circumstances, the role of Mr. Yagami demanded far more time and energy than what Tokyo imagined. Mr. Yagami defined his role as a cultural interrelator between the Japanese and American groups as follows. First, American managers tend to lack cross-divisional communications in daily operations, which his position is intended to promote. His skills are particularly important when the answer to some problem needs to be produced by cross-divisional cooperation. Mr. Yagami said, "I urge them to get together and discuss the matter, taking advantage of their attitude that they would do it if the Japanese said they should." Two things can be inferred from this statement. One is the operation of different ways of thinking between Americans and Japanese about how divisions should be interrelated in daily operations. The other is the possible disorientation among Americans evidenced by their passive attitude when told by the Japanese that they do something. The second observation is also reinforced by the frustrations expressed by some American executives during the interviews.

The second role that Mr. Yagami plays is that of a general consultant. He particularly spends a lot of time interpreting messages from Tokyo and sending messages to Tokyo in the name of American executives.

When he first started as an intercultural spanner, he arranged the internal flow of telexes so that copies of all the telexes from Tokyo were placed on his desk. He went around to the addressees of the telexes to explain their meanings—an unsolicited form of assistance. Mr. Yagami believed that he had then begun to be accepted by American executives as someone on their side, willing to represent them.

Mr. Yagami felt that he needed to demonstrate his position in front of the American executives. So he chose meetings with executives from the head office to object, expressing the local executives' point of view, to some proposals presented by the head office. This was risky for him, but he said he often truly felt like representing American views because he understood them much better than someone from Tokyo. This indicated that Mr. Yagami was close to occupying a third-culture position.

The relations between the head office and the subsidiary.   Established in the early 1980s, the subsidiary grew at an average annual rate of 40 percent, with current employment of over 1000 and annual sales of over half a billion dollars. This size was past the point at which the firm is manageable through personal contact. Therefore, it was necessary to develop good managerial and administrative systems. But even this need developed slowly and quietly, with the result that the local organization went through a transitional period of unfocused movement. The transitional period seemed extremely slow and inefficient to the head office, which was tempted to exclaim, "What on earth is our subsidiary doing?"

The administration of cross-cultural interface during such periods requires especially great energy, time, and creativity. The situation would look entangled and inefficient from a distance. And if it takes place during a trough in the local business cycle, it could be misconstrued as the surfacing of internal problems. Even if the situation were a result of head office strategy, the head office would say, "It is your job on the local scene to adjust the strategy to the local environment."

The typical reaction of Beta's head office in facing the difficulty of the subsidiary was to turn to a more autonomous and independent style by dispatching additional head office staff. The situation usually did not improve rapidly since the newly dispatched staff did not possess adequate skills to manage local managers. Under similar circumstances, some other firms went back to nativization again. The swing between the autonomous, independent style and the combinational, dependent style tended to become greater than necessary. The swing was usually triggered by management crisis. (Other examples are cited in my book, *Cross-Cultural Interface Management.*) Beta Electronics is an example of a firm that has gone back to the autonomous type after some management crisis. Success based on the autonomous type was hard to achieve when the ratio between expatriates and locals was 1:50.

The Japanese became isolated. They had a need to encourage themselves by themselves. However, the more cohesive they became, the clearer was the demarcation between the two cultural groups.

Mr. Yagami insisted that it would be extremely difficult to survive as an intercultural spanner in the organization. It was a no-win situation, he felt, because he was not well understood by the head office, nor was he really accepted by local managers. First, Mr. Yagami felt that an intercultural spanner needed someone high up in the head office hierarchy who would support him in difficult times when the firm swung between Japanization and localization. In the Japanization phase, the head office was bound to say that Mr. Yagami had lost his Japanese orientation and become a nuisance. Bear in mind, however, that intercultural spanning needs to be done by someone. This needs to be understood by the head office. Some local managers develop third culture, too. For instance, the head office used to say that something needed to be done about the U.S. SVP Sales, but apparently he has since become third cultural.

In sum, personnel policy in firms where cross-cultural-interface administration is critical should focus on nurturing good understanding of cross-cultural-interface control, as well as developing good intercultural spanners. The positions that are particularly relevant include those that stand between the head office and the local subsidiary, the top leaders of the local group, and cultural interrelators within the subsidiary. When the head office becomes fully aware of the concept involved, the problem is half solved. Most head offices at the moment still need to learn before they achieve full awareness.

Yam-Busco—a U.S. subsidiary in Japan of the combinational, dependent type

Yam-Busco was set up in Japan approximately fifteen years ago, with 50 percent owned by Busco, 40 percent by Yam and 10 percent by a *sogoshosha*. The president was from Yam and the executive vice president was from Busco, according to the joint-venture agreement. Besides Mr. Alan Tweet, Executive Vice President, there was only one other junior American in this joint venture with 1500 employees.

Mr. Tweet had been in Japan for eighteen months. He also had some prior foreign experience, being stationed in Hong Kong for six months, and had taught at a U.S. university some years ago. Mr. Tweet was about 55 years old, did not speak Japanese, but was well seasoned, with perfect international manners.

To my question of whether Busco had any corporate culture that he was supposedly in Japan to foster, Mr. Tweet replied that there was none, except as expressed in an attempt to nurture a marketing concept. Yam's approach seemed too intuitive for Busco, so that Busco had been trying to implement its marketing concept in Japan. Mr. Tweet felt, however, that the Japanese environment was too different from that of the United States for the American concept to be applied without modifications.

"It's not that we do not have any corporate culture in the U.S.," Mr. Tweet said, "because we say 'he is our kind of a man' or 'he just does not fit in well,' but that we do not use corporate culture as a tool to control foreign subsidiaries. The U.S. firm typically is financially centralized, but otherwise managerially decentralized."

This author had an extensive discussion with Mr. Tweet on the difference between the concept of the firm in the United States and Japan. Mr. Tweet agreed that the salient difference existing in the concept of the firm created a major source of trouble for U.S. firms in Japan. It was possible to obtain agreement from the U.S. head office on how to handle local personnel problems, but impossible to obtain understanding on the problems from the head office.

Mr. Tweet obviously occupied the position of cultural interrelator. He was both the representative of the U.S. parent firm and the executive vice president of the local subsidiary. This meant he could not avoid acting as a watchdog of the U.S. parent, which automatically degraded the level of trust given to him by local managers. He said,

> I avoid problems associated with the "watchdog" concept, first, through stating my position clearly on major issues, and, second, through optimizing the proportion between going for the head office standpoint and for the local viewpoint. I could not go clearly against the head office policy, but on the matters to which I could not agree, I would mention it from the beginning. I would not shift my positions after some head office staff arrived.

Mr. Tweet was one of the top ten executives in the parent company and knew every one of the others well. This meant he was well trusted by his head office—an important and necessary condition for acting as a cultural interrelator.

3.3. Third Cultural Group as Cultural Interrelators

Alpha Electronics America, Inc.—a Japanese subsidiary in the United States of the autonomous, mixed type

As depicted by Figure 2.13, Mr. Takashi Mino is the Chief Executive Officer (CEO) and Mr. William Nelson is the Chief Operating Officer (COO). This means that President Mino is responsible for strategy and long-run decisions, while the American vice president is in charge of daily operations. Excepting the financial manager (J), the rest of the managerial crew—including production, technology, materials, and quality control—are directly under Mr. Nelson. Alpha is 100 percent owned by Alpha KK in Tokyo and produces TV sets in the United States. Since sales are all taken care of by another subsidiary called Alpha America, Alpha Electronics has no sales department.

The critical role of cultural interrelators at Alpha is played by the two-man team of president and vice president, who together form a third-culture spanner. The communications between the two correspond to self-reflexivity, or the thinking of an individual acting as a single intercultural facilitator. The two individuals use their respective experiences to solve common problems together. Between the two, double translations are carried out. One dimension of this is the translation of strategy into daily operations. The other dimension is the mapping from Japanese meaning to U.S. meaning. This is dependent in part upon mutual understanding of personality based on their experience over the past several years.

Let us examine this process in detail. The president is expected to carry out strategy and policy decisions formulated jointly between the head office and the subsidiary. For this, he communicates with the head office. After receiving final suggestions from the head office, the president chooses whether to accept and implement them or to reject them.

In this decision, Mr. Mino expects the participation of Mr. Nelson. To effectively participate, Mr. Nelson needs to understand the advice of the head office. Having been in the United States for more than six years, Mr. Mino is able to explain the head office indications to Mr. Nelson in English to a reasonable extent. For his part, having been with Alpha for six years, Mr. Nelson is able to ask the proper questions to make out the deficiencies in Mr. Mino's explanation. Through their experience, the two have accumulated knowledge

Figure 2.13 Organization of Alpha Electronics.

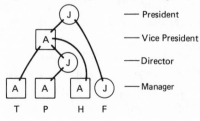

— President

— Vice President

— Director

— Manager

T = Technology, P = Production, H = Personnel,
F = Finance.

about one another as well as their differing national management styles.

When a strategy is finally accepted, Mr. Nelson issues operating orders to his subordinates completely in U.S. terms. Mr. Mino leaves the implementation of these operational orders to Mr. Nelson, the COO. Thus, the third-culture team formed by the two executive officers internalizes head office input and transforms it functionally and culturally into the American output.

Mr. Mino commented, "Transformation should include careful selection of balls the head office throws us. U.S. subordinates would begin to distrust us if we threw every ball we received from the head office to them. We need to re-create our own balls before we throw them to our U.S. managers." The same process was necessary when head office staff visited the local scene. Mr. Mino and Mr. Nelson argued against head office staff to educate them about the local sentiments and viewpoints, as well as to demonstrate their position in front of U.S. managers. The team was able to develop the local viewpoint and leadership by articulating the position of cultural interrelator.

Under these circumstances, it mattered a great deal that the head office trusted the local leaders. When the level of trust deteriorated, the local standpoint would not carry persuasive power. The level of trust depended upon the following: (1) profits and other performance, (2) regularity of expected reports, (3) consideration shown to the key officers in the head office, (4) persuasive communications, and (5) maturity of the subsidiary. Consideration (3) refers to personal communications with certain influential executives who may or may not be directly in charge of the subsidiary. This was important because there were indefinite, unstated authorities distributed widely in the Japanese organizations.

As the level of trust went up, the head office became more tolerant toward local autonomy. As autonomy went up, leadership became easier and more effective.

The watchdog concept is not limited to Japanese subsidiaries. Subsidiaries of any multinationals have problems relating to watchdogs. Unbiased information does not flow to "watchdogs" for obvious reasons. When the president is deemed a watchdog, his leadership suffers. As Mr. Mino said,

The only way to prove that I am not a watchdog is to "bite" head office executives in front of American managers when they are here, though it is funny to claim that one is not a watchdog by biting. I need to support the local sentiments and argue from the local point of view. But this is risky for me. If I repeated this too often, the head office would decide that I was put overseas too long. This would influence my career. Unless you are linked with some influential executive in the head office, the risk would become too high.

From this comment, it is clear that the control of cross-cultural interface would require skills well beyond those of watchdogs.

It is a well-known fact in theories of international business that the interests of the head office and those of the subsidiary differ. But the realities of the differences are not yet well known. Particularly when the performance of the subsidiary is not climbing, the head office's understanding of the subsidiary quickly deteriorates. As a result, the cross-cultural interface within the subsidiary is influenced by the dynamics of relationships between the head office and the subsidiary.

Be it a local national or an expatriate from the head office, the intercultural spanner must follow a "schizophrenic" path. It is not too much to say that how well this is understood by the head office determines the performance of the subsidiary. What prevents the schizophrenic path from leading into a real disease is the development of a common vision to be shared by both cultural groups. This common vision is necessary in our present age of economic conflict.

The Tokyo branch of Big Apple Bank of New York— a U.S. branch in Japan of the autonomous, partially dependent type

The branch was set up in Tokyo in 1972. The U.S. parent is a big bank with 22,000 employees, while the Japanese branch has only one hundred employees, including ten Americans and ten contract helpers. The level of activity at the Japanese branch makes it one of the ten largest foreign banks in Japan. Mr. Jack Wilson, Senior Vice President and CEO in the branch, is 37 years old and holds a B.A. from Harvard and an MBA from Rutgers. At the time of this interview, he had been in Japan nine months without prior experience overseas.

The primary function of the head of a bank branch is usually to develop and maintain good accounts in Japan. In contrast, the head of Big Apple Bank of New York, Japan, is exclusively engaged in internal administration. Mr. Wilson said that dealing with customers was the job of the head of Corporate Division, and that the primary function of the branch head was to manage the heads of the divisions, including Corporate Division. In other words, he was the primary intercultural spanner in the organization. Mr. Wilson has been taking strong leadership in playing this role to date, with assistance from the Japanese senior vice president, Mr. Yoshio Bando. Mr. Wilson said:

> Communication problems at this branch are no greater than in U.S. branches. I listen hard, communicate my mind clearly, and keep my words and actions consistent. I treat Americans and Japanese equally, but it takes longer to communicate with the Japanese. Americans are quick in reaction. I try to be a leader not a commander in chief.

And then he said,

> I understand that in Japan it is undesirable to create confrontation. These days, however, my Japanese staff has come to speak rather freely. I believe I have a good sense of smell. Since I was born and raised as the first of five brothers in a small town in Ohio, I developed a habit of keeping balance in a large family and doing things as a team. When I was young, I used to like team sports.

These words are indicative of his style in administering the cross-cultural interface in the branch.

Regarding decision-making styles, Mr. Wilson said,

> It is not a question of choosing between Japanese consensus and U.S.-style individual decision making. It is a question of classifying what needs to be decided by individual executives in charge. The criteria used in classifying the decisions are qualitative and unstated except those in accounting and operational control. For instance, the decision to extend credit is partly decided by consensus, but there are policies on these decisions. Individual executives may or may not know the qualitative standards. It depends upon their experience and personality.

It was clear that not everything was standardized and stated by policies. It appeared to be within the authority of the executive vice president to formulate policy decisions.

The branch was controlled by the head office through strategic and financial objectives. The primary responsibility of Mr. Wilson was to steer trust and franchise businesses toward the strategic objectives with a view to achieving financial objectives. Mr. Wilson said,

> When environmental change is rapid, business would suffer if the standard of judgment were quarter-to-quarter profits. I would never tell my managers to make more profits. My leadership is focused on setting objectives and standards through internalizing financial objectives and standards agreed upon with the head office.

He went further by saying,

> Some instructions are in order in the area of dealing with the client. I have accepted the Japanese concept of relations. Relations are important both on an individual basis and on an organizational basis. It is up to an individual's brain to judge what relations would lead to long-term profitability.

Thus, Mr. Wilson accepted the Japanese concept of relations but quickly indicated a U.S. orientation by linking it with profitability.

The personnel policy adopted by Mr. Wilson also indicates his brilliant administration of cross-cultural interface. He said,

> The New York Yankees scouted superstars for high performance, while Baltimore developed good team work without superstars. The former approach produced super performance when things went well, but it also had quite a bit of ups and downs. The latter, however, showed a steady growth. I am following the latter pattern here in Japan by selecting the U.S. methods that fit the Japanese environment best.

Mr. Wilson invites his Japanese managers to lunch once every quarter to listen to their thoughts and desires, but he takes care that his U.S. vice presidents are not threatened by his direct contact with their Japanese subordinates. This too helps create special opportunities for cross-cultural communications.

Mr. Bando, Senior Vice President and assistant to successive American CEOs, including Mr. Wilson, had worked for a leading Japanese city bank for thirty years before he joined the Big Apple Bank of New York in 1971. In discussing the differences between the Japanese and U.S. banks, Mr. Bando pointed out that Japanese banks sought size and relations, while U.S. banks looked for a maximum return on investment. For instance, Japanese bankers would exult at the prospect of winning Toyota or Nippon Steel as accounts. U.S. bankers would use profit contribution as the only criterion for good accounts. U.S. banks place some priority on business expansion at an early stage after entry into a foreign market, but after inception the sole standard in evaluating managers becomes net contribution to profits. Mr. Bando explained the reasons behind the difference as follows: in the United States, unlike Japan, the financial institution has not been the center of industry, and its relative position has been low—with 200 to 300 banks going bankrupt every year. The Japanese market particularly has been a difficult one for U.S. banks.

The second salient attribute in the U.S. bank was individualism in work, according to Mr. Bando. You need not worry about this director or that director as long as you did your own work solidly. Work was distributed to each individual and one did not often work in direct collaboration.

Profit orientation also has a bearing on the choice of accounts, the way to create relations, interpersonal relations in the bank, personnel policy, the concept of the firm, etc. Japanese employees apparently accepted the profit orientation in their own ways.

Mr. Bando said that he told the U.S. CEO that human resources were a company's life line, and that he should develop personnel policy to treat employees well. The CEO apparently agreed to this. However, good treatment of employees was conceived of in different ways. The U.S. way did not include the weak or the slow, but was inclined toward teaming up with the strong. This approach would not work in Japan where job hopping would be difficult.

Interesting here, however, was that Mr. Bando did not jump to join the Big Apple Bank of New York. He was sent by his previous city bank to help the American bank upon request by the latter. This would be unusual in another country. The Japanese bank sought the relationship, hoping that it might help somehow in the future. Mr. Bando quickly found, however, that such relations would not produce any substantial fruit.

3.4. Configuration of Young Cultural Interrelators

Theta Machinery Corporation—a Japanese subsidiary of the autonomous, dependent type

When the current president replaced the previous one at Theta Machinery in 1981, he decided to swing from localization to Japanization. This was not due to a policy change in the head office, but to the personality of the president.

In enforcing the basic change of policy, however, management needed to decide how cross-cultural interface was to be administered. It felt that Toyota's so-called *Yajirobe* ("balancing toy") structure, in which every important U.S. line manager was assisted by a Japanese coordinator, would not work for Theta. Management also reviewed Nissan's autonomous type and felt that if applied directly to Theta, implementation by force would harm the existing flows of information. The upshot was to place several young, capable interrelators here and there without any design or structure.

Mr. Yoji Sakuma, one of the several interrelators, was sent two years ago by the Personnel Department at headquarters, where he had had ten years of experience after graduation from the University of Tokyo. He found his role very unclear and difficult to enact. American managers looked at him dubiously. Without knowing any better, Mr. Sakuma called himself Bill and made excuses to walk around between Japanese and American managers at every possible occasion.

Mr. Sakuma needed to create work by himself since no work was given him. His role was to solve problems that would occur as a result of the policy change. No problems immediately struck him, so he walked around to identify and define problems. He quickly found that what he needed most was the trust of the American managers. He needed to create rapport with the American managers so that they would come to him for consultation.

He started to represent the American managers in negotiations with management. Initially, the American managers thought of him as nothing more than an interpreter. Slowly, however, they began to think that they would be able to negotiate better with pig-headed top management in collaboration with interrelators. If their proposals were not accepted by management the first time, they felt that they should get together again with interrelators to develop better strategy. Thus, local managers began to include interrelators as comrades in arms, so to speak. Japanese top managers had strange feelings about interrelators because of the way they had been acting, wondering if they were working for them or for the Americans.

Mr. Sakuma said,

> I sometimes felt it might be the Japanese management that needed coordination by us interrelators. For instance, the Japanese management would feel awkward or a little disgraced to accept something proposed by low-ranking Americans. So we step in and adjust the relations. American top managers probably would not need such adjustments. We do such adjustments very, very delicately, with utmost care. We should not become leaders.

Job-description-oriented American managers were puzzled about whether they should report to the interrelators, send copies to them, or do nothing. The result was that copies were filed with them.

TIM Japan—a U.S. subsidiary in Japan of the combinational, mixed type

TIM landed in Japan in the 1930s and began to manufacture cards in the prewar years. Capital in excess of Y100 billion is 100 percent owned by its U.S. parent. Annual sales have surpassed Y800 billion, with before-tax profits of Y100 billion, accounting for 5 percent of parent sales and profits respectively. Japanese employment is about 17,000.

TIM's pursuit of a universal identity and good corporate citizenry in every host country is characterized by respect for the individual, top customer services, perfection of quality, excellent management, integrity for stockholders, fair transactions, and contribution to society. TIM also operates on the principle of leaving local management to local nationals.

In Japan, too, nativization—including the company president—had progressed until 1983, when some Americanization of top-management positions was revived, including marketing. Delegation of authorities in general, however, has been underway as the local market has become more complex. For instance, pricing and sales through rental were previously uniform throughout the world, but they have come to differ by locale, with variations in forms of sale, including lease and cash sales.

The administrative unit, or middle management, consists entirely of Japanese, except for temporary development personnel from the United States—usually about 200 on two-year assignment. These Americans work *for* TIM Japan, not *with* TIM Japan in that TIM Japan purchases their services from the head office.

Besides TIM Japan, there is the Regional Headquarters of TIM separately in Japan, called TIMRH. TIMRH has a staff of 450, of which 300 are Americans or third-country nationals and 150 are Japanese who have been transferred from TIM Japan. TIMRH controls Asian operations including Japan. TIMRH monitors Japanese operations mainly by business targets. It was explained to the author that TIMRH would not say much as long as business targets were well met by TIM Japan. But there seems to be a lot more behind the scenes, as revealed by the following description.

The planning process starts with a letter sent by the TIM Corporation chairman to the president of TIMRH, who in turn sends a similar letter to the president of TIM Japan. The letter contains next year's budget, including sales and profits. Meanwhile, the bottom-up process begins within TIM Japan with the aggregated numbers reaching the president, who adjusts the top-down and bottom-up budgets. TIM Corporation reserves authority to replace the top executives of TIM Japan. What needs to be done and how things are to be organized are left to the executives of TIM Japan.

Long-range planning of TIM Japan comprises two-year operating cycles and five-year investment cycles. In these annual planning processes, most central is the so-called Contention System, which has been modified and developed over time at TIM Japan.

The Contention System was designed to create contention between line and staff to optimize a balance among imagination, feasibility, and purposiveness. Imaginative ideas are encouraged, but they need to be feasible in face of realities. Direction also matters a great deal for TIM to achieve certain objectives. Each of these needs to be encouraged as well as balanced. After the mutual contention, management decides which way to go.

It generally works as follows. Line managers usually come up with ideas. They are placed in planning perspective and then reviewed by staff. They set ample time for the process. After sufficient dispute and mutual rebuttal, the higher-ranking manager decides which way to go. The staff that takes part in the review depends upon the idea to be reviewed, but it usually is the staff that is part of the line of people who came up with the idea. This means that the participating staff is line staff, not corporate staff. Among corporate staff only legal staff may possibly participate in the contention. Line staff is great in number at TIM. They give advice to both the line manager and his line subordinates.

The Contention System was basically an American idea. Since its inception ten years ago, this checks-and-balances system has been modified and developed into a corporate culture. The System is similar to Japanese *Ringi,* or consensus-seeking processes, in that both are collective decision processes, but in spirit the two are poles apart. The Japanese processes are in a way aimed at avoiding contention partly, if not totally, through administrative cooperation or assistance. Such under-the-table negotiations are totally against the spirit of the Contention System. Negotiations, if any, would center on how the original idea is premodified by incorporating ideas of the staff before the actual contention. These negotiations are Japanese modifications extended from consensus-seeking behavior. This comes from the Japanese reality that interpersonal conflict, once created, tends to last a very long time. Some American managers in TIM Japan commented that Japanese managers took contention personally and carried a chip on their shoulders for a long time.

From the line point of view, one has a feeling of not being trusted. Even when one has full confidence in what one is trying to do, one needs to answer all the questions. Also, these meetings are carried out in English, and some individuals have a great deal of frustration at not being able to express themselves fully.

Some say that this is a democratic system in which everyone can say something. Staff can say whatever they want to say, but the final responsibility for implementation lies with the line. Sometimes, good ideas well conceived by line managers may end up being bent unrealistically by staff. In spite of these frustrations and difficulties, an organizational value has emerged that regards such frustrations as immature. The question of trust also has been redefined as confidence or credibility to be accumulated little by little over time.

Whether the system works or not hinges on the judgment of the final decision-making line manager. As his role increases, his scope of responsibility goes up, requiring him to develop greater knowledge. Staff reviewers also would be more effective if they had line experience. For this reason, rotation between line and staff is frequent at TIM. The organization is also fluid, with the result that ranks and positions are fluid as well. These fluidities make up the incentives for better performance in the Contention System. Thus, the System checks and balances personnel as well as ideas.

4. CONCLUSION

The current strong yen—having appreciated enough to shake the existing structure of international trade—is quickening the pace of Japan's direct foreign investment. Any further expansion in this area will no doubt place additional burdens upon the administration of cross-cultural interface among Japanese investors.

If cross-cultural interface in fact breaks down under these circumstances, it is not hard to imagine the current trade conflict developing into an investment conflict of some sort, e.g., court cases. What would Japanese firms do, confronted with such a conflict? Would they strengthen their administration of cross-cultural interface, adhering to the Japanese concept of the firm? Or would they shift into nominal control of foreign subsidiaries through nativization and the consequent localization of management? And there is always the possibility of some new current arising that would override these problems entirely—but this we must set aside for the moment.

U.S. multinationals, on the other hand, face the opposite problem. They need to assess carefully the consequences of further expansion as multinationals under the current regime of nominal control. Under the current truncated administration of cross-cultural interface, for instance, the head office would not receive and process local information adequately. It is mostly the Japanese executives who go to the United States, for example, to discuss strategy and policy, and not the other way around. The Americans are not the ones accumulating experience on the local scene.

With these existing and latent problems in mind, we can begin to summarize some of the findings, inferences, insights, and conjectures that emerged from this research. We start with some summative comparisons of the U.S. and Japanese administration of cross-cultural interface, and then discuss some of their practical implications.

4.1. Differences Between U.S. and Japanese Subsidiaries in Their Administration of Cross-Cultural Interface

First, the different concepts of the firm between the two countries have resulted in substantially different objectives set by managers in administering their respective cross-cultural interfaces. As a consequence, the basic nature of cross-cultural administration differs significantly between the two country's subsidiaries.

The author recognizes that debates over the concept of the firm have a long history—from the neoclassical Walrasian view emphasizing the maximum consumer satisfaction to the view that the firm is managed to maximize the market value of stocks to theories of managerialism (including the theory of managerial technocracy by such authors as E. M. Dodd, A. Berle, Jr. and G. Means) and the theory of maximizing managers' utilities put forth by W. Baumol and O. Williamson to the most recent theory of management as enforcing a balance among stockholders, managers, and employees, and the theory of labor participation in management.

However, the concept of the firm, as understood by practicing U.S. executives in my interviews in the United States, indicates that management is entrusted by the owners to manage the firm with a view to maximizing profit accruable to the owners through the efficient allocation of resources. Management is rewarded in proportion to their performance in achieving these profit objectives. In this process, employees are considered part of the available management resources. The employees are also rewarded in proportion to their contributions.

In Japan, the concept of the firm is not much different legally, but it makes a world of difference managerially. That is, the firm is considered to be collectively owned by employees, including managers. Collective ownership is a figurative term here, in the sense that what is collectively owned is not divisible among collective owners, since they do not legally possess anything. If one hundred people own, in the usual sense, assets worth $100, each one has a dollar's worth of assets. But if one hundred people "collectively own" assets worth $100, each one does not possess one dollar's worth of assets. Instead, the one hundred people may share any benefits stemming from the assets, but no one can leave the group with his own portion of these assets. But since the firm is still legally possessed by the shareholders, its ownership is in effect split between shareholders and employees. This conception of the firm has made takeover bids very unpopular in Japan. It is considered ungodly to take over a group of employees—an inseparable part of the firm.

Maximizing the owners' profit, though not simple, is at least a more straightforward proposition than maximizing the total benefits to be shared by the employees. The former goal also makes the nature of cross-cultural-interface administration more straightforward. Complications stemming from intraorganizational cross-cultural communications are to be sorted out almost strictly in terms of their contribution to profit.

While the common denominator is clearly profit in this case, in the Japanese conception, the denominator is not always "common" among the "collective owners" who may have different priorities at different times. The situation almost always demands the search for a balance and the willingness to trade benefits over time. This process was depicted in some of the case studies presented above.

A second strong conclusion the author reached during interviews with American managers working for Japanese subsidiaries in the United States and Japanese managers working for American subsidiaries in Japan was that the latter appeared less frustrated than the former. Three quarters of the American managers seemed frustrated. They were frustrated because they were not able to

understand what was really going on and/or to participate effectively in the decision processes through cross-cultural interface. There
were not many such "stray sheep" among the Japanese managers
working for American subsidiaries in Japan.

Did these Japanese then appear exactly the same as the ones in
Japanese corporations? The answer is definitely no. Japanese managers working for American firms in Japan often observed the
difference in the attitudes of American management, particularly in
the areas of personnel policy, corporate objectives, and methods
used to achieve these goals. Their discussion of these matters
revealed a deep understanding of the different forms taken by
American management, though their understanding of the significance and background of these practices lacked equal depth. What
is important is that they clearly have accepted the American style of
management as inevitable. This makes for a contrast with their
American counterparts, who do not even understand the Japanese
styles of management, not to speak of the meanings and values
behind them.

Why has this contrast emerged? No doubt, it has to do with the
dissimilar conceptions of the firm in the two countries. On this
score, we can make the following conjectures:

1. *Japanese concepts and practices may have dimensions that
cannot easily be translated into simple, logical form.* This may be
because they are more complicated than those of a multicultural
society where the common denominator needs to be straightforward. Japanese organizing principles may also simply be more
closely related to cultural intuition rather than logic. In any case, it
would take an enormous amount of time for non-Japanese to develop a good sense of it.

2. *Japanese managers generally exhibit what is recognized as a
low propensity to explain verbally.* This may be the result of poor
preparation for their foreign assignments, but at the base, Japanese culture does not place great emphasis on verbal communication and standardization. It may involve a Japanese feeling that the essence somehow is lost when explanations are put into
words. This point is almost always misconstrued by Americans
for the biased Japanese assumption that foreigners would not

be able to understand things Japanese in any case. The possibility of this interpretation should be explained to all expatriate Japanese well before they leave the head office.

3. *American practices, in contrast, have emerged from the common requirements of a multicultural society, such that they must always be explainable and persuasive in relatively simple terms.* The Japanese sense of social balance may get overlooked in this case, but the Japanese, like other ethnic groups, can live with these practices.

4. *The control of cross-cultural interface in Japanese subsidiaries is based on interpersonal relations attributable to the concept of collective ownership and the resultant sense of balance within the framework of hierarchical orders.* But if cross-cultural interface were administered in the Japanese way, would it really span cultures? Probably not. The resultant frustration on the part of the Japanese could lead to a feeling that local members of the subsidiary are not part of the firm's "collective owners." This often leads to Japanese neglect of orders from the U.S. hierarchy. Some high-ranking American executives complained, for example, that low-ranking Japanese could upset their (American) decisions if they wanted to—unthinkable behavior in an American organization. "The Japanese act like owners," one U.S. executive said scornfully. The Japanese in fact think they *are* "owners," and the Americans think they are not.

5. *The scope of control, in general, depends upon what needs to be achieved, i.e., the objective.* If the objective is demanding, a high level of control is required. American managers working for Japanese subsidiaries observed that the level of control in Japanese subsidiaries was more comprehensive than what they had experienced in American firms. Since the primary objective is more narrowly defined (in terms of profit) in U.S. subsidiaries than in Japanese subsidiaries, it is not surprising that the range of control is narrower in U.S. subsidiaries.

Another reason for more comprehensive management control in Japanese subsidiaries may be that Japanese management is simply more constrained regarding the methods used to achieve their objective—even when the objective itself may not be substantively different from that of U.S. subsidiaries.

A questionnaire was circulated by the author in an attempt to shed some light upon such inflexibilities Japanese management may have as additional constraints in achieving profits. The results indicated that the Japanese impose more constraints upon themselves by trying to avoid open conflict and by performing their jobs in culturally expected ways rather than by job descriptions as will be discussed in Chapter 9.

The narrower dimension, if not the lower level, of control in U.S. subsidiaries was also confirmed by the more frequent use of numerical criteria (sales, profits, etc.) by U.S. firms than Japanese firms. The latter were less satisfied with quantitative performance measurements.

However, it may simply be a question of the dimensions of control exercised by U.S. and Japanese firms. Negandi (1987) reported that local managers in U.S. subsidiaries had less freedom than in Japanese and German subsidiaries because the U.S. firms imposed more demanding and rigid numerical control.

A third important difference between U.S. and Japanese subsidiaries is apparent in the pattern of binational division of labor within the administrative unit. This, in turn, causes substantial differences in the control of cross-cultural interface.

As discussed in the section on organizational structures, the U.S. and Japanese subsidiaries did not differ greatly from one another in binational division of labor at the top-management or policy level. Specifically, the autonomous type was dominant in both.

On the administrative level, from directors to managers, however, the main difference was that the mixed type was rarely found in U.S. subsidiaries and in nearly half of the Japanese subsidiaries. This has to do with the Japanese concept of the firm, since some Japanese must be in the foreign subsidiary to achieve a certain balance, as discussed above, in the administrative unit. It is interesting to note that U.S. firms absorb local input on the policy level only, while Japanese firms take in local input on the administrative level as well. More research is needed to identify exactly what is responsible for this dissimilarity in style of subsidiary control, but we may conjecture that it is a result of the need of Japanese management to control the subsidiary in dimensions other than budget, along with a need to communicate in terms other than words. This will probably be necessary until Japanese firms develop a sufficient number of proficient third-culture interrelators.

Other salient Japanese patterns include the following. The "instructing" type, which is dominant among the ASEAN subsidiaries of Japanese firms, is absent elsewhere, as is the heteronomous learning type. "Learning," no doubt, takes place in the autonomous, or combinational, mixed type, but why is it that this type does not exist under heteronomous management? It is not that the Japanese do not trust foreigners. If this were so, one might argue that the Japanese fear that the culturally non-Japanese would not be able to acquire a Japanese sense of balance. The answer must lie in reasons similar to those for the paucity of combinational management. In contrast, a good U.S. example of the combinational type is TIM.

A fourth conclusion supported by this research is that the greatest problem for Japanese subsidiaries in the United States stemmed from intercultural differences relating to decision making. Especially bothersome were differences in conceptualization, in approaches to problem identification, and in other basic aspects that would not even reach a conscious level in communications within the same culture. As already discussed, this problem was manifest in the frustration felt by local managers who "participated" in the Japanese decision-making processes.

Some of these basic differences were elaborated in the responses to the questionnaire survey in Chapter 9. We found that cultural differences were conspicuous in the concepts of relations, planning, and job. It is well known that interpersonal relations are crucial both in Japan and China. The Japanese inclination to avoid open conflict is a manifestation of their sentiments toward interpersonal relations. The desire to avoid interpersonal conflict has been found stronger with those Japanese who had an overseas experience of three years or more, according to the results of the questionnaire. This suggests that the Japanese in a foreign subsidiary would cover things up if they were perceived to cause some conflict. From a U.S. point of view, this behavior might be seen as an oriental conspiracy or, at best, an underhanded attempt to hide unfavorable facts to save face and avoid interpersonal conflict. This misinterpretation could be extended to other areas as well.

The concept of planning is central in decision making. The Americans and Japanese agree on certain aspects of planning and disagree on others, as will be discussed in the last chapter. Conceptual disagreement is typical in the degree of detail to be included in plans. This must be disturbing when the Americans and the Japanese need to plan together.

The difference in job conception is another source of irritation. Americans feel comfortable with job control based on clear authority and responsibility stipulated by job description. The Japanese, on the other hand, insist on the importance of job flexibility under indefinite, unstated authority and responsibility. Since decisions are made within the bounds of authority and responsibility, it is no wonder if this amplifies misunderstanding between Americans and Japanese.

These differences, however, should not prohibit American and Japanese collaboration entirely. There is some common ground between the two. For instance, they share some aspects of the concept of future, emphasis on organizational interest, participative decision making, emphasis on corporate culture, etc.

Thus, we must conclude that effective organization depends upon how cross-cultural interface is administered. The common interest in directing personnel by corporate culture implies that the effective administration of cross-cultural interface is crucial for both U.S. and Japanese subsidiaries. However, this interest must be understood in the context of the current nature of cross-cultural-interface control, as discussed at the outset of this section.

Discussions so far lead us to the three overlapping objectives for which cross-cultural interface is controlled—the objectives of (1) effectuating specific business functions to be played by the local group, (2) facilitating intercultural understanding for mutual benefit, and (3) creating a functional third culture and hybrid management capable of fulfilling organizational objectives.

Simply put, U.S. firms emphasize the first objective (1), while Japanese corporations place importance on all three, requiring more cross-cultural interface. Yoshihara and Bartlett (1987) insist that Japanese firms are now under pressure to reduce the mounting costs of maintaining so many Japanese expatriates overseas. These appear to be inevitable costs for Japanese operations overseas as long as Japanese firms maintain their interest in transferring the Japanese concept of the firm across national boundaries.

The true common denominator has not yet been identified between the United States and Japan as far as cross-cultural interface is concerned. Will Japan move toward U.S.-style control of the intercultural common denominator variety? The U.S. experience as a multicultural society presents a strong argument. The common denominator approach is persuasive, while the Japanese subtle balance approach is not communicable in a multicultural society. Japan is under great pressure to change; it very likely will change.

4.2. Practical Implications

What can we adduce from the findings of this research about international management, government as well as grass-roots diplomacy, and human resources development? The following are some of the implications of the findings.

International management

1. The head office of the multinational corporation should develop more understanding of the concepts and practices of intraorganizational cross-cultural interface and third-culture facilitation. Though the needs of the U.S. and Japanese firms appear to differ, the benefits accrue, no doubt, to both parties.

2. The multinational corporation should develop active programs to develop third-culture spanners who are able to improve currently insufficient cross-cultural-interface administration.

3. The optimum mix of base and host country personnel for the cross-cultural interface must be set as a means of promoting hybrid management concepts and methods. The apparent needs for this are greater among Japanese firms, but the benefits that would accrue to U.S. firms are much greater than U.S. managers currently anticipate.

4. In order to develop the optimum mix of cross-cultural personnel, the current uniform period (three to four years) to keep managers at overseas posts needs to be broken down into separate two-, four-, and six-year programs. This is more applicable to Japanese firms.

5. The head office needs to develop career programs to use the overseas experience of managers more effectively. If experienced returnees fared well, it would motivate younger managers who would be sent overseas.

6. The multinational corporation needs to develop third-culture facilitators more actively out of local managers. The first step in this direction is to place capable and well-motivated local managers in administrative positions in the head office. The Japanese firms are far behind U.S. corporations in this regard.

Government diplomacy

7. Cross-cultural interface within international organizations such as the United Nations has a lot in common with that of the foreign subsidiary of the multinational corporation. In the former, however, the U.S.-style common denominator approach is essential since the minimum necessary condition is explainability. Also, the interface is typically a multicultural one, which would create nth culture instead of third culture, thus making it difficult to induce bicultural hybridization.

8. Some of the findings regarding the administration of cross-cultural interface also apply to interorganizational negotiation—in other words, to intergovernmental diplomacy. The role of third-culture spanners is crucial in this area. In this regard, suggestions for the development of third-culture spanners within the multinational corporation may be extended to the Ministry of Foreign Affairs and the Department of State.

9. Insufficient mutual understanding of decision-making processes between the United States and Japan also has been a cause of misunderstanding at the intergovernmental level. Conceptual dissimilarities in the area of decision making need to be studied and overcome on this level as well.

10. The role of third culture in bridging societies should be played in part by the Ministry of Foreign Affairs or the Department of State. Therefore, it would be desirable not only to develop third-culture spanners within the ministry or the department officialdom, but also to develop programs to promote the value of third culture. This may help develop leadership among third-culture spanners in the private sector. It goes without saying that

this also has a whole set of implications for educational policies in both countries.

11. The broader cultural success of cross-cultural corporate interface often hinges on an exemplary cultural translation by other well-known social figures (scholars, commentators, writers, etc.). This, in turn, has to do with the underlying drift of public opinion. The miraculous growth rates of the Japanese economy in the 1960s and the early 1970s, for example, helped Japanese management receive credit that was translated into general respect for Japanese management in cross-cultural interface. Governments should keep these relationships in mind when various programs are developed.

Private diplomacy and human resources development

Except for the information contained in our genes, we acquire all information from experience. Our experience involves the processing of stimuli from our environment. The process of getting stimuli from the environment is called communication. Thus, we can say we are the product of experience.

Third-culture spanners are no exception; they too are the product of certain experiences. Since third-culture spanners embody both first and second culture (by definition), they need to experience second culture after they grow up assimilated to first culture. Thus, the experience of second culture constitutes the core of developing human resources for cross-cultural work.

Learning the language and society of second culture is part of the experience of second culture, but living in it helps integrate the experience. Having close contact with the people of second culture is good, though not as good as living in the country of second culture.

This leads us to conclude that the most effective method of expanding the third-culture segment of a population is to develop innovative social systems that motivate the nationals to visit foreign countries and to encourage long-term foreign visitors.

In achieving this goal, grass-roots diplomacy has a great role to play. But governments can only provide roads; its citizens must run on them. We seem to be seeing an increasing number of sister-city agreements, for example. These are good. Cultural exchange, foreign travel, missions, and other things of this sort are all good. We can only hope that they lead to a gradual revolution in awareness and value for both our nations.

BIBLIOGRAPHY

Adler, Nancy J. "Cultural Synergy: The Management of Cross-Cultural Organizations." In *Trends and Issues in OD: Current Theory and Practice*, edited by W. Warner Burke and Leonard D. Goodstein. pp. 163–184, San Diego, Calif.: University of California Associates, 1980.

Azumi, Koya. "Japanese Society: A Sociological View." In *An Introduction to Japanese Civilization*, edited by Arthur E. Tiedemann. pp. 516–535, New York: Columbia University Press, 1974.

U.S. Bank and Corporation Tax Law, §25101, Division 2.

Barbato, Robert J. and Drexel, Richard E. "Americanizing Quality Circles." In *Management by Japanese Systems*, edited by Sang M. Lee and Gary Schwendiman. New York: Praeger, 1982, pp. 491–494.

Barney, Jay B. "Organizational Culture: Can It Be a Source of Sustained Competitive Advantage?" *Academy of Management Review* 11, no. 3 (1986): 656–65.

Baumol, W. J. *Business Behavior: Value and Growth*. New York: Macmillan, 1959, rev. ed., 1967.

Belding, Eser. "Japanese Corporations in Foreign Lands." Paper read at The Academy of International Business Annual Meeting May 1986, in London.

Berle, A. A., Jr., and Means, G. C. *The Modern Corporation and Private Property*. New York: Macmillan, 1932.

Brislin, Richard W.; Lonner, Walter J.; and Thorndike, Robert M. *Cross-Cultural Research Methods*, New York: Wiley, 1973.

California Equal Employment Opportunity Commission. "Discrimination in Employment Is Prohibited by Law." Sacramento, California: Commerce Clearing House, Inc., 1981.

Cherry, Colin. *On Human Communication: A Review, a Survey, and a Criticism*, 3rd ed., Cambridge, Mass.: The MIT Press, 1980.

Christopher, Robert. "The Burden of Success: Japan's Changing Image in the United States," *IHJ Bulletin* 3. no. 4, (1983): 1–6.

Constantino, Renato. *A Third World View of Japan.* Tokyo: The International House of Japan, 1978.

Davey, William G. *Intercultural Theory and Practice: A Case Method Approach.* Washington, D.C.: The Society for Intercultural Education, Training and Research, 1981.

de Tocqueville, Alexis. *Democracy in America,* Garden City, N.Y.: Doubleday, 1969.

Drake, Bruce H. and Moberg, Dennis J. "Communicating Influence Attempts in Dyads: Linguistic Sedatives and Palliatives," *Academy of Management Review* 11, no. 3 (1986): 567–584.

Farace, Richard V.; Monge, Peter R.; and Russell, Hamish M. *Communicating and Organizing.* Reading, Mass.: Addison-Wesley, 1977.

Fayerweather, John, *International Business Management: A Conceptual Framework,* New York: McGraw-Hill, 1969, p. 96.

Franko, Lawrence G. "Doing Business in America: The European Experience." *The McKinsey Quarterly,* 1971, reprinted from *European Business,* Autumn, 1971.

Geneen, Harold with Alvin Moscow, *Managing.* Garden City, New York: Doubleday, 1984.

Gregory, Kathleen L. "Native-View Paradigms: Multiple Cultures and Culture Conflicts in Organizations." *Administrative Science Quarterly* 28, (1983): 359–376.

Gungwu, Wang. "Some Aspects of Southeast Asian Attitudes Towards Japan." *IHJ Bulletin,* 1974.

Hain, Tony. "Japanese Management in the United States." In *Management by Japanese Systems,* edited by Sang M. Lee and Gary Schwendiman. New York: Praeger, 1982, pp. 433–449.

Hanson, Lee. "Boundary Spanning and Cultural Brokers in American Subsidiaries of Korean Parent Companies," a Ph.D. dissertation proposal, University of Washington, 1985.

Hayashi, Kichiro. *Ibunka Intafeisu Kanri* [Cross-Cultural Interface Management], Tokyo: Yuhikaku, 1985.

———. "Crosscultural Interface Management: The Case of Japanese Firms Abroad." *Japanese Economic Studies* 15, no. 1, (1986): 3–41.

———. "Expansion of Japanese Companies Abroad: The Management of Crosscultural Interface." In *Fragile Interdependence: Economic Issues in US–Japan Trade and Investment,* edited by

Thomas A. Pugel and Robert Hawkins. Lexington, Mass.: Lexington Books, 1986, pp. 175–200.

Hofstede, Geert. *Culture's Consequences: International Differences in Work-related Values,* Beverly Hills: Sage, 1980.

Holstein, William; Engardio, Pete; and Cook, Dan. "Japan in America—Special Report," *Business Week* 14 July 1986, pp. 45–55.

Janis, Irving L. *Groupthink,* 2nd ed. Boston: Houghton Mifflin, 1982.

Japan Committee for Economic Development [*Keizai Doyukai*]. Opinion Survey on the Management of Japanese Joint Ventures in the ASEAN Region. Committee on International Economic Policies, July 1977, 32 pp.

Japan External Trade Organization. *Japanese Manufacturing Operations in the United States, Results of the First Comprehensive Field Study.* Tokyo: JETRO, 1981.

"Japanese Owners Resist Union Organization of Memphis Plant." *IBEW Journal* (1983): 10–12 and 62.

Jones, Crystal L. "The Impact of *Texas Department of Community Affairs v. Burdine* on Employment Discrimination." *Houston Law Review* 19 (1982): 981–1001.

Kageyama, Kiichi. "Management Strategy for Coping with International Economic Conflict." *Management Japan* 19 no. 2 (1986): 7–12.

Kim, Ken I. and Lunde, Harold I. "Quality Circles: Why They Work in Japan and How We Can Make Them Work in the United States." In *Management by Japanese Systems,* edited by Sang M. Lee and Gary Schwendiman. New York: Praeger, 1982.

Kitamura, Hiroshi; Murata, Ryohei; and Okazaki, Hisahiko. *Between Friends.* Tokyo/New York: Weatherhill, 1985.

Kohls, L. Robert. *Developing Intercultural Awareness: A Learning Module Complete with Master Lesson Plan, Content, Exercises, and Handouts.* Washington, D.C.: The Society for Intercultural Education, Training and Research, 1981.

Kono, Toyohiro. *Strategy and Structure of Japanese Enterprises.* London: Macmillan, 1984.

Kranish, Michael. "Japan Policy 'Dangerous' Editor Told." *Boston Sunday Globe,* 8 September 1985.

Kuo, Jennifer C. "Race Discrmination." *1982 Annual Survey of American Law,* pp. 515–554.

Lincoln, James R.; Hanada, Mitsuyo; and Olson, Jon. "Cultural Orientations and Individual Reactions to Organizations: A Study of Employees of Japanese-Owned Firms." *Administrative Science Quarterly* 26 (1981): 93–115.

———. "Cultural Effects on Organizational Structure: The Case of Japanese Firms in the United States." *American Sociological Review* 43 (1978): 829–47.

Manglapus, Raul S. "Japan in Asia, Master or Partner?" *IHJ Bulletin* no. 23 (1969): 26–40.

Menzies, Hugh D. "Can the Twain Meet at Mitsubishi?" *Fortune,* 26 January 1981, pp. 41–46.

Miller, H. Anthony and Estes, R. Wayne. "Recent Judicial Limitations on the Right to Discharge: A California Trilogy." *University of California (Davis) Law Review* 16 no. 65 (1982): 65–105.

Mills, Ted. "Worker Participation: The American Experience," *Economic Impact* (1983): 47–53.

Moran, Robert T. and Harris, Philip R. *Managing Cultural Differences,* vol. 1, Houston: Gulf, 1979.

———. *Managing Cultural Synergy,* vol. 2, Houston: Gulf, 1982.

Murata, Kiyoaki. "Problems in International Communication." *IHJ Bulletin* 2, no. 3 (1982): 5–6.

Negandhi, A. R. *International Management.* Rockleigh, N.J.: Allyn and Bacon, 1987.

Nishida, Kohzo. "Japanese Human Resources Management in Transition." Mimeographed. 1986.

Okada, Yoshitaka. "Indigenization Policies and Cultural Differences of Japanese and U.S. Multinational Corporations in Indonesia." Working paper, Graduate School of International Relations, International University of Japan, 1982.

Sakudo, Yotaro. "Nihonteki Keiei wa Ikani Keisei Saretaka" [How has Japanese management been formed?] *Infinity* no. 67 (1985).

Sargent, Alice G. *The Androgynous Manager, Blending Male and Female Management Styles for Today's Organization.* New York: AMACOM, 1981.

Sease, Douglas. "Working for a Japanese Subsidiary: A Life's Thrill— Or a Career Disaster." *Wall Street Journal* 29 August 1985.

Shimada, Haruo. *The Japanese Employment System.* Tokyo: The Japan Institute of Labor, 1980.

Standard Federal Tax Reports, 834CCH, §481[p. 36, 367]—Changes in Accounting Methods.

————, 833CCH, §385[p. 31, 375]—Corporate Interests as Stock.

Thomas, Maxine S. "Mandatory Retirement and Impact Discrmination Under the Age Discrimination in Employment Act: You'll Get Yours When You're 70." *Akron Law Review* 17, (1983): 65–85.

United States–Japan Trade Council. *United States Press Coverage of Japan.* Washington, D.C., March 3, 1980.

U.S. News & World Report. "America vs. Japan, Can U.S. Workers Compete?" 2 September 1985, pp. 40–45.

Watts, William. "The United States and Japan: A New Realism?" *IHJ Bulletin* 4, no. 1 (1984): 1–3.

Wilson, Marilyn and Adkins, Lynn. "How the Japanese Run U.S. Subsidiaries." *Dunn's Business Review* (1983): 32–40.

Williamson, O. E. *Market and Hierarchies: Analysis and Antitrust Implications.* New York: Free Press, 1975.

Yoshida, Mamoru. "Control Systems of Japanese Firms with U.S. Manufacturing Operations." Paper submitted to the Academy of International Business for meeting May 1986 in London.

Yoshihara, H. and Bartlett, C. A., "Top Management by Locals and Internal Internationalization," (Japanese) Sekai Keizai Hyoron, May 1987.

COMMENTARY
ON CHAPTER 2

MIKIO KAWAMURA

*General Manager, Semiconductor Department,
Mitsubishi Corporation*

SOURCES OF CONFLICT

I T IS worthy of note, firstly, that both Americans and Japanese share the same economic system, i.e., a free-market economy. In its simplest terms, this system works according to the logic of business profit. Businesses put together and pay for the necessary resources such as capital, materials, people, and information; create products or services that are recognized as (or expected to be) useful to the society on a competitive basis; make more money than they spent (if they're successful); then pay taxes and dividends. There is no difference of any kind on this philosophical level between the two countries. This writer's fifteen years of business experience in North America and Europe have never contradicted this philosophy of making profit.

Any differences emerge in the area of putting the philosophy into practice. We certainly cannot expect the style of conducting daily business to be identical—dependent as it is on location, people, type of product or service, and social and economic systems. The Americans and Japanese are different in this sense. In recognizing this apparent difference, people tend to conclude that the major problems faced by Japanese businesses in the United States are deeply rooted in this difference, and therefore cannot be solved.

Professor Hayashi conducted a questionnaire survey (discussed in the last chapter) including eleven hypotheses suggesting differences between the United States and Japan that make the management of cross-cultural interface difficult.

As I understand it, the most impressive survey result was that not a few of these hypotheses were challenged. That is, respondents believed American corporations to be closer to the Japanese mentality, and the Japanese more adaptable to American ways than originally expected.

This is a very encouraging signal, suggesting that the perception gap may not be as big as some pessimists claim.

Indeed, most Japanese expatriates understand fully that they are playing games in the opponents' ballpark. The Americans seem superior and more confident. There are also handicaps for the visiting team, including the following:

1. *Their working language is English.* Since the Second World War, Americans have been very close to the Japanese. The American presence is everywhere in Japan. Japanese are eager to learn English, and they may do well with it in simple social situations. But conducting business in English is a completely different matter. One improperly used spoken or written word could easily undermine the Japanese businessman's position. (This could be especially hazardous in lawsuits.) He must be careful in situations of negotiation or instruction on the job. He will be clearly at a disadvantage when engaged in debate or discussion, since the Japanese are brought up in an atmosphere of tacit understanding and have no formal education in debate or speech.

2. *There is no foundation (Nemawashi) for Japanese philosophy in the United States.* The Japanese seem to be experts in *Nemawashi* among themselves, though efforts to instruct Americans in Japanese philosophy appear insufficient. A Japanese expatriate may find himself trying to impart basic Japanese philosophy in one lesson even though the topic he is discussing is a very limited one. But he cannot start from square one in every discussion.

The Japanese expatriate must strive for clarity in his communication with locals. He may be afraid, perhaps subconsciously, that he is at odds in discussing the issue in English, a language in which he may be less eloquent and less persuasive—and therefore, less successful.

3. *They are given limited authority from the head office.* The American subsidiary is a satellite of the Japanese corporate parent, and its activity must be integrated into the parent's total activity. As a result interference is inevitable. The Japanese expatriates are thus put in the difficult position of having to cope with the locals who naturally assume that their boss is fully authorized from the head office.

IDEAS FOR ACTION

In addressing this situation, we Japanese should take the following steps:

- Recognize that, in most cases, the only operative language in cross-cultural-interface management is English. English-language instruction should begin as early as possible in one's life.
- Japanese education should also include the subject of speech/ debate/rhetoric.
- Japanese businesses should be encouraged to hire more American MBAs and assign some of them outside of Japan, as cross-cultural interpreters or spanners, as a part of their business career.
- Business schools should realize that Japanese students with overseas experience are ideally suited to play the role of the next generation's interpreters or spanners.

In conclusion, the Japanese are not an isolated people. They can be just as international as Americans. The Japanese education system should be restructured to teach students in such an international atmosphere. There have been many attempts, in fact, to move in this direction, particularly by private educational institutions. This would help the Japanese become active and expressive, rather than passive, players on the international scene. Americans, for their part, should be understanding of the situation of Japanese expatriates and try to be patient before they speak out.

The final subject I would like to discuss is the concept of Japanese business. In his concluding section, Professor Hayashi indicates that three-quarters of American managers are frustrated with Japanese managers, resulting in high turnover. In looking deeply at the cause of this phenomenon, he reaches the cultural concept of "communal ownership." This writer's observation is slightly different. In my view, a "family compact" is at the foundation of the Japanese firm, with management and employees positioned as if they were kith and kin. What happens when this "family compact" extends overseas?

The Japanese are aware that they are not playing in their home ballpark. Because they are playing to win, however, they must dispatch their available superstars. They are obviously outnumbered in the United States, and inevitably recognize that cooperation with Americans is indispensable. Accordingly, the "autonomous but mixed, or partly dependent" structure is often seen in Professor Hayashi's survey of corporate forms. A top Japanese expatriate is put in the position of representing the parent company, though in most cases the "family compact" defined him as a mere member, not the chief representative of the family itself. Because he must behave as agent of his owner, however, he is inexperienced in his position and is therefore unskillful in his attempt. The "family compact" may be attractive to the locals nonetheless, and a higher-than-normal level of communication will be required to successfully join it.

COMMENTARY
ON CHAPTER 2

KENNETH D. BUTLER
Consultant

CULTURES IN COLLISION

HAVING been engaged in intercultural spanning in a number of ways for the past twenty years, I found Professor Hayashi's thoughts on cross-cultural interface especially interesting. Professor Hayashi defines cross-cultural interface as emerging when two or more people belonging to different cultures come in contact and collide. I would emphasize the "collision" aspect of this contact.

Anyone who has been actively involved in the business relations between the United States and Japan is aware that effective communication is one of our biggest problems. We Americans say something that we think is quite self-evident to our Japanese associates, and they don't seem to understand us. Japanese, as Professor Hayashi has aptly pointed out, do not verbalize their communication in the way we Americans do, so when they attempt to indicate a course of action, or a business strategy, to us, we don't seem to understand.

This lack of understanding has in the past been referred to as a "perception gap," but my own view, which seems substantiated by Professor Hayashi's work, is that it is not so much a *gap* in perceptions as it is a *collision* of perceptions. It has been my experience that due both to cultural and historical factors, Japanese and Americans perceive the world in fundamentally different ways. And this is at the heart of many of the problems we encounter in attempting to interface in a business environment.

At any rate, whether it is an American subsidiary located in Japan, or a Japanese subsidiary located in the United States, we seem to spend most of our working hours trying to determine if we have in fact been understood. The importance of Professor Hayashi's study is that he has gone inside such companies in both countries, and on the basis of empirical research has developed a conceptual framework that allows us to attempt to come to grips with the problems of intercultural interface in much greater depth than can be accomplished by individual managers in either country on a subjective basis.

Professor Hayashi's classifications of the various types of administrative or managerial control adopted by American and Japanese corporations for their subsidiaries, and his discussion of Japanization and Americanization and such, are right to the point and, I think, quite easily understood. I would like to direct the body of my comments primarily to his discussion of "persons of third culture," or cross-cultural-interface administrators, and what this implies.

In my consulting work for American companies in Japan and for Japanese companies entering joint ventures and technical tie-ups with U.S. firms or undertaking local production in the United States, I believe that one of the greatest problems they have had is that within the companies, there has been no one on either side who had the "third culture" skills required to serve effectively as an intercultural spanner. I shouldn't complain, since this is the reason the companies have hired me as a consultant. But usually I have been brought in only after the problems of intercultural business communication have reached an advanced stage. It would have been much better for all concerned if the companies had had their own effective intercultural spanners on the scene right from the start. But is this actually possible?

As Professor Hayashi has defined the qualifications of a third-culture person—command of the languages of the first and second cultures; acquaintance with the knowledge, values, and meanings of first and second cultures at a level where he can translate culturally from one culture to the other; recognition as a legitimate member of at least one of the two relevant cultural groups; plus knowledge and experience in specific business functions—this is quite a range of skills that we are asking our business managers to possess.

There is another problem also. In my experience with American corporations I have found little awareness on the part of top management at company headquarters that any special skills such as these are required to do business in Japan. If a manager happens to know a little Japanese, that is all to the good, but it is not one of the requirements for being assigned to Japan. And in twenty years in Japan, I have only run across one American company that specifically hired an American to work as an intercultural spanner in its subsidiary in Japan. So, at least in the United States, before figuring out how we can meet the need, we must develop an awareness that such a need actually exists. In this regard, I hope that Professor Hayashi's contribution, and the other chapters of this book, receive wide circulation among the top management of American corporations.

On the Japanese side, "intercultural spanners" have existed literally since the early Meiji period. But on the whole these people have not been accorded status within the corporate organization. They have been looked upon as being little more than interpreters, charged with merely the mechanical act of translating English into Japanese and Japanese into English, and have hardly ever been trained as line managers and accorded the level of responsibility within the company required for them to actually engage in intercultural spanning. Professor Hayashi's description of the young cultural interrelators that Theta Machinery Corporation "placed here and there without design or structure" in its U.S. subsidiary is an example of this approach. Lacking status, it was only by chance that any of them actually developed to the point of being effective "spanners," rather than nothing more than interpreters, as they were initially perceived by the American managers in the company.

So, while Professor Hayashi has definitely defined the problem, we still have a long way to go before legions of intercultural spanners are effectively engaged in smoothing out the business relations between our two countries.

THE CONCEPT OF THE FIRM

Professor Hayashi's discussion of the difference in the concept of the firm is a primary example of differences in perception. Both managers and employees in the United States see their relationship to the firm as a contractual relationship. A person is hired to perform a specified job, and his salary and other benefits are determined by how well he performs the job. But as Professor Hayashi had stated, a Japanese joins a firm as if he were being adopted as a son of the family. His job is not specifically defined, and he is expected to exert his efforts for the common good of the group.

Professor Hayashi's account of the perceptions held by Mr. Banting and his Japanese vice president in charge at Gamma Electronics Corporation in the United States are highly revealing of the fundamental differences of perceptions between Americans and Japanese in how a job is to be performed. As Mr. Banting said, in the United States you work hard in the first year on the job to produce evidence that will make the boss glad he hired you. But the Japanese vice president viewed the first year as "a period of settling in," and stated that it had never occurred to him that the results achieved by an individual during the first year should be considered critical in setting one's career with the firm.

Professor Hayashi has described this sort of conflict as being a case of a communication gap in which the Japanese was not even aware of what was required. He makes the point that foreign subsidiaries require intercultural spanners who detect such gaps quickly and bridge them through cultural as well as linguistic translations. While seconding this view wholeheartedly, I would like to suggest that such gaps should not be viewed just as "gaps" in communication, but rather as fundamental differences in perceptions of what a firm is all about and, for that matter, what the world is all about.

Even if Americans and Japanese can be made to understand intellectually that such fundamental differences in perceptions exist, these are still the perceptions that they hold—to a great extent such perceptions are what define a person as being an American or a Japanese. Therefore, the job of the intercultural spanner requires

ongoing efforts on a daily basis to determine when such perceptions are operating to the detriment of the progress of the firm
and, rather than just "bridging the gap," attempting through a process of cultural translation to ameliorate them so that discord does
not arise.

In my experience, this difference in how the firm is perceived is
one of the major hindrances to foreign companies doing business
in Japan. Foreign companies expect to be able to come to Japan and
hire a number of qualified managers and employees, specify each
person's job, and then more or less turn each of them loose to
perform their work on their own responsibility. Even if there is an
awareness on the part of the expatriate management in Japan of the
necessity to create a corporate culture that operates within a
framework that Japanese employees can respond to, making the
home office aware of this need is a major problem.

Confronted all too often with conflicts in cultural orientation that
seem impossible to resolve, many foreign executives have lapsed
into the "This is my order—do it" syndrome, which engenders
mistrust and discord in a variety of ways that often lead to a high
level of frustration on the part of the Japanese employees.

As Professor Hayashi has pointed out, Japanese managers in
American subsidiaries have more or less become accustomed to the
situation they find themselves in. While this is true to a certain
extent, being forced to become acclimated to a different culture
creates a lot of frustration, and the number of first-rate Japanese
managers who are prepared to live with this frustration is, I believe,
decreasing. Therefore, unless greater efforts are made to create
"third *corporate* cultures" in American subsidiaries in Japan, I believe that it is going to become more, rather than less, difficult in the
immediate future for American companies to recruit competent
staff.

What seems to be required as a first step in doing something
about this problem is for American subsidiaries in Japan to bring in
outside competent intercultural-interface specialists to conduct
seminars for both the American and the Japanese managers and
employees of the company. They should explain the underlying
differences in perceptions that result in the wide range of discord
and frustration described by Professor Hayashi in his chapter.

After this is done, an ongoing period of monitoring could be required, in which the outside intercultural-interface specialist interviews key managers, both Japanese and American, to determine if specific differences in perceptions are still acting to the detriment of the successful operation of the business, and if so, conducting specific efforts at cultural translation to improve the situation.

While such problems faced by American companies operating in Japan are great, I believe that differences in perceptions present an even greater problem for Japanese companies operating in the United States. American companies have been operating in Japan for many decades now, and to a certain extent a *modus vivendi* for doing so has emerged. But it has really been only in the past eight or ten years that Japanese companies have begun to set up substantial operations in the United States.

In concluding my comments, I would like to discuss briefly a problem that is implicit in Professor Hayashi's study, but which perhaps deserves even further clarification.

It is well recognized that the ability of the Japanese to operate effectively and efficiently as members of a group in the workplace is one of the key factors that accounts for the success of Japan's economic development in the post-World War II period. The actual reasons why Japanese possess this ability are, I believe, less clearly recognized.

Japanese-style management, reduced to its essentials, is centered on doing what is necessary to create a group that works together for the common good—a group in which individual prerogatives are sacrificed to the common cause, so to speak. The success of quality circles in Japan is an example of how such a group works together. The reason this can be done in Japan is that it is by participation in a group that the Japanese ego, or self, receives its support. A major premise of Japanese management is that a worker will receive a strong sense of support for the self by full participation in a group. I have discussed this subject in an article soon to be published in the United States, and will omit the details here. Suffice it to say that by creating the perfect group, as it were, the top management of Japanese companies provides a setting in which the Japanese employee can give full play to his self and achieve a sense of satisfaction in his work that would be completely foreign to an American worker.

Japanese manufacturing companies, in setting up their operations in the United States, have been fairly successful up to now in transplanting Japanese-type management to American soil. But I believe that in the future, problems—some of which have already been detected by Professor Hayashi—are going to surface that will cause quite a bit of friction. As I see it, the reason for the quite enthusiastic reception accorded Japanese companies in the United States in the past few years stems from the traditional adversary nature of the relations between management and workers in America. Japanese management, by way of contrast, strives to create harmony in the company group, and both American workers and managers were ready for some harmony. The attention paid by Japanese management to workers—the sense that both management and workers are working together for the common good— has appeared as a refreshing concept to Americans.

But Americans have not yet had enough experience in their jobs with Japanese companies to realize that the group approach to the job is, in American terms, a *negation* of the self. Recently the *Yomiuri Shinbun* carried a photo of American workers carrying placards in Japanese protesting the Japanese approach to labor-management relations and demanding that Japanese companies conduct their business in the United States according to "American rules." As the realization that the Japanese approach to management is based on a completely different set of premises sets in, I believe we can expect to see more such pictures of American workers on the picket line protesting the failure of Japanese corporations to respect traditional American approaches to the job.

Therefore, a major problem that top management of Japanese corporations will face in the immediate future is developing an awareness of what is required in effectively managing American workers. To develop this awareness, managers will require all the skills that any intercultural spanner operating on the scene possesses. A few Japanese corporations have attempted to come to grips with this problem by adopting strategies aimed at extensive localization of their management in the United States.

But in doing this they immediately encounter another problem which, if anything, is even more difficult to resolve. A company that is not managed by Japanese is not a Japanese company. This has to do with the modes of communication Japanese employ among themselves, as Professor Hayashi has described. So far, the Japanese have not been able to devise a method of integrating a subsidiary that is totally managed by Americans into the corporate culture of the parent company in Japan. A solution to this dilemma is, I believe, one of the most pressing problems that Japanese corporations face today.

3

A COMPARISON OF JAPANESE AND AMERICAN INTERFIRM PRODUCTION SYSTEMS

TETSUO MINATO
Aoyama Gakuin University, Tokyo

INTRODUCTION

I F WE ARE to set down the issues in the economic relationship between Japan and the United States in the next decade, it is imperative to identify the differences in the production systems of the two countries. It is my belief that the difference lies in the degree of centralization. In the United States, large firms are the axis for a vertically integrated production system. In contrast, the Japanese system revolves around a division of labor between large and small firms, a system that is much more decentralized than the American model.

The American system, with its high degree of centralization, is appropriate for certain situations. It functions better when the environment faced by the firm is changing at a relatively slow pace, and when the financial resources of the large firms are able to achieve a high degree of efficiency through investment. The Japanese situation—a highly decentralized system with slimmed-down larger firms and a very large number of smaller firms connected to them—is appropriate for a different set of environmental conditions. It works best when the tempo of change in the business environment quickens; when the environment requires a more

widely dispersed set of investments; and when the effective use of
the resources of the firm requires decentralized decision making.
There is no one production system that will be best under all
environments; what works well in one situation may fail miserably
in another. Size per se is not the only thing that matters in a
successful and enduring production system.

The American centralized production system and the Japanese
decentralized production system have turned in very different per-
formances over the past few years. This has required a readjustment
of the international division of labor between Japan and the United
States, and is no doubt part of the reason for the trade crisis
between the two countries. World economic conditions have also
changed, reducing the competitiveness of the system based on
internal, centralized production by large firms. The same macroeconomic changes have made the more decentralized form of
production more appropriate. We must understand the trade friction between the two countries in light of these very significant
changes in the economic environment of the world economy.

This difference in performance is often attributed to differences
in plant layout or differences in the use of factory automation. As
part of this research, we visited representative firms in both countries. There seemed to be little difference in these areas when
American and Japanese large firms were compared. Productivity
differences between large American and Japanese firms are probably not a factor in the trade friction between the two countries.

1. THE AGE OF "INTERFIRM PRODUCTIVITY"

Over the last several years, American firms have been aggressively implementing a program of investment in production facilities, in
response to competitive pressures from Japan. These firms are
investing heavily in robots and other automation equipment, and
are assembling extremely efficient computerized production-control systems. For example, GM plans to take a huge step forward in
factory automation by increasing the number of automation devices
in its plants from the current level of 40,000 to 200,000 by 1990,
linking them with a computerized communications network using

its MAP (manufacturing automation protocol) system.[1] American firms have taken the lead in the development of these computer networks, and there is ample reason to believe that large American firms are more productive at the individual factory level than their Japanese counterparts. Nevertheless, in modern industrial society, the production of goods does not begin and end with individual firms; the production process depends on the division of labor between firms. In fact, the proportion of industrial production that depends on such a division of labor has been increasing rapidly in recent years, and "interfirm productivity"—the total productivity of a firm, including its relationships with suppliers—has come to assume a decisive importance.

An additional factor behind the recent increase in the importance of interfirm productivity is the change in the structure of demand in the advanced industrial nations and the change in the product life cycle. We have moved from a uniform demand structure suited to mass production to a differentiated demand structure requiring diverse products and small production lots; the product life cycle has been significantly shortened. The great strides in electronics technology have accelerated the technological revolution, causing the introduction of one new product after another and bringing a need for rapid, flexible production systems. In a study conducted by the Nittsu Research Institute in 1983, for example, the average rate of introduction of new products for the 427 firms responding to the survey was 7.5 percent a year over a three-year period. This is three times faster that the annual increase of 2.5 percent in real GNP during the same period.[2]

To respond to this changing technology and structure of demand, we will have to depend on the productivity of industrial relationships that include relatively small firms. Such relationships will make possible more rapid formulations of strategy and more flexible production systems. The origins of the United States–Japan trade friction lie not in the intrafirm productivity of their respective large firms, but rather in a gap in interfirm productivity. There is a significant relationship between the export record of Japanese industry and the degree of utilization of subcontractors in each industry.[3]

Throughout this chapter, the term *core firm* is used to refer to a single large manufacturer occupying the highest position in the production pyramid and standing above subcontractors and other suppliers. In the Japanese automobile industry, Toyota and Nissan would be core firms. In the electronics industry, the production pyramid is topped by a single "core" manufacturing plant rather than by the corporation as a whole. A literal rendition of the original Japanese term would be "parent firm." In addition, the firms referred to in this paper as *subcontractors* are distinguished by their role in supplying the core firm with what are traditionally referred to as "made-to-order-goods" *(gaichuhin)*, as opposed to "purchased goods" *(konyuhin)*. The term *made-to-order goods* refers to products that owe their characteristics largely to specifications issued by the core firm.

Obviously, there is a division of labor in production between firms in the United States as well as those in Japan. However, Japanese use subcontractors to a much greater extent than U.S. firms. Furthermore, on a more fundamental level, there are intrinsic differences between the industrial systems in the two nations. These differences can be traced to differences in the process that ties firms together and to differences in the processes used to develop, adjust, and maintain these interfirm relationships.

2. A COMPARISON OF SUBCONTRACTING AND PARTS PURCHASE IN JAPAN AND THE UNITED STATES

2.1. The Subcontracting Production System: Partial Integration

The production activities of firms can be divided into two types: production carried out internally, in the firm's own facilities, and purchase from other producers. Thus, firms must decide whether to make or buy the needed output. In the United States, most research has focused on the best way to choose between these two options.

There is a great difference between Japanese and American firms in terms of the degree of vertical integration. As yet, no suitable index has been devised to measure the degree of vertical integration in a given firm. However, value added in production accounts for 46.3 percent of the total value of goods shipped by American manufacturing firms, compared with 32.6 percent for Japanese manufacturing firms as a whole, and only 29.2 percent for Japan's larger firms.[4] This is an indication of the extent of the dependence on external procurement by Japanese firms, especially those with large export operations. According to data available for 1014 manufacturing firms with listed securities, 67.3 percent of the total cost of production was accounted for by purchase of materials. For consumer electronics firms, the figure was 75.1 percent; for automobile manufacturers, 81.6 percent.[5]

Materials purchased from outside the firm include both standardized parts and components and outside orders of components made to specification by suppliers. The proportions of standardized components and made-to-spec components also differ from those in the United States.

In American industry, standardization is more widespread than in Japan, and many components, such as gears, have been standardized and are sold through catalogs. In the firms producing equipment for small and medium-sized firms that we visited in the United States, the assumption that standardized components would be used in production was incorporated into the product right from the design stage, and there were almost no made-to-order parts. Nonstandard components were produced in-house. Basic components that would normally be cast specially by outside suppliers were instead machined to fit from steel plate. This may be an extreme case, but in general, American firms appear to use a large number of standardized components. In contrast, Japanese firms use few such components, with the exception of a very small number of parts, such as bearings. There is a very frequent use of made-to-order goods (*gaichuhin*).

There is an even more important difference between the production systems of the United States and Japan: the Japanese system does not define the production decision in terms of make-or-buy, as is normally the case in the United States. Large Japanese firms maintain very close ties with some of the supplier firms that produce goods to specification; these firms are in effect part of the core firm's internal organization.[6] These partially integrated firms are termed *subcontractors*. This means the parts they make have a status somewhere between that of internally produced and purchased on the open market. For the most part, subcontractors are independent firms that are not receiving capital or personnel from the core firm,[7] but functionally they are partially integrated into the core firm's production process. The core firms enter into a long-term, ongoing relationship with their subcontractors, keep them abreast of internal developments, and exercise some guidance and control over the subcontracting firm's management. Thus, in building their production systems, Japanese firms have, in addition to vertical integration and outside procurement, a third option: that of partial integration with supplier firms.

Outside Japan, aside from subsidiaries that are capitalized in part by their parent firms, there are few supplier firms that are partially integrated into their customer firms. This is particularly true in the United States, where even smaller firms place a great deal of importance on their independence.

2.2. Special Characteristics of the Japanese Subcontracting System

Japan's subcontracting system has a number of characteristics that facilitate communication between firms; this communication is indispensable for the control of subcontractors by parent firms and for making possible an extensive division of labor between firms. These characteristics that facilitate communication can be divided into structural features and behavioral aspects of interfirm transactions. Let us first turn to the structural features that distinguish Japan's subcontracting system.

Figure 3.1   Japanese Production System.

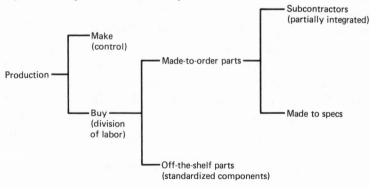

Structural features

1. High dependence on made-to-order goods in the production process
2. Large numbers of subcontractors of high quality
3. Large numbers of specialist subcontractors that depend on one core firm to purchase more than half of their output
4. Single- as well as multiple-level subcontracting (widespread use of secondary subcontractors)
5. Organizations of subcontractors *(Kyoryokukai)* of a single core firm

The high degree of dependence of Japanese firms on subcontractors is possible because the vast majority of firms in Japanese manufacturing are small or medium-sized concerns. Of the over 700,000 small and medium-sized manufacturing firms, 65.5 percent are engaged in subcontracting work.[8] Of those doing subcontracting work, 64.5 percent depend on a single core firm for purchase of over half their output.[9] A further important feature is the widespread use of secondary subcontractors in Japan, which gives rise to production systems with multi-tiered subcontracting. In addition, a core firm often has a cooperative association *(Kyoryokukai)* of subcontracting firms. These are made up of key suppliers selected by the core firm. They exchange information by forming study groups (e.g., to study rationalization of production; to improve quality and production control; or to consider proposals relating to value analysis—VA and value engineering—VE).

Toyota Motor Company, with annual sales of Y6 trillion, spent Y4 trillion on parts and equipment from outside sources. Prior to 1980, Toyota dealt with 200 outside suppliers of components; recently that number has grown to about 250 firms, and Toyota is maintaining long-term, ongoing relationships with nearly all of them. One hundred seventy-four of these firms have been selected as key suppliers by Toyota and have formed a cooperative association of subcontractors. In addition, Toyota deals with about 900 other firms for equipment and other occasional purchases, but these ties are less fixed.

Toyota deals directly with about 250 parts manufacturers, but in addition, each of these firms deals with an average of twenty secondary subcontractors, for a total of about 5000 secondary subcontractors. Each secondary subcontractor deals with six to eight tertiary subcontractors, for a total of about 40,000 tertiary subcontractors. In this way, the number of subcontractors dealing directly with the core firm is limited, but overall production is carried out through the participation of a huge number of firms. This multi-tiered production system results in a pyramidal distribution of production and employment, with the greater part of production being carried out by thousands of small firms.

While the multi-tiered transaction structure in the automobile industry limits the number of firms with direct dealings with the core firm, the situation is somewhat different in the electronics industry, where there is an extremely large number of different parts and components. A core firm in this industry might have direct dealings with as many as 3000 firms. Even in this case, however, the core firm selects about 300 key subcontractors to fill the majority of its orders, and these subcontractors receive detailed guidance from the core firm.

American firms order fewer components from outside suppliers. In the general-machinery field, value-added accounts for 55.0 percent of the value of output; in the electronics industry, the figure is 57.0 percent, and in the precision equipment industry, 64.9 percent. Even in the transportation-equipment field, where outside orders are relatively frequent, value-added accounts for 38.5 percent of the value of output. The proportion of total production expenses accounted for by materials was 50 percent for GM and 60 percent for Ford.[10] In contrast, the average level of value-added for the eleven major Japanese automakers was a mere 16.5 percent of the value of output; furthermore, both Toyota and Nissan spent 82 percent of their total outlays for production on materials.[11] The American manufacturers of finished autos had direct dealings with 3000 to 10,000 suppliers, and secondary subcontracting was rare. The American production system is like an inverted pyramid.[12]

There are also virtually no American organizations of subcontractors serving a single core firm. This is due to the fact that creating such organizations would probably not facilitate the dissemination of information useful to the subcontractors, since American firms dislike to disclose such internal information. In addition, such an association of firms might be seen as a violation of antitrust regulations.

Behavioral features

1. Preference for dealing with a limited number of firms when placing or filling orders
2. Preference for long-term, ongoing relationships
3. Dealings regulated through "tacit understanding" or "logrolling" *(nareai)* rather than documented contracts
4. Preference for close relationships between core firm and subcontractor, which allow extensive exchange of information
5. Close attention by the core firm to the quality of management when selecting subcontractors
6. Acceptance by subcontractors of partial control of their internal management by the core firm
7. Sharing in the fruits of growth

Japanese firms exhibit many special types of behavior in their conduct of business, but ultimately, these may all be viewed as having a single goal: the partial integration of core and supplier firms. Japanese companies are distinguished by their propensity to confine their dealings to a limited number of other firms, and to establish long-term, ongoing business relationships with those firms. These close dealings give rise to an extensive exchange of information between the two parties, and only when this occurs can the partial integration of the two firms take place.

Another important determinant of Japanese firm behavior is the desire to reduce risk. The desire to reduce transaction risk is the underlying reason for the efforts of Japanese firms to maintain close communication with each other. Again, the desire of firms placing orders to maintain some room for maneuver after concluding an agreement, in order to reduce risk or shift it elsewhere, is behind the preference for "tacit understanding" or "logrolling" over contracts while transacting business. Only with partial integration between firms are these sorts of risk-avoidance measures possible.

Close attention by the core firm to the management practices of key subcontractors is also necessary. To ensure that the subcontractor will be able to grow along with the core firm, its management must be of high quality. An additional motive is to ensure that the subcontractor will accurately disclose certain types of information, thus eliminating the possibility of opportunistic behavior by the subcontractor. Furthermore, subcontractors accept this partial integration into the core firm in order to be able to share in the fruits of growth along with the core firm.

3. THE ECONOMIC ACHIEVEMENTS OF THE JAPANESE PRODUCTION SYSTEM

Let us now examine how these structural and behavioral differences between the American and Japanese production systems have influenced the economic performance and international competitiveness of the two nations.

3.1. Cost/Performance: Why Are Japanese Firms Able to Achieve High Output at Low Cost?

Japanese firms did not use some mysterious technique or take advantage of their subcontractors to achieve their high levels of cost/performance. The desire and effort expended to reduce production costs is the same in Japan and the United States; however, there are great differences in the approaches taken to this problem. While cost reduction is made possible in Japan through cooperation between the core firm and its subcontractors, American firms try to obtain the lowest possible price for the components they need through the open competition between suppliers.

There is a very simple reason for the high cost/performance levels achieved under the Japanese production system: the learning that results from long-term, ongoing dealings between core firm and subcontractor; the savings resulting from thoroughgoing specialization in the various production processes; and the production-engineering concepts—value analysis and value engineering—originally borrowed from American firms, and put to practical use through the cooperation of the core firm and its subcontractors.

Clearly, the learning effect that results from the long-term, ongoing relationship between the core firm and its suppliers contributes greatly to reducing costs. In particular, this learning effect is large in Japan because the core firm relationships are stable and the processes that the suppliers use is well defined. In addition, the steps in the production process are allocated among a large number of firms, allowing even a small subcontractor to use advanced, specialized equipment. This in turn means full realization of the advantages of specialization and a division of labor between firms.

In contrast, American firms have contracts covering clearly stipulated time periods, generally less than one year. Once the contract expires, the bidding process starts again from scratch, with no guarantee that prior relationships will be extended; existing suppliers get nothing more than a chance to bid on a larger number of contracts. The risk for the subcontractors is large, and in order to ensure a stable level of orders, they prefer to deal with a larger, more diverse set of firms.

The result is that American subcontractors must not only vary their production activities over a shorter period of time, but must also concern themselves with a more diverse set of processes. Thus, these firms purchase fewer of the specialized material-handling equipment common in Japanese firms, and there is a tendency to prefer multipurpose equipment that can be used to meet any sort of demand.[13] However, recent rapid technological advances have made special-purpose machines many times more productive than multipurpose systems.

Naturally, this tendency toward constant changes in the production activities of a single subcontractor, and the use of multipurpose equipment, lowers the productivity of the production system; there is little opportunity to take advantage of the learning effect; nor are they likely to get the most out of their machines. The longer the production run of a given product, the greater this gap in productivity between American and Japanese firms will grow, leading to a decisive Japanese cost advantage in mass-manufactured products.

The semiannual renegotiation of unit prices for Japanese subcontractors' output is generally accompanied by a *reduction* in price on the part of the subcontractors. Each reduction is small—perhaps 0.5 percent—but the cumulative effect is large. In contrast, renegotiation of prices in the United States generally involves an increase in prices.

In addition, Japanese subcontractors generally try to lower their prices at this time even if an increase in the size of the order from

the core firm necessitates an increase in the subcontractor's productive capacity. In contrast, because of the risks involved in further
investment in plant and equipment when future demand is uncertain, American firms will generally not accept an order that may
exceed their productive capacity unless they can realize a higher
price for their output. In this sense, American subcontractors are
exposed to much more risk than their Japanese counterparts.

An even more decisive source of Japan's cost/performance advantage in mass-produced machinery is production technology, as
developed through the use of value analysis and value engineering.
The key suppliers and core firms work together in pursuit of these
technology gains, share the gains when they are achieved, and see
to it that the new technologies are quickly disseminated among all
the key suppliers.

Among Japanese manufacturing firms, there is a saying that "a 3
percent cost reduction is difficult, but 30 percent is easy."[14] This
reflects the strong effectiveness of value analysis/value engineering.
Suggestions for improvement in the production process and the
use of materials are made in large numbers by on-site personnel.
One automobile parts manufacturer aims for eighteen suggestions
per year from each employee, but in fact receives as many as
twenty-four. Overall, the firm receives several tens of thousands of
suggestions each year.

When a firm must develop a new product to survive in the fierce
competition of the Japanese marketplace, it must set a target price
that is as competitive as possible. The firm then sets unit prices for
made-to-order goods that allow them to meet that price, and notify
the subcontractors. If a subcontractor is unable to make a profit at
the price set by the core firm, the core firm makes various recommendations as to how costs can be reduced, and the subcontractor
also makes suggestions for changes in the design of the product and
improvements in the production process that will allow a profit to
be made at the price set by the core firm. Thus, cooperation
between the core firm and the subcontractor while the product is
still in the design stage allows the core firm's original target price to
be met.

Reductions in production costs made possible by value-engineering improvements on the part of the subcontractor are shared with
the core firm. The rule for distribution of these cost advantages
varies from firm to firm, but the most widespread prac-

tice assigns half of the benefit to the subcontractor during a period of six months to a year. In addition, the benefits of a value-engineering improvement go not only to the firm responsible for its development, but are distributed to all of the other subcontractors through dissemination of the new technology. Most core firms have research circles for their subcontractors, which meet regularly, and the best suggestions for improvements in value engineering are rewarded. Thus, each subcontractor's share in the benefits of an improved process is rather limited. Nevertheless, subcontractors who aggressively pursue improvements in the production process realize greater short-term reductions in production cost and are given preferential treatment by the core firm in placing orders; subcontractors who are not eager to improve their production process face reduced orders or elimination from the group. Thus, subcontractors in Japan have a strong incentive to seek process improvements, and also are able to benefit from improvements made by others.

The core firm has access to certain internal data of the sub-contractor concerning production processes and cost structure. This enables the core firm to provide learning effects, and at the same time permits it to appropriate some of the cost-reducing improvements made by suppliers through value analysis and value engineering. One of the things that impressed us about the American firms we visited was the fact that they had little expectation of receiving suggestions from suppliers regarding value analysis/value engineering. Subcontractors would not consent to disclose any details concerning process improvements. Gaining access to the internal data of its subcontractors would be difficult for an American core firm, and without this data, the American firm cannot determine what sort of profits are being realized by the sub-contractor from process improvements. This also means that the core firm has little reason to encourage suppliers to make process improvements. Ultimately, the American core firm is forced to rely on the bidding process alone in its efforts to discover a fair price for the goods it requires. Also, the product design is naturally complete by the time competitive bidding begins, since the bidding firm must be supplied with all of the necessary specifications in order to determine its price. Therefore, subcontractors have no opportunity to offer suggestions regarding value engineering, and none are expected.

In most of the Japanese firms we studied, the decision to allow a subcontractor to bid on a given contract was not made on the basis of price alone. The cost reductions achieved by a subcontractor are the outcome of long collaboration with the core firm, and all of the purchasing agents we interviewed were extremely confident regarding the underlying factors that determine the prices offered by subcontractors. The purchasing agents maintained: "We have implemented thorough cost-reduction measures. If a new participating subcontractor submits a bid below the price we expect, they must supply a detailed explanation as to how they were able to achieve that price. If they cannot provide this explanation, we know they are just trying to buy their way in and they will not be a reliable low-cost supplier over the long term."

Thus, Japan's high levels of cost/performance come from the efforts made to reduce costs, and the distribution of that knowledge to all of the subcontractors, both of which are the result of the long collaboration between the subcontractors and core firms.

3.2. The Effects of Thorough Quality Control

The current high levels of Japanese product quality, like the high Japanese levels of cost/performance, are the cumulative effect of long-term cooperation between the core firms and their subcontractors. Prior to the 1970s, the level of Japanese product quality was by no means high. The quality-control techniques developed in the United States were known to most large Japanese firms by the early sixties, but had not spread to the small and medium-sized firms.[15] By the late 1960s, the Japanese machine industry had entered an export-driven growth phase. However, the small and medium-sized firms still accounted for over half of Japan's production, and their weak quality control represented a serious limitation to that growth. These smaller firms were introduced to quality-control techniques by the larger firms. One consumer electronics company took subcontractor management personnel on retreats in groups of twenty to thirty at a time. The objective was not only to study quality control, but also to begin changing the management outlook of the subcontractors, from one oriented toward family-type management control to one better oriented to the management of a modern enterprise.

Once modern techniques of quality control were imparted to the subcontractors, the long-term ties between the core firm and its subcontractors made it possible to gradually raise the quality targets. During this period of time, the subcontractors received continuous guidance from the core firm; at the same time, the fierce competition between the subcontractors meant reduction in orders or elimination for those unable to meet the required levels of quality.

The current superior levels of Japanese quality control are the cumulative fruits of twenty years of work. Recently, Japanese firms have begun to measure quality in parts per million (PPM), and in the automobile and electronics industries, responsibility for quality control is gradually being transferred entirely to the subcontracting firms, resulting in a system where no parts are inspected as they come into the core firm *(mukensa)*.

Meanwhile, due to the short-term nature of the relationship between subcontractor and core firm in the United States, gradual improvement of quality is difficult, and the same levels of quality tend to be specified for each round of bids. Even now, in most cases, the Acceptance Quality Level (AQL) is still set at 0.4 percent. Of course, some American firms, such as Apple Computer, have introduced a no-inspection, "ship-to-stock" policy for goods obtained from subcontractors, but this remains the exception.

Professor Steven C. Wheelwright has pointed out that American firms view production cost as being a trade-off with quality, while Japanese firms, through quality control, have eliminated the waste that results from defective output, thus lowering production costs and achieving both objectives at once.[16] The view that lower production costs can be compatible with higher quality is beginning to spread among American firms, giving cause for optimism as to future improvements in American quality control.

3.3. Technological Development: Why Do Japanese Firms Emphasize Refinements?

A division of labor between firms (and within an economy) implies a simultaneous division of the relevant technology. Is there some level at which the technological division of effort between large and small firms leads to an optimal performance in technology? This is clearly an important question.

American economists such as Kenneth Galbraith and Robert D. Buzzell have pointed out that highly integrated firms show high performance in the development of new technology.[17,18] In fact, this is true in the field of research itself, which demands large investments and many first-class personnel. However, things look very different when one considers the entire new-product-development process, including in the definition the transformation of technology into a marketable product to the creation of a demand for that product among end-users. Creating competitive products requires more than good basic research; it requires good applied technology, including related technology. It also requires the ability to adjust rapidly to shifts in consumer demand. Except in certain types of basic research requiring extensive funding, individuals and small firms are the best sources of innovative ideas. In *The State of Small Business 1984,* published by the U.S. government's Small Business Administration, small and medium-sized enterprises were singled out as "idea generators." Inventive, innovative corporate cultures are easier to mobilize in these firms. Large and small firms differ in the types of research at which they excel, and thus the two types of firms can play complementary roles in the development of new products.

In recent years, large Japanese firms have begun limiting the scope of their in-house research in order to cope with the acceleration of technological progress and somewhat limit the huge investments required. For example, NEC limits its own new-product research to the key components that differentiate the product, and leaves nearly all other research as well as production to its subcontractors. The fine segmentation of labor between firms in Japan encourages technological specialization, and some of the subcontractors possess greater technical capabilities than the core firm in their chosen areas of production. Furthermore, many large Japanese firms have recently been moving toward consignment of all production processes to the subcontractors. This accumulated experience in OEM (Original Equipment Manufacture) production has resulted in striking increases in the subcontractors' level of expertise in production control as well as in process technology. This in turn has done much to raise the level of Japanese product quality.

The fact that each subcontractor works within a well-defined area of the production process means that opportunities for process improvements are open to even the smallest firm. All of the technical improvements accumulated through the subcontracting system end up in the final product, making it very competitive in the international market.

Still, these technological improvements are primarily refinements rather than breakthroughs. The long period when Japanese firms were preoccupied with catching up with the advanced nations of the West has left a legacy of emphasis on improvements to existing technology, rather than on the development of original technology. For over a decade, the core firms have been increasing their R&D spending enormously in an attempt to overcome this barrier, but so far they have not produced many real technological breakthroughs.

Meanwhile, the huge R&D expenditures of large American firms have combined with huge government outlays on defense-related R&D to give the Americans a leading position in basic research. However, there is little research cooperation between firms, and while basic research receives much attention, researchers have little incentive to improve existing technologies. Furthermore, the huge investments in defense-related research and the huge demand for military products diverts research attention from the satisfaction of consumer demand. Indeed, the American firms (even the smaller firms) we visited that had high-level technological capability were primarily emphasizing production for the military. The United States has by far the greatest R&D resources of any nation, but it seems that not enough of it is applied to the development of consumer products.

3.4. Why Is the Cycle of New-Product Development Two Years in the United States and Six Months in Japan?

Just as the division of research and development work between core firm and subcontractors has resulted in high levels of technological performance, so the close ties between firms have played a major role in accelerating the pace of new-product development. Japanese subcontractors are involved in the development of a new product from the ground up; they do not simply execute blueprints provided by the core firm. Detailed design of many components is often provided entirely by the subcontractors, who also provide many proposals for improvements in the product.

At least in their specific area of production technology, subcontractors have surpassed the core firm, and this accumulated wisdom, acquired by the subcontractors on the factory floor, is unavailable to the engineers of the core firm as they assemble their designs for the product on the drawing board. Getting this factory-floor wisdom of the subcontractors into the product design at the very beginning results in products that are more functional and have lower production cost.

Orders for dies are placed with the subcontractors while the patterns are still at a tentative stage, allowing design changes and improvements to be incorporated by the subcontractor along the way. This flexible capability of the subcontractor, along with the marked reduction in the time required for the core firm to produce the patterns, plays a large part in the shortened product-development cycle. Japanese firms are able to produce dies of all types in about half the time needed in the United States and elsewhere, and some subcontractors have reduced the required time by an additional 50 percent through extensive use of CAD (computer-assisted design) systems and specialized equipment. In addition, there are many contractors specializing in the trial runs needed for the development of new products. Thus, by mobilizing the capabilities of a large number of firms early in the new-product-development cycle, product quality is enhanced and development time is reduced. The result is a product life cycle of around six months in technology-driven fields such as office automation and audio-visual equipment. In contrast, the foreign product life cycle is around two years, and this difference in the rate of introduction of new products is reflected in their competitiveness in the international marketplace.

Again, the primary reason for the Japanese advantage in this area lies in the relationship between the core firm and its key subcontractors. Dealings with the subcontractors are not determined through a process of competitive bidding, and the price of the work is not contracted ahead of time. Subcontractor prices are set at a reasonable level based on the core firm's detailed understanding of the subcontractor's cost structure, and subsequent design changes can be matched by adjustments in the price.

3.5. Flexible Production

The "Just in Time" (JIT) inventory method shuns the holding of inventory at the production site in favor of deliveries of just the right amount of materials, at just the right place and time. This system was developed by Toyota and has spread beyond the automobile industry to find use in a broad portion of Japanese industry. The JIT method not only reduces inventory holding costs, but also makes it easier for firms to engage in diversified production. In order for the system to work, components must maintain a level of quality that eliminates the need for testing, deliveries must be on schedule, and the suppliers must be capable of responding flexibly to changes in the pace of production.

The time from core-firm order to subcontractor delivery has fallen to one month in Japan; in some segments of the electronics industry, the cycle is down to two weeks, and late deliveries have dwindled to zero. In the American firms we surveyed, order-to-delivery times of eight to ten weeks were most common, twice as long as in Japan; delivery delays were common, and purchasing agents for American core firms spent significant amounts of time monitoring the delivery schedules of subcontractors. Long delivery times present not only purchasing-control problems, but reduce the ability of the firm to respond to changes in the marketplace. In the current environment of rapidly shifting demand and high market uncertainty, the ability to adapt rapidly has a tremendous impact on firm performance.

How have Japanese firms achieved this overall reduction in delivery time and the precise coordination of delivery schedules with production? The answer lies in the limited number of subcontractors with which the core firm must deal, and the advance notification of production schedules given by the core firm to the subcontractors. Every six months, subcontractors usually receive rough outlines of the core firm's management objectives and planned production schedules for that period; three months in advance, they get a specific but nonbinding notification of the planned order's size. The final figure is contained in documents issued two to four weeks before production is to begin, but again, these documents specify only the number of units needed by the core firm; the actual number, size, timetable, and destination of deliveries is determined by the *kanban* system. The number of units specified in the preproduction documents and the number actually called for through the *kanban* system may differ within plus or minus 10 percent; any discrepancies will be adjusted for during the next period.

This system of nonbinding advance notification by the core firm, in combination with the day-to-day contacts maintained with the subcontractors, acts to reduce the risk associated with changes in the core firm's needs for supplies. Japanese firms also rotate personnel frequently between the sales, production, and purchasing functions, and the resulting lines of communication keep the differences between estimated and actual orders small. Thus, the risk faced by the subcontractor is relatively slight. Furthermore, the fact that the core firm is dealing with a relatively small number of key contractors means that communication among firms is simplified, and fluctuations in core-firm production are more easily dealt with.

In American firms, the sales, production, and purchasing functions are handled by specialists, and there is almost no exchange of personnel between these functions. The scope and limitations of the responsibilities within each functional area are clearly defined with little overlap, making it difficult to initiate cross-functional contact or cooperation. As a result, large discrepancies arise between projected and actual costs, and there are large fluctuations in the level of orders to suppliers. At the same time, each subcontractor has dealings with a large number of other firms, making it difficult to respond quickly to changes in the production of one core firm.

The relatively long delivery times of American firms necessitate greater adjustments to ongoing changes in the environment. Furthermore, American subcontractors prefer to deal with a large number of customers through legally binding contracts, in order to reduce the risk of fluctuations in the orders of each core firm. However, long-term relationships based on explicit contracts come up against the barrier of "bounded rationality," as O. E. Williamson has noted.[19] Reducing risk by broadening one's customer base impedes close day-to-day communication between core firm and supplier, and reliance on legally binding contracts makes subsequent adjustment of order size impossible. Ironically, this very fact adds to the risk involved in interfirm transactions in the United States.

3.6. Functional Distribution of Risk

The idea that Japanese core firms use their contractors as a buffer against business shocks is still widespread. Recently, an opposing view of the core firm as taking on the risk faced by the subcontractors has begun to gain attention.[20] Both of these views are one-sided and do not really explain the distribution of risk among Japanese firms.

Regardless of size, Japanese firms show strong risk-avoidance tendencies. In fact, the conduct of Japanese firms is determined by an underlying drive both to avoid risk and to distribute responsibility for risk. Japanese and American firms differ in the ways they attempt to reduce and distribute risk. Japanese firms prefer to reduce risk through close communication and exchange of information among firms. This Japanese preference leads to multilevel organizations of business entities, and such structures can be seen in the wholesaling and retailing sectors as well as in the manufacturing sector. Japan's often-criticized multilevel distribution system is not a relic from Japan's past—it acts to provide information that can help in the reduction or distribution of risk.[21]

Thus, Japanese firms act to reduce risk by seeking large amounts of information. In contrast, American firms act to reduce risk through dealings based on clear contracts.

In Japan, risk is distributed between large firms and the small and medium-sized enterprises, because the cost to each of absorbing risk of a given situation is not the same for both types of firms. Core firms practice lifetime employment and cannot easily lay off workers, while the small and medium-sized firms have more latitude in adjusting their workforce and production levels to follow fluctuations in the business cycle. These smaller firms face a relatively smaller cost in absorbing short-term business-cycle risk; this capability is a source of bargaining power for the smaller firms; for some small firms, this ability to absorb short-term risk is the key to their competitiveness.

However, once the impact of such factors as the business cycle extends beyond the short term, the very existence of some medium-sized and small firms may be threatened. Absorbing this type of risk is relatively less costly for the core firm, which can act as a "haven of last resort" for the subcontractors, especially those with whom it has the closest ties. The core firm can then distribute risk by continuing to place orders with the subcontractors at the minimum level required to sustain each firm. In this way, the core firm can insure its subcontractors against risk. To retain these benefits, subcontractors will prefer to maintain a large percentage of their business with one main core firm, even as they attempt to increase the number of other firms with which they deal.

Large Japanese firms generally try to avoid major fluctuations in income in favor of smooth, steady earnings growth. In order to reduce losses in down cycles, it is not unusual for a core firm to call for lower subcontractor prices; in compensation, the core firm will try to provide the subcontractors with more favorable terms when business trends improve.

Behind the smooth functioning of this structure for risk reduction lies the long-term, ongoing relationship of the core firm with its contractors, and the mutual trust built up through close interfirm communication. In addition, there is a tacit understanding that the core firm will not impose unsustainable levels of risk on its subcontractors, and will act as a haven of last resort for the subcontractors in times of emergency.

3.7. Reducing the Cost of Communication

In order to maintain this close, organic linkage between core firm and subcontractor, a great deal of communication, coordination, and guidance must take place between parties. Naturally, maintaining this information flow involves large costs. If steps were not taken to reduce these communication costs, they would eventually increase to the point where the system would break down, preventing the kind of superior Japanese international competitiveness we see today. Again, one could say that the Japanese production system is inherently information-intensive, providing an incentive to devise a system to lower the resulting communication costs. Firms with such a system will have a significant advantage in the information-intensive industrial society of today. This new industrial environment now includes a more diversified demand, shortened product life cycle, proliferation of different products, accelerated pace of technological change, emergence of complex sets of related technologies, and increased technological uncertainty. This environment requires more and better information and information collection than at any time in the past.

How have Japanese firms managed to reduce their communication costs? In contrast to the multifirm, multilevel Japanese production system, the American production system accomplishes most production with just two levels: core firm and first-level supplier. This difference in the subcontracting systems of the two nations also implies important differences in the structure of their communication systems. The American production system involves direct lines of communication from the core firm to all the subcontractors, while the Japanese system employs a multilevel system, with the core firm maintaining contact (almost as if it had information terminals at the various firms that it deals with) at each level.

Clearly, the Japanese system involves lower communication costs. As Kenneth J. Arrow has shown, communication costs increase with the number of contact points.[22] Organizational researchers such as Herbert Simon and Oliver E. Williamson have also stressed that multilevel organizations have the ability to greatly reduce the cost of information transmission. In the Japanese multilevel system, there is a single firm at each level that deals and communicates with a comparatively small number of supplier firms; that single firm deals with its suppliers on a close, daily basis, ensuring the accurate, complete transmission of information and guidance. This greater efficiency of the multilevel system in the transmission of information can be seen not only on the level of costs but also in terms of the level of detail the system can support.

Since there are only two levels in the American system, American core firms must deal with many thousands of subcontractors directly, making it difficult to carry out frequent, close communication. For example, the core firm must rely on a large number of standardized criteria to evaluate subcontractors; while these criteria provide a measure of objectivity, they do not allow the core firm to evaluate equally important but less easily quantified information about the subcontractors, such as their future potential.

The long-term, ongoing relationship between core firm and subcontractor in Japan also can greatly reduce these information costs. Since it does not need to begin many new relationships with subcontractors, the cost of investigating the trustworthiness or technical capability of the firm is eliminated. In the United States, core firms must go through the process of carefully describing and advertising upcoming contracts, and must process bids from all participating firms. In Japan, the core firm merely awards the contract to the supplier with the most suitable cost structure and technical level. Kenneth J. Arrow states that another special attribute of communication cost is that "it is probably less costly to continue using established communication channels than to open new ones."[24] The long-term, ongoing relationship of the Japanese core firm with its subcontractors seems to be quite effective in reducing communication costs.

The Japanese subcontracting system is itself an information channel. The subcontractors make internal data available to the core firm, and innovations developed by one subcontractor are disseminated to the others via the purchasing agents in the core firm. In addition, the subcontractors' cooperative association acts as a channel to funnel information from the core firm to the subcontractors, and helps to disseminate information on process improvements to the community of subcontractors as a whole.

There is yet another factor working to reduce the costs of moving information and goods between the core firm and its subcontractors: this is the limited land area of Japan. In particular, the construction of factories in major industrial centers makes this communication easy. Unfortunately, Japan is now reaching a limit to further plant expansion on these industrial zones; this has led to a recent trend toward locating factories in rural areas farther from the major cities, complicating the communication process. However, when the core firm relocates a factory in a rural area, production facilities of the subcontractors are built near it; if only the subcontractor's plant is relocated, the organizational portions of the firm necessary for contact and exchange of information with the core firm are kept near the core firm's facilities. Relocation of production facilities to rural areas is facilitated by the recent widespread use of facsimile machines by small and medium-sized firms, and the advent of rapid-mail and delivery services that can deliver material anywhere in Japan within twenty-four hours.

Furthermore, the purchasing departments of the Japanese core firm are quite decentralized, and the purchasing department in a single factory has a great deal of freedom in carrying out local procurement of materials and overseeing the activities of subcontractors. Normally, the purchasing department at the headquarters of the core firm deals only with large-scale purchases with substantial potential to reduce unit costs; the determination of overall firm purchasing policy; and the administration of the subcontractors' cooperative association. Smaller orders of materials or the selection and supervision of key subcontractors is left to the purchasing departments of the individual production facilities. In the Japanese automobile industry, purchasing is controlled by the headquarters, and purchasing departments at the factory level are not allowed as much autonomy, but personnel from the head office are often stationed at the factories. This means that in practice, purchasing in each region is carried out by personnel who are familiar with the subcontractors located in that area. Obviously, this purchasing-control structure works to keep the subcontractors and the core firm's factory in close communication.

The sheer size of the United States and the wide dispersion of production facilities results in higher shipping costs and makes close communication difficult. American subcontractors deal with many customers, and the core firms deal with many subcontractors, resulting in little incentive for core firms and subcontractors to coordinate decisions on plant location. IBM's Colorado plant, for example, deals largely with suppliers located in Ohio, Kentucky, and Indiana.

This wide geographic dispersion of suppliers means very few opportunities for face-to-face communication; one such contact in two to three months was not uncommon among the firms we visited. Most business was conducted by telephone and sometimes via personal computer, but since most suppliers did not possess facsimile equipment, plans and diagrams from the core firm had to be sent through the mails, a time-consuming process. In contrast,

Japanese purchasing agents meet personally with representatives of important suppliers at least once a week, and nearly all plans and drawings are sent instantaneously via facsimile equipment.

Close communication between core firm and supplier is also made more difficult in the United States because of the very centralized and overspecialized character of the purchasing function in most American firms. For example, in the Ford assembly plant we visited, all purchasing was controlled by the purchasing department at headquarters, and such basic information as the origin of the parts used in assembly was not known at the factory level. Thus, information concerning factory-level needs cannot be transmitted to the subcontractors, while subcontractors have no direct way of submitting suggestions to the factory level if they have ideas for improvements. There is no way to develop potential suppliers located in the vicinity of the factory.

4. CHANGING TRENDS AND IMPROVEMENTS IN THE U.S. AND JAPANESE PRODUCTION SYSTEMS

4.1. Change in the U.S. Production System and Barriers to that Change

American firms are beginning to realize that the strong international competitiveness of Japanese companies stems not from unfair dumping, but from differences in the performance of their respective production systems. These firms have begun to implement a thorough restructuring of the American production system in order to revitalize the international competitiveness of American industry.

The automobile industry has become the greatest focus of these efforts. In order to regain its position as the leading maker of small cars, GM has invested the huge sum of $5 billion to establish the Saturn Corporation. The procurement policies of this new venture include the following objectives: (1) long-term relationships with parts suppliers; (2) limiting the number of parts suppliers; and (3) establishing a "strategic procurement system" coordinated with the automobile assembly line. These and other measures are a real attempt to implement the Japanese production system in the United States.

At the American auto plant we visited, a company representative spoke straightforwardly. "We are trying to copy the Japanese subcontracting system," he said. "But there are some things that cannot be adapted in an American context."

Which portions of Japan's production system would prove helpful for American firms? Which *can* be adopted? How will they have to be modified to fit the context of American industry? These are questions on the minds of automotive-firm managers.

There is a growing awareness in American industry that the differences in competitiveness between Japanese and American firms spring from the long-term nature of the relationship between the Japanese core firm and its subcontractors, as well as the lower communication costs the Japanese system affords. American firms are moving to eliminate these differences. For example, the preparation of documents involved in the production of a single American automobile costs about $200. In order to reduce this figure, documents are being standardized and bar codes applied to parts to form a computer-controlled, paperless transaction system. In this and other ways, the automobile industry is moving to improve the ways firms deal with each other. An Automotive Industry Action Group (AIAG), which includes the subcontractors and the large auto firms, has been formed with the aim of improving the relationships between the core firms and suppliers, as well as improving the management of the subcontractors.

4.2. Reduction in the Number of Business Relationships

American companies have begun to realize that they have dealings with too many other firms. Most of the purchasing agents at the American firms we visited stated that they felt it was necessary to sharply reduce the number of suppliers with which they dealt, and to establish close ties with a limited number of selected firms. For example, GM has announced its intention to reduce the number of its suppliers by half.[26] However, this will not necessarily be easy, because both core and supplier firms are reluctant to increase their dependence on dealings with any single firm. For example, IBM has a policy of keeping its dependence on any single supplier to less than 30 percent, and most other core firms also try to keep this figure at 20 to 30 percent or less. At the same time, a representative of a spring supplier for GM stated, "GM is reducing the number of suppliers it deals with from twenty to around five. We are confident that our competitiveness will put us into that group, but the increase in orders from GM will make us more dependent on them, which we do not like.'

Another way to reduce the cost of transactions between firms is to increase the degree of vertical integration. Vertical integration reduces the firm's flexibility in production, but when the number of items produced by the firm is limited, vertical integration can be effective. An American manufacturer of industrial ventilation fans reduced its dependence on outside suppliers from 77 percent to 50 percent through the installation of modern equipment such as automated presses, welding robots, and robot painting booths. They even installed a system for quick change of dies. However, this meant a loss of business for the subcontractors who formerly performed such jobs as metal bending and painting. In Japan, if a firm loses out as a first-level supplier, it can always try to regroup as a secondary supplier. In the United States, there is no such opportunity, since few firms go past the first level of supplier. Without this multi-tiered system of suppliers, there is a greater social cost of adjustment when a firm is cut out of a given supply relationship.

Probably the best way for a U.S. firm to deal with the need to strengthen the ties between firms would be for the core firm to choose a small number of key suppliers from its total number of suppliers, and strengthen its ties with them. For example, one American manufacturer of electronic measuring instruments, which deals with as many as 11,000 suppliers, has chosen forty-five key suppliers and is reaping benefits by working closely with them on quality control and delivery scheduling.

A new-venture firm in the field of computer peripherals has also adopted the Japanese system on a large scale. This company was formed in 1981 and has a Japanese-style no-layoff policy. To help reduce the risk of fluctuations in its sales, it subcontracts as much as 75 percent of the value of its output. The firm deals with 272 suppliers, and has formed close ties with seventeen of them. Four of these suppliers produce all their output for the core firm, which guarantees their level of orders. This demonstrates that the adoption of Japanese management practices necessitates a Japanese-style approach to supplier relationships as well.

Japanese production-control and procurement methods were also introduced at Matsushita Electric's Chicago color television plant, purchased from the troubled Quasar. Even though the changes were only partial in nature, the level of quality has risen and the plant's performance has improved dramatically. The number of suppliers has been reduced from 1000 in the days when the plant was run by Quasar to 200. Thirty of these are key suppliers doing 20 percent or more of their business with Matsushita. By concentrating the number of suppliers in this way, close working relationships have become possible, the purchasing staff has been reduced by half to twenty-five, and transactions costs have been reduced. The plant's policy on selecting suppliers places greatest importance on the subcontractor's performance and the quality of its management.

One of the subcontractors to the Matsushita plant, a firm supplying molded plastic parts, does nearly 50 percent of its business with that one factory. It is rare for an American firm to depend so much on one customer. A representative of this firm mentioned three advantages of its relationship with Matsushita: the ability to maintain a good working relationship, close geographical proximity, and scale economies resulting from large orders. In addition, business with Matsushita is stable, while the firm's orders from American automakers fluctuate very widely.

4.3. Extending and Deepening Working Relationships

American firms are also beginning to recognize the need to step up product development and bring the subcontractors in on the new-product-development process. Some firms have begun to use "early sourcing" schemes to allow suppliers to participate in the design stage. Still, the standard American practice of choosing subcontractors on the basis of the bids they submit means that many small product details must be determined prior to bidding. This makes it impossible for most suppliers to participate in product design, and if the unit price is also determined in advance, adjustments after production has started are also impossible.

In Japan, the key subcontractors are specialized firms depending on the core firm for 70 percent or more of their business; these firms have little problem maintaining confidentiality about the core firm's new products. In the United States, suppliers have business dealings with a large number of firms. This makes core firms reluctant to reveal new-product information at an early stage. In order to solve these problems, a thorough restructuring of the process through which prices are determined, as well as deepened ties between firms, will be necessary. In other words, the current competitive-bidding process must be discarded. In its place, firms must adopt a system of negotiation and agreement based on accumulation of data on subcontractor production costs and on accurate exchange of information. Both sides must make accurate disclosure of production costs. The goal for Japanese core firms is a unit price based on the agreement of both parties, and because of this they pay close attention to the character and management of their suppliers. This helps to eliminate the possibility of opportunistic supplier behavior.

In order for trust to exist between core firm and supplier, business dealings must be long-term and continuous, and purchasing policies must be stable. However, American purchasing agents are generally specialists who are promoted or jump to better jobs elsewhere on the basis of short-term results. The result is unstable purchasing policies, which hamper the creation of relationships based on trust. The notable improvement over the last year or two in the American auto industry's parts-procurement process is due to reduced job turnover among purchasing agents, and thus to an increased knowledge of the situation faced by each supplier.

The overly centralized character of the purchasing function should also be changed by allocating more purchasing authority at the local factory level. Outside purchasing will also be more effective if purchasing practices are tailored to the region in which the plant is located, and potential local suppliers developed. If efforts such as these continue, the current large gap in interfirm productivity between the United States and Japan will narrow.

In order to hasten this process, small and medium-sized firms as well as core firms will have to change their outlook. Large firms that must compete with the Japanese have a strong desire to improve their production systems, but change is slow in coming to the smaller firms and those that face little direct import competition. There is also a lingering misconception on the part of some American firms that their production systems and efficiency are the world's best.

5. CHANGING THE SOURCES OF FRICTION INHERENT IN JAPAN'S PRODUCTION SYSTEM

As we have seen, long-term business dealings with a limited number of suppliers result in many beneficial economic effects, and have been responsible for Japan's rise to superior economic competitiveness. At the same time, this model of business dealings limits opportunities for new firms to participate and functions to close off markets. Furthermore, these business relationships rely less on contracts and more on custom and "logrolling," and foreign firms, unfamiliar with Japanese business customs, are left with an even stronger impression that participation in the Japanese market is difficult.

Nevertheless, in their search for long-term advantage, Japanese core firms keep competition among suppliers alive by changing 3 to 5 percent of even their key suppliers each year. Suppliers of more standardized components are changed even more often. Among the American firms we studied, the typical case of supplier rotation was 15 to 20 percent annually. However, some American firms are similar to Japanese core firms in this respect. Hewlett-Packard changes 3 to 5 percent of its suppliers each year, and most of these changes are the result of changes in the firm's product line. This sort of stable relationship with the core firm's suppliers is not limited to Japan; rather, entry to Japan's markets is made difficult by presumptions that they are closed, and by the lack of information concerning Japan's business customs. The head of the purchasing department for one of Japan's major automakers pointed out to us that nearly all Japanese automakers have purchasing offices in De-

troit, but that they receive virtually no sales attention from American
auto-parts suppliers, and that there is little effort by the American
firms to adapt their products to Japanese auto specifications, or to
reduce costs.

The long-term business relations common to Japan are not a
remnant from premodern times, nor are they a product of some
feudal Japanese mentality. As we have seen, from the standpoint of
both core firm and supplier, the Japanese production system is both
profitable and logical. In view of the magnitude of the benefits
conferred by this system, it is hardly reasonable to expect Japanese
firms to change it. Rather, it would make more sense for American
firms, especially manufacturers of accessories and standardized
parts, to deepen their understanding of Japanese business customs
in order to penetrate the Japanese market. At the same time,
Japanese firms must move to change not the system of supplier
relationships itself, but rather the source of core firm power that
might permit the core firm to gain control of the system of supplier
relationships.

One reason we must be concerned about this control is the effect
that it might have on the trade friction with the United States. But
there is a more basic reason for this concern. This kind of control
exercised by the core firm over the suppliers has no legal basis,
such as capital participation by the core firm. As long as the core
firm continues to grow, the subcontractors will continue to enjoy
the long-term fruits of growth. The system thus will be supported by
its suppliers, but if growth stops, the core firms will be unable to
control their suppliers. That could lead to chaos.

The competitiveness of Japanese firms depends upon the productivity of the subcontracting system, and a loss of cooperation
from the subcontractors would represent a life-or-death issue for
the core firm. This has already occurred, with core firms losing
their ability to survive after a slowdown in growth led to their
abandonment by the subcontractors. Thus, Japanese core firms have
emphasized the maintenance of growth at all costs in order not to
fall into such a situation. This pressure to grow, combined with
support for failing firms, helping them to move into higher-growth
fields, has contributed greatly to the rapid changes in Japan's industrial structure. For example, Canon moved out of the camera

field, which had exhausted its growth potential, and into the high-growth field of office-automation equipment. Cameras now account for only a third of Canon's sales.

Once this strong growth push is turned outwards into international markets, however, the natural result is trade friction. Japanese firms have greatly expanded their production capacity in existing fields in order to maintain their high rates of growth, and this tendency may be the source of the unending trade friction. In order to alleviate this problem, the excessively strong growth pressures probably will have to be weakened. For this, a new source of control for the Japanese production system must be found. The strong points of Japan's excellent production system must be retained, but in order to promote international economic harmony, the source of control for the Japanese production system must move from sharing the fruits of growth to sharing strategic information.

In actuality, many of Japan's subcontractors have consolidated their managerial resources and their degree of reliance on one core firm has dropped markedly. These firms have turned from the pursuit of economies of scale to the pursuit of economies of scope, and the information needed for this has become important to the subcontractors. A section head in a purchasing department at Sony told us that core firms can now effectively control subcontractors even with only a few percent of their business, because of the subcontractors' eagerness to work with core firms that have the ability to produce many new, market-leading products. Subcontracting firms are strongly attracted to companies at the leading edge of technology, such as Sony, Matsushita, and Japan IBM, because working with these core firms allows them to absorb the latest technical advances and marketing developments.

Reform of the American production system, particularly the use of computer networks, should greatly reduce their transaction costs. At the same time, Japanese firms have little further room for cost reduction, and little initiative to install computer networks to further reduce their communication costs. As long as Japan does not reform its production system, the gap between American and Japanese firms should shrink; if the Japanese system of subcontractor control by the core firms can be changed, the strong pressure for Japanese core firms to grow could be eased, lowering their export expansion.

Still, there is a need to make short-term adjustments to the current competitive strength of Japanese firms. This will be accomplished by the current high value of the yen. However, the considerable ability of the Japanese firms to adapt will reduce the long-term potential for control of trade frictions through exchange rates. Long-term, record-breaking high values for the yen would be needed for continual reduction of trade surplus, with inevitably large adjustment costs needed for both the economy of Japan and the United States. In order to compensate for the high competitive strength of Japanese firms with relatively low adjustment costs, the excess productive capacity of Japanese export industries must be restricted uniformly. The best way to achieve this is to reduce the number of working hours for the Japanese core firms and their subcontractors.

NOTES

1. "Kojou Kakumei no Nami" [Trends of Factory Revolution], *Nihon Keizai Shinbun [The Japan Economic Journal]*, 19 December 1985, p. 8.

2. Nittsu Research Institute, *Butsuryu Sai-kouchiku no Dokou ni Kansuru Chosa Hokokusho* [Surveys on the Restructuring of Physical Distribution Systems], March 1983, p. 6 (mimeo).

3. Tetsuo Minato, "The Japanese System of Subcontracting and Interfirm Communication" in *Linkage Effects and Small Industry Development,* (mimeographed) (Asia Productivity Organization, May 1986), pp. 43–35.

4. For the United States, *Census of Manufacturers 1982* and for Japan, *Kogyo Tokei-hyo 1984* [Census of Manufacturers, MITI].

5. Japan Development Bank, *Keiei Shihyo Hando Bukku 1985* [Handbook of Financial Data of Industries].

6. Ken-ich Imai et al., *Naibu Soshiki no Keizaigaku* [Economics of Internal Organization] (Tokyo: Toyo Keizai Shinposha, 1982) p. 45 and Susumu Nakamura, Chusho-kigyo to Dai-kigyo [Small Business and Large Business] (Tokyo: Toyo Keizai Shinposha, 1982), p. 8.

7. The Survey of Shoko-chukin Bank suggests that only 22.9 percent of subcontracting firms have capital participation from their core firms. Shoko-chukin Bank, *Shitauke Kigyo no Shin-tenkai* [New Stage of Subcontracting Firms] (Tokyo: Shoko-chukin Bank, March 1983), pp. 25–26.

8. Small and Medium-Sized Enterprise Agency, MITI, *Kogyo Jittai Kihon Chosa Hokokusho* [The Sixth Surveys on Basic Structures of Industries] (Tokyo: MITI, March 1984).

9. Shoko-chukin Bank, op. cit., p. 28.

10. *The U.S. Census of Manufacturers, 1982.*

11. **Number of Plants and Suppliers: The United States and Japanese Car Assembly Company**

	Plants[a]	Suppliers[b]
General Motors	147	12,500
Ford	67	7,800
Chrysler	36	4,000
Toyota	11	250
Nissan	9	170
Honda	6	140

Source: For the United States Company, *Kojou Kanri* [*The Journal of Plant Management*], vol. 28, no. 7, July 1982, p. 39.
[a]*Not including overseas plants.*
[b]*These figures are car parts companies dealing with the car assembly companies directly.*

12. Japan Development Bank, op. cit.

13. Professor Masataka Ikeda pointed out the same things on British industries, "Eikoku no Sabu Asenburi Shitauke Kigyo no Jittai" [Surveys on British Subassembly Type Subcontractors], *Shoukou Kinyu* [The Journal of Shoukou Chukin Bank] February 1986, pp. 3–18.

14. The slogan was first used in Matsushita Electric Company and is now often used by many other companies.

15. Sei-ichi Kato et al., eds., *Keizai Kozo to Chusho Kigyo* [Economic Structure and Small Business] (Tokyo: Do-yu-kan, 1976), p. 113.

16. Steven C. Wheelwright, "Japan—Where Operations Really Are Strategic," *Harvard Business Review* 81, no. 4 (July–August 1981): 67–74.

17. John K. Galbraith, *American Capitalism* (Boston: Houghton Mifflin, 1957), pp. 69–70.

18. Robert D. Bazzell, "Is Vertical Integration Profitable?" *Harvard Business Review* 83, no. 1, (January–February 1983): 92–102.

19. Oliver E. Williamson, *Market and Hierarchies,* (New York: Free Press, 1975), pp. 21–23.

20. Masahiko Aoki, *The Economics of the Japanese Firm* (Amsterdam: North-Holland, 1984), pp. 26–31.

21. OECD, *Economic Surveys,* Japan 1985, pointed out that the complexities and inefficiency of Japanese distribution systems are restricting Japanese imports.

International Comparisons of Distribution Systems

	Japan	*US*	*UK*	*France*	*Germany*
The ratio of wholesale to	5.2	1.7	1.5	1.4	1.5
retail sales[a]	(1979)	(1977)	(1974)	(1981)	(1978)
Number of shops per	13.6	5.9	6.4	11.3	5.6
thousand persons	(1979)	(1977)	(1980)	(1979)	(1979)
Productivity in retail and	2769	4014	2805	3317	3025
wholesale trade[b]					
(Y thousand, 1980)					
Small (1 or 2 persons)	61	43	40	66	50
shops as percentage of	(1979)	(1977)	(1971)	(1980)	(1979)
total shops					

Source: OECD, *Economic Surveys,* Japan 1985, p. 42.
    [a]*This ratio is the value of wholesale trade transactions divided by the value of retail sales. Therefore the greater the number of stages in wholesale transactions, the larger this ratio will be.*
    [b]*Real GDP per capita at 1975 prices.*

22. Kenneth J. Arrow, *The Limits of Organization,* (New York: W.W. Norton, 1974), pp. 42–43.

23. Harvert A. Simon, *The Shape of Automation,* (New York: Harper & Row, 1965), p. 100 and Oliver E. Williamson, *Corporate Control and Business Behavior,* (Englewood Cliffs, N.J.: Prentice-Hall, 1970), p. 20.

24. Kenneth J. Arrow, op. cit., p. 41.

25. "Kokusai Butai ni Tatu Jidosha Buhin Gyokai" [Internationalization of Auto Parts Suppliers], *Nihon Keizai Shinbun* [The Japan Economic Journal], 17 December 1985, p. 8, Tokyo.

26. "Nihon ni Manabe" [Learn from Japanese Industries], *Nihon Keizai Shinbun* [The Japan Economic Journal], 21 May 1982, p. 5, Tokyo.

COMMENTARY
ON CHAPTER 3

JOHN P. STERN
*Executive Director, U.S. Electronics Industry,
Japan Office*

RELATIONSHIP BETWEEN CORE COMPANIES
AND SUBCONTRACTORS

I AM HAPPY to be able to participate in what I regard as a very timely discussion of Japanese and American parts-supply systems. The discussion is particularly timely for me because I recently spent some time with seventeen executives from U.S. companies that produce analytical instruments, one of America's most competitive exports to Japan.

As the group visited a number of Japanese instrument makers, many of the Americans were most interested in discussing the Japanese company's relationship with its subcontractors. The Japanese companies, in turn, were very interested in the relationship of the American companies to subcontractors in the United

The U.S. Electronics Industry Japan Office ("Office") is a joint project of the American Electronics Association (AEA), the Electronic Industries Association (EIA), the Scientific Apparatus Makers Association (SAMA) and the U.S. Department of Commerce. The Office was founded in June 1984 as the first permanent office in Japan of a U.S. manufacturing sector trade association. The goal of the Office is to increase the share of the Japanese market held by U.S.-made electronics products. The Office is located at the Nambu Building 3rd floor, Kioicho 3-3, Chiyoda-ku, Tokyo, Japan 102. Telephone (03) 237-7195. Facsimile (03) 237-1237.

States. The Japanese companies wanted to know more about sub-contractors in America because their production in Japan relied heavily on subcontractors. A lack of subcontractors in the United States would impede the decision of a Japanese company to pro-duce in the United States. The Americans, in turn, wanted to know how the Japanese companies maintained quality control among hundreds of subcontractors. Many of the Americans reported that their companies were abandoning the use of subcontractors and were doing more work "in-house." The high cost of subcontractors in the United States and the difficulty of maintaining quality control were given as the major reasons why some U.S. companies were producing more of their product entirely by themselves.

One of the Japanese companies we visited said that it was easier to maintain communications with its subcontractors in the Kansai area than in the more sprawling Tokyo area, and therefore they were successful in using subcontractors in the Kansai area. This amused the Americans since companies in the United States may have to deal with suppliers many thousands of kilometers away, as both Professors Roehl and Minato have pointed out. It might be interesting to examine whether new Value-Added Network services in Japan that link suppliers and core firms have been successful in using telecommunications technology to change the way Japanese firms do business. I suspect that business among Japanese core firms and their suppliers remains based heavily on face-to-face contact, despite the availability of advanced information-handling technology.

Professors Minato and Roehl suggest that the Japanese sub-contractor system works best when the business environment is healthy and improving. What happens when the business environment is plagued by a high yen exchange rate and slowed domestic growth? Both Professors Roehl and Minato agree that neither the large firm nor the small firm willingly bears the risk of a business downturn. Willingly or not, however, it appears that at least in the Japanese *electronics* industry subcontractors have been squeezed by their core firms as one way for the core firms to maintain their pricing structure in the face of a sudden increase in the value of the yen. Professor Minato comments that "subcontractor prices are set at a reasonable level based on the core firm's detailed understand-ing of the subcontractor's cost structure. . . ."[1] He also adds that "there is a tacit understanding that the core firm will not impose unsustainable levels of risk on its subcontractors, and will act as a "haven of last resort" for the subcontractors in times of emergency."[2] Nevertheless, in every month of 1986, at least ten Japanese electronics subcontractors filed for bankruptcy. MITI lectured executives of the larger Japanese electronics firms on their duty to avoid forcing their subcontractors into bankruptcy. Japan's largest electronics trade association, the Electronic Industries Association of Japan *(Nihon denshi kikai kogyo kai),* held seminars for its 650 members concerning the Fair Trade Commission's *(Kosei torihiki iin kai)* fair dealing guidelines for negotiating with subcontractors.[3]

Whether the core firm and its subcontractors are all one happy family, or whether the core firm uses its subcontractors as a buffer for business recessions—or whether the subcontractor has power over the core firm—the role of technology held by the subcontractor is an important one. Chapters 3 and 4 provide important information on the growth of technology among subcontractors and the role that new technology plays in keeping the subcontractor healthy.

MOVEMENT OF CORE FIRMS OVERSEAS

One of the greatest problems facing the Japanese parts-supply system is the movement of Japanese core firms overseas to avoid the high yen and trade friction. It is characteristic of the vitality of the Japanese government that the Medium-Sized and Small Enterprises Agency *(Chusho kigyo cho)* announced in June 1987 a new system of loans and funding to allow Japanese subcontractors to develop new technology. This system may help Japanese subcontractors weather the recession caused by the high yen and trade friction. It is designed to help subcontractors that do more than 20 percent of their business with a single firm, and that have already lost at least 10 percent of their business or expect to lose at least 15 percent of their business because their core firm has moved overseas.[5]

Whether the subcontractor system is unique to Japan or is a form of business found in the United States and other countries, there will be increasing debate in Japan about whether it can be maintained and perhaps even whether it should be maintained. The closing of the curtain on Japan's postwar era may mean a new role for Japan's subcontractors—or it may mean the end of an industry.

NOTES

1. See p. 104–105.
2. See p. 108.
3. The Electronic Industries Association of Japan ("EIAJ") has published a Japanese-language handbook on the subject that can be viewed at the EIAJ headquarters, Tokyo Chamber of Commerce and Industry Building, Marunouchi 3-2-2, Chiyoda-ku, Tokyo 100.
4. For further details, see *Tsusansho koho* [MITI Daily Bulletin], June 16, 1987, p. 5.

4

A COMPARISON OF U.S.–JAPANESE
FIRMS' PARTS-SUPPLY SYSTEMS:
WHAT BESIDES NATIONALITY
MATTERS?

THOMAS ROEHL
University of Washington

INTRODUCTION

I T MAY seem paradoxical to write about United States–Japan decision making without focusing directly on the problem of the different characteristics of the pool of U.S. firms versus those of the Japanese. Why, one might ask, look at the variation within these two samples, and ignore the important and significant differences between them? I do not dispute the importance of the differences between the average system in the sample of U.S. firms and the average for their Japanese counterparts. The differences have been well documented by many recent books and articles on these subjects. For the convenience of the reader, I have provided a bibliography of works in English that cover this topic. My co-researcher, Professor Minato, has added his contribution to this comparative literature as Chapter 3 of this book. Not wishing to merely repeat his insights, I have chosen to focus on the differing competitive environments and firm strategies faced by the Japanese and American firms we interviewed. This permits me to look at the samples of Japanese and American firms for differences in not just the country variables, but variations in other factors as well—

factors that might also change the appropriate type of business transaction for a given parts-supply relationship. We can then be sure that we are looking at a difference between the United States and Japan that is indeed a difference of country characteristics. This approach also permits us to consider the use of principles from both the economics literature on cooperative games and the business-strategy literature on developing and managing cooperative ventures.

If we are to suggest changes in the current system to managers in the two countries, we will have to keep in mind these same environmental and firm variables. If these managers are American, it will be useful to present the ideas as more universal principles, rather than seem to be advocating that they "copy" the Japanese. I thus believe this approach can have both analytical and practical benefits.

Initial studies of the parts-supply system tended to look exclusively at the national differences. As we begin to study the parts-supply relationship in more detail, however, we are discovering that there are significant variations within the country samples, variations between industries, and between firms in the same industry. Professor Asanuma's recent paper (Asanuma 1985) has documented differences in the parts-supply systems for electronics and automobile firms in Japan that can be attributed to the differences in market conditions and the environment faced by individual firm managers. Using data from the interviews conducted in 1985 by Professor Minato and myself, we have an opportunity to extend the sort of comparison begun by Professor Asanuma to an international level. This chapter thus considers three types of variables that should influence the type of parts-supply relationship that develops: the nationality of the firm; the nature of the competitive environment in which the firm must operate; and the resources (managerial, technical, as well as financial) available to the firm to create and implement its parts-supply strategy. Given the results from this discussion, a second part of this chapter looks at the incentives for *creating* and *maintaining* both the market-driven and cooperative types of parts-supply systems, using principles from the economics literature and business-policy literature.

1. COUNTRY-SPECIFIC VARIABLES

In comparing the parts-supply systems of the United States and Japan, it is important to identify various elements that might be different in the two countries. It does not help managers who are trying to develop more appropriate systems for parts supply to simply lump all these factors under the label of one country or other. It seems useful to discuss the different competitive situations faced by United States and Japanese firms in three areas: differences in the growth patterns of the economies in the postwar period; the differing conditions of uncertainty in the two economies; and the different economic and business-institutional relationships that support parts-supply relationships in the two countries.

1.1. Economic Growth

Japanese economic growth in the postwar period has been substantially higher than that of the United States. This has made it more likely for the Japanese to develop new types of long-term parts-supply relationships. When we asked Japanese firms about new commitments in their parts-supply relationships, they frequently answered that they made little change unless there was a new and growing sector they needed to add to their stable of parts suppliers. Growth in the overall scale of operations allowed some establishment of new long-term relationships. When we talked to firms that were not growing as fast (e.g., those in heavy industry), we found them extremely unlikely to make additions to their group of parts suppliers. Previous commitments had to be maintained.

This raises an important point: firms must feel confident that they will be able to live up to the commitments that such long-term parts-supply relationships require. Growth of the firms' own output—even if that growth might be in several areas—permits them a certain flexibility in maintaining these relationships. If nothing else, a parts supplier that formerly did most of its business with the shipbuilding division, for example, can at least apply some of the same skills to the aerospace or automobile divisions. Without that expected growth, parts suppliers will find greater uncertainty in the relationship, especially at the early stages when both sides must make a commitment, giving up alternatives in expectation of future sales. At this early stage in the development of the parts-supply system in postwar Japan, most of the firms could take advantage of high growth rates, reducing the costs of systems development. It is not clear that firms in the current Japanese environment could duplicate the smooth development of the system. This also supports the position that U.S. firms that will have the easiest time in developing similar long-term parts-supply systems are those that currently face a rapidly growing demand able to provide support for both parties. It is not surprising that most of the firms that we found exhibiting these long-term relationships with parts suppliers in the United States (e.g., Boeing and Hewlett-Packard) had fairly high rates of growth in demand at that critical time.

1.2. Uncertainty

In the discussion of economic rationales for long-term business relationships below, uncertainty will play an important part in the justification for rejecting a purely market-based parts-supply system. At this point, it is important to compare the uncertainty found in the Japanese economy and that of the United States economy in the postwar period. I will argue that at three levels—those of the personal, corporate, and national economy—Japanese businesses faced what they perceived as a higher level of uncertainty. Given this higher perceived level of uncertainty, we would expect the Japanese firms to develop, on average, better systems of dealing with such uncertainty; the payoff was higher. As conditions in the two countries are now more similar, one would expect this uncertainty factor to encourage U.S. firms to develop systems to deal with this uncertainty, even if there were no Japanese models to emulate.

There are two elements to the uncertainty that matter to the participants in the parts-supply system: variations within a trend; and changes in that trend. This distinction is an important one in the Japanese case, since in the era of fast growth (1950–1974), the first uncertainty predominates, while in the later period (1974 to date), changes in the trend (international wage differences; oil prices; technology) predominate for more firms. The lower growth rate and the lower rate of change in the industrial structure of the U.S. economy in the first period (1950–1974) gave an American firm justification to put a lower premium on systems for parts supply that dealt better with uncertainty.

That picture changed substantially after 1975. The differentials in growth rates between Japan and the United States narrowed; the swings in those growth rates became more dependent on global factors such as oil prices and trade pattern shifts. This has led to more similar national environments in the two countries.

The second type of uncertainty, radical changes in the overall trend, has also influenced the two countries, although they start from different bases. In both countries, firms have been faced with more frequent and more significant changes in the demand for certain product characteristics by their customers and in the technology available for production. The earlier Japanese experience in dealing with wide variations in demand around a growth trend will give Japanese firms an advantage in dealing with this increasingly important aspect of uncertainty, making the Japanese parts-supply system more malleable than its American counterpart. While it is usually asserted that the Japanese systems developed for the high-growth period make it less able to deal with a slower pace of change (Roehl 1983), in this case, experience seems to be more transferable.

It is tempting to generalize from the greater variation in the national economy to argue that Japanese firms, on the average, face greater levels of uncertainty in their own competitive environments as well. There is no doubt that the industrial structure of the Japanese economy changed faster than its U.S. counterpart during the first period, but as we will show below, the individual firm and industry characteristics varied much more within the American samples.

1.3. Individual Characteristics (Culture)

Management scholars (Sullivan 1983) have frequently cited Hofstede's international comparison of national characteristics to justify Japanese business patterns. Hofstede found "tolerance for uncertainty" as one of the key factors that differentiates cultures, and his study showed the Japanese to be one of the highest among the respondents on this factor (Hofstede 1980). Since individual managers make the decisions about the type of parts-supply relationship to be developed, these cultural characteristics will make the Japanese likely to perceive the above uncertainty in their economic environment as more significant than their American counterparts. Japanese will not only have more uncertainty in their economic environment, but they will also be more concerned about that uncertainty. Those searching for a culture-based explanation that is consistent with rational economic behavior of the participants can use this Japanese characteristic to justify the risk sharing that has developed as part of long-term parts-supply relationships. Given that the post-oil-shock economy has even more uncertainty than the period in which most of these relationships were developed, this cultural characteristic has given the Japanese a head start on the development of supply systems to cope with the increased uncertainty in the business environment after 1975.

1.4. Institutional Differences

Japanese long-term labor contracts (granting permanent employment) are perhaps the most important institutional difference that affects the costs of developing and maintaining the parts-supply relationship. The same uncertainty that justifies risk sharing in the parts-supply relationship has been shown by Aoki and others (Aoki 1985) to justify a risk-sharing relationship for labor-supply relationships as well, providing an economically rational justification for the permanent employment contracts. Once this system is in place, it reinforces the effects of uncertainty. As I will argue, when purchasing managers are likely to remain with the same firm for a long period of time, it is easier to achieve a smooth flow of information; experience from previous exchanges enable firms to deal more effectively with the uncertainty factors mentioned above. If promotion—as opposed to performance appraisal, which is continuous—is a long-term process as it is in most Japanese firms, a purchasing manager can be more easily credited with the rewards of a successful parts-supply relationship that is not market-based. Several American purchasing managers cited this longer period of evaluation as necessary for development of the long-term system.

The growth, uncertainty, and institutional factors presented in this section, while not necessarily cultural, are certainly country-specific. There were enough significant differences within the American and Japanese samples, however, that we had to consider firm-specific variables as well. The following section presents some of these firm-specific factors.

2. ENVIRONMENTAL VARIABLES

Not all firms in the two countries had the same type of parts-supply system. Interviews in both countries identified some common factors that explained part of the variation within each of the country samples. The following factors appeared frequently enough to be cited as most important:

- large core firm output relative to supplier capacity for parts production
- stability of technology
- location of potential scale economies in production
- uncertainty about future product mix
- ability of corporate culture to support long-term commitments

Given the additional costs of managing the long-term parts-supply relationship, there must be sufficient volume over time to justify the more complex business relationship. This includes repetition, as Williamson suggests (Williamson 1979), but also the size of the order relative to the capacity of the parts supplier. Both in questionnaire studies in the United States (Schmitt and Connors 1985) and in interviews with Japanese producers, the assurance of volume relative to capacity was important in getting commitment from parts suppliers for such a long-term relationship. If the firm cannot guarantee that level, it is unlikely to attract interest from the quality of suppliers necessary for success in this type of parts-supply system.

The expected future growth of the firm is perhaps just as important as current volume. While current growth is important in attracting suppliers, future growth matters to the core firm as well. As a Japanese heavy-industry purchasing manager put it, "In the current market, we would not think of taking on new suppliers; we no longer are able to guarantee that they will get the volume necessary to make such business profitable." One would expect that the wide variety of products made by the diversified Japanese companies would permit them to develop a parts-supply system with more flexibility. Indeed, a manufacturer of jigs for aerospace units of a heavy-industry firm can use the same sort of products with other units when aerospace demand drops. Within our sample, however, diversified firms seemed no more likely to have developed long-term relationships. As Asanuma points out, relationships and technologies are often developed that are only useful to certain product lines. In that case, adjustment has higher costs.

Entry into the ranks of suppliers is not determined only by overall demand, however. No matter how slow the growth, new suppliers can enter when the product requires different technology. Though Boeing has not increased its volume substantially over the last decade, increased use of new materials has required that it develop new suppliers. The same can be said of Hewlett-Packard as it moved into computers. Existing commitments to firms do not automatically lead to cooperation in the development of new technologies; it must be technologically and economically feasible for the firms. In Japanese firms, we found more willingness to try to work with existing firms, but even there, it is more defensive in nature. When demand changed for an auto firm that had made a commitment to buy parts from a supplier, for example, the firm felt an obligation to find new products to maintain that commitment. That approach is not always successful, however, and may not receive enthusiastic support from the parts supplier, who may find other firms willing to commit to its current technology.

Economies of scale often justify the internal production of particular parts, but interviews often indicated that some technology required more or less volume than was available in house. On one extreme, economic size may permit a firm to provide competitive sources of technology, even as it makes long-term commitments. Toyota might have two headlamp sources but make each produce only for a given model, or perhaps even as specialized as a left headlamp of a particular model. Note that this strategy permits alternatives to market competition even as it maintains the competition between suppliers of the similar technology. American firms tended to use market competition when these conditions were met.

On the other extreme, there are frequently cases when the core firm alone is not of sufficient size to exhaust the scale potential. Graphite for use in composites for planes can also be used for sports equipment; parts for electronics firms frequently have wide use in the industry (Asanuma 1985). Although one possible response might be to produce the parts internally and sell to outsiders, the short response times of the Japanese electronics industry or the joint technology development of composites and airframes may still provide benefits from close cooperation with suppliers. There are also benefits to suppliers. Given the commitment required to achieve the scale economies (either in resources or in assumption of risk), a supplier would be more likely to undertake the business if offered a long-term commitment from the user firm. This is just as true for the manufacturer of rare metal forgings used in aerospace as it is for the Japanese producer of printed circuit boards for a Japanese electronics firm.

While not truly a scale-economy factor, parts-supply relationships must often take advantage of portfolio effects as well. When a silicon-wafer manufacturer makes a crystal, it finds that the product has different characteristics along its length, requiring a variety of final-product customers to avoid substantial waste. Because carefully developed business relationships with customers are required to assure that the chips will be appropriate, long-term relationships are consistent with scale economies. Alloys that cannot be made to tight specifications also require a variety of customers for a metal fabricator to allocate output efficiently. Here it is the production process rather than diversification of customers per se that makes it unlikely that the company would choose to be totally dependent on one firm.

When firms are less confident about the future product line of the firm, they are less likely to make a total commitment to that firm. This does not mean that long-term relationships cannot be developed, just that both sides want to limit that commitment, providing a rationale for participation in multiple parts-supply relationships. Asanuma points out that the level of the commitment is higher in automobiles than electronics in Japan. Cars are more predictable, with longer product life cycles and less change in technology. We found similar evidence in areas like precision machinery and heavy industry. Participation in several concurrent long-term supply relationships seemed to be more likely, however, when the parts-supply firm had some independent technology to offer to various suppliers. The technology gave the firms, we speculate, the bargaining power to insist that concurrent relationships be maintained.

A final factor is the overall corporate culture of the core firm. If the competitive strategy of the firm encourages long-term commitments, it is likely the firm will feel more comfortable with less than arm's length relationships in parts supply as well. The Japanese electronics industry gives a good example of this impact on parts-supply strategy. We interviewed three companies, Sony, Matsushita, and Sharp. Only Matsushita had really tight parts-supply relationships. As Itami and Roehl have noted (Itami and Roehl 1987), these three firms take very different competitive strategies, even though they are in the same industry. Sony is the first to market with innovative products, and expects to fall behind as a product matures. Matsushita, often criticized in Japan as a copycat *("Maneshita"),* takes technology initiated by firms like Sony and, through a fast response and effective marketing, expands the market for the products. Once the products have become relatively standardized, Sharp becomes a major player, capitalizing on its low cost of production to gain competitive position in more mature markets. For entirely different reasons, Sony and Sharp find close supplier relationships less important than Matsushita. Sony can win on technology alone, and does not expect to maintain large market share in an individual product for as long a period. Both make a major commitment by a supplier less likely, and the firms that supply Sony show correspondingly less commitment. At the other extreme, Sharp can depend on standardized parts that are not expected to change as much. Thus, it must be able to change suppliers if cost warrants, and it operates in a market with less uncertainty. Matsushita faces an entirely different situation. Because it must respond quickly to trends initiated by others, it must place a premium on flexible supply relationships. Uncertainty is greater, and fast response to changed market conditions is key. Continual adjustment of its product portfolio is key to its competitive position, and this requires suppliers who are able to adjust quickly. Dependence on more market-oriented relationships, as in the Sharp case, is out of the question for Matsushita. Matsushita's stronger commitment to its suppliers, and its ability to develop supplier capabilities follows once these overall strategy differences are made clear—one supplier of circuit boards now does a substantial amount of assembly, giving the overall system more capability to respond to market movements. The greater loyalty on the part of Matsushita suppliers also follows, given the increased potential for profit implicit in the long-term relationship Matsushita must develop to carry out its strategy.

The difference is also apparent in the American sample. Suppliers to Hewlett-Packard and IBM gave very different stories about the type of parts-supply relationship they faced. IBM changed suppliers frequently, while Hewlett-Packard worked more closely with suppliers. IBM strategy has always been to produce a large proportion of the equipment in house. Hewlett-Packard, along with most precision-equipment manufacturers, operates on lower volumes, and depends on active support from suppliers at the design stage. Variations in production volume within its product line are more common. As in the Japanese electronics case, these two firms in similar markets exhibit differences in parts-supply systems consistent with the predictions set out above.

3. ECONOMIC EXPLANATIONS FOR COOPERATIVE STRATEGIES: CAN A MARKET SYSTEM JUSTIFY SUCH RELATIONSHIPS?

If we take as a starting point the market orientation of most parts-supply relationships in the United States, we must examine factors in the environment and in the operation of markets that force firms to even consider these more cooperative and long-term relationships. After all, the market system has the advantages of maintaining competitive pressure among suppliers, making it possible for the firm to adjust to lower-cost suppliers as they appear in the market, without the costs of maintaining a complex business relationship with the firm's many suppliers.

Writers considering the internal organization of the Japanese firm, however, have developed a rationale for the cooperative relationship that has developed between workers and stockholders. In justifying the new theory of the firm as a cooperative relationship in which workers, managers, and shareholders all have stakes, writers like Masahiko Aoki have had to show that such stakeholder cooperation is more efficient than a more market-oriented solution. Their analysis is useful in understanding the cooperative relationships between parts suppliers and the firm purchasing the parts (the *core firm,* to use Asanuma's terminology). Both Aoki and Asanuma have assumed that the core firm, through its manager, controls the relationship, and the parts firm or supplier of labor services (the worker) operates in a market exchange with little long-term commitment. Aoki makes the case for the worker/ stockholder pair—and it is easy to show for the supplier/core firm pair as well—that when some of the assumptions of market exchange are called into question, such cooperative relationships can lead to greater efficiency in economic organizations.

3.1. When Cooperative Relationships Yield Greater Efficiency: Four Conditions

There are four conditions Aoki cites as important in driving the participants of this market exchange toward cooperative relationships (Aoki 1984, p. 30). Reworded to apply to the problem of parts-supply relationships, the conditions can be stated as follows:

1. Since both sides want to avoid risk, risk-bearing cost is reduced if a contract can compel both parties to share the burden rather than forcing one to assume all risk.

2. Substituting for the market, purchasing managers can be given the authority to allocate and monitor the resources of the parts-supply firms, making sure that they perform their job effectively.

3. Since the parts market is changing frequently (i.e., it is often in disequilibrium), adjusting to new conditions requires skills not found easily in the market model.

4. Forming and implementing production systems requires information exchange that cannot be expected from market exchange, so that a cooperative parts-supply system is necessary for informational efficiency.

I will discuss each of these in turn, drawing on the interview information to illustrate the theoretical points presented.

Risk-sharing contracts

Aoki stresses the importance of risk as a key determinant of economic institutions. Conventionally, microeconomists have assumed that the shareholders willingly take the risk in a firm; implicitly, writers on the parts-supply relationship have also said that one side or the other takes all the risk. Japanese Marxists say that all the risk falls on the small-parts suppliers *(Shiwayose)*, while American writers suggest only the core firm is risk-bearing. In almost all our interviewing, however, we confirmed that nearly all the participants expressed an aversion to risk, and expected the other side to bear some of the risk in the parts-supply relationship. Even many Americans who had been comfortable with the assumption of all the risk in the past now find this less attractive: Boeing, formerly willing to bet the company at each stage, now searches out partners for its newest planes.

The purchasing manager as a monitor

The stockholders of the two companies—and also the workers in the two firms—have the potential for sharing in the benefits of the supply relationship, but if arm's-length exchange predominates, the supplier firm has the incentive to take advantage of the one-time contract to shift the gain to its advantage. It may ask to delay shipment; it may not ship the required quantity or quality. These complaints are frequently heard about East Asian suppliers who bid on American firms' tender offers. Monitoring costs of such behavior are high unless the purchasing manager can monitor a relatively small number of firms in relation to his volume. Conversely, suppliers might worry about the core-firm commitment to the relationship, which would require monitoring as well. Successful monitoring requires sufficient knowledge of the supplier firm (or the core firm) to know when the change is legitimate. This requires the substantial reduction in suppliers that we have seen in every attempt, American or Japanese, to develop a cooperative parts-supply relationship.

The purchasing manager's compensation or promotion depends on the performance of the overall system. This is even more true in the long-term parts-supply relationships that require cooperation.

There would seem to be an incentive to skew the returns to the core firm, but the overall efficiency of the system forces the parts manager to consider the parts supplier as well, since supply disruptions or lack of new-product-development coordination will have an effect on the performance of his unit. An efficient monitor is one that has a commitment to the smooth functioning of the relationship as a whole. Preferably, the monitor's rewards should be tied to the ongoing performance of the system (Roehl 1983). In that sense, the parts manager, even though he is a manager of the core firm, may be the best available monitor of the business relationships between the firms, both of which have incentives to try to skew the returns to their own advantage once the long-term business relationship has been developed.

It is easier for the Japanese purchasing manager to perform this function, since he is likely to stay with his firm for a longer period of time. At least one purchasing manager in the United States indicated that it was unlikely he would stay in his job very long, since pay was a function of volume handled, and an increase usually required moves to a larger firm. In contrast, many of the Japanese purchasing people we talked to had worked in the same firm, often the same division, for many years. Here a Japanese characteristic, permanent employment, permits lower-cost monitoring of these complex business relationships. It should not be surprising that the American firms that have such longstanding parts-supply relationships (e.g., Hewlett-Packard and Boeing) are firms that promote from within and have strong company loyalty on the part of their management employees. As Minato points out, the close proximity of suppliers to the core-firm plant makes possible a more frequent contact with suppliers by the monitors (see pp. 110–111). Still, when we asked Japanese parts-supply firms where they sent their products, the list, except for the auto industry, was often national. An overnight delivery service picks up a set of electronics parts at a small plant south of Tokyo for NEC's plant in the north of Japan. The progressive die technology of this small firm was sought out by the NEC plant manager, even though it was not nearby. American firms like Hewlett-Packard make use of just-in-time systems that source from fairly distant places, taking advantage of the delivery services. Thus, unless the part is heavy and/or hard to transport, firms may find other ways to communicate—Boeing computer information exchange—

to substitute for the daily personal exchange that is common in the Japanese monitoring system.

Adjustment costs

Classical economic analysis does not emphasize the move from one equilibrium to another. If the adjustments in technology and market demand are as important as we have suggested above, the costs of getting from one stable situation to another—the move from one equilibrium to another—will be an important element in evaluating the efficiency of a given parts-supply system. A short-term contract is by definition attractive and distributes gains equitably between parties; otherwise, the parties would not have negotiated it. Even with both parties initially satisfied, however, when conditions change, each party will at least consider how best to benefit from the change. This is to be expected, but it can lead to attempts to redistribute gains from the contract, even if the overall contract still makes sense. This opportunistic behavior on the part of both parties is damaging not just for this particular contract, but also forces people to be more cautious at the contract stage as well, trying to anticipate these problems.

Information efficiency

Aoki stresses the importance of information exchange among the various people within a given organization, indicating that this exchange of information between members of the team is important for the efficient operation of the firm. This is just as important for the various actors in the parts-supply relationship. Whenever we encountered firms that found the market approach unsatisfactory and had developed close, long-term business relationships with their suppliers, we found that the smooth flow of information was an important factor in their decisions. This was just as true for the American firms as it was for the Japanese. The U.S. computer-workstation manufacturer emphasized the close sharing of information about its new products and the new technologies of its disk drive suppliers. Toyota stressed the importance of informing its suppliers of the patterns it expected in the market for its automobiles. In all cases, this permitted the firms to be responsive to changes and, perhaps just as important, to plan for change in a way that presented fewer opportunities for opportunistic behavior, changing the distribution of the gains. This permitted all parties to concentrate on expanding the potential profits from the business relationship. Rather than being presented with a fait acompli when the auto manufacturer changes output, the supplier is alerted with some lead time.

The principles presented in this section are quite different from the standard explanations for parts-supply systems, but as has been demonstrated, it is quite possible to build a rationale for these systems based not on any cultural or national characteristics, but solely on the ability of these systems to minimize the costs for firms trying to set up an efficient parts-supply system. While I would not want to argue that this explanation is the only possible explanation for the development of these parts-supply systems, it is important to note that changes to this less traditional (from an American point of view) form of parts supply do not require a culture-specific explanation. Thus, an appeal to even the most chauvinistic manager can be made on economic grounds that do not challenge the conventional business principles of that manager.

4. BUSINESS STRATEGY CONSIDERATIONS

The economic approach is not the only way to organize a discussion of the problem of parts-supply relationships. In the business-policy and international management literature, essentially the same questions are being asked as scholars attempt to evaluate the costs and benefits of international cooperative relationships (Lorange and Contractor 1987). For these scholars, the problem can be posed in a different way, focusing on the internal decision making of the firms involved. If we use the approach of this literature to look at parts-supply relationships, we have to pose the following three questions as we search for successful systems to manage the parts supply process:

1. Can firms find ways to supply parts consistent with both firms' overall strategy?

2. Can technology transfer be managed so that both firms gain?

3. Can the parties agree to a responsive and flexible system for decision making necessary for this parts-supply relationship?

4.1. Meshing Strategies

Even when a firm tries to use new types of organizations for in-house production, it still must be conscious of the effects on its wider strategy. The example of the American chain-saw firm that became so productive through new production techniques that it was unable to maintain employment levels without better marketing skills is a good example. This problem is even more important when the production arrangements require interfirm relationships. Toyota's commitment to just-in-time production systems and close supplier relationships is considered by some to be one reason Toyota was so slow to introduce new models with front-wheel drive. The influence of parts-supply decisions on other areas of strategy can surely not be neglected in the decision-making process.

When a firm chooses to purchase on the open market, the solution becomes a simple one: no one makes any commitment, and each order is judged individually. If it is in the interest of the firm, the supplier can choose to accept it, and the firm ordering can choose a supplier with full information about the state of the world at that point. In such standardized products as semiconductor chips, even a firm like Matsushita, committed to long-term relationships, feels no obligation to commit to a long-term, sole-source supplier contract.

If the firm makes a longer-term commitment, however, it deploys some of its resources. A company that accepts subcontracting work to the aerospace industry, whether a Japanese sheet-metal fabricator or a rare-metals fabrication firm supplying parts to Boeing, will have to make a commitment to substantial equipment that does not have wide use outside the industry. This constrains the firm's overall strategy. It must hire people with skills in this area, and must use financial resources to acquire equipment that has little use outside the aerospace industry. In talks with even the Japanese suppliers to Toyota, the constraints that this commitment imposed was volunteered by the people interviewed, indicating that even under the

Toyota system, with its strong support for the suppliers, the different company strategy goals have to be kept in mind. In this case, the worry is not that Toyota will cut off orders, but rather that the requirements of the core firm will change, making the commitment of resources less valuable. Toyota officials told us that they have had to anticipate the potential changes in their parts requirements, and both alert the potentially affected firms early and provide training in the production of alternative products. Firms involved in metal fabrication are thus trained in some plastics applications, and firms making carburetors have to be introduced to new engine-related parts due to the increase in the use of fuel injection. In the market prototype of parts supply, such firms would merely be exchanged for new suppliers. But if Toyota were to do that directly, it would cast into doubt the ability of the firm to mesh its strategy with those of its suppliers. Firms that do not make the adjustment, even after advance notice and assistance in adjustment, of course, are still dropped from the parts-supply system. But adjustment assistance is required from the parts-supply system, and perhaps the guarantee of a "soft landing" as a lower-level supplier to the system even if the firm fails to adjust.

4.2. Technology Transfer

In both the international business literature and the more traditional explanations of subcontracting relationships in Japan, there has been a clear assumption of a one-way flow of technology from the core firm to the venture partner. The key issue then becomes the ability of the partner to acquire important technology from the parent, and the ability to the core firm to price the transfer of technology appropriately to maintain its competitive position.

While these issues are also important in a discussion of parts-supply relationships, two additional characteristics make the management of technology significantly different. First, the flow of technology permits a payoff shared by both partners, namely a successful product or series of products over time that provides profits and growth for both firms. Second, both sides must accept a division of labor in developing technology, that is, each partner will develop what cannot be duplicated easily by the other firm. These characteristics permit the partners to deal more easily with issues of technology transfer than conventional wisdom suggests, reducing the potential for opportunism that many suggest would doom such relationships.

In transfer of technology to overseas competitors, the core firm usually gives up the right to sell products in those markets in exchange for the payment for the transfer. With parts supply, this is not necessarily the case. When Toyota teaches a stamping plant to change dies faster, or when an American aerospace company works with a supplier of blades for the turbines to help that firm understand the related technologies that constrain the design, it need not fear that the company will become a competitor; it need not feel that its core skills are being challenged. Of course, contracts may have to prohibit sales to competitors for a period. A semiconductor ingot manufacturer that designs equipment with a machinery firm requires an agreement that the equipment not be sold outside for a period of time.

Each party in the exchange is rewarded if the exchange of technology is progressing smoothly, in the form of increased sales of the product. This joint production is also a convenient monitoring tool for both parties, permitting each to check on the performance under the contract. We thus observed, both in Japan and the United States, a much greater willingness to commit a technology exchange in these business relationships than for conventional licensing relationships usually studied in the literature.

One additional characteristic of the technology relationship seems important to the management of the parts-supply relationship. Let me call it *mutual technology hostage taking:* each side permits the other to develop independent sources of technological expertise not found in the other partner's technology portfolio. This is obviously more important for the parts supplier, since the core firm will almost by definition have some expertise not found in the supplier.

This technology hostage taking seems to take two forms, depending on the characteristic of the core firm strategy. Either a core firm can choose to be involved in the development and design of the parts or it can choose off-the-shelf parts and make the core of its strategy the effective and unique *combination* of these standardized parts. The U.S. computer-workstation manufacturer buys its disk drives from a single firm, committing itself to outside purchase of all these hardware parts. Since the core firm has made no effort to acquire the expertise to make disk drives in-house, the supplier firm contemplating a major investment to serve that growing customer's desires will not be worried about losing the business to an internal source. The core firm is hostage to the technology it has identified in the disk drive manufacturer, yet firm managers felt quite comfortable with the arrangement, knowing that they had identified the firm that was most likely to give them the quality component they required and respond to requests for future design improvements. The firm was content to build its strategic advantage around the operating system of the workstation, the combination of the purchased elements.

In other cases, more frequently in Japan, the core firm chooses to "lose" the ability to do certain functions. The electronics and the automobile industry managers emphasized the evolution of their production system, with the core firm eventually specializing in design and final assembly, and with other skills either being spun off—the Matsushita pattern—or developed with and by their suppliers—the Toyota model. This development coincided with the establishment of the long-term supply relationships by these firms. While the firm managers often justified the decision as a means of dealing with the rapid growth in demand with their limited labor pool, they simultaneously developed a system that, in effect, helped guarantee the return of their supplier firms by encouraging them to specialize in the technology necessary to efficiently perform more narrowly defined production processes. Contrary to a market process, where the firms would have to develop this on their own, Toyota initially supplied technology—often even the machines and retired managers to begin the process—and was a continuous supplier of related technology through the long-term supply relationship.

Note that given the decision of Toyota to get out of many types of technology, a means for technology and production technique exchange between supplier firms becomes more important. This in turn helps justify the supplier associations that have recently become more prominent as a vehicle for periodic exchange of information among sources of technology in the supplier firms. This has an extra benefit for the system as a whole: each supplier profits by successfully handling well a narrowly defined technology or production technique. Since profitability depends only on that narrow skill, managers tend to spend all their time concentrating on that narrow job, something that the larger firm could not afford to do. We heard this especially from parts suppliers in the auto industry in Japan, an extreme example being the decision of a sheet-metal firm to further subcontract for production of an ash tray form valued at a few cents. Even though it could have easily produced it itself, it felt that improvements would have too small a value to a firm its size to warrant the necessary attention.

American firms tend to have less confidence in this system, however. While the smaller firms like the workstation manufacturer do not attempt to take an insurance policy through in-house production capacity, interviews in both the auto and aerospace industries indicate that even those American firms that utilize this hostage-taking strategy want a fallback position. In the auto industry, this involves doing some of the production in-house but with sufficiently low capacity to retain some dependence. In the aerospace industry, Boeing chooses to do a wide enough variety of work in-house—in addition to final assembly—so that it has the ability to tool up relatively quickly if a supplier is not able to meet Boeing standards. In this case, the basic skills necessary for other Boeing production elements are sufficiently general, so that this option is possible.

4.3. Decision Making

The conventional wisdom of decision making, at least in the Japanese parts-supply relationship, says that the core firm is able to control, even exploit, the firms that supply parts to the firm. Decision making in the conventional American parts-supply relationship is not much different. The open-bidding system gives full control to the firm purchasing the parts and gives access to all firms that have potential to produce the parts, insuring against inaccurate pricing. Almost by definition the parts-supply relationship requires a substantial degree of control by the purchasing firm due to its ability to assess the market demand for the final product. Still, we found substantially more sharing of decision-making responsibility than would have been expected. Much of this follows once the mutual hostage nature of the technology is recognized.

When either technology or market demand changes quickly, the ability to respond quickly with new products has a payoff for both supplier and core firm. Unless the decision making brings in the suppliers at an early stage, it may be difficult to make the fast adjustment necessary. A change in technology may require a redesign of a product (a new level of integrated circuit density), while consumer tastes in such electronics products as VCRs require constant adjustment of product line to keep a marketing edge. Even such a mundane product as plastic cabinets for electronic equipment requires new molds and fast production startup if the final VCR or TV is to reach the market in a timely manner. Matsushita's suppliers, whether in the United States or Japan, get involved in the product planning early and are given information on the projected market size. The suppliers are in turn expected to suggest ways to make the product more reliably and at lower cost. Japanese suppliers cited cases where the design of a plastic cabinet had been changed on their suggestion to eliminate an especially costly production element. With total core firm control or an open-bidding process, there is less core firm flexibility in adjusting to these changes in market demand, and this flexibility may well have to be added in house.

The close working relationship often requires a degree of decentralization of decision making on the part of firms. Interviews in an American auto plant far from Detroit indicated that the plant managers could not choose suppliers themselves. The purchasing agents felt they had better information and contacts with local firms. The centralization of purchasing in Detroit, however, did not permit the local decision makers, who had superior information to develop the decision-making relationships, the necessary freedom. This centralized purchasing pattern is based on long runs of standardized products, and is used by Toyota as well. Yet, as the firms move to more frequent adjustments in production, some ability of the individual plants to develop and manage parts-supply relationships has greater value. The value of quick adjustment and flexibility begin to have higher payoffs than the scale economies based on central purchasing. Asanuma points out (Asanuma 1985) that this plant-level purchasing independence has always characterized the electronics industry in Japan, an industry known for rapid changes in technology and customer demand.

5. CONCLUSION

Those scholars who have praised the parts-supply system in Japan are clearly not incorrect. In a world with increased uncertainty and greater capability to customize products resulting from advances in information and computerization, a system that permits suppliers and core firms to work more closely together has obvious advantages. What this paper has hopefully shown, however, is that the path that the Japanese took to the current system, while not reproducible, does share sufficient characteristics with systems developed in U.S. firms. By identifying not just the country-specific factors, but also the factors in the environment that shaped these business relationships, we've tried to show that alternative paths to the same flexible and successful manufacturing and parts-supply relationships are available to American firms as well. While this chapter has focused on alternative types of outside sourcing to the relative neglect of the equally important "make or buy" decision, I hope it helps both scholars and business people understand the costs and benefits of developing various paths toward a production system that takes full advantage of the characteristics of the changed production environment.

BIBLIOGRAPHY

Abegglen, James C., and Stalk, George, Jr. *Kaisha: The Japanese Corporation.* New York: Basic Books, 1985.
This book looks at the wider issue of corporate strategy in Japan, and is the best presentation of the ties between production and the rest of corporate strategy. A must read for anyone who wants to understand the supply system, since it operates within corporate strategies of firms that Abegglen has described better than anyone.

Aoki, Masahiro. *The Co-operative Game Theory of the Firm.* London: Oxford University Press, 1984.
This important book gives a clear explanation of the theory of firm behavior that does not require the classical assumptions about the entrepreneur. Instead of the assumption of a risk-

loving set of stockholders, Aoki presents a strong argument that the workers and stockholders as a group can more effectively provide for a system that gives each group the maximum benefits from their resources. While the book is technical in parts, a noneconomist can read around them and still profit from his insights. While Aoki says little about interfirm relationships here, the analysis is just as applicable to these relationships.

Asanuma, Banri. "Transactional Structure of Parts Supply in the Japanese Automobile and Electronic Machinery Industries: A Comparative Analysis." *Socio-Economic Systems Research Project,* Kyoto University, Technical Report No. 1, July 1985.

This paper tries to describe some propositions that permit a scholar to predict what type of parts-supply systems will develop. Limited to Japanese data, he still gives perhaps the best analysis to date of the rationale for specific relationships within a parts-supply system. Good description of the terms used by other writers. Professor Asanuma is now working on a comparative paper.

Contractor, Farok, and Lorange, Peter. *Cooperative Strategies in International Business.* New York: JAI Press, 1987.

Germides, Dimitri, ed. *International Subcontracting: A New Form of Investment.* (OECD Development Centre Studies). Paris: OECD, 1980.

The current discussions are about intracountry parts supply, but the issues described in this book about the global parts-supply relationships will eventually have to be addressed by scholars of the parts-supply systems, so this book gives good background.

Hayes, R. H. "Why Japanese Factories Work." *Harvard Business Review.* 59 (July/August 1981): 57–65.

One of the earliest attempts by American scholars to point out the importance of the system of production in Japanese competitiveness.

"High Tech to the Rescue." *Newsweek* (16 June 1986), pp. 100–108.

A recent newsmagazine article on the topic, indicating the danger of automation, or any one element of production as a panacea for increased productivity. Shows that many U.S. firms are now focusing on the system as a whole rather than particular blockbuster solutions.

Hofstede, G. *Culture's Consequences*. Beverly Hills, Calif.: Sage, 1980.

Itami, Hiroyuki, with Roehl, Thomas. *Mobilizing Invisible Assets*. Cambridge, Mass.: Harvard University Press, 1987.

MacKnight, Susan. "U.S.–Japan Competition in Motor Vehicle Parts." *JEI Report* #48A, 1984 (21 December 1984).

Description of the competitive situation in one of the industries most discussed in parts-supply relationships. Gives much data necessary for discussion of the wider questions of appropriate parts-supply systems.

McMillan, Charles J. *The Japanese Industrial System*. Berlin: Walter de Gruyter, 1984.

Good description of the overall industrial system, though more from an internal-organization aspect than from overall strategy or interfirm relationships. Good, readable description of how the production process is organized in Japan, linking it to the rest of the organization.

Ministry of International Trade and Industry. *Outline of Small- and Medium-Scale Enterprise Policies of the Japanese Government*. Mimeo, January 1983.

The Japanese government is involved in the regulation and promotion of smaller industries. This publication describes the policy. The 1986 White Paper on Small and Medium-Sized Enterprises, now available only in Japanese, also describes government policy. A summary in English is available in *White Papers of Japan: 1987*.

Miyazaki, Hajime. "The Rat Race and Internal Labor Markets." *Bell Journal of Economics* 8 (Autumn 1977): 394–418.

An early description of the problems with the classical theory of market operation when there are different characteristics of participants.

Monden, Yasuhiro. *Toyota Production System*. London: Industrial Engineering and Management Press, 1983.

Description of the Toyota system, with an emphasis on the internal operations of the system, and the mechanics of the tracking system.

Monden, Yasuhiro; Shibakawa, Rinya; Takayanagi, Satoru; and Nagao, Teruya. *Innovations in Management: The Japanese*

Corporation. Norcross, Ga.: Industrial Engineering and Management Press, 1985.

Short, crisp articles about various parts of Japanese management that give much detail if sometimes little analysis. Monden's article on *Kanban* and Yoshihara's article on the transferability of Japanese production innovations to foreign subsidiaries are useful for understanding the parts-supply relationships.

Moxon, Richard W.; Roehl, Thomas W.; and Truitt, J. Frederick. "International Cooperative Ventures in the Commercial Aircraft Industry: Gains Sure, But What's My Share?" In *Cooperative Strategies in International Business,* pp. 255–277, edited by Farok J. Contractor and Peter Lorange. Lexington, Mass.: D.C. Heath: Lexington Books, 1988.

The paper looks at cooperative strategies in aerospace, showing that the ventures can be better understood if we consider three major factors that dictate the form of cooperation: meshing the strategies; managing the technology and information flow; and means of control.

Nakatani, Iwao. "The Economic Role of Financial Corporate Grouping." In *The Economic Analysis of the Japanese Firm,* edited by Masahiko Aoki, pp. 227–259. Amsterdam: North Holland, 1984.

The best case for a risk-aversion argument for industrial groupings. Nakatani argues that the members who choose to join industrial groups give up some profits to gain the assurance of stable growth in their business relationships. He does not talk about the parts-supply relationship, limiting his comments (due to lack of data, probably) to the relationships between larger firms in the Japanese economy.

Ohno, Tai-ichi. "How the Toyota Production System Was Created." *Japanese Economic Studies* 10 (Summer 1982): 83–104.

The only description in English that I know of by the Toyota manager who put together the *Kanban* system. His books in Japanese are well read.

Roehl, Thomas W. "An Economic Analysis of Industrial Groupings in Post War Japan." Ph.D. dissertation, University of Washington, 1983.

While the dissertation addresses the relationships between larger firms rather than that between large firms and parts suppliers, its discussion of the interfirm relationships from a rational-actor perspective may be useful for researchers on industrial groupings as well.

Roehl, Thomas W. "A Transactions Cost Approach to International Trading Structure: The Case of the Japanese General Trading Companies." *Hitotsubashi Journal of Economics* 24 (December 1983): 119–135.

Using the Williamson typology of transactions types, this article shows how the trading companies achieve efficient exchange of goods for their customers. The argument is that the type of transactions relationship that the trading firms develop depends critically on the characteristics of the transactions themselves, and not just on the fact that the trading companies are involved.

Roehl, Thomas W., and Schmitt, Thomas G. "The Kanban Inventory Control System: The Myth of Zero Inventory." In *Proceedings of the Academy of International Business: Asia-Pacific Dimensions of International Business,* edited by Steven Dawson. Honolulu: University of Hawaii East West Center, 1983, pp. 656–667.

My earlier attempt to try to describe the relationships between firms that are necessary to make the internal *Kanban* system operate effectively. The discussion of the influence of land-price differentials has not been well received, but the second half of the paper, describing the way the system handles the inevitable problems of managing the Japanese type of supply relationships, forms the background of this chapter.

Sato, Yoshio. "The Subcontracting Production (Shitauke) System in Japan." *Keio Business Review 21 (1983),* pp. 1–25.

Description of the development of the subcontracting system in one industry, plus a description of the current level of subcontracting, with good, up-to-date data.

Schmitt, Tom, and Connors, Mary. "Supplier Attitudes Toward the Establishment of Just-in-Time Delivery Relationships—a Survey of Manufacturing Firms in the Northwest." Discussion paper, Graduate School of Business Administration, University of Washington in Seattle, 1985.

Survey of supplier firms to Hewlett-Packard showed six worries concerning the implementation of zero-inventory systems: desire for diversification; poor customer forecasts; engineering

changes required; quality-assurance levels required; high cost
of small batches; long distances.

Schonberger, Richard J. *Japanese Manufacturing Techniques.* New
York: Free Press, 1982.
A readable description of the Japanese system, less technical
than Monden's book. It uses information about Japanese subsidiaries in the United States to discuss the potential for application to U.S. conditions.

Sugimori, Y.; Kusunoki, K.; Cho, F.; and Uchikawa, S. "Toyota Pro-
duction System and *Kanban* System: Materialization of Just-in-
Time and Respect for Human System." *International Journal of
Production Research* 15 (November 1977): 553–564.
One of the early descriptions by Japanese of the system as it was
developing at Toyota.

Sullivan, Jeremiah J. "A Critique of Theory Z," *Academy of Management Review* 8 (January 1983): 132–142.

Takeuchi, Hirotaka. "Productivity: Learning from the Japanese,"
California Management Review 23 (Summer 1981): 5–19.
Useful to put the issues of parts supply into a wider framework
of productivity as an element of corporate strategy.

Wheelwright, S. C. "Japan—Where Operations Really Are Strategic."
Harvard Business Review 59 (July/August 1981): 720–733.
This article (along with that of Hayes) really got the discussion
started in the United States, questioning the minor role manufacturing has had in U.S. corporate strategy. Strong emphasis
on the relationships between manufacturing and the rest of
Japanese corporate decision making.

COMMENTARY
ON CHAPTER 4

KONOSUKE ODAKA
Hitotsubashi University, Tokyo

INTRODUCTION

PROFESSOR MINATO argues that greater emphasis by the Japanese on closer intraindustry linkages between assemblers and parts suppliers has been the cornerstone of the successful performance of their industries. This implies that the recent gap in economic efficiency between U.S. and Japanese firms can be largely accounted for by the differences in intraindustry organizational structure. This hypothesis is certainly plausible, but I am not as yet totally persuaded by the argument. It requires empirical substantiation.

A related, and yet conceptually separate, issue of considerable importance is the firms' policy on their parts procurement (the so-called make-or-buy decision), as it calls for high-priority attention by the management in a discrete process industry such as machine building. Indeed, the two countries differ significantly in the extent to which the assemblers rely on "subcontractors" for the supply of parts and various manufacturing services. It has been repeatedly pointed out, for example, that the U.S. auto manufacturers have traditionally been more highly integrated, which at one time was taken as a sign of modernity.

Note, however, that assemblers may be less dominant in their relations with their suppliers if the latter command a stronger technological as well as economic position, e.g., in the production of sewing machines. Moreover, I suspect that financial considerations are also conducive to certain forms of intraindustry organization; rapidly growing assemblers, which face severe financial constraints, may opt to depend more heavily on external sourcing of their intermediate inputs. One might also argue that the Japanese subcontracting firms are functionally equivalent to an autonomously behaving, internal division of a gigantic U.S. firm, and that therefore the difference is only superficial.

In any event, it is a legitimate, and perhaps rewarding, question to analyze empirically why U.S. machinery manufacturers are more highly integrated than their Japanese counterparts. My tentative hypothesis is that the difference is largely ascribable to historical as well as institutional factors.

MARKET CONDITIONS

My attention has been drawn especially to Roehl's argument that the U.S. companies tend to rely completely on market mechanisms in their interfirm economic transactions, whereas the Japanese counterparts recognize the inadequacies of the market for covering the cost of risk and of information gathering. I wonder how these differences have come about.

Aside from these behavioral questions, there is a noteworthy difference in market conditions themselves. The U.S. market is not only vast in its size but is also highly oligopolistic, which may have worked against the American firms in developing new products and/or responding quickly to the needs of their customers.

For instance, Chuck Sabel and his associates describe how the large, oligopolistic textile-machine industry in the United States, because of the firms' lack of sensitivity to a new economic environment, lagged behind their new competitors in Europe.[1] Susan Helper has noted in her dissertation research that the U.S. automobile assemblers acted to minimize the suppliers' bargaining power from the 1950s to the 1970s, thus suppressing the latter's incentives and capabilities for innovation. According to her, it was not until 1980 that, under pressure from imports, the U.S. automakers began to move toward two-way relationships with their suppliers in such a way that the latter's unique capabilities were honored and their independent R&D activities encouraged.[2]

By contrast, Japan has relied heavily on the export market from the beginning of its modern history, and has thus proved to be highly vulnerable to fluctuations in world demand. This must have led to a relatively higher level of uncertainty and thus contributed to the development of an institutional mechanism to mitigate its undesirable effects.

Noteworthy in this connection is Roehl's insight that the firm's relative position in the market with regard to its technological leadership affects the structure of assembler-supplier relationships (recall the contrast he draws between Sony, Panasonic, and Sharp).

Finally, one should not minimize the weight of historical heritage in understanding the behavioral differences in the two cultures. Jin-ichi Konishi has noted that the mark of Japanese groupism was already apparent in the ancient days. According to him, the Japanese literary art is characterized by (1) the absence of a class concept and (2) the avoidance of conflict between group and individuals.[3] I find his remarks highly suggestive.

NOTES

1. Chuck Sabel et al., "How to Keep Mature Industries Innovative," *Technology Review,* vol. 90, no. 3, April 1987, pp. 26–35.

2. Susan Helper, "Supplier Relations and Innovation in the Auto Industry" (Ph.D. diss., Harvard University, 1986).

3. Jin-ichi Konishi, *Nihon bungei shi* [History of Japanese Literature], vol. 1 (Tokyo: Kōdansha, 1985) pp. 35–39.

COMMENTARY
ON CHAPTER 4

YOSHIO SATO
Keio University

T HE THEME of interfirm division of labor is now receiving worldwide attention. The Japanese interfirm production systems are part of the larger socioeconomic, cultural systems, and it is opportune to compare these systems with those of the United States.

Japanese production systems have been reorganized in the wake of changing socioeconomic patterns brought about by a shift from a high-growth to a low-growth economy. These systems also have been influenced by a shift toward what is referred to as an internationalized and information-oriented society. Professors Minato and Roehl, through the use of common standards and methods, have identified changing features of these systems.

FIVE CONTROVERSIES

As a researcher in the same field, I wish to point out the following five controversies:

First, Professor Minato insists that gains from growth shared between the core firm and subcontractors is the basis of mutual trust. But the relations between firms, in my view, are dependent upon certain premises. We must carefully consider, for instance, whether the industry is growing, whether subcontractors can comply with the demands from the core firm, and whether other severe conditions are satisfied.

Second, as Professor Minato also points out, General Motors manufactures 50 percent in-house and Toyota only 20 percent. How do we account for this difference? However, "in-house manufacturing" may need to be redefined once it is noted that the Toyota group includes ten wholly owned parts suppliers within its household. We must analyze this problem within the context of the historical circumstances of the Japanese auto industry.

Third, behind the high efficiency of the Japanese subcontracting system is severe competition among parts suppliers under the carrot-and-stick policies of the core firm. In this respect, we should not overlook the use of the prominent position by the core firm and its use of unfair trade practices. We must look closely into the "excessive" nature of Japanese competition.

Fourth, I do not object to praising Japanese interfirm efficiency and productivity and the resulting international competitiveness, but we must also examine how the fruit of this productivity has been distributed among the actors. Without such analysis, we would only be addressing half the issue.

Fifth, the international transfer of Japanese interfirm productivity must be analyzed through further studies of "buy or subcontract" in the United States and Japan. Particularly, we must look at how Japanese auto manufacturers develop and manage their interfirm systems in the United States, and what the most significant barriers to this development are.

5

FORMULATORS AND LEGISLATORS OF INTERNATIONAL TRADE AND INDUSTRIAL POLICY IN JAPAN AND THE UNITED STATES

MASAO SAKURAI
Aoyama Gakuin University

INTRODUCTION

I N THIS STUDY, first, a comparative examination is made of the processes whereby the United States and Japan make laws, as we believe that these processes have an impact on the outcome of the arguments over U.S.–Japan trade problems as well as discussions of trade-related legislation in both countries. Second, we seek to identify both the nominal and actual formulators of policy and bills and sponsors of bills, within the context of differences in the lawmaking process that arise from differences in political institutions, as well as the nature of the influence of the persons involved in policy formulation and preparation of bills and resolutions, such as members of the Congress or Diet, majority leaders, congressional staff and outsiders, such as pressure groups and lobbyists. Third, we distinguish the roles of bureaucrats and members of the legislatures between the two nations in the international trade and industrial policy-making process, and the legislative process, and in so doing reveal the relative ease or difficulty in making law in the two countries.

The underlying intention is to contribute to the analysis of the implementation of industrial and trade policy in the United States and Japan, and to elucidate the issues related to corporate behavior in both countries.

1. BASIC POLICY-FORMULATION PROCESS AND LEGISLATIVE PROCESS

1.1. The Political System of the Two Countries

In Japan, the power of the national assembly (Diet; *kokkai*) to propose a law is more limited than that of the administrative part of the government. The Japanese Constitution and the Diet Law provide that the sponsor of bills can be either a Diet member, the Cabinet, a Standing Committee *(jonin-iinkai)* or a Select Committee *(tokubetsu-iinkai)*. The reason that the power of the national assembly is limited is that the Cabinet *(naikaku)* is made up of leaders of the majority party, and the ruling party occupies an extremely important position. Therefore, the probability is extremely high that a bill proposed by the Cabinet will be made into law.

In the United States, because of the principle of balance of powers, only members of Congress can propose bills. The President does not have such power, and is limited to suggesting necessary legislation through such statements as his State of the Union message, the Economic Report of the President, and his Budget Message.[1]

1.2. The Law-Making Process in Japan

Coordination at the ministerial level

Interaction with the principal divisions concerned. The smallest subdivision in a ministry *(sho)* or agency *(cho)* possessing a bill-drafting function is the lowest administrative subunit, the division *(ka, shitsu*[2]*)* or subdivision *(kakari)*. The scope of opinion exchanges is expanded to other ministries to the greatest possible extent, and consideration is given to the method of contacting the ruling Liberal–Democratic Party *(jimin-to,* hereafter referred to as "LDP"), the time required to do so, the election pledge of the LDP, and coordination with other ministries. (See Figure 5.1.)

There is a strong tendency for bills to concern more than a single ministry, as a result of which there are frequent occasions of joint sponsorship, competition for sponsorship, conflicts of opinion as to which ministry is to be in the leading position, and encumbrances arising from sectionalism. When there are difficulties in achieving

Figure 5.1 Legislative Process in Japan. [Asano, Ichiro, *Horitsu-jorei* [Law and Regulations.] (Tokyo: Gyosei, 1984). pp. 78–79.]

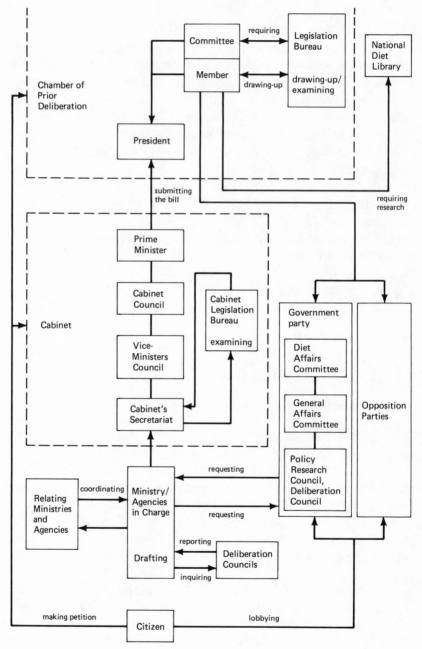

compromises among ministries, this problem is frequently resolved at the initiative of divisions *(bukai)* within the Policy Research Council of the LDP.

Inquiring of the deliberation councils. Japan's deliberation councils *(shingi-kai)* were created as institutions that would secure broad-based expertise from the public in order that political affairs be based on the sentiments of the people, and that the administration of government be equitable. Among them there are some that wear the invisible mantle of the mechanisms of bureaucracy, or are dominated by certain industries possessing self-seeking motivations, and pressure groups. Because the deliberation councils are based on law, ultimate responsibility for them resides in the Diet.

When a bill is to be prepared subsequent to reporting from a deliberation council, the ministry or agency concerned has a bureau or division head present at a council meeting to provide an explanation of the bill and seek the opinions of the council members. Frequently the gist of a bill that is being prepared is already expressed in the language of the official's report or advice.

Intraministerial coordination. A bill that has been drafted by a ministerial bureau and is to be submitted to the Cabinet Council *(kakugi)* is first presented at conference by the competent bureau heads *(kanbukaigi),* at which time it is reviewed and revisions are suggested.

Review by the cabinet legislation bureau and the Ministry of Finance

Cabinet legislation bureau. There is a Legislation Bureau in the Cabinet. Review of the bills and proposed cabinet orders *(seirei)* is done by a joint body of counsellors *(sanjikan)* from all parts of the Legislation Bureau.

Legislation bureau of the houses of the Diet. Other bureaus besides the Cabinet Legislation Bureau exist in the House of Representatives and the House of Councillors. These bureaus are concerned with administrative tasks related to legislation within the jurisdiction of the Standing Committees *(jonin-iinkai)* and tasks not delegated to other bodies.

Preparation for cabinet legislation bureau review, and the review. Each ministry and agency, by August 31, submits its budget request for the following year to the Ministry of Finance, and at the same time submits its proposed budget bill to support the request to the Cabinet Legislation Bureau and Cabinet Secretariat. The review by the Cabinet Legislation Bureau generally requires a long period of time.

Review by the LDP

Division (bukai). The ministries submit their draft bills to the appropriate division *(bukai)* of the LDP Policy Research Council, and after review by that body it is referred to the Policy Deliberative Council and others in turn. Because prior consideration is given to the stance of the LDP, when a draft bill is submitted to council division it is approved in its original form in most cases.

Policy research council. The Policy Research Council *(seimuchosa-kai)* obtains explanations of draft bills from division chairmen, and comments from deliberation councils.

General council. Ordinarily when a draft bill is sent to the General Council from the Policy Research Council, the General Council undertakes a highly advanced political review.

Diet affairs committee. Review of draft bills by the Diet Affairs Committee *(kokkai-taisaku-iinkai)* is done solely from the viewpoint of getting the bill through the Diet over possible objections by opposition parties.

The cabinet council

Vice-ministers council. The Vice-Ministers Council *(jimu-jikankaigi)* has the responsibility of overall coordination of matters requiring Cabinet approval, most of which concern bills.[3] When there is the possibility of confrontation from different parts of the nation over a bill's expected effects, and this becomes the subject of sectionalist conflict among ministries, the coordination is performed by the LDP Policy Deliberation Council.

Parliamentary vice-ministers council. The Parliamentary Vice-Ministers Council *(seimu-jikan-kaigi)* holds hearings primarily on issues for which they would report to the Cabinet.

The cabinet council. Bills are submitted for the above-mentioned LDP review. The process whereby a government-sponsored bill passes through the ministry and LDP reviews and is finally submitted to the Cabinet Council (where each ministry is represented) for the decision-making act, i.e., for final approval, constitutes the "policy-determination process" in Japan.

Diet deliberation

House of prior deliberation. Bills that have been reviewed by the Cabinet Legislation Bureau are processed within the ministry concerned and then submitted to the Prime Minister for Cabinet Council deliberation. The Cabinet and LDP Diet Affairs Committee decide on which House and at what time a bill is to be introduced in the Diet. The Diet is managed by a "reading" system in committee, and all bills are to be decided on the floor (the American system can be seen here). A government-sponsored bill is referred to committee by the Bills Division of the House, where it is introduced, and it is there that the actual review is undertaken. Regarding government-sponsored bills, the minister in charge of the relevant committee gives an explanation of what is proposed, and responds to interpolation.

Floor (hon-kaigi). Government-sponsored bills that have been presented in the Diet after review and approval in committee are sent to the other House immediately after adoption (approval) in the first House. When a bill has passed through the same law-making process in the second House as it had passed in the first House and has been approved, it becomes law. Bills that have become law are proclaimed by the head of the second House after he reports to the Cabinet.

1.3. The Law-Making Process in the United States

Legislative process

The legislative process is depicted in Figure 5.2.

Figure 5.2 Legislative Process in the United States. [Prepared from *How Congress Works*. (Washington, D.C.: Congressional Quarterly, 1983) p. 43.]

This graphic shows the most typical way in which proposed legislation is enacted into law. There are more complicated, as well as simpler, routes, and most bills never become law. The process is illustrated with two hypothetical bills, House bill No. 1 (HR 1) and Senate bill No. 2 (S 2). Bills must be passed by both houses in identical form before they can be sent to the president. The path of HR 1 is traced by a solid line, that of S 2 by a broken line. In practice most bills begin as similar proposals in both houses.

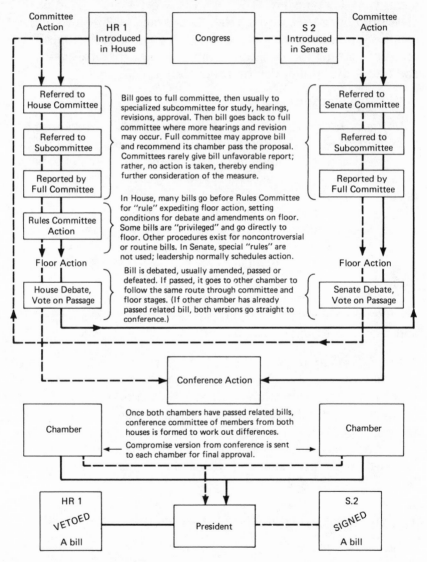

Compromise bill approved by both houses is sent to the president, who can sign it into law or veto it and return it to Congress. Congress may override veto by a two-thirds majority vote in both houses; bill then becomes law without president's signature.

Congressional decision making

The main characteristics of the decision-making process in the U.S. Congress are as follows:

- decentralized power structure and numerous committees
- multiple decision making
- bargaining and coalition building
- congressional cycle (two-year deadline of the congressional term)[4]

Leaders affecting decision making and legislation

Congressmen; legislators. The following three differences between the two chambers are probably the most important:

- The House is more than four times the size of the Senate.
- Senators represent a broader constituency than do respresentatives.
- Senators serve longer terms of office.

The Senate is comparatively less concerned than the House with the technical perfection of legislation and is more involved with cultivating national constituencies, formulating questions for national debate, and gaining general public support for policy proposals. A result of the generalist role is greater reliance by senators on knowledgeable personal and committee staff aids for advice in decision making. A House member, on the other hand, is more likely to be an expert himself on particular policy issues. If not, he often relies on informed colleagues rather than staff aids for advice on legislation. Consequently, Senate staff aids generally have more influence over the laws than do their counterparts in the House.[5]

Leadership structure of congress. The leadership structures in both houses have great influence over the course a bill may take; few important bills become law without the support of the majority leadership. In the Senate, the majority leader is the most influential officer, because neither the vice president nor the president pro tempore holds substantive powers over the chamber's proceedings. The primary role of the majority leader is to program and to expedite the flow of his party's legislation.

Among the informal congressional groups, there are caucuses, party committees, and numerous other informal groups that play a significant role in the legislative process.[6]

Congressional staff. For the standing committees, the professional staff (consisting of not more than eighteen, six of whom may be selected by the minority) is appointed on a permanent basis solely on the basis of fitness to perform the duties of their respective positions. The number of staff members is far more than that of staff members assigned or employed in the Japanese Diet or more than the total number of Diet members of Japan.[7]

Pressures on members. In making their legislative decisions, members of Congress are influenced by numerous pressures, as follows:

- The Executive branch. The president's role as legislative leader derives from the Constitution. This function has been broadened over the years. The president presents to Congress, each year, in addition to his State of the Union message, two other general statements of presidential aims: an Economic Report and a Budget Message.
- The media. Of all the pressures on Congress, none is such a two-way proposition as the relationship between legislators and the media.
- Constituent pressures. Although there are many pressures competing for influence on Capitol Hill, it is still the constituents, not the president or the party or the congressional leadership, who grant and can take away a member's job.[8]
- Washington lobbyists. Of all the pressures on Congress, none receives such widespread publicity and yet is so dimly understood as the role of Washington-based lobbyists and the groups they represent. Lobbyists and lobby groups play an active part in the modern legislative process. Commercial and industrial interests, labor unions, ethnic and racial groups, professional organizations, citizen groups, and representatives of

foreign interests have sought by one method or another to exert pressure on Congress to attain their legislative goals.[9]

2. DECISION-MAKING PROCESS OF INTERNATIONAL TRADE AND INDUSTRIAL POLICY AND ITS LEGISLATIVE PROCESS

2.1. The Process in Japan: The Case of the Ministry of International Trade and Industry

Significance, evolution, and issues in international trade and industrial administration

The Ministry of International Trade and Industry (*tsusan-sho;* hereafter referred to as "MITI") is the most important part of the central government making policy and laws relating to international trade and industry. The following is a summary of the administration in MITI.

Outline of international trade and industrial administration. The purpose of international trade and industrial administration is to contribute to the formation of smoother external economic relations; to develop and improve the domestic economy; to create employment opportunities; and to improve the livelihood of the people through policies for industry and international trade, as well as for natural resources and energy, technology, small and medium-sized enterprise, and related areas. Recent emphases in international trade and industrial administration have been as follows:

- energy policy
- external economic relations
- industry and technology
- small and medium-sized enterprise
- regional policy[10]

Thus, the area of concern to MITI is of a very wide range. MITI occupies a central position in the government with regard to these policy areas, and because it also develops and carries out policies that are related to similar activity by other ministries, every aspect of the national life is influenced by MITI. In the past, international trade and industrial policy was primarily concerned with providing authorizations and approvals according to the relevant laws. Today, administrative activities by MITI pay closer attention to market functions, supply generalized indicative plans ("visions") to industry, promote technological development through financial and taxation systems, and is deeply involved in "soft" aspects of industry, trade, and life in addition to "hard" aspects.[11] When circumstances so require, MITI assumes its responsibility as the leading ministry in economic affairs, encompassing both domestic and external issues, on the basis of strong confidence of industry and both Japanese and foreign bodies concerned.

Industrial policy. Industrial policy is defined here as policy meant to supplement the market mechanism, seeking to arrive at the optimum overall solution(s) without intervening in the decision-making process at the level of the firm in conformity with the market mechanism, in order to realize a desirable industrial structure from a long-term viewpoint.[12]

The Industrial Policy Bureau *(sangyo-seisaku-kyoku)* seeks to promote overall industrial policy on the basis of plans with regard to industrial structure, industrial organization, and industrial adjustment.

The following concerns lie behind the above policies:

- realization of internationally optimized industry relations through maintenance and creation of international comparative advantages from long-term and vitalistic viewpoints
- optimization of resource allocation where imperfections in the market mechanism impede high-risk development
- countermeasures for key constraints of resources, energy, land, water, etc., which impede industrial and economic activities
- countermeasures for pollution and other external diseconomies resulting from industrial activity
- promotion of orderly investment and other activities overseas so as to contribute to good external economic relations

Regarding the emphasis in methods used to implement industrial policy, note should be made of how there has been a historic change from direct and regulatory activity to indirect, leadership-providing activity. In particular the following five methods are to be noted.

1. Issuance of "vision" type documents. These include "Vision of Industrial Policy for the 1980s" (March 1980) and "Outlook and Issues for Industrial Structure in the 1980s" (November 1980).

2. Policy-oriented finance. For example, the Export-Import Bank of Japan, established in 1950, has provided low-interest long-term finance especially to sectors identified as having strategic importance, or to export industry.

3. Taxation. Preferential measures such as tax exemptions, accelerated depreciation, authorization of buildup of internal reserves and the like has been used for selective strategic objectives such as the promotion of exports.

4. Direct action by the government. This includes research and development by government agencies and measures to reduce risk to private firms in efforts at development of technology.

5. Administrative guidance *(gyosei-shido)*. This has included export restraints, price policy, influence on investment, and so on.[13]

Basic decision-making processes

The policy-formulation process at MITI can be explained in chronological sequence as follows (see Figure 5.3).

In the routine course of their activity, MITI officials come into contact with companies, industrial organizations, politicians, and others, whereby they collect, analyze, and store information. They also participate in a wide variety of specialized study groups. The concept of a policy is often generated in these processes (Figure 5.3, ①, pp. 172–173).

In order for the concept to be realized, first, it is necessary for either a proposal to be drafted by an assistant to the division head in the division most immediately concerned, such as the Trade Policy Bureau, International Economic Affairs Department, Tariff Division; or the division drafts a policy proposal based on instructions from the minister, bureau director-general, or head of the Secretariat (ordinarily, this takes place in spring) (③–⑤). This proposal is

Figure 5.3   International Trade and Industry Policy Making and Its Legislative Process. [Prepared on the basis of hearings in the Ministry of International Trade and Industry.]

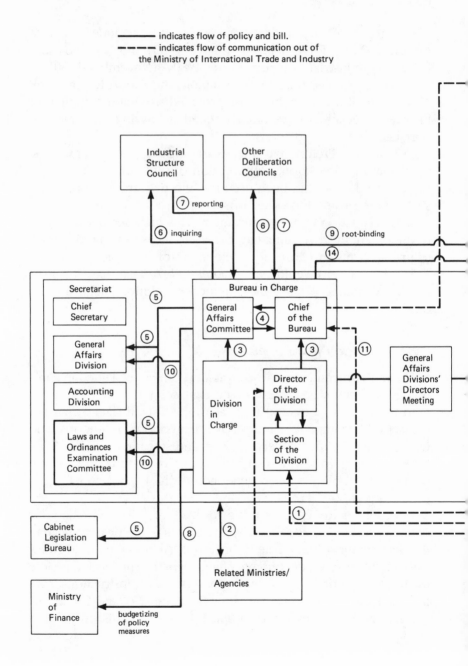

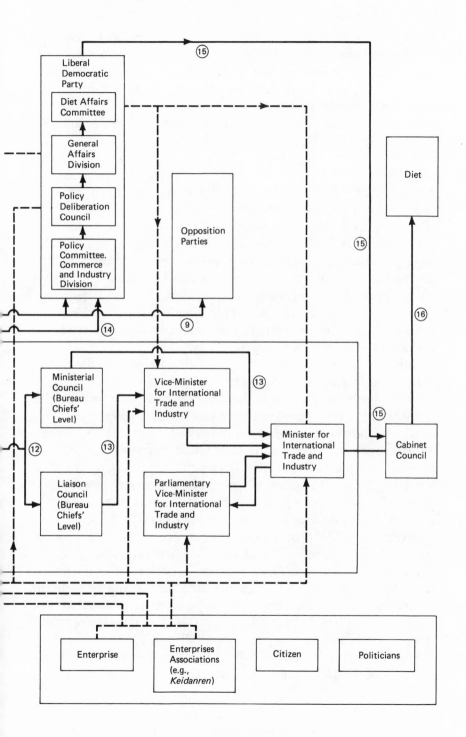

forwarded to the Laws and Ordinances Examination Committee mentioned before, which must approve the proposal if it is to be carried out. If the proposal will require a budget appropriation, this is studied by the division most directly concerned (generally, this takes place in June or July).

Second, discussions are begun by the bureau in charge and the Cabinet Legislation Bureau (⑤).

Third, parallel to the above, MITI seeks the opinion of the suitable deliberation council *(shingi-kai),* which may be, for example, the Industrial Structure Council (such contact is normally made in or about July). More recently, however, it has become common for officials at the level of director-general of a bureau, or head of an agency (such as the Natural Resources and Energy Agency) or the minister himself to establish an advisory committee dedicated to serving the office of the official concerned. One example would be the International Enterprises Study Committee, which provides advice to the chief of the Industrial Policy Bureau (⑥–⑦).

Fourth, a draft bill seeking to translate the policy into reality, is prepared in the relevant bureau.

Fifth, that bureau contacts the Accounting Division of the Secretariat regarding the budgeting (⑩).

Sixth, the bureau contacts the General Affairs Division in the Secretariat for final coordinating measures, and has the draft reviewed by the Cabinet Legislation Bureau. At the same time, contact is made with the ruling party (LDP), and in particular with key members of the party's Policy Research Council, in the process known as informal contact. When deemed necessary, appropriate contact is made with opposition parties. Such *nemawashi* (root-binding) with politicians is done *sub rosa* (⑨).[14]

Seventh, after the plan (or draft bill) is approved by the administrative division chief's committee *(shomukacho-kaigi),* a group made up of division head level persons), a committee of the ministry's bureau heads, and an administrative coordinating group (bureau head level), the approval of the Minister of International Trade and Industry is obtained, and with the drafting now complete, the document becomes a policy or a bill (⑪–⑬).

Eighth, MITI submits the bill to the Commerce and Industry Division of the LDP's Policy Research Council for review (⑭).

Ninth, the bill, after overall review, it goes to the Cabinet Council for its approval (⑮).

Tenth, the Cabinet submits the budget proposal and accompanying bill for the new policy to the Diet (⑯).

Special features and problems

The Diet and committee system.   It would be no exaggeration to state that at present the floor is almost completely dominated by ritual. For review by the Diet, bills are referred to its committees. The committees (and the Standing Committees in particular) today have neutral roles in the law-making process, reviewing the assorted benefits that would accrue from the law and coordinating technical aspects of law making, as well as the side effects of these two. The most important committee related to the ministry is the Standing Committee on Commerce and Industry. With regard to making laws related to international trade and industry, this is the quintessence of the functioning of the Diet as a law-making body. This committee, nevertheless, is by no means free of defects and problems. First of all, the standing members of the Standing Committee on Commerce and Industry cannot be said to have adequate specialized knowledge. It is painfully evident that Standing Committee members in particular cannot cope well with the intense changes taking place in Japan and abroad. Second, there is a tendency for the Standing Committee on Commerce and Industry to preserve rather than prevent dominance by MITI technocrats. Third, it is all too easy for an unhealthy relationship to arise wherein MITI technocrats identify themselves with special-interest (industrial) groups. If this happens, the law-making mechanism could become a hotbed for acquisition and protection of *riken* (rights and interests).

Ruling party.   The MITI technocrats cannot carry out their policies without close liaison with the LDP. This means that for MITI to protect and enlarge its organization and functions, to create special corporations under its protective wing, to acquire additional authority, and to secure budget allocations, it is necessary to keep in close contact and be on favorable terms with the LDP, and especially

with the Commerce and Industry Division in the Policy Research
Council.

Deliberation councils. In order that the interests and opinions
of others may be reflected in the process of formation, approval,
and implementation of policy by MITI, the deliberation councils
(shingi-kai) have been started. As of October 1985, the number of
councils that have been established within MITI are as follows:
twenty to the Ministry; one to the Agency of Industrial Science and
Technology; six to the Natural Resources and Energy Agency; two to
the Patent Agency; and four to the Small and Medium-Sized Enterprises Agency. It may well be necessary to review the situation in
connection with those committees where it is patently clear that
compromises between conflicting interests cannot be worked out
because of domination by one or another interest group.

Private enterprises. It is a commonplace phenomenon for MITI
and private enterprises or industrial groups to go hand in hand. The
larger the enterprise involved, the more likely this is the case. The
communication process from enterprises to MITI is schematically
shown in Figure 5.3.

Pressure groups. When the activities of social organizations in
the legal process are examined, what stands out sharp and clear is
the presence of big business and organized labor. These are the two
groups from outside the Diet that are most prominent when important legislation is pending. The presence of agriculture, small business or consumer groups is inconsequential relative to these two.
The most important organizations representing big business are the
Japan Federation of Economic Organizations *(Keidanren),* the Japan
Federation of Employers' Associations *(Nikkeiren),* and the Kansai
Federation of Economic Organization *(Kankeiren).* Mention may
also be made of the Japan Association of Corporate Executives
(Keizai-doyukai), the Japan Iron and Steel Federation *(Tekko-
renmei)* and the Japan Foreign Trade Council *(Nippon-boeki-kai).*
These organizations make use of the high level of funding and
powerful leaders that they have, to exert influence on administrative affairs and lawmaking.

The most prominent labor organizations are the General Council
of Trade Unions of Japan *(Sohyo)* and the Japanese Confederation of

Labor *(Domei)*. They have tended to lose influence in the legislative process.

The process of holding "public hearings" has been tried as a means of having the variety of social interests represented fairly in the lawmaking process, but the experience with this in committee work in Japan to date leaves much room for doubt about its real efficacy.

Government-affiliated organizations. There are three types of organizations affiliated with MITI. They are public-benefit corporations *(idealer Verein; koeki-hojin)*, specialized agencies *(tokushu-hojin)*, and voluntary bodies *(nin'i-dantai)*. Of the first, there are as many as 700. The specialized agencies constitute the "largest suzerainty in the central government." MITI provides substantial subsidies to these affiliated organizations, and in practice MITI policy is implemented through their activities.

2.2. The Process in the United States

The formulation process of international trade and industry laws in the United States is shown in Figure 5.4 (pp. 178–179).

One of the major characteristics of this process is that the TPSC (Trade Policy Staff Committee) plays an integral role for policy coordination. The TPSC is composed of officials dispatched from United States Trade Representative (USTR) and other main economic ministries. The Function of the TPSC is only to prepare draft bills and, if they desire to submit them to Congress, to look for a sponsor in the two houses.

3. COMPARISON OF BOTH COUNTRIES

Which country's institutions and legislative process is superior might be a peripheral issue, and we should recognize that the countries' political systems are basically different. We can indicate the basic differences as follows.

3.1. Function of the State

In Japan, the government is concerned with the precise setting of substantive goals. On the other hand, the United States government

Figure 5.4 International Trade Legislation Process in the United States. [Prepared from hearings by Theodore W. Kassinger, Esq., of law firm Vinson & Elkins (Washington, D.C.) in Nov. 1985 and Sept. 1986.]

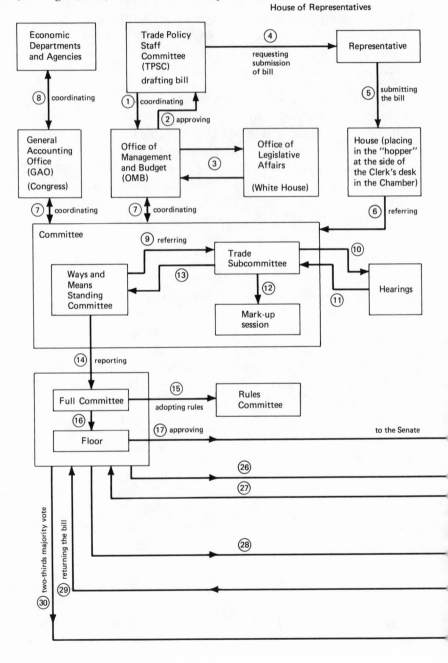

Senate

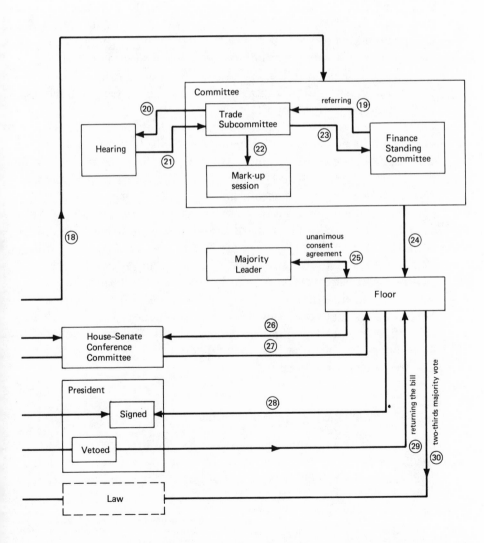

seems to concern itself with the forms and procedures of economic competition, but not with substantive matters. For example, the United States has numerous laws and regulations concerning the anti-trust implications of the size of firms, but it does not concern itself with which industries should exist and which industries are no longer needed.[15]

3.2. Substantial Legislator

According to the Japanese Constitution, "the highest organ of state power" is the Diet. But as a practical matter, the Diet's power is somewhat circumscribed. The Japanese Constitution and the Diet Law provide that the sponsor of bills can be either a Diet member, the Cabinet, a Standing Committee, or a Select Committee. Almost all important bills, however, are usually introduced by the Cabinet. On the other hand, similar sponsors in the United States are limited to the members of the two Houses.

The Japanese may rely generally on law, but these laws, compared with those of the United States, are relatively short and highly generalized. Concrete meaning is given to these laws through bureaucratically originated cabinet orders, ministerial ordinances, rules (*tsutatsu,* etc.), and administrative guidance. It is the bureaucrats in Japan who draft most of the legislation that is introduced to the Diet and virtually all the legislation that is eventually adopted. It is also the bureaucrats who basically decide how this legislation will be administered. In this way, substantial political power and legislative power reside with the bureaucracy. Neither individual Diet members nor the committees are given such enormous staffs as the United States generously gives to its congressmen. Partly for that reason, very little legislation originates in the Diet itself. And its committees might be at best of little service to the United States congressional committees.

3.3. Decision Making and Policy Change

As far as differences between the two systems in terms of decision making are concerned, the strategic level of policy development in Japan reflects the high position of the bureaucrats. The career civil servants—the elite bureaucrats of Japan—make major policy innovations in the system. In the United States, decision making might be centered in the parliamentary assembly, while national decision making is dominated by the elected members of the professional class, who are usually lawyers, rather than bureaucrats.

The process of policy change is also manifest in quite different ways. In Japan, change is marked by internal bureaucratic fighting and conflict among related ministries. In the United States, change might be marked by strenuous parliamentary contests over new legislation and by election battles.

3.4. Rules in Congress

First, the rules of the U.S. Congress are especially sensitive to the rights of minorities. On the other hand, Japan's rules seem to be sensitive to the rights of majorities.

Second, the U.S. Congress is also responsive to external groups and pressures; in Japan, the government also seems responsive to those groups.

Third, the U.S. Congress is a collegial, not a hierarchical, body. Power does not flow from the top down, as in a corporation, but in practically every direction. Congressional policies are not "announced" but are "made" by shifting coalitions that vary from issue to issue. In Japan, coalitions are rather fixed.

3.5. Role of Economic Ministries

In Japan, the government gives the greatest precedence to economic policy, which is considered carefully by the officials of economic ministries, that is, the Ministry of Finance, MITI, the Ministry of Agriculture, Forestry and Fisheries, the Ministry of Construction, and the Ministry of Transportation, plus the Economic Planning Agency. In particular, "industrial policy" might take priority over any other policies because of the predominant concern with the structure of domestic industry and with promoting the structure that enhances the nation's international competitiveness.

On the other hand, the United States is usually thought of as having economic policy but not "industrial policy".[16]

3.6. The MITI Technocrats and Their Organization

Japanese who have passed the higher civil service examinations
are considered the "best brains" in Japan. In MITI, as in the Ministry
of Finance, there is a high concentration of such persons, compared
with the situation at other ministries.

Career officials in MITI are assigned to major areas in the ministry
as soon as they have completed their short training period, where
they are groomed as elite generalists. Often they are sent overseas
to study at this time, to schools such as Harvard, Yale, and Stanford,
and to Cambridge and Oxford, or seconded to embassies or institutions such as the Institute of Developing Economies (*Ajia
Keizai Kenkyujo*) where they can acquire additional experience,
including experience abroad. After that, they are promoted to director of division, chief of department, chief of Bureau, director-
general of agency and vice-minister.[17]

The authority to formulate and decide on policy is delegated to a
group of relatively youthful technocrats. The Laws and Ordinances
Examination Committee *(horei-shinsa-iinkai)* is exceedingly important as a means of ensuring democratic processes within the ministry. It is virtually impossible for any important policy to be adopted
without the approval of this body; decisions made by these men are
not overruled by their superiors.

Meetings of this committee are held according to absolute rules
of reason, without regard to the identity of the person who introduced an issue, or to the identity of Diet members supporting
one or another position, or other sources of bias.[18] And yet no
matter how democratic the process whereby this group reaches its
decisions on policy, it is unavoidable that the process is conditioned
by delicate political considerations of the highest order.

No change is expected in the importance of this committee or in
the way it functions to formulate and coordinate MITI policies,
acting on the basis of the total situation within which policy is made
and implemented.

However, if the proposals that become the basis of laws regulat-
ing international trade and industry are taken as giving direction to
the intent of the Diet as formed by MITI technocrats—i.e., as providing a fixed framework—it can mean that MITI has that much
more potential power. Since the vast majority of important bills in
Japan are sponsored by the government and created by the tech-

nocrats, there is also the ever present possibility that MITI's policy making has nothing to say to the masses or the weak, since its policies are made to promote the "economy" or logic for the strong.[19]

For the formulation and approval of policy in MITI to be judged as right and proper it must be the work of "outstanding technocrats." In keeping with the tendency for MITI to acquire greater prominence in the total workings of the government, it is necessary for the MITI technocrats who have control of the rational mechanisms of MITI policy making to have a strong say in the legislative process. Further, in the immediately related processes of drafting proposals for bills, members of the ruling party cannot compare with these officials in regard to the vast store of information the latter have collected through soundly functioning, sophisticated mechanisms, or in regard to experience and knowledge. It is therefore indispensable for these career officials to participate in the law-making processes by exercising a strong hand in leadership. In that the underlying quality of these technocrats can be seen as a pervasive rationality *(Rationalität)* in the procedures they abide by, their objectives, and their methods, they can be considered more suitable for the role of law making than are politicians.

3.7. The United States Trade Representative and Other Bodies

In the United States, the making of decisions on trade and economic policy is concentrated in Congress. More than the Department of Commerce, the USTR, the TPSC or other bodies, it is the Congressmen, the congressional staff and specialists, including many practicing lawyers, who have power. Rather than debate policy within one of the departments of government (different from within MITI), the debate is between members of Congress, in Congress, and through the election process.

Finally, in Japan, when a bill is sponsored by MITI it is rarely shelved. But in the United States, if technocrats sponsor an important bill there is a high probability that it will be scuttled by Congress.

Table 5.1 compares the legal cultures of the two countries in summary form.

Table 5.1
Comparison of Legal Cultures in the United States and Japan

	United States	Japan
1. Consciousness lying at the basis of life	Assertion of individual rights	Harmony inside group
2. Conflict of interest	Settle in court	Settle by negotiation, private/public
3. Competition	Individual vs. individual	Group vs. group
4. Adherence to	Provisions of law	Mores behind provisions (social norm as its setting)
5. Sanction to rule violator	Indemnity and/or restitution	Recovery of emotional loss
6. Basis of conscience	Universal justice	Harmony inside group
7. Sponsor of presenting bill	Congressmen only	Cabinet (bureaucracy), Diet member, Standing Committee, and Select Committee
8. Law is regarded as	Instrument to assert rights	Last resort
9. Juridical system	Diverse (federal and state)	Single national
10. Administrative authority	Public servant	Respectable/dependable/ paternal administrator (*okami*)

Source: Japanese Ministry of International Trade and Industry, Study Committee on Transnational Corporations, *Waga-kuni-kigyo no kaigai-jigyo-katsudo ni-kakawaru sosho; be-ikoku ni-okeru saiban-kankatsu-ken to sotatsu no mondai o chushin to-shite* [Disputes Arising From Foreign Operations of Japanese Enterprises: With Special Reference to Jurisdiction and Service of Process in the United States], March 1984; and prepared from *"Nichi-bei ho-bunka no hikaku kento kenkyu-kaigi (1–2)"* [Workshop on comparative analyses of Japan–U.S. legal culture] *Jurisuto* [Jurist], no. 760, 762, March 1, 15, 1982.

NOTES

1. The work of the Congress is initiated by the introduction of a proposal in one of four principal forms: bill; joint resolution; concurrent resolution; and simple resolution. The bill is the form used for most legislation, whether permanent or temporary, general or special, public or private. A joint resolution may originate either in the House of Representatives or in the Senate. Joint resolutions become law in the same manner as bills. A concurrent resolution is used merely for expressing facts, principles, opinions, and purposes of the two Houses. A simple

resolution is used for the operation of either House alone. *How our laws are made.* Presented by Mr. Rodino. Revised and updated by Edward F. Willett, Jr., Washington, D.C., U.S. Government Printing Office, 1980, pp. 6–8.

2. A *Shitsu* (literally, "room") is an organizational unit within or approximating the division.

3. Although this body has a strong coordination function as an assisting organization to the Cabinet, as well as Parliamentary Vice-Ministers Council, it has no statutory basis.

4. In more detail, see Walter J. Oleszek, *Congressional Procedures and the Policy Process,* 2d ed. Washington, D.C., Congressional Quarterly Inc., 1984. p. 12 et seq.; *The Bill Status System for the United States House of Representatives.* Committee on House Administration. July 1, 1975. p. 19; U.S. Congress, *Legislative Status Steps.* Washington, D.C., U.S. Government Printing Office, 1974. (This flowchart—40 cm × 80 cm—is hung on the wall of the room of Professor Charles Tiefer, Office of the Clerk of the House, who permitted me to make a photocopy.); and R. D. Davidson and Walter J. Oleszek, *Congress and Its Members.* 2d ed. Washington, D.C., Congressional Quarterly Inc., 1985. p. 349 et seq.

5. In more detail, see, "Committees and Subcommittees of the 98th Congress," *Congressional Quarterly Weekly Report,* special report, 2 April 1983; Steven S. Smith and Christopher J. Deering, *Committees in Congress.* Washington, D.C., Congressional Quarterly Inc., 1984; Sula P. Richardson and Susan Schjelderup, *Standing Committee Structure and Assignments; House and Senate.* Washington, D.C., Congressional Research Service, 1982. Report no. 82–42 GOV., 76–77; and W. J. Oleszek, *op. cit.*

6. In more detail, see Steven and Deering, *op cit.;* Robert L. Peabody, *Leadership in Congress.* Boston, Little, Brown, 1976. p. 336; and Richardson, Sula P., *Congressional Research Service;* and Davidson and Oleszek, *op. cit.*

7. In more detail, see, *How Our Laws Are Made,* p. 11; Stevens and Deering, *op. cit.; Congressional Staff Directory, 1982.* Mount Vernon, Va.; Oleszek, *op cit.;* Norman J. Ornstein et al., *Vital Statistics on Congress, 1984–1985.* Washington, D.C., American Enterprise Institute, 1984. Chap. 5; and Davidson and Oleszek, *op. cit.*

8. David Mayhew, *The Electoral Connection.* New Haven, Yale University Press, 1974.

9. On membership in various groups, see, National Opinion Center, *General Social Surveys, 1972–1984; Cumulative Codebook,* Washington, D.C., Congressional Research Service, July 1984; and Davidson and Oleszek, *op. cit.* On lobbying techniques used by interest groups, see Kay Lehman Schozman and John T. Tierney, "More of the Same: Washington Pressure Group Activity in a Decade of Change," *Journal of Politics,* May 1983, p. 350; and Davidson and Oleszek, *op. cit.*

10. *Tsusho-sangyo-gyosei-kenkyuu-kai* [Study Group of International Trade and Industry], ed., *Tsusho-sangyo* [International Trade and Industry] Tokyo: Gyosei, 1983. p. 21.

11. Professor Vogel indicates that "the success of [MITI] is derived not from statutory rules but from its efforts at administrative guidance and from the voluntary cooperation of the business community." Ezra F. Vogel, *Japan as Number One: Lessons for America.* Cambridge, Mass.: Harvard University Press, 1979, p. 73.

12. *Tsusho-sangyo-gyosei-kenkyuu-kai,* ed., *op. cit.,* pp. 76–77; and see also Yoshihide Ishiyama, "Industrial Policies of Japan and the United States—Their Mechanisms and International Implications," pp. 236–237, in this book.

13. *Gyosei-shido* is generally defined as "that, without coercive force, which restricts rights of nationals and puts them under obligation, induces them to make certain commission or omission so as to perform certain administrative objectives, within the limits of function or competence endorsed by law based on which the administration was organized." (Answer by Mr. Tsunoda, Director of First Department of the Cabinet Legislation Bureau in the Standing Committee on Trade and Industry of the House of Councillors held on 26 March 1974.)

14. Nothing gets done unless the people involved agree. The Japanese call this *nemawashi* (root binding). Just as a gardener carefully wraps all the roots of a tree together before he attempts to transplant it, Japanese leaders bring all members of society together before an important decision is made (*Time* magazine). Even in a labor field, unions play a role in aggregating worker opinion on issues directly affecting them as part of the root-binding process in the firm. Vogel, *op. cit.,* p. 154.

15. Chalmers Johnson, *MITI and the Japanese Miracle: The Growth of Industrial Policy, 1925–1975.* Stanford, Calif.: Stanford University Press, 1982, p. 19.

16. For a definition of "industrial policy," see p. 170.

17. According to the study of Professor C. Johnson, the internal MITI rank order is as follows: (1) vice-minister; (2) chief, Industrial Policy Bureau (before 1973, the Enterprise Bureau, which was created in 1942); (3) director-general, Natural Resources and Energy Agency; (4) director-general, Medium and Small Enterprises Agency; (5) director-general, Patent Agency; (6) chief, International Trade Policy Bureau; (7) chief, Machinery and Information Industries Bureau; (8) chief, Minister's Secretariat; (9) chief, Basic Industries Bureau; (10) chief, Industrial Location and Environmental Protection Bureau; (11) chief, Consumer Goods Industries Bureau; and (12) chief, Trade Bureau (the old Trade Promotion Bureau). Chalmers Johnson, *op. cit.,* p. 79.

18. Speech by Mr. Urata, Masutaro (at that time, an assistant to the member of Laws and Ordinances Examination Committee and presently member of the committee) Takano, Hajime, *Tsusan-sho no yabo* [Ambitious MITI]. Tokyo, Nikkan-kogyo-shimbunsha, 1980. p. 17.

19. Shibata, Masuo, "Gyosei no kokoro" [Mind of administration], *Tsusan janaru* [MITI journal], October 1976, p. 52.

BIBLIOGRAPHY

On Japan

Asano, Ichiro. *Horitsu, jorei; sono riron to jissani* [Law and Rule of Local Public Body: Theory and Practice]. Tokyo: Gyosei, 1984.

Gikai ni-okeru rippo-katei no hikaku-ho-teki-kenkyu [Comparative Studies on Legislative Process in Congress]. Tokyo: Keiso Shobo, 1980.

Gyosei-kiko-zu, 1985-nen-ban [Government Organization, 1984] edited by Somu-cho. *Gyosei-kanri-kyoku* [Management and Coordination Agency. Administrative Management Bureau]. Tokyo: Gyosei-kanri Kenkyu Center, 1985.

Hatakeyama, Takemichi, *"Sangyo-seisaku to gyosei-shido"* [Industrial Policy and Administrative Guidance], *Koho-kenkyu*, no. 44, 1957.

Higashi, Chikara. *Japanese Trade Policy Formulation*. Forewords by Yasuhiro Nakasone, and Michio Watanabe. New York: Praeger, 1983.

Ikeda, Masaaki. *"Rippo-katei-ron no mondai-ten."* [Problems of Theory of Legislative Process] *Iwanami's Contemporary Law*. vol. 3. Tokyo: Iwanami Shoten, 1965.

———. "Rippo rippo-katei" [Legislation and the Legislative Process] *Nippon-koku-kempo-taikei*. Tokyo: Yuhi-kaku, 1971.

Johnson, Chalmers. *MITI and the Japanese Miracle: The Growth of Industrial Policy, 1925–1975*. paperback ed. Stanford, Calif.: Stanford University Press, 1982.

Kaplan, Eugene J. "Perspectives on Government-Business Interaction in Japan," in *Asian Business and Environment in Transition: Selected Readings and Essays,* edited by A. Kapoor. pp. 323–337. Princeton, N.J.: The Darwin Press, 1976.

Kobayashi, Naoki. *Rippo-gaku kenkyu; riron to dotai* [Studies on Legislature: Theory and Dynamics]. Tokyo: Sanseido, 1984.

Kojima, Kazuo. *Horitsu ga dekirumade* [How Laws Are Made], 4th ed. Tokyo: Gyosei, 1981.

Murakawa, Ichiro. *Nippon no seisaku-kettei-katei* [Policy-Making Process in Japan]. Tokyo: Gyosei, 1985.

Nagai, Mikihisa. "Nichi-bei-kan no sangyo-seisaku rongi," *Refarensu* [Reference]. National Diet Library: August 1983.

"Naikaku to kanryo" [Cabinet and Bureaucrats], *Hogaku-semina* [Jurisprudence seminar]. Special issue, 1979.

Narita, Yoriaki. *"Gyosei-shido."* [Administrative Guidance] *Iwanami's Contemporary Law*. vol. 4. Tokyo: Iwanami Shoten, 1966. pp. 131–168.

"Nichi-bei ho-bunka no hikaku kento kenkyu-kaigi 1–2)" [Workshop on Comparative Analyses of Japan–U.S. Law Culture] *Jurisuto* [Jurist], nos. 760, 762, March 1, 15, 1982.

Otake, Hideo. "Gendai-seiji ni-okeru dai-kigyo no eikyo-ryoku (1–

3)" [Impact of Big Business on Contemporary Politics] *Kokka-gakkai-zasshi,* vol. 91, no 5/6, 9/10, 1978, vol. 92, no. 1/2, 1979.

Taguchi, Seiichi. *"Rippo-katei-ron."* [Theory of Legislative Process], in *Iwanami's Contemporary Law.* vol. 3. Tokyo: Iwanami Shoten, 1965, pp. 209–241.

Tsusho-sangyo-gyosei-kenkyu-kai [Study Group of International Trade and Industry Administration], ed. *Tsusho-sangyo* [International Trade and Industry]. Tokyo: Gyosei, 1983. 2 vols.

Tokuyama, Jiro. "The Japanese Notion of Law: An Introduction to Flexibility and Indefinitude," in *Asian Business and Environment in Transition: Selected Readings and Essays,* edited by A. Kapoor. pp. 276–301. Princeton, N.J.: The Darwin Press, 1976.

Yazawa, Shujiro. *"Tsusan-sho ni-okeru seisaku-kettei-katei."* [Policy-Making Process in the Ministry of International Trade and Industry], in *Towareru Tsusan-sho* [Ministry of International Trade and Industry in Question]. Tokyo: Ootsuki-shoten, 1983.

On The United States

American Political Science Association. *The Legislative Process in Maine,* by Kenneth T. Palmer and others. Washington, D.C.: American Political Science Association, 1973.

Ayres, Robert U. "Industrial Policies: An Analysis," *Economic Impact* (U.S. Information Agency), pp. 29–34. no. 51, March 1985.

Bell, George Alfred. *The Legislative Process in Maryland: A Study of the General Assembly.* College Park, Bureau of Governmental Research, College of Business and Public Administration, University of Maryland, 1958.

Berry, Jeffrey. *Lobbying for the People: The Political Behavior of Public Interest Groups.* Princeton, N.J.: Princeton University Press, 1977.

Ceaser, James W.; O'Toole, Laurence J.; and Thurow, Glen. *American Government: Origin, Institutions, and Public Policy.* New York: McGraw-Hill, 1984.

Chamberlain, Joseph Perkins. *Legislative Process: National and State.* New York: Appleton-Century, 1936.

Cohen, Stephen D. *The Making of United States International Economic Policy: Principles, Problems, and Proposals for Reform.* 2d ed. New York: Praeger, 1981.

Congressional Quarterly Service. *Legislatures and the Lobbyists.* 2d ed. Washington, D.C.: Congressional Quarterly, 1968.

Danforth, John C. "The Need for Reciprocity Legislation." *Economic Impact* (U.S. Information Agency), pp. 25–27, no. 43, March 1983.

Davidson, Roger H., and Oleszek, Walter J. *Congress and Its Members.* 2d ed. Washington, D.C.: Congressional Quarterly, 1985.

Davies, Jack. *Legislative Law and Process.* St. Paul, Minn.: West Publishing, 1975.

Deakin, James. *The Lobbyists.* Washington, D.C.: Public Affairs Press, 1966.

Downs, Anthony. *Inside Bureaucracy.* Boston: Little, Brown, 1967.

Farmer, Hallie. *The Legislative Process in Alabama.* University of Alabama. Bureau of Public Administration, 1944–1947.

Fisher, Joel M., and Bell, Charles G. *The Legislative Process in California.* Washington: American Political Science Association, 1973.

Fox, Jr., Harrison, W., and Hammond, Susan Webb. *Congressional Staffs: The Invisible Force in American Lawmaking.* New York: The Free Press, 1977.

Froman, Lewis Acrelius. *The Congressional Process: Strategies, Rules and Procedures.* Boston: Little, Brown, 1967.

———. *Congressmen and Their Constituencies.* Chicago: Rand McNally, 1963.

Galloway, George B. *The Legislative Process in Congress.* New York: Crowell, 1953.

Gordon, Glen. *The Legislative Process and Divided Government: A Case Study of the 86th Congress.* Amherst: Bureau of Government Research, University of Massachusetts, 1966.

Gray, Virginia; Jacob, Herbert; and Vines, Kenneth N., eds. *Politics in the American States: A Comparative Analysis.* 4th ed. Boston: Little, Brown, 1983.

Gross, Bertram M. *The Legislative Struggle: A Study in Social Combat.* New York: McGraw-Hill, 1953.

Guild, Frederic Howland, and Snider, Clyde F. *Legislative Procedure in Kansas.* Lawrence: Bureau of Government Research, University of Kansas, 1946.

Hall, Donald R. *Cooperative Lobbying: The Power of Pressure.* Tucson: Ariz., The University of Arizona Press.

Holtzman, Abraham. *Interest Groups and Lobbying.* New York: Macmillan, 1966.

Hormats, Robert D. "The Presidency in the High Competition, Hi-Tech Eighties," *Presidential Quarterly,* Spring (1983): 225–260.

How Congress Works. Edited by Mary L. McNeil. Washington, D.C.: Congressional Quarterly, 1983.

How Federal Laws Are Made. Washington, D.C.: WANT Publishing Co., 1983.

Jewell, Malcolm Edwin, and Patterson, Samuel C. *The Legislative Process in the United States.* 2d ed. New York: Random House, 1973.

Kassinger, Theodore W. *The Congressional Trade Policy Process.* Mimeographed. Paper submitted to Brookings' Seminar for Korean Executives, 1985.

Kirkpatrick, Samuel A. *The Legislative Process in Oklahoma: Policy Making, Peoples, and Politics.* Norman: University of Oklahoma Press, 1978.

Kofmehl, Kenneth. *Professional Staffs of Congress.* 3d ed. West Lafayette, Ind.: The Purdue University Press, 1977.

Levitan, Donald, and Mariner, Elwyn E. *Your Massachusetts Government.* Newton Centre, Mass.: Government Research Publications, 1984.

Loewenberg, Gerhard; Patterson, Samuel C.; and Jewell, Malcolm E., eds. *Handbook of Legislative Research.* Cambridge, Mass.: Harvard University Press, 1983.

Mandelker, Daniel R.; Netsch, Dawn C.; and Salsich, Peter W. *State and Local Governments in a Federal System: Cases and Materials.* 2d ed. Charlotteville, Va.: The Michel Co., 1953.

Marcuss, Stanley J., ed. *Effective Washington Representation.* New York: Harcourt Brace Jovanovich, 1983.

McCracken, Paul W. "Does the U.S. Need an Industrial Policy?" *Economic Impact* (U.S. Information Agency), no. 46, Feb. 1984:8–13.

Michigan State University, East Lansing. Institute for Community Development and Service. *The Legislative Process: A Bibliography in Legislative Behavior.* Compiled by the Michigan Senate Fellows. East Lansing, 1966.

New York City. *The Green Book, 1985–1986. Official Directory of the City of New York.*

———. *The Red Book, 1985–1986.*

O'Conner, Robert E., and Ingersoll, Thomas G. *Politics and Structure; Essentials of American National Government.* 3d ed. Monterey, Calif.: Brooks/Cole, 1983.

Office of the Republican Leaders. *Manual of Legislative Procedure in the United States House of Representatives.* 5th ed. Washington, D.C. 1983.

Ogura, Kazuo, *"Keizai-masatsu no horitsu-gaku"* [Legal Problems of Japan-U.S. Economic Conflicts], in his *Nichi-bei keizai-masatsu* [Japan–U.S. Economic Conflicts]. Tokyo: Nippon Keizai Shimbunsha, 1982.

Oleszek, Walter J. *Congressional Procedures and the Policy Process.* 2d ed. Washington, D.C.: Congressional Quarterly, 1984.

Olson, David M. *The Politics of Legislation: A Congressional Simulation.* New York: Praeger, 1976.

Pastor, Robert A. *Congress and the Politics of U.S. Foreign Economic Policy, 1929–1976.* Berkeley: University of California Press, 1980.

Patterson, Samuel C. *The Role of the Labor Lobbyist.* Paper presented to the American Political Science Association. Washington, D.C., 1962.

Petlit, Lawrence K. comp. *The Legislative Process in the U.S. Senate.* Chicago: Rand McNally, 1969.

Redman, Eric. *The Dance of Legislation.* New York: Simon and Schuster, 1973.

Reid, T. R. *Congressional Odyssey: The Saga of a Senate Bill.* San Francisco: W. H. Freeman, 1980.

Reitman, Jerry I.; Bettelheim, Judith; and the Staff of Academic Media. Directory of Registered Federal and State Lobbyists. lst ed. Orange, N.J.: Academia Media, 1973.

Riddick, Floyd M. *Senate Procedure: Precedents and Practices.* Washington, D.C., U.S. Government Printing Office, 1978.

Rudder, Katherine E. *Power From the People.* Mimeographed. Prepared exclusively for the American Embassy in Tokyo. 18 p. [n.d.]

Schultze, Charles L. "Industrial Policy: A Dissent." *The Brookings Review,* Fall (1983):3–12.

Schwab, Susan C. "Japan and the U.S. Congress; Problems and Prospects." *Journal of International Affairs* 37, no. 1 (1983) pp. 123–139.

Sinclair, Barbara. *Majority Leadership in the U.S. Congress.* Baltimore: The Johns Hopkins University Press, 1983.

Smith, Steven S., and Deering, Christopher J. *Committees in Congress.* Washington, D.C.: Congressional Quarterly, 1984.

Underwook, Cecil H. *The Legislative Process in West Virginia.* Morgantown: Bureau for Government Research, West Virginia University, 1953.

University Reference System. *Legislative Process, Representation, and Decision-Making: An Annotated and Intensively Indexed Compilation of Significant Books, Pamphlets, and Articles.* Selected and processed by the Universal Reference System. Prepared under the direction of Alfred de Grazia, and John B. Simeone. Princeton, N.J.: Princeton Research Publishing Co., 1967.

U.S. Government, *Senate Manual Containing the Standing Rules, Orders, Laws, and Resolutions Affecting the Business of the United States Senate.* Prepared by Jack L. Sapp under the direction of John B. Childers. Washington, D.C.: U.S. Government Printing Office, 1981.

U.S. General Accounting Office. *Industrial Policy: Japan's Flexible Approach.* Prepared by the Comptroller General. Report to the Chairman, Joint Economic Committee, United States Congress. 23 June 1982.

U.S. House of Representatives. *How Our Laws Are Made.* Revised and updated by Edward F. Willett, Jr., esq. Presented by Mr. Rodino. Washington, D.C.: U.S. Government Printing Office, 1980.

U.S. House of Representatives. *The Constitution of the United States of America, as Amended.* Unratified amendments. Presented by Mr. Rodino. Washington, D.C.: U.S. Government Printing Office, 1978.

U.S. House of Representatives. *Our American Government; What Is It? How Does It Function?; 150 Questions and Answers.* Washington, D.C.: U.S. Government Printing Office, 1981.

U.S. Senate. *Senate Legislative Procedural Flow (and Related House Action).* Prepared by Harold G. Ast, Legislative Clerk under the direction of J. Stanley Kimmitt, Secretary of the Senate. Washington, D.C.: U.S. Government Printing Office, 1978.

U.S. Senate. 98th Congress. 1st Session, *Standing Rules of the Senate (pursuant to the adoption of S. Res. 274 and S. Res. 389, 96th Congr., Nov. 14, 1979, and Mar, 25, 1980, respectively) and Congressional Budget and Impoundment Control Act of 1974, as amended*. Washington, D.C.: U.S. Government Printing Office, 1983.

Vogler, David J. *The Third House: Conference Committees in the United States Congress.* Evanston; Northwestern University Press, 1971.

The Washington Monitor. *Congressional Yellow Book.* (loose-leaf) (n.d.).

Wescott, Robert F. "U.S. Industrial Approaches: A Review," in Adams, Gerard, and Klein, Lawrence R., eds., *Industrial Policies for Growth and Competitiveness.* pp. 8–13 Lexington, Mass.: Lexington Books, 1983.

Wiggins, Charles W. *The Legislative Process in Iowa.* Ames: Iowa State University Press, 1972.

Woll, Peter. *American Government; Reading and Cases.* 8th ed. Boston: Little, Brown, 1984.

Zimmerman, Joseph F. *The Government and Politics of New York State.* New York: New York University Press, 1981.

Zysman, John, and Cohen, Stephen S. "Double or Nothing; Trade and Competitive Industry. *Foreign Affairs* 62, no. 4 1983: 1113–1139.

COMMENTARY
ON CHAPTER 5

MASUTARO URATA
*Natural Resources and Energy Agency**

I N THE LAST few years, legislation concerning Japanese industrial
policy has changed. In short, internationalization has become a
key word in domestic policy making for industries, and every effort
has been made to make legal measures acceptable in the international world, with the basic thrust of making policies about the
market and the business activities more indirectly.

Such a switch from the direct approach to the indirect approach
is remarkable, first of all, in policies directed at growing industries
and technological development.

It is well known that during the period of recovery after the war
and the following period of high growth of the Japanese economy,
several laws were established to permit low-interest loans, tax incentives, and other measures in specified industries that were expected to grow. Such laws giving direct incentives to production
and investment of specified industries have disappeared in the last
decade or so. Instead, laws facilitating technological development
in general, without specifying certain industries, are now playing a
large role. Priority is given especially to fundamental technological
development. The Act for the Facilitation of Research in Fundamental Technologies of 1985 is a good example.

*This is a personal opinion, and not an official view of MITI.

To support technological development in general, it is desirable not only from the standpoint of the government's neutrality toward the industry and indirectness toward the market, but also as a contribution to the accumulation of basic technologies, which is at the core of the world economy's development.

In the area of declining industries, the basic idea is not to support the survival of the enterprises of the declining industries, but to convert them into other business fields. This will stamp out protectionism and contribute to the maintenance of the competitive economy. More important is that the aim of the government's support has switched from adjusting production, investment, and other business activities to relieving the serious impact of industrial adjustment on employment and local economies. Such changes in industrial adjustment legislation can obviously be seen in the series of laws, enacted in 1987, concerning measures for facilitating employment and for revitalizing depressed local economies.

Such changes in the trend of industrial-policy legislation are, in a way, a reflection of the maturity of the Japanese economy and society, as well as a manifestation of Japan's efforts to harmonize itself internationally. As policy areas such as fundamental technological development, and measures to facilitate employment and local development become common in other countries, legislation in these fields is expected to grow in Japan as well.

6

MISSION TO MANAGE:
THE U.S. FOREST SERVICE AS A
"JAPANESE" BUREAUCRACY

JOHN O. HALEY
*Associate Dean and Professor, University of
Washington School of Law*

INTRODUCTION

THE PRESTIGE and power of the Japanese bureaucracy have been constant themes in studies of Japanese patterns of governance. Views vary from Robert Ward's understated textbook description that "since the Meiji restoration . . . the bureaucracy has been very important in the Japanese political system" (Ward 1967, 161) to Dan Henderson's hyperbolic quip that in Japan, "rather than a rule of law, a rule of bureaucrats prevails" (Henderson 1973, 195, cited with approval in Johnson 1982, 37). Some might quibble about the accuracy of such descriptions for all agencies at all levels of government in Japan, but few if any disagree with the characterization of the Ministry of International Trade and Industry

I am indebted to the assistance of David A. Hearth, a third-year law student of the Harvard Law School. As noted below, Mr. Hearth is responsible for the extensive research on the use of consensus groups in U.S. Forest Service Region Six, particularly the summary of the Hardesty Mountain dispute. See Hearth, A Process Analysis of United States Forest Service Consensus Groups in Region 6, unpublished paper, Harvard Law School. I must also thank Jeff M. Sirmon, who as the Regional Forester of the Pacific Northwest Region, organized and invited me to participate in a Field Seminar for Educators in July 1985. The seminar introduced me to the Forest Service and its striking similarities to a Japanese bureaucracy.

(MITI), the Ministry of Finance, and the other premier economic bureaucracies as able elites with a strong sense of mission, dominating both the formation and execution of policy and jealously protecting all prerogatives and power.

Normative evaluations aside, American views have changed little during the past four decades. Writing in 1947 as a critic of bureaucratic influence, again with select ministries in mind, John Maki saw the Japanese bureaucracy as a small, elite group sharing "a common training, a common tradition, a common ideology and a common desire to monopolize what the group regarded as the skills of government" (Maki 1947, 396). While offering a more favorable assessment, Hugh Patrick and Henry Rosovsky agree that "Japanese ministries have a tradition of considerable autonomy and independence of views and jealously guard their powers" (Patrick and Rosovsky 1976, 48).

Comparison is implicit in such observations. Throughout the literature there runs an underlying but rarely stated assumption— "but it is different elsewhere." Whether praised or criticized, the role and characteristics of bureaucracy in Japan are generally viewed as exceptional. Yet remarkably little has been written evaluating such assumptions or subjecting them to explicit comparative analysis. For most observers the special role of the Japanese bureaucracy is simply taken for granted or, if explained at all, characterized as a product of a distinctive history and cultural tradition.

The purpose of this chapter is to rethink such assumptions and, in so doing, to identify at least the most important institutional and cultural factors that help to explain the role of the bureaucracy at least in Japan. The ultimate objective, however, is to understand better the dynamics of bureaucratic behavior in all cultures, not just Japan. With this aim, I have selected the United States Forest Service as a focus for comparison; for despite significant differences in personnel and function, in organization and behavioral dynamics, the Forest Service bears a remarkable resemblance to the elite Japanese economic bureaucracies.

To preview my conclusions, let me state that as in Japan's economic bureaucracies, an emphasis on personnel training to instill a sense of tradition and loyalty, of mission and commitment characterizes the Forest Service. Also like the Japanese bureaucracies, the

Forest Service has reacted to the challenges posed by litigation over its policies and practices by accommodation and, at least in one of its nine regions, an innovative program for decision making by consensus. These similarities suggest that the function of the agency as manager of resources is a determinative factor in both internal organization and external response. Although the ease and skill with which Japanese bureaucracies use consensus-building techniques demonstrates the influence of cultural patterns as a source of models and approaches, the thrust of my argument is that similar operating premises—such as the view of the managerial mission of an agency—produce similar patterns of behavior. I will begin, however, with a brief analysis of basic institutional contrasts between Japan and the United States as an introductory summary of some of the more salient contrasts observed in studies of public administration in Japan.

1. THE JAPANESE BUREAUCRACIES

The obvious sometimes bears repeating: many of the differences between patterns of governance and the role of the bureaucracy in the United States and Japan stem from differences between the American presidential system and parliamentary systems generally. Consequently, many of the features considered from an American perspective as distinctively Japanese are more accurately viewed as reflections of distinctively American institutional arrangements. One of the best examples is the policy-making or legislative role of the bureaucracy. Bureaucratic participation in setting the agenda and determining the content of legislation is a prevailing feature in all industrial states today (see Aberbach, Putnam and Rockman 1981, 84–114). In parliamentary systems, however, the bureaucracy exerts an especially strong influence on legislation. Often-cited statistics on the dearth of private or members bills as opposed to government-sponsored initiatives in Japan are, for example, as common to other parliamentary systems generally as to Japan in particular.

Routinely 85–90 percent of all legislation enacted by the Diet originates in the ministries and is actually drafted by career bureaucrats (Seki 1984, 25). Chalmers Johnson sees in such data evidence that "the influence of former bureaucracts within the Diet has tended to perpetuate and actually strengthen the prewar pattern of bureaucratic dominance" (Johnson 1982, 47). However accurate Johnson's conclusion may be on other grounds, the bureaucracy's influence on legislation does not provide its proof.

The Japanese experience does not appear to be significantly different from that of the United Kingdom, Germany, France or other parliamentary systems. As Brian Smith notes, in the United Kingdom as a matter of course legislation is planned and drafted within the administrative department with jurisdiction over its subject after consultation with affected interests (Smith 1976, 86). Private-member bills in the United Kingdom are thought to constitute a "very small proportion of the work of Parliament, and then only those which embody policies acceptable to the government are passed" (Smith 1976, 86). In the Federal Republic of Germany as well, 75 percent of all legislation is estimated to originate in the ministries (Lowenberg 1967, 267). Much the same is true for France (Ehrmann 1983, 307; Suleiman 1974, 302–5).

A second characteristic of bureaucratic influence Japan shares with European parliamentary regimes is the presence of the bureaucracy in the ruling political party. A constant theme in most of the literature on Japan is the number of former bureaucrats within the ruling Liberal Democratic Party (LDP). One consequence is the greater deference they foster to the bureaucracy in lieu of parliamentary leaders or such nongovernmental bureaucracies as labor unions under Labor Party governments in the United Kingdom, Australia, and New Zealand. The extent of political leadership drawn from the elite bureaucracy therefore seems distinctive to Japan. This feature is readily explained, however, by the near monopoly of power the elite civilian bureaucrats enjoyed under and immediately after the Allied Occupation. The ruling political parties of postwar Japan were created by members of this elite. The contrast between the postwar and wartime careers of Yoshida Shigeru and Konrad Adenauer or between Kishi Nobusuke and Ludwig Erhard provides a telling reminder that the political leaders of immediate postwar Japan were predominantly drawn from the prewar or wartime civil bureaucracy; in postwar Germany, they were either prewar political figures untainted by Nazi affiliation or political newcomers. As both John Maki (1947) and Chalmers Johnson (1975) emphasize, the principal source of bureaucratic power in postwar Japan was the decision of Occupation authorities as to who were to be the appropriate conduits for Occupation rule. Bureaucratic influence in the postwar political process was thus more a product of Occupation policies than a legacy of a more distant past.

Gradually, almost imperceptibly, however, the postwar constitutional order has worked to reduce this influence. Not since the elections of 1949, in which thirty-seven bureaucrats, including twenty-five recruited by Prime Minister Yoshida, made their political debut, and 1952, in which 139 depurgees and 48 former bureaucrats were elected, has any election in Japan resulted in a significant gain for ex-bureaucrats in the Diet (Reed 1987, 9; Sato and Matsuzaki 1986, 232). Since then, the number of ex-bureaucrats entering the Diet has rarely exceeded a dozen (Sato and Matsuzaki 1986, 232). As the careers of Kakuei Tanaka and Yasuhiro Nakasone illustrate, the power at the periphery of career politicians and former staff members with strong local bases of support has slowly increased from election to election during the postwar period at the expense of the bureaucracy at the center.

Yet, even granting the influence of former bureaucrats in the Diet, postwar Japan approximates other parliamentary systems. For the Federal Republic of Germany, for example, Aberbach, Putnam & Rockman (1981, 277, note 16) cite statistics showing that in 1973 about 38 percent of the members of the Bundesrat were government officials on leave. Of the members of the Bundesrat elected a decade later, over 10 percent were high civil service officials in federal, state, or local governments at *the time of* their election (Schweitzer et al. 1984, 399). With about 20 percent of the LDP members of the Japanese House of Representatives identified as former bureaucrats (Fukui 1984, 393), Japan is thus comparable to the Netherlands (Aberbach, Putnam and Rockman 1981, 277, note 16).

Bureaucratic dominance in Fifth Republic France appears even stronger, as evidenced by the observation (Suleiman 1974, 31, quoting Quermonne) that 34–41 percent of the members of the

National Assembly can be identified as "members of the administration." This influence is also reflected in the careers of Giscard d'Estaing and Michel Debré (Gournay 1984, 83). In contrast, only 3 percent of British members of Parliament and no U.S. congressmen are estimated to have a career background in the civil service (Aberbach, Putnam and Rockman 1981, 277, note 16).

From the American perspective, the power and influence of the Japanese bureaucracy seems impressive also for its reach. The scope of bureaucratic intrusion into the economic and social life of Japan is often described as if it were several degrees greater than the United States or other industrial democracies. The Japanese bureaucracy thus appears to be "monolithic" (Henderson 1973, 200).

Such observations are equally flawed, however. Government in the United States is far more intrusive than in Japan. Excluding perhaps family registration and the neighborhood police, there is little if any evidence that the average Japanese citizen has any more contact with government than his or her American counterpart. The volume and intrusiveness of governmental controls in the United States—from taxation through consumer and environmental regulation—seems in fact to be far more extensive than in Japan.

The weekly volume of new regulatory enactments alone in the United States appears to be in excess of the *annual* quota of all new legislation and regulations promulgated by the Japanese government. Thus Japanese firms operating in the United States have had to make major adjustments, developing significantly larger legal departments for their limited operations in the United States than for all of their home office activities in Japan (Miyazawa 1986).

Perhaps what makes the Japanese bureaucracy appear monolithic is the stable simplicity of governmental organization in Japan. We speak of the bureaucracy in Japan in the singular, but we can hardly even describe accurately the variety of government agencies at the municipal, county, state, and national levels in the United States.

A fourth feature noted by nearly all who have studied the Japanese bureaucracy does stand out: a sense of mission. As quoted above (Maki 1947, 396), a "common tradition" and "common ideology" are distinctive to the Japanese bureaucracy. Ezra Vogel, writing in 1979, observes:

The esprit that unites a ministry's five hundred or so elite bureaucrats rests on a sense of group mission. Although not immune from political pressures, bureaucrats do not hesitate to unite against politicians who obstruct their perceived mission. Responsibility for success in any important matter rests with a work unit, and all in the unit are judged by their unit's contribution to the ministry. Superiors do not promote someone who cannot win the liking and cooperation of his peers, for an individual's value to his unit is determined by his capacity to work effectively with his peers, his superiors and his subordinates. Each bureaucrat is personally identified with the mission of his work unit and the ministry as a whole. (Vogel 1979, 56)

Chalmers Johnson amply demonstrates the accuracy of such conclusions in his study of the Ministry of International Trade and Industry. "Whatever its roots," he states, "MITI's spirit has become legendary" (Johnson 1982, 56). However, absent from these and other descriptions of the spirit and sense of mission of MITI and other economic Japanese bureaucracies is a clear delineation of precisely what that mission is. Nor is it certain that Japanese bureaucracies at all levels of government share a similar esprit found among officials in MITI, the Ministry of Finance and other economic ministries. Nonetheless, a sense of cohesive spirit and mission as members of the national bureaucracy and especially of particular elite ministries or agencies is cited as another distinctive characteristic of public administration in Japan.

The importance of mission to the role of Japanese bureaucracy is not, however, simply a matter of ministerial élan or internal consensus as to objectives. Rather it is the sense of managerial responsibility that the Japanese bureaucracy in general and the economic bureaucracies in particular appear to share. This factor above all others, I believe, sets Japanese governmental agencies apart at least from the regulatory policing agencies in the United States, to which the Japanese bureaucracies are usually compared, if not from "managerial" bureaucracies in other industrial democracies. In brief, the managerial mission of the Japanese economic bureaucracies establishes an underlying premise that has had as much to do with their organization and behavior as history or other cultural factors.

For example, in a recent comparison of American Occupational Safety and Health Administration (OSHA) inspectors and their counterparts under the Swedish Workers Protection Board (Arbetarskyddsstyrelsen, or ASU), Steven Kelman notes a very different sense of commitment, which he identifies as mission. The Americans, he writes, "know what they are supposed to do; most are go-getters about it, and a few are gung-ho" (Kelman 1984, 109). Kelman sees this as evidence that a "sense of mission is easier to infuse the clearer and operationalizable [sic] the organization's goals are." The contrasts between the American and Swedish inspectors, especially Kelman's finding of greater hostility of the Americans toward private industry and the less rigid attitudes of the Swedish inspectors, can better be explained, I would argue, by differences in mission rather than degrees of commitment. Regulatory agencies such as the FTC, OSHA, and the EPA are designed to operate as prosecutorial agencies. Operating under extensive and often vague delegations of authority, they proscribe conduct considered as a matter of public policy to be inappropriate, and then they identify and prosecute violators. These agencies function as policemen within an otherwise "free" market. Similar tasks can be performed, however, under a radically different conception of an agency's mission: to manage rather than to police. The authority to define standards and the powers to assure conformity may be identical in either case, but if the role is that of manager, not policeman, the hierarchy and pervasiveness of responsibility change the nature of relationships with outside constituencies, the patterns of interaction, and the attitudes of all concerned. Industry becomes subject to direction and can be expected to comply, even though the legal capacity to coerce may be weaker. The end result may be the same, but the officials are less likely to be as hostile or as rigid in working out solutions with industry. Both in terms of purpose and organization it is therefore important to distinguish the independent regulatory agency from the more inclusive managerial ministry or department.

Many comparisons of Japanese and American bureaucracies, especially those that center on MITI and other economic ministries in Japan, thus fail to take adequately into account the unique dominance of independent, single-cause policing agencies in the United States. Oft-cited contrasts between Japanese and American bureaucratic behavior do not appear so stark when the Japanese Fair Trade is compared to either the Federal Trade Commission or the Federal Cartel Office in Germany, or in comparisons between the Japanese

Ministry of Agriculture, Forestry and Fisheries and the U.S. Department of Agriculture.

In short, the nature of the organization and its function—whether it is a comprehensive department or a single-cause agency, whether its purpose is to promote or to regulate, to manage or to police— appear to be at least as important a set of variables in influencing bureaucratic behavior as such "cultural" factors as shared values or a common sense of history and tradition. Culture is of course relevant and should not simply be treated as a residual element. Along with the expectations and values that permit or deny a managerial mission to bureaucracies, the operating premises and the internal "culture" created by institutional design are, however, the determining cultural factors.

The challenge then is to find an American agency that differs in almost all respects from at least a stereotypic Japanese bureaucracy except in organization, function, and mission to see if it indeed manifests similar patterns of administrative behavior. For this purpose, the United States Forest Service is surely one of the best cases in point.

2. THE UNITED STATES FOREST SERVICE

It is difficult to imagine an administrative agency in the United States that at first blush would appear as far removed from a Japanese bureaucracy as the United States Forest Service. The model Japanese bureaucrat is almost universally portrayed as a product of elite university education—i.e., a graduate of the law faculty of the University of Tokyo—heir to the samurai *kanson mimpi* tradition, a generalist with a strong psychological or cultural tendency toward cooperative, collective behavior (see, e.g., Craig 1975). In contrast, the United States forester is nearly always pictured as a product of rural America, a graduate of a land-grant "state" university, and heir to the American tradition of rugged individualism. Yet the Forest Service is noted for "a strong sense of tradition whose mission has remained essentially unchanged since its inception" (Frome 1984, 33, citing Gold 1981, 5–6). "Cohesiveness and loyalty" are considered its primary characteristics (Frome 1984, 33). In the words of Harold K. Steen, "Of the many Forest Service traits, esprit de corps is the most outstanding. Pride in one's work and loyalty to the agency did not dissipate after the first old timers retired; rather, they became a part of the Forest Service mystique and a part of the ranger's personality" (Steen 1976, vi).

The esprit de corps of the Forest Service is not accidental. With Japan's elite bureaucrats, the U.S. Forest Service shares a mission of resource management in the public interest as well as a process of selection and socialization in which "tradition" and "loyalty" are consciously emphasized to produce conformity to agency goals. The end product is a shared capacity to influence, adapt, and respond to changing public demands by adjusting immediate objectives and programs without sacrificing the central mission that defines the agency and its ultimate aims. Like the economic ministries in Japan, the Forest Service maintains both its prestige and powers with a jealous care that requires it to adapt to changing public demands.

The origins of the U.S. Forest Service are to be found in the reaction to the massive transfer of public lands to private owners in the 1860s and 1870s. During this period a series of statutes—the Homestead Act of 1862, the Mineral Land Act of 1866, the Timber Culture Act of 1873, the Desert Law Act of 1877, and the Timber and Stone Act of 1878—"designed," in Michael Frome's words, "to encourage, assist, and reward ordinary Americans who would open frontier lands . . . were short-cut and subverted, leading to fraud, land thievery and land speculation, through which something like one-half of the nation's forests passed into private ownership" (Frome 1984, 17). In response, in 1881 a Division of Forestry was established in the Department of Agriculture, headed in 1886 by the government's first professional forester, the German-born Bernhard Edward Fernow. Credit for the establishment of the Forest Service, however, goes to Fernow's successor, Gifford Pinchot, who, when appointed Chief of the Division of Forestry in 1898, headed only a minuscule staff. Frome states that Pinchot began with only eleven employees (Frome 1984, 19) but citing Pinchot's diaries, Steen claims sixty (Steen 1976, 53). Whatever the actual number, in 1898 the Division employed only a small fraction of the Department of Agriculture's 2500-plus employees. Benefiting from Pinchot's close personal relationship with Theodore Roosevelt, in 1905 the new director won a decisive political battle in the enactment of the

Transfer Act, which brought all forest work, including forest lands previously administered under the Department of Interior, under the Division and established the U.S. Forest Service.

Since 1905 the Forest Service has defeated all attempts, even those with strong presidential backing, once by Franklin Delano Roosevelt and most recently Jimmy Carter, to relocate this authority in other departments (Steen 1976, 237–245; LeMaster 1984, 105–129). The primary task of the new Forest Service was to manage the nation's forest reserves (soon renamed national forests). For the ensuing half century, as one observer noted:

> The Forest Service administered nearly 200 million acres of forests, rivers, mountains, and ranges with little legislative guidance nor much interest from the public and frequently, tremendous pressure from exploiters of range, timber, and mineral resources. The Forest Service acted both as protector and as arbitrator. (Frome 1984, 21)

The service also grew, reaching a peak in 1980 with a total of 61,279 employees (21,421 permanent full-time, 15,815 permanent part-time, and 24,043 temporary employees). In 1984 the total had decreased to 49,220, but permanent full-time employees increased to 30,030 (Forest Service Annual Report 1984, 5). Today it is not only the largest bureau in the Department of Agriculture, but also one of the largest in the entire federal civilian bureaucracy.

Of the Forest Service's total work force, 93 percent work in the national forest system, 6 percent are engaged in research, and less than 1 percent are in state and private forestry. The largest category is technical operations. The majority of professional employees, the second largest category, are foresters and civil engineers (Forest Service Annual Report 1984, 5). The nearly 6000 professional foresters in the Service comprise the core from which are selected the district rangers, who, with principal responsibility for field operations, constitute the inner elite of the Service, akin to the law-trained generalists in a Japanese bureaucracy.

The Forest Service today manages 155 national forests through 147 administrative districts divided into nine regions, of which economically the most important is Region Six. Region Six comprises all of the national forests in the states of Washington and Oregon. Because of extraordinarily propitious conditions for timber production, it generates over half of the Forest Service's total revenues from timber sales.

The Service is organized hierarchically under the "Chief" in Washington, D.C., who has been traditionally selected from career officials in the Service. Despite the Service's centralized organization, it allows extensive administrative discretion at the local level. District rangers have traditionally exercised considerable authority and experience relatively little control from authorities at the center in planning activities (Chadwick 1987). A trend toward greater central control in the 1960s and 1970s has apparently been reversed, with a return to a more decentralized, "feudal" pattern of decision making (Chadwick 1987). Some, particularly lawyers on the outside, criticize the lack of central direction (e.g., Netzorg 1987), but members of the Service take pride in the administrative freedom of the Forest Service, especially as contrasted with its principal bureaucratic rivals at the national level—the Bureau of Land Management and the National Park Service (Beitia 1987). In this respect too the Forest Service resembles a Japanese bureaucracy. As Yoshihisa Ojimi describes decision making in MITI, "Lower-level subordinates have a great deal of influence" and "give their opinions freely and generously" (Ojimi 1975, 103). Yet like MITI, seldom do the actions of subordinates in the Forest Service fail to reflect the intentions of their superiors.

3. INSTILLING COHESION, LOYALTY, AND CONFORMITY

As in the case of Japanese bureaucracies, the Forest Service goes to considerable effort to instill a sense of identification with the agency and to foster cohesion and loyalty as well as unconscious conformity with Forest Service practices and goals. The process begins with recruitment in the selection of personnel. The Service seeks those who are most likely to fit into the agency's patterns and discourages anyone who is not highly motivated, depicting the life of the forester in discouraging terms. As described by Hubert Kaufman:

> Recruiting publicly tends to deter the impatiently ambitious, the seekers after the easy job and the comfortable and stable life, and men who grow restless at the thought of positions within the framework of a large organization, with all the administrative borders and frustrations this entails. (Kaufman 1960, 165)

However stark the warnings to potential recruits, the Service attracts the best and brightest of forestry graduates each year (Elkins 1957, cited in Kaufman 1960, 168).

Again paralleling Japanese patterns, the Forest Service placed special emphasis on mentor training for each new recruit. Each supervising officer is expected to work with new junior foresters to provide closely supervised, on-the-job training. In the course of this training, the tradition and mission of the Forest Service and the importance of its tasks to the nation's welfare are continuously affirmed (Kaufman 1960, 173). This early training process also provides an opportunity for supervisors to identify those who seem most appropriate for advancement. Thus those slated to move upward in the hierarchy are identified early in their careers.

Finally, the Forest Service has developed an "environment" that fosters identification of its members with the agency, subsuming the individual's interest into that of the organization as a whole. In Kaufman's words:

> In addition to picking and advancing men likely to be receptive to communications from the leaders of the agency, and to "training into" these men the capacity and willingness to adhere to preformed decisions announced by the leadership, the Forest Service enjoys—largely as a result of its deliberate efforts, but partly in consequence of fortuitous circumstances—an environment conducive to an almost automatic tendency to conform to those decisions. That environment is a set of conditions promoting identification of the members of the Forest Service with the well-being of the organization, linking their own positions and welfare and futures with those of the agency, fusing their perspectives with those of their colleagues and superiors. It is a set of conditions that sets them apart from all people "outside" the organization, binds them intimately with other organization members; that "injects into the very nervous systems of the organized members the criteria of decision that the organization wishes to employ," and thereby vastly increases the probability that each of them will "make decisions, by himself, as the organization would like him to decide." Without realizing it, members of the Forest Service thus "internalize" the perceptions, values, and premises of action that prevail in the bureau; unconsciously, very often, they tend to act in the agency-prescribed fashion because that is the way that has become natural to them. (Kaufman 1976, 176)

Ezra Vogel's description of Japanese bureaucrats, quoted above, thus applies almost word for word to the Forest Service.

It should be noted that history and tradition are not irrelevant. Although we should question simplistic explanations of the present in terms of the past, such explanations are themselves factors. History and tradition are legitimizing devices. Thus for contemporary bureaucrats in Japan to claim to be heirs of the samurai tradition is more of an ideological than an historical statement. It justifies more than it determines that role. Like that of Japanese bureaucracies, the Forest Service's repeated emphasis on its tradition is instrumental in the development of cohesion and loyalty.

The development of solidarity and a sense of shared aims and cohesion in the Forest Service thus parallels the process for internalizing agency purposes and goals in Japanese bureaucracies. However, unlike Japan, where this process is repeated throughout the government and in the private sector (see Rohlen 1974), the Forest Service experience is generally regarded as unusual. As a result of the process, however, members of the Forest Service, like Japanese bureaucrats, develop a strong sense of loyalty and identification with a special tradition, which enables them to lay special claim as stewards of the national forests for the public good. As a former district ranger and forest supervisor explained:

> Although the Forest Service considers itself disinterested with respect to forest uses, it believes that it knows best. The scattered public [and, one might add, private] interests do not understand forest management. . . . Any opposing parties will have a fight on their hands if they question Forest Service authority. (Chadwick 1987)

Again Vogel's description of Japanese ministries holds true for the Forest Service:

> The high quality and integrity of the bureaucrat, the respect of the Japanese public, and the self-contained nature of a ministry enables bureaucrats to be relatively free from political pressure and to work for what they consider the good of the country. As a result, the Japanese government has enjoyed high-quality leadership with considerable continuity and long-term perspective regardless of the rapid changes in political leaders. (Vogel 1974, xxv)

4. RESPONSE TO LITIGATION AND NEW SOCIETAL DEMANDS

The parallels between the Forest Service and the Japanese economic bureaucracies are most poignant, however, in their responses to the changes in societal concerns and in the consequent challenges posed by legislative demands and environmental litigation in the 1960s and 1970s.

Despite conflicts over the allocation and use of the resources under their supervision, both the economic bureaucracies in Japan and the U.S. Forest Service enjoyed broad public support for their respective managerial roles during the 1950s. In Japan, a national consensus gave overwhelming priority to economic growth and deference to the managerial role of the economic bureaucracies in directing the effort to achieve this goal. Armed with an array of left-over Occupation regulatory controls, notably the Foreign Exchange and Foreign Trade Control Law *(Gaikoku kawase oyobi gaikoku bōeki kanri hō)*—Law No. 228, 1949—and new-found influence in the ruling political party, the mid-1950s marked the pinnacle of bureaucratic power in Japan. By the end of the decade, this power had begun to dissipate (see, e.g., Apter and Sawa 1984). Success eroded consensus for growth and gave industry a measure of independence from bureaucratic controls. Attempts to win passage of legislation to increase the legal powers of the economic bureaucracies to command failed repeatedly. Increasingly, MITI and other economic bureaucracies resorted to indirect means of persuasion (Johnson 1982, 247). The era of guidance cartels had begun, and consensus became the "crux" of economic policy (Murakami 1982, 42).

Unlike managerial oversight of a market economy, in which private firms and consumers are the primary actors, the managerial role of the Forest Service was intrinsic to its supervision of the national forests. Until the 1960s, however, the Forest Service enjoyed a notable degree of autonomy in carrying out its tasks. The Service operated under a broad and almost standardless delegation of policy-making authority. The Transfer Act of 1905 merely directed the Service to manage the "occupancy and use" of the national forest land "and to preserve the forests thereon from destruction" (Wilkinson and Anderson 1985). The Service received little guidance and almost no direction from sources outside the Department of Agriculture, and within the Service regional and local staff personnel enjoyed considerable discretionary authority and freedom. Thus there was considerable variance in policies and plans among different regions and parts of a forest, although rarely if ever were they incompatible with general Forest Service aims (Wilson 1978, 467). Although the Service did not have direct or indirect representation in Congress through the election of former members, it maintained close ties with the congressional delegations from districts in which national forest land was located and carefully fostered its "Smokey the Bear" public image. The result was an extraordinarily good reputation. "I know of no service," remarked Senator Hubert Humphrey in 1960, "which has more dedicated people or a group of more conscientious or better-trained public servants who are more willing to make the necessary sacrifice to have a good program" (Humphrey 1960).

As in Japan, an aura of quiet order hid serious conflicts over the use of the resources of the forest and the realization of their economic value. Not all uses were compatible, and not all Forest Service practices were deemed appropriate.

In the 1960s, conflict could be contained no longer, and the authority and prestige of the Forest Service and Japanese economic bureaucrats were increasingly challenged. These challenges took acute form in political demands for new policies and an increasing volume of lawsuits attacking allegedly favored private industrial interests at the expense of the public welfare. These suits did more than rebuke the agencies; they attacked their integrity and mission as custodians of resources on behalf of the nation as a whole.

In Japan, the lawsuits addressed the failure of the national bureaucracies, particularly the Ministry of Health and Welfare and MITI, to protect the public from the hazards of chemical wastes, water and air pollution, and drugs. In their wake small unknown villages—such as Minamata—and strange illnesses with frightening names became international symbols of the captivity of economic government policy-makers by private industrial interests. The response by Japanese officials is well known (Upham 1987; Gresser et al. 1981; Huddle and Reich 1979).

Earlier when a dispute arose involving a client industry or firm, officials had customarily moved quickly to assist in securing a settlement. With their paternalistic concern and authority unquestioned, their efforts at mediation and "guided" consensus usually worked. In 1955, for example, officials from the Ministry of Health and Welfare successfully mediated a settlement between the manufacturer of powdered milk alleged to have contained arsenic causing the death of 130 infants and injuring nearly 12,000 other victims. No suits were brought.

Two decades later, however, the inadequacy of the settlements became a national scandal. The times had changed. Although generally less directly involved than local officials and political leaders, various ministries quickly became deeply involved in attempts to resolve the major pollution suits of the 1970s by mediation. However, mediation and efforts to reach consensus without any significant change in policy no longer worked. The result was an increase in litigation and widely publicized attacks on bureaucratic inaction.

Once conflict and litigation appeared likely to become a recurrent pattern, officials responded similarly with institutionalized mechanisms for administrative resolution and compensation (see Upham 1987). As early as 1968, for example, efforts began to establish a special administrative forum for resolution of pollution disputes. These culminated in the 1978 law for the Compensation of Pollution-related Health Damage *(Kōgai kenkō higai hoshō hō)*, Law No. 111, 1973 (see Gresser 1975).

The reaction was predictable. In the 1920s Japan had witnessed a similar pattern of official response to social conflict and a rising volume of lawsuits with institutionalized procedures for formal conciliation *(chōtei)* (see Haley 1982). The cultural determinants of this reaction are equally evident. In a sense, Japanese officials and political leaders rediscovered tradition, finding in Tokugawa trial procedures forms of dispute resolution that could be adapted to the Westernized legal system of an advanced industrial state. Although innovative, they were consistent with values, habits, and expectations shared generally within Japanese society. The conciliation statutes did, however, reflect conscious choices and top-down decisions designed to satisfy bureaucratic aims. Neither formal conciliation in the 1920s nor administrative schemes for compensation of injuries caused by pollution sprang from popular demand. Nor did they replace litigation or end conflict (Haley 1982).

Mediation and attempts to find substitutes for litigation are aspects of a broader administrative reliance on consensus in both making and enforcing public policy. As evidenced by "administrative guidance," the emphasis on consensus building is generally considered a dominant characteristic of bureaucratic behavior in Japan. Like mediation, it too fits comfortably in the Japanese "tradition." Reliance on consensus to avoid confrontation and conflict is not, however, a product of bureaucratic power. Rather, it generally reflects the inability of officials to assure compliance by command and an erosion of bureaucratic influence (Haley 1986).

Seldom if ever in Japanese political history has the power of those who govern matched their authority to rule. Historically, the recurring obstacle for Japanese governance has been the centrifugal pull of local centers of power and the incapacity of rulers at the center to institute an effective system of pervasive bureaucratic control. The paradox of semi-autonomous communities and the ideology of the absolute state, of the *mura* and the *jōkamachi,* provides the dominant theme of the Japanese tradition. As claimants to the Japanese tradition, the Japanese bureaucracies thus are bound at least to some extent by the shared values, habits, and expectations that legitimize their role as managers but also denies them the power to exercise autonomous control. Reliance on consensus in Japan has been and continues to be a matter of necessity.

The resort to mediation and consensus by Japanese bureaucracies is telling in comparison with the Forest Service. Although, as noted, differences in the nature of the resources they manage helps to explain the greater managerial autonomy of the Forest Service; nonetheless, many routine decisions by the Service do involve conflicting interests. Trees may not talk back, but lumbermen and environmentalists do. The experience of the Service in dealing with these conflicts thus has important parallels and contrasts with the bureaucrataic managers of Japan's economy.

Beginning with the controversy over the Forest Service's clear-cutting practices on the Monongahela National Forest in West Virginia in the early 1960s, the Forest Service timber-management policies came increasingly under unprecedented attack. The number of lawsuits challenging Forest Service practices rapidly increased. Although the exact number of lawsuits filed against the Forest Service between 1975 and 1985 is unknown, over one hundred judgments are reported. Many more, one estimates, were settled. In 1985 the agency was forced to defend more suits than throughout its first half-century.

The observations by Richard D. Pardo of the Society of American Foresters are as applicable to MITI as the Forest Service:

To the foresters, lawsuits are at best a time-consuming nuisance. More often they are viewed as an attack on professional competency, and may even carry the implication of moral wrongdoing. In almost every case, there are out-cries that the lawyers and the judges, who probably are unable to tell a juniper from a jack pine, are telling the foresters how to practice forestry. (Pardo 1976, 44)

So challenged, however, both MITI and the Forest Service sim-ilarly attempted to channel if not control the legislative response. Despite initial efforts to thwart or blunt attacks and defend previous policies, both agencies proceeded to change and adopt policies that satisfied public demands without, however, sacrificing their es-sential managerial roles. For MITI this meant close involvement in setting new antipollution policies and efforts to prevent loss of jurisdiction. The establishment of a relatively weak Environmental Protection Agency in Japan thus represented for MITI at least a partial victory.

The Forest Service was more successful. The legislative action to meet environmentalist as well as commercial concerns began with the Multiple-Use Sustained-Yield Act of 1960. The statute attempted to reconcile both interests by implicitly equalizing range, timber, watershed, and fish and wildlife protection, giving no single use a priority over the others. Drafted with close Forest Service involve-ment, the Act left intact the Service's ultimate discretion. Two stat-utes followed in 1964 and 1969 in response to increased public support for environmental concerns. The first was the Wilderness Act of 1964, which removed large areas of land from commercial and general recreational use. The most important legislation, however, was the 1969 National Environmental Policy Act (NEPA), which significantly altered the Forest Service's previous practices. First, the Service was required to prepare Environmental Impact Statements (EIS) before any wilderness or roadless areas could be altered. Second, the Act mandated increased participation by other government agencies and the public in the Service's decision-making process. Third, the Act required the Service to obtain more information and data about each area's resources. Finally, the Act made the planning process more centralized and hierarchial.

Continued conflict over national forest uses and consequent litigation led Congress to intrude further in the Forest Service's management. Two more broad-ranging statutes were enacted, di-recting the Service as to the management of particular uses and mandating the most comprehensive and detailed plans for national forest use in the nation's history: the 1974 Forest and Rangeland Renewable Resources Planning Act (RPA) and the 1976 National Forest Management Act (NFMA) (Williamson and Anderson 1985; LeMaster 1984). The Forest Service cooperated with Congress in the passage of each of these statutes, with representatives from the Service sitting with the joint committee to work out the final compromises. Although they reflected criticism of the agency, none circumvented its ultimate authority to manage the national forest or established an outside agency to oversee or rival its jurisdiction. Like the pollution legislation in Japan, the RPA and NFMA reflected a congressional solution, but unlike the Japanese pollution laws, the RPA and NFMA as comprehensive planning statutes left the Forest Service in control.

The similarities between the Japanese economic bureaucracies and the Forest Service do not end with their responses to the challenge of environmental litigation and their co-option of the issues in legislative initiatives. Both have tended also to deal with the disintegration of public consensus as to their role as resource managers and the policies they were pursuing by redefining their approach and method without sacrificing their ultimate mission. Instead of managers by directive they have increasingly become managers by mediation and consensus. Consequently, both MITI and Forest Service officials have had to become more sensitive to the diversely competing claims for resources and the political expression of these claims. The Forest Service in particular began to place greater emphasis in attracting new specialists to its staff, men and women trained in wildlife preservation, recreational use and sociology—to balance the predominance of timber-management professionals. Notable also is the Forest Service's resort at least in one region to consensus as a means to reduce confrontation and to avoid what it views as destructive polarization.

5. RESORT TO CONSENSUS

The Forest Service has long been familiar with informal mediation and resort to consensus in developing local community and political support (Chadwick 1987) as well as in resolving contained, local disputes involving its constituencies. The considerable discretion given district rangers has permitted them to take into account local concerns and interests, particularly those of small communities economically dependent upon the timber resources of the adjacent forests and customary uses of neighboring forests, worked out with informal consultation and compromise. In this context, as noted with respect to the Japanese experience, mediation and deference to consensus can best be viewed as a product of paternalistic concern and an exercise of unchallenged authority and power.

Reliance on consensus to deflect challenges to Forest Service policies and to avoid confrontation and litigation thus represents a significant departure from past practice. By accepting outside participation in decisions over competing uses of areas of the forest, the Forest Service surrenders autonomous control over the policies to be implemented and risks a loss of its authority. It is not surprising, therefore, that, in the words of a former district supervisor, one finds "a tension between the old instinct to win and the new determination to seek a better way of doing things" (Chadwick 1987).

Although the use of formal consensus-building techniques may now be practiced throughout the Forest Service, the first examples appear to have originated in Region Six in 1980 as the result of the efforts of Bob Chadwick, former district ranger and Forest Service supervisor of the Winema National Forest. Apparently influenced by the Klamath Indians, with whom he had close contact, as well as earlier experiences, Chadwick decided to use a consensus-building process in resolving a dispute over a decision to extend logging into roadless areas. Meeting with representatives from the forest-products industry and environmental groups, Chadwick was successful in achieving agreement on almost all the issues (Chadwick 1981). In 1982 a similar process was successful in resolving the Blue River controversy in the Willamette National Forest. The approach was repeated in at least five other significant disputes in Region Six; among the most important were the Hardesty Mountain and Bull Run controversies in Oregon.

5.1. The Hardesty Mountain Dispute

Located in the Willamette National Forest about twenty-five miles from Eugene, Oregon (home of the University of Oregon), Hardesty Mountain is a wilderness area of deep canyons, dense Douglas fir forests, and varied plant and animal life, including the endangered bald eagle and spotted owl. With twenty miles of low-elevation trails affording spectacular views of the Cascade Mountains, Hardesty provided a popular recreational area for outings from Eugene and other nearby communities.

Timber sales in the area had been a source of conflict for over a decade. After passage of the Multiple-Use Sustained-Yield Act in 1960, the Forest Service designated the area for multiple use. Although excluded in the 1964 Wilderness Act, it was included in 1983 in the House of Representatives version of proposed wilderness legislation for Oregon. Ultimately, however, the area was excluded in the Senate version and in the final bill enacted in 1984 as the Oregon Wilderness Act. The statute as enacted reflected Forest Service hopes that the area not be withdrawn completely from productive use. After the legislation was enacted, the Forest Service authorities decided that, with the exception of about 3000 acres set aside under its own Willamette National Forest Plan, the remaining land should continue to be subject to multiple use despite strong opposition from environmental groups in the region. The dispute soon came to a head. Bark beetles had begun to attack timber blown down in a windstorm, forcing the local district ranger to decide whether to not disturb the area, at least for the time being, and risk further infestation or to take advantage of the need for salvage logging to open new roads. The opportunity "to capture the area" was too attractive to miss. Thus, planning began for three substantial timber sales plus a limited helicopter salvage operation. Many groups and individuals in the area expressed adamant opposition and began to mount organized efforts to prevent the sales. Trees were spiked (in order to ruin saws and thus lower the value of the trees) and bake sales were organized to raise funds for the opponents. In an effort to avoid further escalation of the dispute, the district ranger somewhat "arrogantly but sincerely" approached the public, inviting interested groups and individuals into the area for field trips and asking for their input. The result was deferral of the three timber sales and any new road construction, but with agreement that limited salvage operations could proceed along existing roads. The Forest Service also decided to explore the idea of using a consensus committee to resolve the underlying, longer-term issues.

A number of environmental groups opposed to these interim

measures decided to boycott any further discussions. Others, such as the local Sierra Club chapter, decided that, since road-area salvaging would not damage the environment, they would accept the measures, with the hope that they could use this "concession" as a bargaining chip in negotiations to limit timber sales elsewhere in the area (Desmond 1987).

A "consensus group" was established. In addition to Bob Chadwick as facilitator, the group included two local district rangers and two other Forest Service representatives, a representative of the Bureau of Land Management, a local county commissioner, the local state representative, a University of Oregon herbarium professor, as well as representatives from the principal environmentalist organizations willing to participate—the Oregon Wildlife Federation, the Lane County Audubon Society, and the Many Rivers Group Sierra Club—the Northwest Timber Association, and a local logging firm. Meeting every two weeks for a period of five to six months, they agreed in the end on boundaries that reduced the area in dispute to about 15,000 acres and on protection of 6000 acres as a "core" wilderness area for wildlife habitat and semiprimitive recreation.

Toward the end of the process, a consortium of environmental groups that had refused to participate put forward an additional proposal. This was deferred without any changes in the original agreement (Desmond 1987).

5.2. Bull Run Watershed

The second example involved a dispute over Forest Service logging within the Bull Run Watershed (until 1977 the Bull Run Reserve) of the Mt. Hood National Forest outside of Portland, Oregon. Originally a nearly 140,000-acre area set aside by the federal government in Oregon's first federal timber reserve, Bull Run was established to protect Portland's water source. In 1904 the Bull Run Trespass Act prohibited all private entry. In the 1970s the City of Portland built the first entry and accessary roads and water-distribution facilities. Since then, Bull Run has provided a substantial portion of the potable water for Portland. Requiring little or no treatment, its quality had been a source of legendary pride among Portland residents. Although the Forest Service manages the area, the reservoirs, dams, and distribution facilities in the watershed are under the control of the City of Portland Water Bureau, giving the Portland City Council legitimate claim to some voice in how the watershed is administered yet without authority to control Forest Service decisions (Mt. Hood National Forest 1984, 2).

Prior to 1976 the Service managed the area with a watershed and commercial forest. In 1958 the Comptroller General had advised the Forest Service that multiple-area activities were permitted throughout the Reserve as long as Portland's water supply was protected. Subsequently over 42,000 acres were opened for public use, with road construction and logging permitted throughout the area. In 1973, a neighboring landowner, angered over the reserved use of an all-but-abandoned logging road adjoining his property, protested and filed suit. After extensive hearings, in 1976 a federal judge enjoined all logging-area recreational use in the entire reserve.

Reflecting the political influence of the Forest Service, both the Portland City Council and the U.S. Congress responded by protecting the Forest Service's activities. The Council passed a resolution (No. 31232) to permit recreation and logging in the original 42,000-acre area. Congress then enacted legislation that reduced the Reserve to about 95,000 acres, renaming the area the Bull Run Watershed Management Unit (Mt. Hood National Forest 1984, 2).

Public outcry over the perceived despoiling of the watershed continued, however, fueled by fears of harm to the quality of Bull Run water. In December 1983, after a severe storm blew down trees across a 5000-plus-acre area, affecting 287 million board feet of timber, the Forest Service issued plans not only to sell the blow-down but also to clear out several thousand more acres. Several environmental groups then joined in filing an administrative appeal against the Service's plans. Soon the City Council became involved, and the Forest Service again found itself involved in a major political controversy. After extended efforts to negotiate a solution failed, the Service initiated a series of meetings with environmentalist groups, representatives from the City Council, the Water Bureau, and the timber industry. The results were summarized by *The Oregonian* (13 September 1985) under the headline "Consensus Eases Bull Run Tensions":

What happened in this instance is a remarkable departure from the progress of many environmental controversies. After four environmental groups appealed the Forest Service's environmental assessment of plans to deal with the blowdown, the stage was set for confrontation and litigation. Instead, the Forest Service and appellants decided to form what was called a "consensus group" to discuss issues and concerns and attempt to resolve them. Also involved in this group were representatives of the timber industry, city and congressional offices.

This effort does not mean one side co-opted the other or that strongly held views were discarded. As one participant put it, "We explored ideas and adjusted our conclusions a little bit at a time."

In the end, a representative of the Oregon Environmental Council and a Forest Service staff member jointly reworked the initial portion of the Forest Service's salvage plan. The result was a prescription for salvage-logging some 580 acres—about 10 percent—of the downed timber, focusing on species such as true firs particularly susceptible to rotting. Forest Service officials emphasize that logging techniques will be aimed at minimizing disruption of the ground that could damage water quality.

Although isolated examples, both the Hardesty Mountain and the Bull Run disputes illustrate Forest Service resort out of political weakness to decision making by consensus as a means to avoid confrontation. In each instance the Forest Service shifted its position in the process to assume the role of mediator between industry and environmental interests. Its overriding concern was to preserve public and political support for its authority to manage. To achieve this end, it was willing, if reluctant, to compromise on particular policies. Although organized differently and less pervasive, the Forest Service adopted a pattern of negotiation and more formalized attempts to resolve conflict by consensus that paralleled the Japanese experience. Above all, decision making by mediation and consensus was a means of protecting the agency's mission to manage.

6. MISSION AS AN ORGANIZING PRINCIPLE

In conclusion, the factor that seems best to explain both the organization and behavior of the U.S. Forest Service as a "Japanese" bureaucracy is its managerial mission. This provides the underlying premise around which cohesion and loyalty are developed and determines the response of the agency to external challenges.

Citing Kaufman's study of Forest Rangers on the inculcation of values, Michael Hill notes:

> The Forest Service has a fairly clear objective: The maintenance of publicly controlled forests in the United States. In possessing this objective, it is in some respects in conflict with those elements in American political life which are opposed to public enterprise. Its continued existence depends upon maintaining the integrity of its general goals and fighting off challenges to its activities. (Hill 1972, 83)

Hill rejects, however, the notion that the development of central goals and the staff's internalization of the agency's objectives are determinants of success, implicitly distinguishing the Forest Service from multifunctional agencies. Hill ignores, however, the variety of demands upon the Forest Service and the multiplicity of functions it performs. His point is better made by distinguishing agencies with managerial roles as opposed to regulatory objectives. The parallels between the Japanese economic bureaucracies and the Forest Service result, I suggest, from neither the clarity nor the alleged narrowness of their objectives, but rather the shared premise that their tasks are managerial. These otherwise dissimilar bureaucracies assume similar patterns because both operate on the basis of similar premises.

Although perhaps exceptional within the American framework, the Forest Service illustrates the importance of a mission to manage as a significant factor in determining agency behavior. Differences between bureaucratic performance in Japan and the United States can thus be explained by the pervasive acceptance of managerial responsibility by the Japanese economic bureaucracies in contrast to the narrower regulatory focus of at least the stereotypical American government agency. The prevalence of a managerial mission among Japanese bureaucracies and its broad acceptance by the Japanese public (and its denial in the United States) are, of course, tied to cultural factors. Nevertheless, as illustrated by the U.S. Forest Service, similar institutional functions and managements do produce similar consequences even in distinctively different cultural environments.

BIBLIOGRAPHY

Aberbach, Joel D.; Putnam, Robert D.; and Rockman, Bert A. *Bureaucrats and Politicians in Western Democracies.* Cambridge, Mass.: Harvard University Press, 1987.

Apter, David E., and Sawa, Nagayo. *Against the State: Politics and Social Protest in Japan.* Cambridge, Mass.: Harvard University Press, 1984.

Beitia, Frank. Telephone interview 13 March 1987. Mr. Beitia is the former Grasslands and Watershed Supervisor, Caribou National Forest.

Chadwick, Bob. "Consensus Resolves Polarization," *Forest Planning* (1981):4–6. Chadwick is the former supervisor of the Winema National Forest.

————. Interview by John O. Haley and David A. Hearth, 24 March 1987.

Craig, Albert M. "Functional and Dysfunctional Aspects of Government Bureaucracy." In *Modern Japanese Organization and Decision-making,* edited by Ezra Vogel. pp. 3–32. Berkeley, Calif.: University of California Press.

Desmond, Jack. Telephone interview with David A. Hearth, 4 March 1987. Desmond is a member of the Many Rivers Group, Sierra Club.

Ehrmann, Henry W. *Politics in France.* 3rd ed. Boston: Little, Brown, 1983.

Frome, Michael. *The Forest Service.* 2nd ed. Boulder, Colo: Westview Press, 1984.

Fukui, Harahiro. "The Liberal Democratic Party Revisited: Continuity and Change in the Party's Structure and Performance." *Journal of Japanese Studies* 10, no. 2 (1984):385–435.

Gournay, Bernard. "The Higher Civil Service in France." In *The Higher Civil Service in Europe and Canada.* Washington, D.C.: Brookings Institution, 1984.

Gresser, Julian; Fujikura, Kōichirō; and Morishima, Akio. *Environmental Law in Japan.* Cambridge, Mass.: M.I.T. Press, 1981.

Haley, John O. "The Politics of Informal Justice: The Japanese Experience 1922–1941." In *The Politics of Informal Justice,* edited by Richard Abel. vol. II, pp. 125–147. New York: Academic Press, 1982.

————. "Administrative Guidance versus Formal Regulation: Resolving the Paradox of Industrial Policy." In *Law and Trade Issues of the Japanese Economy,* edited by Gary Saxonhouse and Kozo Yamamura. pp. 107–128, Seattle: University of Washington Press.

Henderson, Dan Fenno. *Foreign Enterprises in Japan.* Chapel Hill: University of North Carolina Press, 1973.

Hill, Michael J. *The Sociology of Public Administration.* New York: Crane, Russak & Company, 1975.

Huddle, Norie, and Reich, Michael. *Island of Dreams.* New York: Autumn Press, 1975.

Humphrey, Hubert H. *Congressional Record.* 1960, Vol. 106, pp. 12,083, 12,084.

Johnson, Chalmers. "Japan—Who Governs? An Essay on Official Bureaucracy." *Journal of Japanese Studies* 2, no. 1 (1975):1–28.

————*MITI and the Japanese Economic Miracle: The Growth of Industrial Power.* Palo Alto, Calif.: Stanford University Press, 1982.

Kaufman, Hubert. *The Forest Ranger: A Study in Administrative Behavior.* Baltimore: Johns Hopkins Press, 1960.

LeMaster, Dennis C. *Decade of Change: The Remaking of Forest Service Statutory Authority During the 1970s.* Westport, Conn.: Greenwood Press, 1984.

Loewenberg, Gerhard. *Parliament in the German Political System.* Ithaca, N.Y.: Cornell University Press, 1967.

Maki, John M. "The Role of the Bureaucracy in Japan." *Pacific Affairs.* (1947):391–406.

McKean, Margaret A. "Pollution and Policymaking." In *Policymaking in Contemporary Japan,* edited by T. J. Pempel. pp. 201–238, Ithaca, N.Y.: Cornell University Press, 1977.

Miyazawa, Setsuo. "Legal Departments of Japanese Corporations in the United States: Organizational Adaptation to Multiple Environments." *Koho University Law Review,* no. 20 (1986):99–162.

Mt. Hood National Forest, U.S. Forest Service, U.S. Department of Agriculture. *The Bull Run Protection Plan: Past, Present and Future of Portland's Water Supply,* 1984.

Murakami, Yasusuke. "Toward a Socioinstitutional Explanation of Japan's Economic Performance." In *Policy and Trade Issues of the Japanese Economy: American Japanese Perspectives,* edited by Kozo Yamamura. pp. 3–46, Seattle, Wash.: University of Washington Press, 1982.

Netzorg, Leonard. "Leonard Netzorg on Law" (Interview). *Evergreen* 4, no. 4 (1987):2.

Ojimi, Yoshihisa. "A Government Ministry: The Case of the Ministry of International Trade and Industry." In *Modern Japanese Organization and Decision-making,* edited by Ezra Vogel. pp. 101–112, Berkeley, Calif.: University of California Press, 1975.

Pardo, Richard D. "The Complacency of Congress in Crisis." In *Crisis in Federal Forest Land Management,* edited by LeMaster and Popovich. *Proceedings of Symposium,* Denver, Colo., Nov. 4–5, 1976, pp. 43–47.

Patrick, Hugh, and Rosovsky, Henry. *Asia's New Giant: How the Japanese Economy Works.* Washington, D.C.: Brookings, 1976.

Reed, Stegven. "Confused Voters and Contentious Politicians: The Five General Elections 1947–1955." Paper presented at Annual Meeting, Association for Asian Studies, April 1987, in Boston.

Rohlen, Thomas P. *For Harmony and Strength.* Berkeley, Calif.: University of California Press, 1974.

Sato, Seisaburo, and Matsuzaki, Tetsuhisa. *Jimintō seiken.* Tokyo: Chuō Koron, 1986.

Schweitzer, C. C., et al. *Politics and Government in the Federal Republic of Germany: Basic Documents.* Leamington Spa, Great Britain: Berg Publishers, 1984.

Seki, Mamoru. "Naikaku teishutsu hōritsuan no rippō katei" [Drafting Process for Cabinet Bills], *Jurisuto,* no. 805, (1984):25–39, translated by Daniel F. Foote in *Law in Japan: An Annual* 19 (1986):168–87.

Smith, Brian. *Policy-making in the British Government: An Analysis of Power and Rationality.* Tatowa, N.J.: Littlefield, 1976.

Steen, Harold K. *The U.S. Forest Service: A History.* Seattle: University of Washington Press, 1976.

Suleiman, Ezra N. *Politics, Power and Bureaucracy in France: The Administrative Elite.* Princeton, N.J.: Princeton University Press, 1974.

Upham, Frank K. *Law and Social Change in Postwar Japan.* Cambridge, Mass.: Harvard University Press, 1987.

U.S. Department of Agriculture, *Forest Service Annual Report.* Washington, D.C.: Forest Service, 1984.

Vogel, Ezra F. "Introduction: Toward More Accurate Concepts." In *Modern Japanese Organization and Decision-making,* edited by Ezra Vogel. pp. xiii–xxv, Berkeley, Calif.: University of California Press, 1975

———. *Japan As Number One: Lessons for America.* Cambridge, Mass.: Harvard University Press, 1979.

Ward, Robert E. *Japan's Political System.* Englewood Cliffs, N.J.: Prentice-Hall, 1967.

Wilkinson, Charles F., and Anderson, H. Michael. "Land and Resource Planning in the National Forests." *Oregon Law Review* 64, nos. 1 and 2 (1985):1–373.

Wilson, Carl N. "Land Management Planning Processes of the Forest Service." *Environmental Law* 8 (1978):461–77.

COMMENTARY
ON CHAPTER 6

ROBERT McILROY
University of Tokyo

INTRODUCTION

THIS empirical evidence that, given similar *organization, function* and *mission,* American bureaucrats behave similarly to Japanese bureaucrats is reassuring. It is reassuring because it implies that Japanese bureaucratic success stories, such as MITI, can be replicated in the United States. All we have to do is give our hypothetical American bureaucracy a Japanese-style *organization,* and Japanese-style *function,* and a Japanese-style *mission.*

Organization, function, and mission are interrelated. For example, a bureaucracy's ability to influence legislation (function) will affect its sense of managerial responsibility (mission), which in turn will affect its ability to attract and retain competent personnel (organization). This suggests that we cannot replicate a MITI just by copying one of these three attributes. Rather, all three attributes are part of a package.

THE POWER TO MAKE DECISIONS

It seems to me that the most important feature of the package is power. This would fall mostly in the category of function, I suppose. I mean the power to make decisions that will have a substantial effect on economic society. I myself worked for a short time in the

U.S. Department of Commerce, so I know what it is like for a bureaucrat to be utterly without such power. You spend a lot of time thinking about what your retirement benefits will be.

Perhaps I may offer the Department of Commerce as evidence of the proposition that, where bureaucrats have no power, it is impossible to create an excellent bureaucracy. By "power," I do not mean absolute, dictatorial power, of course, but simply the ability to participate, as a significant player, in the important decisions that government makes. MITI bureaucrats have this kind of power, as Professor Haley points out. In the United States, congressional staffers have this kind of power to a surprising degree, as Professor Sakurai points out. I suspect that, where this kind of power is provided, all the attributes of an excellent bureaucracy tend to fall into place.

But is it possible, in the United States, to give a federal bureaucrat this kind of power? The major obstacle, it would seem, is the separation of the executive and legislative branches. Since most of the federal bureaucracy belongs to the executive branch, most federal bureaucrats are far removed from the most conspicuous exercise of governmental power, namely the law-making function. Federal bureaucrats do get to write regulations, but this is very different from writing laws. Precisely because the executive and legislative branches are separate, the legislature writes its laws in great detail, leaving very little scope for variation at the regulation-writing level. Speaking from experience, I should say that writing federal regulations is largely an exercise in tedium.

But Professor Haley's chapter shows that, despite this obstacle, it is possible for a Japanese-style bureaucracy to exist in the federal government, indeed in its executive branch, and that the name of this bureaucracy is the United States Forest Service. This holds a significant lesson, and it raises an interesting question.

A LESSON

The lesson is that there are no "cultural" barriers to creating, in the United States, the same cohesive spirit and sense of mission as is found in the most elite Japanese bureaucracies. The relevant "cultural" factors, such as a common sense of history and tradition, can be and are in practice created by institutional design, both in Japan and in the United States. To use Professor Haley's example, it is un-

likely that the "samurai spirit," per se, predetermines the behavior
of any MITI bureaucrat; but the leaders of MITI may refer to the
samurai tradition as a means of legitimizing and strengthening the
sense of mission they are trying to inculcate in young bureaucrats.
The United States Forest Service, I assume, uses the hero figures of
Gifford Pinchot and Theodore Roosevelt in much the same way.

The significance of this lesson goes beyond governmental
bureaucracies, I believe. In commercial organization as well, "cultural" factors are less of a barrier to international cross-fertilization
than is commonly thought. Japanese companies in the United States
should not be shy about introducing such Japanese practices as
chôrei (a greeting ceremony held every morning before work
starts), *shaka* (singing the company song), and even *rajio taisô* (a
mid-afternoon break, when everyone stands beside his desk or
work station and does limbering-up exercises in time to music).

A QUESTION

But to return to Professor Haley's comments, the question it
leaves in my mind is, how many other federal bureaucracies are in a
position to emulate the United States Forest Service and become a
Japanese-style bureaucracy?

Few, if any, I should think.

The key to the Forest Service's success has been, as Professor
Haley points out, that it has a "managerial role," or, to reuse the
wording I used above, that its bureaucrats have "the power to make
decisions that will have a substantial effect on economic society."
How did it manage to get and keep such power, in spite of the
legislative branch? The answer to this question holds the key to
whether the Forest Service can be emulated by other federal
bureaucracies.

THE VALUE OF MANAGING AN ECONOMIC ASSET

The Forest Service's power lies in its ownership of a huge asset,
namely the national forests. Of course, the federal government
owns many assets, from governmental office buildings to military
facilities, but the national forests are different in that they are

primarily an economic asset. Since the United States is not a socialist country, such assets are rather rare. But to the extent that they exist, they have to be managed, and the manager has to be given broad managerial powers, largely beyond the day-to-day supervision of the legislative branch.

This suggests that, in the United States, the only federal bureaucracies that are in a position to emulate the Forest Service and become Japanese-style bureaucracies are those that have, or can be given, the ownership of huge economic assets. But there are very few candidates, and those few candidates that exist, such as the Tennessee Valley Authority, are anathema to conservative politicians, so that it would seem to be impossible for them to maintain the kind of close relationship with the legislative branch that the Forest Service has succeeded in maintaining.

Thus, as Professor Haley acknowledges, the Forest Service is an unusual case. It was able to develop a "mission to manage" mainly because it was given a valuable economic asset to manage. Moreover, the particular economic asset that it was given to manage, namely the national forests, was an economic asset that even conservative politicians have been willing to leave in the public sector.[1] Without the asset, I suspect that many of the Forest Service's unique institutional arrangements would not survive.

Take mediation and consensus-building, for example. It only works because the private-sector protagonists, namely lumbermen on the one hand and environmentalists on the other, know that they have to maintain a good relationship with the Forest Service over the long term, because the Forest Service is the owner, not only of the particular asset that may be in dispute, but also of nearly 200 million acres of similar assets all over the country. To lumber companies and environmental groups that operate on a nationwide scale, the importance of maintaining a good relationship with the Forest Service over the long term is greater than the importance of any particular local dispute. Thus they are willing to cooperate and to compromise, and of course these are the keys to successful mediation and consensus-building.

When I worked in the Department of Commerce, I was handling antidumping investigations. Theoretically, I suppose, we could have called in the private-sector protagonists, namely the injured American manufacturer on the one hand and the foreign manufacturer doing the alleged dumping on the other, and tried to mediate. But what incentive would there have been for either side to cooperate or to compromise its position? Neither side had, or wanted to have, a long-term relationship with the antidumping investigators of the Department of Commerce. Quite the contrary, both sides hoped they would never have to deal with us again. Thus, as a natural consequence of what Professor Haley might call our mission to prosecute, we were unable to use tools such as mediation and consensus-building, which are available to bureaucracies that have a mission (and an asset) to manage.

A RIDDLE

The riddle with which I should like to close my comments is this. I think I can understand why the United States Forest Service is such a successful bureaucracy—because it has a mission to manage, and also an asset to manage. The asset is the Forest Service's power base. But MITI has a mission to manage without any asset to manage. Where is MITI's power base over the long term? MITI no longer enjoys the extraordinary legal powers that it had during the 1950s and 1960s, and therefore MITI bureaucrats no longer have the basic wherewithal to create the *jinmyaku* (personal bonds) and *kinmyaku* (money bonds) that in the past tied them to political and industrial circles. We hear a lot about sunset industries, but I wonder whether MITI is not a sunset ministry.

NOTE

1. Professor Haley suggests that this unique situation originally arose as the result of history—the development of the American frontier in the nineteenth century and the scandals that accompanied it—but now it is more the result of the Forest Service's bureaucratic survival tactics, including co-option of legislative initiatives, "Smokey the Bear" public relations, and the use of history and tradition as legitimizing devices.

7

INDUSTRIAL POLICIES OF JAPAN AND THE UNITED STATES— THEIR MECHANISMS AND INTERNATIONAL IMPLICATIONS

YOSHIHIDE ISHIYAMA

IBM Japan, formerly Associate Professor, Aoyama Gakuin University

INTRODUCTION

I N THE EARLY 1980s in the United States, concern arose over industrial policy or "industrial targeting" of other countries, particularly Japan. Several government agencies published reports, and academics stimulated debates, on how the United States should respond to foreign industrial policy. It may also be recalled that the necessity of strong industrial policy in the United States was one of the contentious issues in the presidential election fought between Ronald Reagan and Walter Mondale in 1984.

One area of public discussion has been how the United States should respond to foreign industrial policies. The overwhelming majority of Americans are clearly not in favor of industrial policy, although they are in general unaware that there already exists a sort of industrial policy in the United States. Many U.S. economists

Most of this paper was written while the author was an associate professor at Aoyama Gakuin University. The views expressed in the paper are purely personal and do not reflect those of IBM Japan. The author is grateful to Professor Thomas Pugel of the Graduate School of Business of New York University for his comments on an earlier draft.

231

either discount the influence of government policy on industry or the possible harm done by government intervention in foreign countries. As an example of the former, Charles L. Schultze, former Chairman of the Council of Economic Advisors, argues:

> Those who attribute Japan's economic success principally to MITI's industrial policy seem to be suggesting that without MITI the huge 30 to 35 percent of GNP that the Japanese invested in the past several decades would have gone mainly into such industries as textiles, shoes, plastic souvenirs, and fisheries. This is nonsense. Given the quality of Japanese executives, those massive investment funds probably would have wound up roughly where they actually did.[1]

As an example of the latter, Professor Paul Krugman of the Massachusetts Institute of Technology states:

> This paper asks whether the United States should "get tough" with regard to other countries' industrial policies. . . . It would be possible in principle for the industrial policies of foreign governments to do the U.S. economy serious harm, but there is no evidence that they have done so in practice.[2]

What these statements convey is an impression that many American economists, and also the general public, maintain that even if an industrial policy is introduced, there is no guarantee that it will achieve results superior to the free-market mechanism. The presumption behind this view is that discriminatory government policies are distortionary, leading to misallocation of resources. As a result, the appropriate policy response to industrial policies in foreign countries is no industrial policy at all.

However, there is an important minority of economists that advocates a well-coordinated, strong industrial policy. First of all, Professor John Zysman of the University of California (Berkeley) emphasizes that we should recognize the presence of industrial policy in the United States, in addition to unintended sectoral effects of macroeconomic policies.

> [P]olicy measures with explicit and intended sectoral effects . . . have played a role in shaping the postwar U.S. economy. . . . Procurement and research and development policies have intentionally influenced the aeronautics industry. . . . More recently, the complicated set of price controls, taxes, and direct

regulations on the use and distribution of oil have affected the operation of the energy industry. . . . . [T]he United States has had an industrial policy, whether by default or intent, in several important industries.[3]

Professor Daniel Okimoto of Stanford University also argues that the U.S. government has neither let the free market take its course nor treated all industries the same:

The government's rate of effective taxation has . . . fluctuated widely across industrial sectors. Electrical machinery has borne a higher tax burden than the automobile or shoe industries. And the steel and automobile industries have been given protection from foreign imports while semiconductors have not. All this points to the fact that, notwithstanding rhetorical disclaimers, the U.S. government has in fact backed its way into a tacit industrial policy—one that has protected many of its declining industries from the full force of international competition.[4]

As we shall argue in the following sections, the United States can be seen to have an industrial policy, according to an adequate definition of that term. The statement that the United States has an industrial policy is not particularly enlightening, however. As the *Economic Report of the President* of 1984 pointed out, the relevant question is whether the proposal of introducing a more systematic industrial policy into the United States is a good idea.[5]

The competitive difficulties of U.S. industries have been known for some time. Traditional industries like steel have been in a long-term decline, and some emerging industries are having trouble growing at a speed Americans would like. The important factor has been competition from Japan. In trying to interpret these difficulties, one view maintains that they reflect long-run structural changes in the world and U.S. economies, not just cyclical deteriorations as a result of the high value of the dollar and the budget deficit. This view goes on to argue that the government can serve individual industries not only by having the right macroeconomic policies but also by introducing a coherent, well-coordinated industrial policy into the existing policy framework.

However, the recommendation of industrial policy does not automatically follow from the competitive difficulties of the United States. As already mentioned, most Americans tend to go to the other extreme of advocating, in addition to good macroeconomic policies, the elimination of government intervention and the consequent unleashing of private, free-market forces. Also, they usually reject the view that the United States has been deindustrializing, by citing evidence that the productivity growth in the U.S. manufacturing sector compares favorably with that in other industrial countries, and that the share of manufacturing output in GNP has stayed more or less constant in the past years.

Whatever the assessment of these opposing views may be, the issue of an appropriate response remains. If the competitive difficulties of some U.S. industries in the international marketplace are attributed to "unfair" Japanese industrial policies, then the United States may protest and demand the abolition of those policies. Antagonism may then arise between the United States and Japan, since Japan can respond that industrial policy is a legitimate instrument for developing future industries and smoothing the disinvestment process in declining industries.

So far, the United States has refused to adopt a stronger, more broad-based industrial policy, tending to resort to various trade-protection measures to deal with the competitiveness issue. Frequently these measures are seen as a legitimate response to the "unfair" industrial policies of Japan. But they are, and have been, a source of conflict between the two countries as well. In any event, the appropriateness of the United States response to Japanese industrial policy should rest on the evaluation of actual policies pursued in the United States and Japan.

From the standpoint of Japan, the mechanism through which industrial policy works will have to be explained in a more transparent way to the United States and modified in response to legitimate criticisms from the United States. Although a fair amount of work on Japanese industrial policy has been done by both American and Japanese economists, it is still unclear, beyond the enumeration of policy measures, what aspects of the economic and social organization of Japan make its industrial policy fairly effective in Japan. Such obscurity seems to contribute to gross misunderstanding about Japanese policy in the United States.

The changing nature of Japanese industrial policy also requires accurate explanation. In recent years, corporations in Japan have become more and more resourceful, and as a consequence the influence of the Ministry of International Trade and Industry (MITI) has waned. The fact that Japan's industrial policy has been evolving with new economic conditions, into a more market-oriented one should be understood. Nevertheless, MITI still remains a considerable power, and ministry officials are now trying to streamline their policies in ways that are more acceptable internationally.

From the standpoint of maintaining healthy relationships between the United States and Japan, the area of industrial cooperation or collaboration seems to be of increasing importance. Industrial cooperation ranges from the exchange of technological information to joint research and development to joint ventures. This is not a mere theoretical possibility—it is already in progress. The exemplary case of collaboration is NUMMI, a joint venture by Toyota and General Motors that is providing an excellent opportunity for an American auto manufacturer to produce automobiles with quality and efficiency. Ironically, it may not have happened without the perceived threat of import restriction by the United States. Of course, it is not at all clear that many firms, both American and Japanese, want to engage in industrial collaboration. Nevertheless, the two countries seem to be so complementary in natural resources and types of human capital, including researchers, designers, and managers, that the potential area of collaboration seems to be quite extensive.

Although such industrial collaboration will certainly form a welcome development in bilateral relations and help diffuse the trade dispute and protectionism, it may have an added dimension in the following sense. In the current environment, it is vital to have a healthy and dynamic industry in the United States, in order to maintain the basic economic, political and international security of the postwar world. Sustained world economic growth through free trade and capital movement is an essential ingredient in such an order, and the United States has been, and continues to be, its guardian. Other countries may perform greater roles, but they could not replace the United States in the foreseeable future.

Without doubt, the responsibility for maintaining a strong industrial base in the U.S. economy resides with the United States itself. But Japan, as the second-largest economic power in the West, also has a legitimate interest in this area. Americans will have to understand the concern of some Japanese about the erosion of industrial base in the United States, which may not show up clearly in macroeconomic data but is at least suggested by certain trade figures and episodes suggesting the "deindustrialization" of America.

1. THE MEANING OF INDUSTRIAL POLICY

As is clear from the preliminary discussion, the meaning or definition of industrial policy is not a trivial question. A valid definition should serve to eliminate unnecessary controversies.

When Professor Zysman states that the United States has had an industrial policy, he is referring to policies that are intended to serve nonindustrial objectives such as national security, but have an unintended effect of promoting certain industries. Unintended differential effects across industries have also been observed in the supposedly general policy of reducing the tax burden through the accelerated cost-recovery system (ACRS) adopted in 1981 in the United States. ACRS was policy aimed at and applied to all industries, but has turned out to have highly skewed effects across industries, which is why it was viewed as a virtual or unintentional industrial policy.

While it seems justified to include general economic policy with unintentional industrial effects in the broad definition of industrial policy, it is too broad to include policies that are commonly conceived as aggregate or macroeconomic. For example, monetary restraint may affect the housing industry more adversely than other industries, but one would not wish to label monetary policy a type of industrial policy. The presence of differential effects on industries is the key to defining industrial policy, but the judgment as to the presence or absence of such effects is a matter of degree, not an a priori distinction.

The distinction between intentional and unintentional raises the question of whether the definition of industrial policy should include a characterization of its objective. Professor Chalmers Johnson of the University of California (Berkeley) defines industrial policy inclusive of its objective as "the government's explicit attempt to coordinate its own multifarious activities and expenditures and to reform them using as a basic criterion the achievement of dynamic comparative advantage for the American economy."[6]

Professor Sidney Weintraub of Texas University takes issue with the latter part of this definition for mixing definition with objective.[7] To be sure, achieving dynamic comparative advantage has been one of the stated objectives of Japanese industrial policy, but it does not have to be the single objective common to all industrial policies of various countries.

In Japan, such objectives as the development of "knowledge-intensive" industries and the smooth adjustment of declining (structurally depressed) industries, which are not identical with the achievement of dynamic comparative advantage, have also been stated by policy makers. Similarly, in the United States, the computer, electronics, and aircraft industries have been promoted by the Department of Defense within the stated objective of maintaining national security—but at the same time with considerable industrial and commercial impact. If the definition is narrowly tied to the single objective of "dynamic comparative advantage," these policies will have to be dropped from the comparison of industrial policies in Japan and the United States, which will unduly narrow the scope of discussion.

Thus, in the following discussion industrial policy will be defined as "any governmental policy that is aimed at or results in changing the allocation of resources among industries in a significant way from what the market mechanism will dictate." Note that this definition deliberately omits the policy objective and tries to comprise virtual or unintentional policies, as well as commonly perceived industrial policies, with explicitly stated objectives.

What this definition excludes are activity-specific policy and regional policy. Activity-specific policy refers to measures that promote certain activities of firms, the typical example being tax credits for R&D. Regional policy usually means special incentive measures to invest in certain regions. These two policies are not included because they usually apply to all industries, although in practice policy benefits may be made use of only by certain industries. (Again the line of distinction cannot be drawn very sharply.) However, federal government expenditures on R&D in aeronautics, for example, will have to be classified as an industrial policy because it partially explains the strength of the aircraft industry in the United States.

Trade protection extended to certain industries is an important industrial policy, according to our proposed definition. Import barriers for fledgling industries—tariffs and import quotas—are now insignificant in both the United States and Japan, but their role as an instrument of industrial policy for smoothing the contraction of declining industries remains important.

In a thorough study of Japanese industrial targeting, the U.S. International Trade Commission (ITC) defines industrial policy as follows (the term "industrial targeting" rather than industrial policy is used by ITC, but it refers to virtually the same thing—it is simply a concentrated form of industrial policy):

> Industrial targeting . . . means coordinated government actions taken to direct productive resources to help domestic producers in selected industries become more competitive. These government actions can be incentives or restrictions, such as subsidies, tax incentives, import barriers, or other market-distorting actions.[8]

This definition contrasts with ours in its characterization of industrial policy as a coordinated policy aimed at promoting a certain set of selected industries. On this definition, the United States cannot be said to have an industrial policy; in the United States a policy of systematically promoting selected industries has never been implemented. In practice, however, the two definitions may not be so different, since coordination and systematicity of Japan's industrial policy stressed in the ITC definition will weaken as the economy matures and the private sector becomes more resourceful.

Another notable feature of the ITC definition is its strong presumption that industrial policy is likely to be market-distorting. This view is typical to many Americans, but may not be entirely correct. Japanese are likely to object to such a view, particularly if recent industrial policy is the subject of argument, because subsidies, tax incentives, and import barriers that existed once on a significant scale have largely been phased out and MITI now emphasizes the role of industrial policy as a complement or supplement to the market mechanism. In fact, it can be argued that, except for import barriers in the early years of postwar development, Japan has avoided an extensive use of subsidies and tax incentives to industries. MITI has always emphasized this point, and recently this view was also upheld by an American analyst. Professor Gary Saxonhouse of the University of Michigan found that in the 1970s direct subsidies to industry in Japan were an extremely small proportion of GNP, and that R&D grants from the government were smaller and tax credits and special depreciation allowances less generous than in other industrial countries, particularly the United States.[9]

Saxonhouse also notes that during the late 1970s and early 1980s the loans extended to firms in emerging industries by the much-discussed Japan Development Bank were very small, and the rate of interest charged on these loans was less than one percentage point below commercial rates (although he neglects the fact that the regulated financial markets have kept interest rates low generally). This suggests that what has been important in Japan is not any instrument or instruments of industrial policy, but the structure of a policy that makes the use of instruments effective even if they represent relatively small amounts of public expenditures.[10]

It is such a policy structure and the environment in which industrial policy is made that should be the real focus of discussion. This has not been explored sufficiently so far. The analysis of this policy structure goes beyond the realm of defining industrial policy, but it is in fact an essential and most interesting aspect of understanding how policy is conducted in Japan.

So far we have concerned ourselves with industrial policy aimed at promoting emerging industries. However, this leaves out the increasing importance of policies aimed at smoothly phasing out declining industries that have lost competitiveness.

After the two oil crises and sharply higher energy costs, the Japanese economy finds itself facing the same problem of declining industries that has troubled other advanced countries. When a number of industries producing basic materials lost their competive edge internationally, MITI drew up the bill dealing with "structurally depressed industries" and "stabilization plans" aimed at reducing capacity, creating a special credit guarantee fund, and controlling import volumes.

The United States also faces the problem of declining industries. The U.S. steel, textile, and apparel industries have continued to decline and have repeatedly relied on import restraints on other countries, which has generated international political tensions and put pressures on the United States. The United States and Japan can probably learn from each other's experience in adopting policies for declining industries.

2. RECENT INDUSTRIAL DEVELOPMENT IN JAPAN
   AND THE UNITED STATES

Until very recently, Japan has been in the process of catching up with other more advanced industrial countries. Having started from a level far below the United States, it had to concentrate its financial and human resources in key industries.

The Japanese strategy of rapid industrial development was once beautifully explained by the then vice-minister of MITI in a 1972 OECD meeting:

> The Ministry of International Trade and Industry decided to establish in Japan industries which require intensive employment of capital and technology, industries that in consideration of comparative cost of production should be the most appropriate for Japan, industries such as steel, oil refining, petrochemicals, automobiles, aircraft, industrial machinery of all sorts, and later electronics, including electronic computers. From a short-run, static viewpoint, encouragement of such industries would seem to conflict with economic rationalism. But, from a long-range point of view, these are precisely the industries where income elasticity of demand is high, technological progress is rapid, and labor productivity rises fast. It was clear that without these industries it would be difficult to employ a population of 100 million and raise their standard of living to that of Europe and America with light industries alone; whether right or wrong, Japan had to have these heavy and chemical industries.[11]

This tradition of creating comparative advantage has been much weakened by MITI's shift in emphasis from heavy and chemical industries to "knowledge-intensive" industries, which broadly coincides with so-called high-technology industries but is a rather elusive concept.

Some MITI officials now maintain that they have abandoned the criterion of dynamic comparative advantage. For example, the MITI vice-minister since the summer of 1985, Mr. Shinji Fukukawa, stated that the current policies strengthen the "basic technological base" and that they no longer promote specific industries.[12] However, it is obvious that MITI currently pursues a policy of promoting the information-processing industry. Just as MITI encouraged the steel industry in the 1950s (because steel is used as input by a number of other industries and good steel was considered the building block of an industrial economy), high-quality, inexpensive computers can be thought of as the basis of an "informatized" economy, in which a number of industries depend on computer-assisted manufacturing and information processing. Of course, this consideration alone would not justify special governmental encouragement. This policy seems to have been justified by the lack of weakness of investment by private companies—owing to either the large uncertainty about future demand without government commitment or the inappropriateness of external economies. If this interpretation is correct, considerations or criteria of both dynamic comparative advantage and external economies are involved here.

MITI's recent emphasis is well represented in the "vision" of the future industrial structure of Japan, which is usually forged through the Industrial Structure Council, a permanent institution composed of industrialists, academics, former MITI officials, and journalists. It is this council that formally approves of and publishes the consensus "vision" reached by MITI and industry. It is well known that such a vision, because it is a vision, does not have coercive power. Still, it is a result of a vast amount of information gathering by MITI and lengthy discussions between MITI and industry. MITI officials frequently emphasize that the process of discussion is as important as the vision itself. MITI and the Council still identify quite a few industries or activities for promotion. In 1982 the activities identified as high-priority areas were (1) VLSI (very large-scale integration) research and application, (2) laser-beam technology, (3) computer-software capability, (4) high-speed computational systems, and (5) a fifth-generation computer. These areas can be considered as concrete forms of the "vision" of developing "knowledge-intensive" industries proposed earlier in 1980 by the Council. The plan envisaged by the Council can also be considered a vision of product quality and the direction of R&D.

Owing partly to MITI's active industrial policy and partly to the inherent vitality of private corporations, Japanese steel, automobile, and consumer-electronics industries have made great strides, rapidly increasing their share of the world market during the 1970s. High-tech industries such as machine tools, semiconductors, and computers developed rapidly in the late 1970s and 1980s. The development of the semiconductor industry in Japan and the export of semiconductors to the United States have been so rapid that in June 1985 the U.S. Semiconductor Industry Association petitioned the office of U.S. Trade Representative to force the Japanese to buy more American chips and set floor prices for their exports. This petition has subsequently led to a year-long negotiation between the U.S. and Japanese governments, and resulted in an accord in July 1986 establishing a monitoring system for prices of Japanese-made microchips—not only in the United States but also in third markets—and improving the access of American chip manufacturers to the Japanese market. (Major Japanese semiconductor manufacturers expressed dissatisfaction with this accord, but signed an agreement with the U.S. Department of Commerce requiring them to submit cost and profit data in return for a suspension of investigations into dumping charges.)[13]

The reason for such an intervention in free trade is obvious. Semiconductors are essential components of computers, robots, and other sophisticated machines, and computers are finding uses across a wide spectrum of industries (and, of course, by the military). In short, semiconductors are the fulcrum of all the high-tech industries and the key to modern technology, which explains the actions of the U.S. government even with Japan's relatively low share of the U.S. semiconductor market.

As we will see in more detail later, the rise of Japan's semiconductor industry owed much to the determined effort by MITI to organize a research cooperative for VLSI technology and to mobilize the policy instruments at its hand. Now that the basic semiconductor industry has been firmly established, the focus is shifting to the development of laser-beam applications, computer software, and artificial intelligence, as already mentioned. MITI also aims at developing the aeronautics and space industries, although precise plans have not been drawn up in this area.

Some doubt the capability of the Japanese in making breakthroughs at these state-of-the-art frontiers of technology. In general the Japanese are regarded as excellent adapters and innovators when the basic concept is already given. And it is true that Japan still has a long way to go until it can challenge the U.S. supremacy in information processing and aeronautics. The nature of competition also seems to change at the frontiers. Despite this, however, no one has anticipated the massive high-tech sector that exists in Japan today. The question of whether Japan will repeat in more advanced technology what it has done with the steel, automobile, and machinery industries is, at least, being posed seriously.

It should not be forgotten that the current Japanese industrial scene is not sunny everywhere. Coal-mining and textiles have long been declining industries that required government assistance. In 1978, when it became clear that higher energy costs and the structural changes in demand had rendered a number of old-line manufacturing industries much less competitive internationally, MITI enacted the Law on Temporary Measures for the Stabilization of Specific Depressed Industries. Under this law, fourteen sectors were designated "structurally depressed industries." They included open-hearth and electric-furnace steel, aluminum smelting, nylon filament, polyester filament and fibre, ammonia, urea, shipbuilding, phosphoric acid, cotton and wool spinning, etc. (The law expired in 1983, but its essentials were kept in the revised law, called the Law on Temporary Measures for the Structural Improvement of Specific Industries, which was extended for five years.)[14] Under this law MITI drew up detailed plans for capacity and employment reductions, created a special credit guarantee fund (to which both the government and industry contributed funds) for companies in weak financial conditions having difficulty obtaining loans from banks, and allowed industries to set up cartels.

For products in declining industries it is natural to expect rising imports. Aluminum is an example of such a product. It appears that MITI and Japanese manufacturers try to discourage imports by using informal means in some sectors; for instance, MITI discouraged sharp increases of imports of urea and soda ash. Import restrictions take various forms—from assignment of informal quotas to foreign exporters to issuance of MITI letters to trading corporations. The lack of transparency seems to dissatisfy many U.S. manufacturers in those industries that stand at comparative advantage. The slow pace of contraction of many of these industries, trade disputes, and MITI's muddling through the process suggest that Japan is no different from many advanced countries in the difficulties it is experiencing with structural adjustment.

Let us turn our attention now to U.S. industry. Understandably, the maintenance of a strong industrial base in the United States has been a serious concern of government officials and knowledgeable people. James Schlesinger, former Defense Secretary and currently at the Georgetown Center for Strategic and International Studies, laments the fact that American society underwent an adjustment of internal values that led to the weakening of the social order—

meaning reduced incentives for capital formation and little encouragement of strategic investment in creating new capabilities and new markets.[15]

The low rate of capital formation in the United States has been rectified to some extent by the Reagan Administration, but U.S. manufacturing capability is still the concern of senior officials. For example, Lionel Olmer, former Undersecretary of Commerce, made a very careful study of the competitiveness of U.S. industry while he was in office.[16] In his study, he rejects the notion of "deindustrialization" of the United States, but warns that even after the dollar returns to a more reasonable level the challenge from other industrial countries will continue to grow. He also warns against the apparent change in U.S. corporate strategies—away from export-oriented strategies to more transnational ones, a shift evident in the recent expansion of foreign procurement and sourcing. Nevertheless, American mainstream opinion usually rejects these concerns as overstated. For example, the *Economic Report of the President* of 1984 cites 1973–1980 average growth in manufacturing output of 2.4 percent for Japan, 1.8 percent for the United States, 1.3 percent for France, and 1.0 percent for Germany.

In the deindustrialization debate, however, the more important issue is the competitiveness of the high-technology sector. The *Economic Report of the President* seems to reflect this concern in its reference to the declining share of the United States in the trade of high-tech products: its share among industrial countries' exports fell from 30.3 percent in 1962 to 23.9 percent in 1980, and Japan's share rose from 4.1 percent to 12.3 percent during the same period. However, the analysis of the *Economic Report* does not go further, ending with the optimistic note that the United States is still the largest exporter of high-tech products. Nor does it make any reference to rapid import penetration into the United States. Decline of the U.S. share in high-tech trade can of course be interpreted in various ways. This decline may just be part of a natural evolutionary process in which other countries have caught up with the United States from low levels after the war. Or, more recently, it may have been strongly influenced by the high value of the dollar and rapid economic expansion in the early 1980s in the United States. Clearly, these factors have been at work, but the overwhelming impression appears to be that these factors alone cannot explain the following facts cited in the above-mentioned report by Lionel Olmer.

1. The U.S. trade balance in manufacturing has moved from a surplus of $11 billion in 1981 to a deficit of $81 billion in 1984, a swing of $92 billion in only three years.

2. The manufactures trade deficit in 1984 reached an unprecedented 10 percent of manufacturing output; before the 1980s the highest deficit share was 2 percent.

3. The volume of U.S. exports in manufactures in 1984 was 14 percent below the 1981 level; manufactures imports climbed an astonishing 53 percent over the same period.

Even if the major cause of these drastic changes were attributed to macroeconomic forces, it would be rather pointless to make a plea for the "correction" of macroeconomic policies, which is warranted in itself, but would take a long time if ever to bring into being given the political reality. In the meantime, individual depressed industries tend to resort to protectionism of one kind or another, and the external debt of the United States continues to accumulate. Ultimately, the United States will have to become a poorer country through the deterioration of its terms of trade to make the interest payments abroad.

From the standpoint of the Japanese, there are two remarkable features about the recent behavior of U.S. corporations that have an important bearing on their competitive strength. One is the surge of mergers and acquisitions, which seems to be a diversion from the badly needed modernization of production facilities and are regarded with disfavor by many Japanese; another is an emerging spirit of cooperation among firms in the form of joint research projects, which bear resemblance to research cooperatives in Japan.

The first of these two cannot be explained by a few simple reasons; it is a very complex phenomenon. Nevertheless, it seems clear that a combination of a buoyant economy following the Reagan tax cut and deregulation of industries greatly accelerated mergers and acquisitions. The phenomenon has become so prevalent that the 1985 *Economic Report of the President* assigned a whole chapter to it.

The standard argument for mergers and acquisitions rests on the realization of greater efficiency of production facilities and the expected synergy effects in technology and, perhaps, management. In addition, the greater exposure of corporations to takeovers might result in an increased effort on the part of management of corporations susceptible to takeovers. There are also criticisms, however. Frequently bidders seem to pursue quick paper profits by manipulating share prices of their corporation or the targeted corporation, or both. Even in cases where a real synergy effect is sought, acquiring firms may be waiting until a company's growth is confirmed by the marketplace and then rushing to buy it—a strategy that is not likely to succeed in the long-run.

Often, managers faced with hostile takeover attempts must purchase the would-be acquirers' shares or shares of their own corporation at a premium over the market. Thus, for both acquirers and defenders takeover attempts are very exhausting and wasteful in terms of financial resources and time, as they neglect the fundamental requirement of investing in technology, production lines, and manpower.

In contrast to such a negative view, the 1985 *Economic Report of the President* emphasized the benefits of takeovers and suggested that no regulatory policy is needed. As a reason, however, it only reiterated abstract, theoretical benefits without citing any concrete evidence like the birth of new products or the acceleration of R&D as a result of acquisitions.

More encouragingly, American corporations, facing stiff competition from abroad of late, have started to cooperate in joint research projects, albeit in an embryonic form. Andrew Pollack, who watched this phenomenon closely, has the following assessment:

> The move represents a fundamental shift in attitude on the part of American corporations, which long prided themselves on doing their own product research and development. But many companies are now beginning to think they can no longer afford the time and money to do all research themselves, especially when manufacturers of other countries are cooperating with each other.[17]

Probably the best known of such joint research efforts are the Microelectronics and Computer Technology Corporation (MCC), which consists of 21 entities, including Boeing, Advanced Micro Devices, Bell Communications Research, Digital Equipment Corporation, and RCA, and is engaged in research in computer and semiconductor technology; and the Semiconductor Research Corporation (SRC), which has thirty-three members, including IBM, ATT, Burroughs, Texas Instruments, Du Pont, General Electric, and

General Motors, and is sponsoring research in semiconductors. Lesser-known projects, according to Pollack, are the Center for Advanced Television Studies (ten members); the Guided Wave Optoelectronics Manufacturing Technology Development Program (six members); the International Partners in Glass Research (seven members); Pradco, involved in the design of new boiler pumps for power plants (four members); and the Software Productivity Consortium (fourteen members).

The U.S. government is behind these cooperative projects; the Department of Commerce has been acting to bring companies together. Although there are no tax or other financial assistances offered to these projects, the government has extended support in the form of looser antitrust restrictions by enacting the National Cooperative Research Act of 1984. Although the success of these joint research projects is not guaranteed, as with those in Japan, they are surely adding a precious new dimension to the experience of pooling resources and sharing information by U.S. corporations.

In addition to these joint research efforts, the U.S. government itself has been active in the following areas:

1. In the 1960s the U.S. government actively supported the development of integrated circuits. The United States had to respond to the Russian challenge in space ("Sputnik") and missiles. This support was instrumental in the subsequent development of the semiconductor industry in the United States.

2. Since 1981, the Department of Defense has been developing VHSICs (very high-speed integrated circuits). This ten-year program was set up to do research in the area of advanced lithography, fabrication-technology devices, and ultimately aims at the production of small but very high integration, very high-speed chips and their application to weapons.

3. In 1983, the Defense Advanced Research Projects Agency (DARPA) of the Department of Defense started a program to develop a "supercomputer," which bears some resemblance to the Japanese "fifth-generation" computer project in the sense that the supercomputer exhibits elements of "artificial intelligence." Unfortunately, the information about the budget size and the progress of the program are not available in an accurate form.

4. The Department of Defense is also engaged in a Manufacturing Technologies Program (Mantech). This program, receiving about $200 million in fiscal 1984, aims ultimately at the development of lower-weight, high-performance military aircraft, but in the process has fostered the industry of numerically controlled machine tools. This is an example of a governmental R&D program that has had direct relevance to private industry.[18]

These R&D efforts are similar in nature to the development of jet aircraft in the 1950s and 1960s, which led to the supremacy of the U.S. aircraft industry today. In the eyes of many Japanese, such efforts are nothing but an extension of industrial policy.

In the United States in fiscal 1984, the R&D budget of the federal government was about $45 billion, 50 percent of which went into industry. In contrast, in Japan, in the same year, the central government R&D budget was only a little over Y1 trillion, with most of it going to government agencies and universities. At the average exchange rate of about Y240:$1 in 1984, the United States had a budget ten times larger than Japan.

Credit allocation to preferred industries or activities is usually a major instrument of industrial policy, and the United States is no exception. In the United States, a variety of forms of credit allocation have developed over the years, with emphasis on housing and agriculture. There is no public financial organization that supplies low-cost funds for businesses' fixed investment or R&D, however. The Export-Import Bank is notable for promoting exports of U.S. corporations. Although the size of its loans is not large, corporations producing commercial aircraft, power-generating equipment, and energy-related equipment have been the major beneficiaries.

3. INSTITUTIONAL BACKGROUNDS OF INDUSTRIAL POLICY

In this section we contrast the institutional setups for implementing industrial policies in Japan and the United States. The difference between the two countries remains substantial.

Japanese-type policy implementation has two distinct characteristics—the use of the "visions" and the dependence on collaboration by private firms, in addition to subsidies, special tax measures, and special financial arrangements.

MITI makes use of the "visions" of the future industrial structure. The famous Perspectives and Tasks of Industrial Structure in the 1980s is an example of the vision indicating a broad policy orientation endorsed by the government of the Industrial Structure Council. Visions are not mandates based on law, but they nevertheless play an important role for both government and private industry as a guide to the direction in which the economy is moving.

Because the vision represents a consensus view of the participants of the Industrial Structure Council, there are generally no objections from private firms to specific policy measures promoting selected industrial sectors. The vision is also the result of sharing detailed information about the state of industry provided by MITI, supplementing or rectifying whatever inaccuracies may be contained in information gathered by private firms. As a result, the government and private firms come to share the same information about industry.

Perhaps the ultimate power of MITI derives from its statute-writing ability. When MITI recognized the importance of computer technology and information processing, as far back as the early 1950s, it started to develop the industry by a series of laws. In 1957 MITI enacted the Law on Extraordinary Measures for the Promotion of Electronics Industries. In 1971, the Law on Extraordinary Measures for the Electronics and Machinery Industries came into force, combining the machinery industry with the electronics industry. In 1978, a revised law, called the Law on Extraordinary Measures for the Promotion of Specific Machinery and Information Industries, replaced and extended the 1971 law. It was under these laws that MITI officials drew up detailed development plans for industries and initiated research cooperatives.

The ability to draft legislation of this kind, thus, seems to be the power base of MITI officials, many of whom are graduates of law schools. Officials try to influence discussions in the Industrial Structure Council and policies of governmental financial institutions like the Japan Development Bank. However, the democratic process requires that major policy changes or initiatives be approved in the Parliament by statutes. Because statute writing requires both professional legal ability and detailed knowledge about industry, MITI officials have to be relied on. This explains why MITI acts as an information clearinghouse and industries usually comply with the ministry's request for information.

Institutionally, Japan is characterized by a number of intermediate organizations at the connecting points between MITI and individual firms. The following are the most notable examples.

1. *Japan Electronic Computer Corporation (JECC)*. JECC is a computer-leasing company created in 1961. In the early years of computers, the rental system was dominant. This required computer manufacturers to raise large amounts of funds to recoup production costs, but Japanese manufacturers were not able to shoulder this financial burden. In order to foster the growth of the domestic computer industry, the government persuaded seven domestic manufacturers (Oki, Toshiba, NEC, Fujitsu, Hitachi, Mitsubishi Electric, and Matsushita) to join together and create a company to purchase computers from these firms and lease them to end-users. Although JECC is a purely private company, the governmental Japan Development Bank (JDB) extended considerable low-interest loans to it. In the 1960s JECC purchased around 50 percent of its equipment from domestic manufacturers, and the JDB loans financed about 20 percent of all purchases. In this sense, JECC played a truly instrumental role in the development of the computer industry. (In fiscal 1984, JECC's equity capital stood at Y65.7 billion, with revenue of Y187.4 billion. In fiscal 1981, it purchased computers worth Y184.2 billion, and the outstanding loan from JDB amounted to Y46 billion.)

2. *VLSI Technology Research Cooperative*. This was a well-publicized joint-research cooperative that existed over the period fiscal 1976–1979. MITI wished to develop manufacturing technology of VLSIs as a key to future computer systems. Because the government does not give subsidies to individual firms directly, MITI needed a public-purpose research organization, and persuaded five companies, Fujitsu, Hitachi, Toshiba, Mitsubishi Electric, and NEC, to form a cooperative. The total project budget was Y73.7 billion, of which the government subsidy amounted to Y29.1 billion (39.5 percent of the total); the rest was funded by those five companies. The cooperative had a legal basis in the Mining and Manufacturing Technology Research Cooperative Law.

The research was largely conducted at individual laboratories of the five companies, but some basic research was done at the Cooperative's laboratory, by staff of the Electrotechnical Research Laboratory of MITI's Agency of Industrial Science and Technology. Note that companies cooperated only in basic research; they did not cooperate on product designs and processing technology. Even so, the Cooperative was successful in developing basic technologies from which companies involved could benefit later in developing specific products.

The Cooperative was effectively terminated in 1979 and now exists only as a management organization for about one thousand patents. Royalties for patent use were repaid to the government budget until 1987; they now accrue to the individual companies. The Cooperative was also successful in the sense that it complemented the relatively low mobility of research personnel in Japan.

3. *The Institute for New-Generation Computer Technology (ICOT).* ICOT is another well-publicized nonprofit organization created in April 1982. Its objectives are set at developing the operating systems, in which Japan lags behind the United States, and the hardware of the new-generation computer. The project period is ten years, and the total budget is expected to be around Y100 billion. (The amount of government subsidy in this total cannot yet be estimated at this state.) In 1982, MITI launched the ten-year Research and Development Project of Basic Technology for Future Industries. Targeted technologies in this project include superlattice devices for high-speed calculation and three-dimensional integrated circuits. The new-generation computer project can be positioned within this broader and ambitious project.

As in the VLSI project, researchers have been attracted from private firms including NTT (which was privatized in April 1986) and MITI's Electrotechnical Research Laboratory. Most of them engage in research at ICOT on a leave-of-absence basis.

4. *The Information-Technology Promotion Agency (IPA).* IPA is a corporation created under a special MITI approval in 1970, based on a law specifically enacted for its creation. The organization was created out of concern about the lagging development of software in Japan. IPA covers such areas as the development and use of advanced programs that private corporations cannot easily afford by

themselves. Information-processing firms and software houses frequently need to borrow to develop software programs but lack property that can be used as collateral. It is the function of the IPA to guarantee such borrowings, as long as they are registered members of the IPA.

The law creating the IPA was conceived as fundamental in preparing the Japanese economy for informatization. Strictly speaking, the stated objectives of this law were not only to create the IPA but also to facilitate the use of computers and the distribution of software programs. After fifteen years, in 1985, MITI enacted a new law that expanded the 1970 legislation, making the original law even more fundamental in promoting the information industry. The title of the law was accordingly changed to the Law on the Promotion of Information Processing.

It is generally understood that this law is based on the recognition that information processing will eventually be the largest industry in Japan and indeed the pivot for further development of the entire economy. It is this idea that led MITI to concentrate its maximum effort in acquiring the necessary funding from the Ministry of Finance.

5. *The Japan Development Bank (JDB).* JDB, a well-known governmental bank, also played a major role in the early postwar industrial development of Japan. Its role has been diminishing recently, however, as Japan's industries get more and more resourceful.

It is important to note that this bank is independent of the bureaucracy and politicians. Because its capital is funded entirely by the government and borrows money from the government's postal savings and trust funds, it can make loans at concessionary rates. The JDB loan decision frequently signals the extent of government support behind it, and private banks tended to follow the signal. This makes it a very effective channel for funneling money into prospective industries. The staff of the bank enjoy freedom from political pressures and can make decisions on economic rationality with a time horizon longer than that of commercial banks.

In 1985, the JDB lent Y435 billion to industry for investment purposes. This should be contrasted with the net supply of funds for the same purposes by private financial institutions, which, according to the Bank of Japan's *Economic Statistics Annual* amounted to

Y15.75 trillion. Moreover, most of the loans made by the JDB are directed at the development of energy and urban environment. These facts indicate that the JDB now plays only a limited role as an instrument of industrial policy.

6. *The Industrial Structure Council.* This council represents many governmental councils, and has been touched upon already. The most important aspect of this council is that it not only gathers information and discusses industry issues based on common knowledge but also irons out conflicting views and interests of members. Once a concrete policy recommendation is agreed upon in this council, it can normally be implemented without resistance from any parties that may suffer. In this sense, the council's deliberations are a form of democracy Japanese-style.

The Vision of MITI Policy in the 1980s was originally published in March 1980 by the Industrial Structure Council.[19] This document was submitted by the Council to the MITI Minister. It begins with an analysis of the world and Japanese economies, makes reference to the country's energy security, the aging of the population, the quality of life, and extends to a vision of the desirable future industrial structure and the role of industrial policy. The document enumerates four considerations for the development of Japan's industrial structure: dynamic comparative advantage, national needs such as housing, medical, and cultural services, energy efficiency, and national security. Thus, the scope of the vision is quite broad. Nevertheless, the importance of "knowledge-intensive" industries for sustained economic growth is stressed.

A unique aspect of Japanese policy implementation is the organization of private firms into research collaboration under the leadership of MITI. Both the VLSI and the new-generation computer projects clearly indicate the unique nature of Japan's industrial policy, which is directed at strengthening the private sector and contributing to its international competitiveness without weakening competition within the country.

The VLSI joint-research cooperative and the next-generation computer project are two well-known examples, but there are also a number of lesser-known cooperatives. The legal foundation was provided for by the 1961 Law on Research Cooperatives for Mining and Manufacturing Technologies, under which a group of private corporations can apply for government approval by submitting documents describing the R&D plan and financial and technological capabilities needed to support it.

Once the approval is granted to such a cooperative, it normally enjoys special depreciation of the machinery and equipment used for the research, concessionary loans from government financial institutions like the JDB, and an outright subsidy from the government.

But Japanese government-business cooperation in joint research programs has not always been successful. Two cases may be interesting to look at in this respect. First, the Japanese machine-tool industry is now very competitive, but has become so largely independently of MITI's policy. In the late 1970s, MITI coaxed twenty firms into the Research Cooperative on Laser-Using Complex Manufacturing Systems, which existed for the period 1977–1983. However, the industry is now dominated by companies that did not participate in the program. Second, the program for the development of fourth-generation computers over the period 1976–1983, which led to the creation of the Electronic Computer Basic Technology Research Cooperative in 1979, intended to manufacture computers comparable to the IBM series, possibly leapfrogging over them, but has apparently failed.

Thus, MITI officials have to tread a difficult path in order to organize research cooperatives and lead them to success. They must persuade private firms to join together and negotiate with the Ministry of Finance for special budget measures. Furthermore, they must now clearly state the criteria for membership (because foreign-based firms may complain about the absence of transparency), and keep the projects accountable to both antitrust critics and foreign governments.[20] Such is the process of coordination of industrial policy.

In contrast to the Japanese framework, the U.S. government does not systematically promote an industrial policy; it does not generally select specific industries for support. It focuses instead on broad objectives such as capital formation and technological advancement. Only certain industries may benefit from policy in practice, but it is regarded as inadvertent.

Industry-related policies in the United States have included the accelerated cost recovery system (ACRS); the 10 percent investment tax credit; preferential tax treatment for capital gains; a tax credit of 25 percent of incremental R&D expenses; government spending on basic research; development projects such as the manufacturing-technology program under the auspices of the Department of Defense; and the government procurement program, also centered around the Department of Defense. These policies do not, however, constitute a systematic industrial policy, and this absence is partly attributable to the way the government is organized. The federal political system in the United States is such that the two major parties, the Republicans and Democrats, frequently alternate in power, inevitably resulting in politicization and instability of policy.[21] For example, strict environmental protection rules may be introduced by one administration, only to be abolished later by another administration. Stability and continuity in policy might be maintained if officials performed their duties within the government as lifelong careers, but in the United States numerous senior officials leave the government when one administration goes out of power.

Under such a political and governmental system, officials may well have difficulty in obtaining real information from corporate managers about the states of their industries; corporate managers will be very reluctant to trust government officials and discuss detailed information with them on a regular basis. But such constant exchange of information between the government and industry—and its use by officials for the general interests of industry—is one of the essential elements of successful implementation of industrial policy, as has been exemplified in the case of Japan.

As a matter of principle, however, there is no objection to the government's stepping in when there are market failures. There is a strong presumption that R&D is one area where the market does not generate socially optimal amounts of investment, does not avoid duplication of effort, and does not properly develop industries with dynamic gains like learning-curve improvements and broad external economies. However, there is also no guarantee that government intervention will generate outcomes superior to the market. Obviously, then, we have to look at some concrete cases.

The launching of the VHSIC (very-high-speed integrated circuit) program in the United States is said to have depended on the initiative of a handful of officials in the Department of Defense. The program is organized in four phases, and it has been reported that fourteen prime contractors, including General Electric, Honeywell, 3M, Hughes, RCA, IBM, Texas Instruments, and Westinghouse, submitted research proposals for awards.

Like Japan's Fifth-Generation Computer Technology program, it is premature at this stage to make any definite assessment about such a program. However, there appears to have been an acceleration of research efforts, and some commercial applications can be expected. It also appears that it has been successful in introducing the concept of government–industry and intercompany cooperation, and public opinion at large in the United States has not been unfavorable. Nevertheless, it will be curious if the Department of Defense has to bear the responsibility for maintaining the competitiveness of the U.S. manufacturing industry; to many Japanese it looks as if the Manufacturing Technologies Program is being sponsored by the Department of Defense. The natural agency for such tasks would be the Department of Commerce, with some reshaping.

R&D expenditures in the United States, both public and private, dwarf those in Japan, and the competence and originality of American researchers have earned world renown. The orientation of Americans toward high risk and high profit is also visible in the vitality of venture businesses and the large amounts of money flowing into them. What is lacking or weak in the United States, however, is the far-sighted development of commercial applications of basic R&D and the achievement of product quality and reliability at reasonable costs. For the United States, then, an industrial policy focused on these two areas is more important than an improved R&D policy. A policy with such a focus implies government assistance to the improved production or process technology, which is basic to many manufacturing industries, and not a preferential treatment of or pork-barrel spending for certain industries.

Yet too many Americans think of industrial policy in terms of government officials choosing industries for policy promotion and giving them subsidies, special loans, and preferential tax treatments. Industrial policy need not be this. It can be implemented through a process of discussion in a governmental committee representing a wide variety of interest groups and neutral persons like professors. The flow of industrial information between government and industry can be improved. Government officials can play the role of mediators, not dictatorial planners of the direction of industrial development. Politicization of industrial policy can also be kept to a minimum if the policy process is transparent and statutory foundations are secured. Neither economic planning nor politicization is inherent in industrial policy *per se.*

The Congressional Office of Technology Assessment, in its thorough study of the electronics industry and industrial policy, has concluded that the fundamental reason why there has been no coherent industrial policy in the United States is the widespread belief that corporate executives rather than government officials have not only the ability but the right to make decisions that affect business activities.[21] The study also questions the business community's attitude of not taking the Commerce Department seriously. The Office of Technology Assessment urges Americans—quite correctly in the author's view—to take a more positive view of industrial policy and start to alter the political and institutional realities so that the government can implement a more coherent industrial policy.

4. GOVERNMENTAL SETUPS COMPARED

The implementation of industrial policy in Japan described above is predicated on the organizational setup of MITI, and it is informative to review the organizational chart represented in Figure 7.1. It is grid-like, with cross-sector concerns such as trade, industry, industrial location, and energy, as well as sector-specific concerns. There are eight internal bureaus of MITI, including the minister's secretariat. These bureaus comprise what is called the "main ministry," but the Agency of Natural Resources and Energy, the Agency of Industrial Science and Technology, etc., also perform important functions. The latter maintains numerous research institutes conducting basic and applied research.

There are three sector-specific bureaus—Basic Industries, Machinery and Information Industries, and Consumer Goods Industries. The cross-sector Industrial Policy Bureau is the key organization for general industrial policy plans based on business trends. It drafts policies on industrial structure and works out business-stimulating measures.

Figure 7.1   Ministry of International Trade and Industry (MITI).

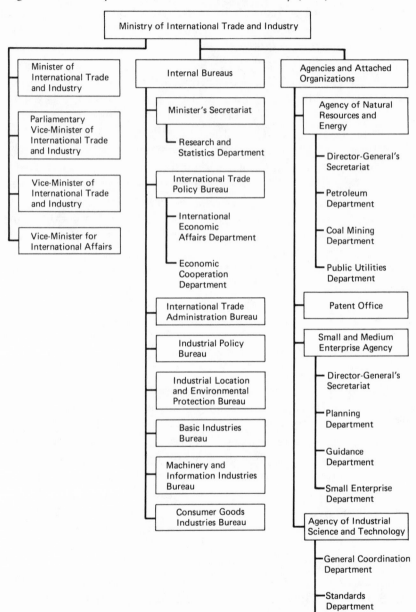

In these bureaus officials plan a number of industrial-development programs over a span of ten years. This would be impossible if they did not pursue lifelong careers and lacked detailed information. One of the elements that distinguish Japan's industrial policy is its continuity over such a long time horizon.

In contrast to Japan, the United States does not have an institutional setup to implement a coherent industrial policy. Without intermediate organizations, the government lacks a constant means of communicating with industry, and the government-industry relationship tends to be one of direct confrontation.

If we look at the organization of the Department of Commerce in Figure 7.2, we realize that its functions are largely limited to either research and compilation of statistics or routine administration like standards and patent records.

5. CONCLUSION

It is not obvious that the overall industrial base of the United States has been eroding. There are a few corporations whose competitive edge with corporate firms in other countries is still overwhelming. IBM, for example, spends annually for R&D an amount five times the total expenditure of Japan's new-generation computer project over a ten-year-period. Neither is it clear whether industrial policy can play an effective role in the United States, given the existing political and institutional context.

Nevertheless, the foregoing discussion suggests that some positive role can be expected for U.S. industrial policy in correcting some problems of the U.S. economy and restraining unfounded criticism of "unfair" trade practices of foreign countries. An appropriate macroeconomic policy is of course necessary, but it will not be enough to cope with the diverse circumstances of individual corporations and industries.

This conclusion hinges, of course, on a reorganization of the government, particularly the Commerce Department, and of government–industry relations in the United States. With historic and social conditions very different from those of Japan, the United States will find it difficult to emulate Japanese-style industrial policy. Still, some aspects of Japan's policy could be emulated—the least

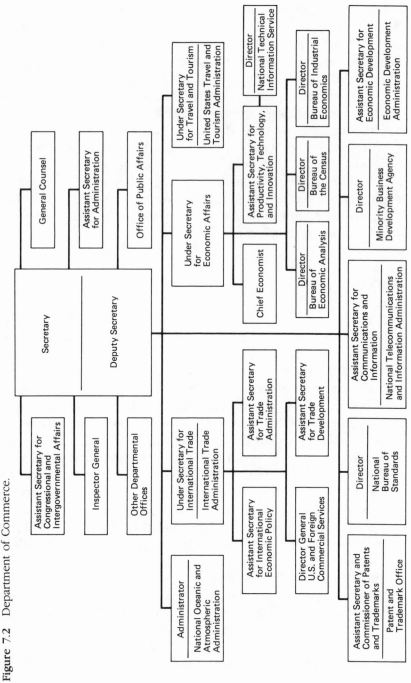

Figure 7.2 Department of Commerce.

controversial and most acceptable would be the creation of a governmental committee as a permanent body for discussing industrial issues and enhancing research cooperation among private firms.

The Japanese experience suggests that the implementation of industrial policy requires continuity of the government bureaucracy. If there is too much politicization of economic policy in the United States, then it seems natural to recommend at least some reorganization of the existing setup in the government so that the positions of Commerce Department officials can carry greater authority.

It was once reported that President Reagan was favorable to the idea of creating a Department of International Trade and Industry (DITI). But it is not clear that the mere creation of a department that looks similar on the surface to Japan's MITI is useful. What is more essential in the United States is the reorganization of the governmental system and a change in the government-business relationships.

It may also be recalled here that the Reagan Administration created the Commission on International Competitiveness of U.S. Industry in June 1983. This consisted of academics, industrialists, labor union representatives, and bankers, and was chaired by John A. Young, Chairman of Hewlett-Packard. Membership is thus very similar to that of Japan's Industrial Structure Council. The Commission, after a study of about a year and a half, published a report entitled *Global Competition—The New Reality* in January 1985. The report issued a number of warnings about the performance of the U.S. industry. For example, it rejected the views that once the value of the dollar was corrected the U.S. trade deficit will be eliminated (citing the fact that the deficit increased in the face of depreciation of the dollar in the 1970s) and that the manufacturing sector's deterioration should not be cause of concern because of the development of the services sector. The recommendations of the report included (1) the creation of the Department of Science and Technology, (2) increased incentives for R&D by the private sector, and (3) the promotion of technology and the manufacturing industry.

In the eyes of most Japanese, some of these recommendations are quite appropriate and should be implemented. However, the report is insufficient in its neglect of the prime importance of enhancing production or process technology for the United States.

It is also unfortunate that the Committee has not been established as a permanent organization; it was dissolved after publication of the report.

So much for U.S. industrial policy. What can be said about Japan's industrial policy? Despite the advancement of Japanese industry, MITI will continue to wield considerable influence over industry, particularly in developing the information industry in the broad sense, in the manner already described. Even now industrial policy plays a positive role as a spearhead for future industries, a coalescing point of diverse interests of industries, and as a remedy for risks and long lead time in certain investments. However, MITI's policy is not simply the enhancement of basic R&D; it ultimately aims at increased international competitiveness of individual firms. The Japanese public will then come to question more rigorously what public interests industrial policy serves, because, after all, industrial policy is implemented not only through suasion, administrative guidance, and "visions," but also through budget and tax expenditures, however modest they may be. Foreign countries will also come to scrutinize Japan's industrial policy more than hitherto because of the already advanced level of Japanese industry. MITI's current task resides in responding to these domestic and international concerns and modifying its industrial policy accordingly.

NOTES

1. See C. L. Schultze, "Industrial Policy: A Dissent," *Brookings Review* (1983).
2. See P. R. Krugman, "Foreign Industrial Targeting: Should the United States Respond?" *Brookings Papers on Economic Activity,* no. 1, 1984, pp. 78, 80.
3. See J. Zysman and L. Tyson, eds., *American Industry in International Competition* (Ithaca, N.Y.: Cornell University Press, 1983), pp. 20–21.
4. See D. Okimoto, "Political Context" in *Competitive Edge,* ed. D. Okimoto et al. (Stanford, Calif.: Stanford University Press, 1984) p. 123.
5. Council of Economic Advisors, *Economic Report of the President,* 1984 (Washington, D.C.: U.S. Government Printing Office), p. 88.
6. See Chalmers Johnson, "Introduction: The Idea of Industrial Policy," in *The Industrial Policy Debate,* ed. C. Johnson (Institute for Contemporary Studies, 1984).
7. See Sidney Weintraub, "Industrial Policy and International Trade" in *Portfolio: International Perspectives: Industrial Policy and International Competitive-*

ness vol. 11, no. 3, U.S. Information Agency. After an examination of various definitions, Professor Weintraub comes to the conclusion that "the essence of any definition must be the extent to which government measures are directed at the industry or sector level." This statement seems to be quite appropriate in its emphasis on the differential effect on industries, and comes very close to the author's definition that appears below.

8. See U.S. International Trade Commission, *Foreign Industrial Targeting and Its Effects on U.S. Industries, Phase I: Japan,* (Washington, D.C.: U.S. Government Printing Office, October 1983).

9. See G. R. Saxonhouse, "What Is All This About 'Industrial Targeting' in Japan," *The World Economy* 6 (September 1983): It is worth noting that Saxonhouse makes the following controversial point that Japanese industrial policy has been a substitute for, and not a complement to, the market mechanism: "What effective elements of industrial policy exist in Japan are an effort to overcome the difficulties which might result from the long-time absence of well-developed capital markets. . . . In the same way that industrial policy in Japan operates to ensure that the concentration of capital in the country does not lead to a misallocation of resources, the widely discussed government-sponsored cooperative research-and-development projects of Japan must be understood as a substitute for what is believed to be achieved in other industrialised countries, particularly in the United States, as a by-product of well-functioning markets for experienced scientific and engineering manpower" (p. 270). Although the substance of such a statement is understandable, the author is troubled by Saxonhouse's usage of the terms "substitute" and "complement." It may be accepted that the United States has the best-functioning capital markets, particularly its equity market, to direct capital to promising industries. But Japan also has a very well-functioning private banking system to do the same thing. Thus, it is not clear whether Japanese industrial policy can be equated with the role of the equity market in the United States. It will be fairer now to consider that market mechanisms in the United States and Japan are both efficient in different ways, but are each not free from shortcomings. If this view is accepted, at least in theory, it provides grounds for industrial policy as a complement to the market mechanism.

10. In their thoughtful study, T. Pepper, M. E. Janow, and J. W. Wheeler achieved this insight. See *The Competition: Dealing with Japan* (New York: Praeger, 1985) p. 71.

11. See OECD, *The Industrial Policy of Japan* (Paris, 1972) p. 15.

12. An interview conducted by the Japan Economic Research Center *(Nihon No Inobēshon [Innovation in Japan],* August, 1986.

13. See *The Japan Economic Journal* 12 July 1986.

14. For details of this and other related laws, see Sueo Sekiguchi and Toshihiro Horiuchi, "Myth and Reality of Japan's Industrial Policy," *The World Economy* 8 (December 1985).

15. See J. R. Schlesinger, "Whither American Industry?" in *The American Economy in Transition,* ed. M. S. Feldstein (Chicago: University of Chicago Press, 1980) pp. 554–556.

16. See L. H. Olmer, *U.S. Manufacturing at a Crossroads* (Washington, D.C.: U.S. Department of Commerce, 1985).

17. Andrew Pollack, "A New Spirit of Cooperation," *New York Times* 14 January 1986.

18. See Charles P. Heeter, Jr., et al., *The U.S. Approach to Industrial Policies and Practices* (Government Research Corporation, 1984) p. 17.

19. MITI and the Industrial Structure Council, *The Vision of MITI Policies in the 1980s.*

20. The government contributions are made in the forms of consignment payments and conditional loans to research cooperatives. Conditional loans may not be repaid, as in the case of the VLSI Technology Research Cooperative, if the patents generated by the cooperative do not yield enough returns. Patents belong either to the cooperative or to the government, and licensing of those patents to nonmember firms, including foreign-based ones, is available under MITI review.

21. Professor Daniel Okimoto states, "The American government's reluctance to tailor policies to the special circumstances of individual industries is also based on the fear of opening a political Pandora's box. If policymaking is already highly politicized in America, the chances are that it would become even more so if greater use were made of industrial policy; the formulation and implementation of industrial policy, almost by definition, expands the role of the government and stretches the boundaries within which interest groups operate." See D. Okimoto, op. cit., p. 127.

22. See Office of Technology Assessment, *International Competition in Electronics* (Washington, D.C., U.S. Government Printing Office, 1983), p. 496.

8

THE IMPLEMENTATION OF INDUSTRIAL POLICY IN THE UNITED STATES AND JAPAN: TAX REFORM AND CORPORATE TAXATION

THOMAS A. PUGEL

Associate Professor of Economics and International Business, New York University

INTRODUCTION

C ORPORATE taxation has a major impact on competitiveness through its effects on after-tax rates of return and thus the incentives to invest in various corporate activities. Corporate taxation is a potentially powerful instrument of industrial policy, and one that is used to some extent by all industrial countries. Industrial policy has been defined in various ways, but it is here taken to refer to the use of government policy instruments that have a distinct differential impact on the allocation of productive resources across industries. Over time the use of these instruments affects growth or rationalization in particular industries or sectors of the economy.

The original version of this chapter was written while the author was a Visiting Professor at the School of International Politics, Economics and Business of Aoyama Gakuin University. The author is grateful for the professional assistance provided by Yoshihide Ishiyama in the research of this topic, for comments by J. Mark Ramseyer, and for the financial support provided by the Research Institute of the School of International Politics, Economics and Business of Aoyama Gakuin University.

265

Industrial policy can include not only policy instruments that have a limited application to specific industries, but also macroeconomic or general policy instruments that create substantially different supply-side effects across industries.

This chapter examines corporate income taxation as an instrument of industrial policy. The chapter has two major goals. First, it provides a summary of the systems of corporate taxation in the United States and Japan and a comparison of the use of corporate taxation as an instrument of policy toward industry in the two countries. This set of topics is taken up in section 1, where the general tax systems are discussed and the major features of corporate taxation are described. The role of corporate taxation as a policy instrument is explored by focusing on the effective rate of taxation of corporate profits. The conclusions of this discussion are that, by the early 1980s, effective rates of corporate taxation were substantially higher in Japan than in the United States, and that the variation of tax rates across industries and assets in Japan was substantially lower than in the United States.

The second and more important goal is an examination of the process of the formation and implementation of tax policy as an example of the process of forming and implementing industrial policy in the two countries. Section 2 provides an overview of the typical process of tax revision in each country. Section 3 provides an extended discussion of efforts in the mid-1980s toward a major reform of the tax systems in both countries.

The last section of the chapter discusses the implications of the comparisons of taxation and tax-reform efforts. It provides insights regarding several important issues in the formation and implementation of industrial and other economic policies.

The discussion shows that both countries have industrial policies, and that both use tax policy to some extent as an instrument of industrial policy. In both countries decisions about the use of tax policy as an instrument of industrial policy are influenced both by concepts of the national interest and special-interest politics. Both countries make only limited use of tax policy as an instrument of industrial policy, but the reasons for the limited use differ somewhat. In Japan a rather coherent framework for applying industrial policy exists and could be used to guide such use of tax policy.

However, the increasing importance of other policy goals and the constraints imposed by the continuing government budget deficits impose severe limits on this use. In the United States no conceptual framework for pursuing an activist industrial policy exists. Decisions to implement tax (and other) policies that benefit certain industries are ad hoc. In addition, U.S. tax policies are subject to rather abrupt shifts, and the use of tax policies to benefit certain industries sometimes involves the use of general tax rules that create other, unintended effects across industries.

The comparison also demonstrates other differences between the United States and Japan in the formation and implementation of policy. Power is diffused in the United States, with Congress playing a major role. Power resides largely in the ministries in Japan, although the complexity of the loci of power appears to be increasing in Japan. Policy conflict in the United States is often manifested in Congress, where lobbying by special interests can overwhelm broader national economic interests. Policy conflict occurs largely between (and within) ministries in Japan. The process is also subject to special-interest pressures in Japan, and the Liberal Democratic Party increasingly is influencing some outcomes. Close business–government cooperation in the area of taxation is not now evident in Japan. Nonetheless, Japan has not experienced the wide swings in corporate tax policy that have occurred in the United States. The decline in the use of tax policy as an instrument of industrial policy has been rather gradual in Japan.

Acceptance of open conflict is greater in the United States than in Japan, and this difference appears to influence differences in both the processes and the outcomes of the tax-reform efforts in the two countries. The outline of the tax-reform package in the United States changed substantially several times during the process of enactment, but the acceptance of conflict eventually resulted in the enactment of a comprehensive reform. The outline of the proposed tax-reform package in Japan has been known for several years and changed little during this time. However, a failure to achieve consensus on one of the major elements of the package delayed its enactment. After open conflict developed, the package was withdrawn, and subsequently a more limited package, including only two of the four original major elements, was enacted.

1. OVERVIEW OF TAX SYSTEMS AND CORPORATE TAXATION

The United States and Japan both have highly developed systems of taxation. In order to provide a framework for the subsequent discussion of corporate taxation and tax-reform efforts in the United States and Japan, this section begins with an overview of the tax systems of the two countries.[1] Table 8.1 shows the major sources of tax revenues (for all levels of government combined) in each country for selected years from 1955 to 1983.

In the United States the individual (or personal) income tax raises about a third of total tax revenues, and its share has been rising slowly. In 1955 corporate income taxes accounted for a fifth

Table 8.1
Distribution of Tax Revenues as Shares of Total Tax Revenues, and Total Tax Revenues as Shares of GDP, United States and Japan, 1955–1983 (in Percentages)

Country and Share	1955	1960	1965	1970	1975	1980	1983
United States: Shares of Total Tax Revenues							
Individual income	33.09	32.70	30.53	35.20	32.98	36.94	37.12
Corporate	20.29	17.17	15.81	12.71	10.79	10.17	5.52
Social security	11.03	14.38	16.40	19.30	24.48	26.14	28.71
Property, inheritance, and gift	13.49	14.28	15.31	13.61	13.28	10.08	10.62
Goods and services	22.10	21.47	21.94	19.19	18.47	16.67	18.02
United States: Tax Revenues as Share of GDP	23.63	26.51	26.31	29.79	29.63	30.35	29.03
Japan: Shares of Total Tax Revenues							
Individual income	24.49	17.10	21.68	21.46	23.90	24.31	25.57
Corporate	18.40	28.04	22.20	26.29	20.65	21.81	19.62
Social security	12.71	13.82	21.78	22.30	28.99	29.11	29.95
Property, inheritance, and gift	9.86	9.31	8.07	7.58	9.09	8.19	9.39
Goods and services	33.95	31.53	26.25	22.36	17.31	16.34	15.20
Japan: Tax Revenues as Share of GDP	17.09	18.19	18.35	19.71	21.00	25.91	27.71

Source: Adapted from Organization for Economic Cooperation and Development, *Revenue Statistics of OECD Member Countries, 1965–1984* (Paris: OECD, 1985), Tables 3, 11, 13, 15, 21, 23, 25, 112, 113, 115, and 116.

of all tax revenues. This share fell to a tenth by 1980, and the tax reduction of 1981 resulted in this share falling to about a twentieth by 1983. Social security contributions have risen dramatically since 1955, while there have been small declines in the shares of property, inheritance and gift taxes, and taxes on goods and services.

In Japan individual income taxes account for about a fourth of all tax revenues, although this share was somewhat lower in the 1960s. Corporate taxes account for about a fifth of tax revenues, and this share has been rather steady since 1975. Social security contributions also rose dramatically since 1955 in Japan, while the share of property, inheritance, and gift taxes has been rather stable. The share of taxes on goods and services, all of which fall on specific items, has fallen dramatically since 1955. There is no broad-based tax on goods and services in Japan at the national or local level.

Table 8.1 also shows tax revenues as a share of gross domestic product (GDP). The share has risen in both countries since 1955. In 1955 the share was substantially lower in Japan, but by 1983 the shares were nearly equal.

Table 8.2 shows the distribution of tax revenues by type of tax and by level of government for both countries in 1983. Central (federal or national) government taxes account for 69 percent of tax revenues in the United States and 74 percent in Japan.

This chapter largely focuses on taxation at the federal or national level. This is the major part of taxation in both countries. In the United States each state and many localities control their own taxes. Any consideration of U.S. taxation at the state and local level thus is very complex. In Japan most prefecture and local taxes are subject to control at the national level, and many are uniform throughout the country. Although consideration of prefecture and local taxes would thus be manageable for Japan, symmetry is maintained by focusing on national taxes. In both countries current tax-reform efforts are occurring at the federal or national level, and this provides the basic justification for the chapter's focus.

1.1 Individual Income Taxation in the United States and Japan

Before examining the systems of corporate taxation in the United States and Japan, several features of the individual income tax in each country, especially those affecting saving and the after-tax return on financial investments, should be mentioned. In the United States a major feature of the personal income tax is the deductibility of interest expenses, especially interest on mortgages. Several other features of the tax system, including a lower rate for taxing realized long-term capital gains, tax-deductible and tax-deferred individual retirement accounts (IRAs), and a limited exclusion for dividends received, have favored saving and financial investment. Nonetheless, it appears that the U.S. system favors current consumption, personal borrowing, and home ownership.

In Japan the individual income tax allows a deduction for interest expenses only against noninterest investment and business income, and only if the indebtedness was incurred to finance the investments of business. Several features of the system favor saving and financial investment. Interest received on various small savings accounts, postal savings accounts, and certain other financial investments has been exempt from taxation. A tax credit exists for special savings deposits to be used for housing purchases, and high-income individuals can elect to have taxable interest and

Table 8.2
Distribution of Tax Revenues, Central Government and State and Local Government, United States and Japan, 1983 (in Percentages of Total Tax Revenue)

Country and Tax	Central	State and Local
United States	69.26	30.74
Individual income	31.16	5.96
Corporate	4.00	1.52
Social security[a]	28.71	—
Property, inheritance and gift	0.65	9.97
Goods and services	4.73	13.29
Japan	74.26	25.74
Individual income	17.69	7.88
Corporate	12.74	6.88
Social security[a]	29.95	—
Property, inheritance and gift	3.26	6.13
Goods and services	10.61	4.59

Source: Adapted from Organization for Economic Cooperation and Development, *Revenue Statistics of the OECD Member Countries, 1965–1984* (Paris: OECD, 1985), Tables 137 and 148.
[a]*All social security contributions attributed to the central government.*

dividends received taxed separately at rates lower than their marginal tax rates on other income. A tax credit of 10 percent (reduced to 5 percent for high-income individuals) applies to dividends received. Although other realized capital gains are taxable, capital gains on securities transactions are not taxed. Thus, the individual tax system in Japan favors saving by enhancing the after-tax returns to various financial investments.

1.2. Corporate Taxation in the United States and Japan

Corporate taxation began in the United States in 1909 as an "excise on the privilege of doing business as a corporation." Currently the corporate income tax is usually justified as a separate tax either because the corporation is viewed as managed by its officers and directors, and thus not actually controlled by its shareholders, or because protection is needed against the avoidance of personal income taxation through the use of a corporation.

Taxation of corporate profits began in Japan in 1899. A major reform occured in 1940, and another in 1950. The reform of 1950 was based on the recommendations of the Shoup mission during the Occupation. Several recommendations were of major importance to corporate taxation. Based on modern public-finance economics, the mission recommended that the corporation be viewed as an aggregation of shareholders and not as an independent taxable entity. In principle, the corporate tax was then a prepayment of the individual income tax, and an attempt should be made to minimize double taxation of corporate income. The mission also recommended reductions to the minimum level possible of the large number of special tax treatments of different sectors, industries, and firms that existed at that time. The reform of 1950 did eliminate most of the special tax treatments, but a large number of tax breaks (often called "special taxation measures") were then introduced into the tax system during the next two decades.

The Japanese tax system has several features to reduce the double taxation of corporate income. The individual income tax exempts capital gains on securities transactions and offers a tax credit for dividends received. In addition, a lower corporate tax rate for the portion of income paid as dividends was instituted in 1961.

Corporate taxation in both the United States and Japan involves a complex set of provisions. The next subsections provide an overview of the major features of corporate taxation in these two countries, focusing on provisions relevant to industrial policy or to current efforts toward tax reform.

Statutory tax rates

Small changes in statutory rates of taxation of corporate profits have occurred periodically in both the United States and Japan. Since 1979 the top tax rate in the United States has been 46 percent, with four lower rates (15, 18, 30, and 40 percent) applying to income brackets for smaller amounts of profit.

Japan has a split-rate system. Large corporations have been paying a rate of 42 percent plus a 1.3 percent surcharge on profits that are retained, and a rate of 32 percent plus a 1.3 percent surcharge on profits that are paid to shareholders as dividends. The surcharge was enacted as a temporary two-year measure in 1984, but was extended in 1986. Smaller corporations with smaller profits pay 30 percent plus a 1 percent surcharge on retained profits and 24 percent plus a 1 percent surcharge on profits paid out as dividends. Lower tax rates also apply to cooperatives and public-interest corporations, such as corporations set up to pursue joint research and development (R&D) or corporations used to coordinate disinvestment in declining industries.

Depreciation

The tax rules applying to allowable depreciation have a major impact on the determination of taxable profits and thus on the amount of corporate income taxes paid. Before 1981 depreciation allowed by the U.S. tax system was based on the concept that an asset should be depreciated over its useful life. Various rules also permitted depreciation to be accelerated in relation to this useful life. In 1981 a major change occurred with the adoption of the accelerated cost-recovery system (ACRS). Four broad categories of assets are recognized under ACRS. Automobiles, trucks, and R&D equipment are depreciated over a three-year period, most other equipment over a five-year period, long-lived utility equipment, railroad tank cars, and coal-utilization equipment over a ten-year period, and buildings and certain other long-lived equipment over a fifteen-year period (subsequently increased to nineteen years). Thus, the depreciation period became largely unrelated to, and generally shorter than, an asset's useful life. The change in 1981 was partly justified as an "adjustment" for inflation, but the arbitrary shortening has no real relation to the issue of inflation.

In Japan the useful life of an asset continues to guide the period used for depreciation, based on a set of about 400 asset categories whose useful lives were last subjected to a full-scale review in 1966. A corporation can apply to alter the depreciation period if the useful life is expected to be shorter than that shown in this set.

Special accelerated depreciation for designated plant and equipment is one of the tax breaks applied to Japanese corporations. This tax break is used to stimulate the purchase of particular types of assets, and the list of designated plants and equipment is revised periodically. The goals pursued and the types of plants and equipment promoted are diverse.[2]

Investment tax credit

The United States adopted a general investment tax credit (ITC) in 1962. This provision, although ended temporarily several times, was made "permanent" in 1981. Under the 1981 law, assets eligible for three-year depreciation under ACRS receive a 6 percent ITC. Other depreciable assets receive a 10 percent ITC, but most buildings are not eligible for an ITC. The amount of ITC that can be claimed is limited according to the tax owed. Under the 1981 law, the full value of the asset could be used to calculate depreciation, but changes enacted in 1982 require a reduction of the asset value for depreciation by one-half the amount of the ITC received.

Japan has no general ITC, but a specific ITC applies to investment in certain equipment related to energy conservation or pollution reduction by declining industries and by certain small and medium-sized enterprises. This ITC is also limited according to the tax owed.

R&D expenditures

Most R&D expenditures can be treated as current expenses, rather than capitalized and depreciated, in both the United States and Japan. In 1966 Japan introduced a tax credit, currently 20 percent, for the increase in R&D expenditures over the largest previous amount spent.[3] The credit is limited to 10 percent of the income tax otherwise owed. In 1981 the United States introduced a tax credit of 25 percent for increases in R&D expenditures over the average of the expenditures in the three previous years, with no specific limit.[4]

Tax-free reserves

Deductions for reserves in excess of the amounts justified by the economic situation of an industry are permitted under certain circumstances in both countries. In the United States the major beneficiaries are financial institutions. In Japan tax-free reserves have been used more widely. As with special depreciation, the goals pursued and the industries benefiting are diverse.[5] For instance, tax-free reserves currently are offered for the early repurchase of computers and for the guarantee of software, two reserves with a clear relationship to the promotion of high-technology industry. But other tax-free reserves are related to environmental protection, nuclear power, and other energy development. Indeed, tax-free reserves are used most intensively by several Japanese industries outside of the manufacturing sector, namely financial institutions, public transportation, and utilities. Their use by financial institutions has been declining.[6]

Export promotion

Substantial tax breaks for exporting existed in Japan from 1953 to 1972.[7] Almost no incentives now exist—the exception is that small and medium-sized enterprises can set up tax-free reserves related to overseas market development. In addition, a special deduction is permitted in relation to foreign sales of technical services.

In 1971 the United States instituted a tax break for exports called the Domestic International Sales Corporation (DISC). In 1984, in response to findings that DISC violated the General Agreement on Tariffs and Trade, the United States replaced it with the Foreign Sales Corporation, which serves as a tax incentive for U.S. exports by permitting U.S. corporations to shelter part of their U.S. export profits in foreign affiliates.[8]

Other provisions

Several other provisions of corporate taxation in the United States should be mentioned. In the United States net losses can be carried back three years and carried forward fifteen years. In Japan losses can be carried back one year and carried forward five years, but the carryback provision was temporarily ended (for two years) beginning in fiscal year 1984, and this curtailment has been extended.

In 1981 the United States adopted new rules to facilitate leasing used to transfer tax benefits (such as the ITC) between corporations, but such leasing was limited somewhat by further changes in 1982. Also, the United States imposes a minimum tax (of 15 percent at the margin) to prevent excessive use of the various preference items permitted under U.S. tax law. For a variety of technical reasons, this minimum tax has not been particularly effective.

Special tax rules apply to energy and natural resources in the United States, with immediate expensing of exploration and development costs and percentage depletion applying to a number of extraction activities. In Japan various special tax-free reserves, deductions, and exemptions promote prospecting, developing, and extracting foreign natural resource deposits.

1.3. Effective Corporate Tax Rates

The complexity of the provisions of the corporate tax makes it difficult to determine its effects on after-tax rates of return and on investment decisions. A useful summary measure of the effects of the corporate tax system used by many researchers is the effective rate of taxation of corporate economic profits. Such effective rates can be measured and evaluated at the aggregate level—for the entire corporate sector—or they can be used to compare the effects of the corporate tax system across different industries. The aggregate analysis is often used to examine the effects of corporate taxation on aggregate real investment and on the macroeconomic performance of a country. The comparison across industries is often used to analyze the effects on the composition of real investment across industries. Although the latter is more clearly related to issues of industrial policy, both are related to the overall industrial performance of the country. In addition, any comparison of corporate taxation between countries is further complicated by differing concepts and definitions used in the systems of corporate taxation in different countries.

Various features of a tax system create effective rates of corporate taxation that differ from statutory rates. In the United States accelerated depreciation and the ITC have tended to reduce the effective rate below the statutory rate. Other provisions have had a smaller impact at the aggregate level but some importance in creating variations across industries. In Japan the various tax breaks applicable to corporations have had an impact both at the aggregate level and across industries.

While no data exist that provide a perfect comparison of effective corporate tax rates in the United States and Japan, a reasonable comparison at the aggregate level can be obtained using data drawn from each country's national income accounts. The strength of this data is that definitions are very similar between the two countries, but the weakness is that the items measured do not conform exactly to the economic concepts desired. Table 8.3 provides one measure of average effective rates of taxation of corporate income at the aggregate level, namely corporate taxes as a share of corporate operating surplus, for the United States and Japan from 1971 through 1983.

The following conclusions seem reasonable given the information shown in Table 8.3. In the early 1970s the effective rate of corporate taxation was lower in Japan than in the United States. In 1974 Japan enacted a general increase in corporate taxation, and at about the same time began to curtail many tax breaks benefiting Japanese corporations. The rates shown for 1974 and 1975 may be biased somewhat by the recessions that occurred in both countries at that time, but by the late 1970s the effective rates of taxation were roughly the same in the two countries, and perhaps even slightly higher in Japan. The 1981 tax reduction in the United States, and especially the introduction of ACRS, caused a substantial decline in effective tax rates in the United States. By the early 1980s the average effective tax rate in Japan was substantially higher than that in the United States.

This analysis is confirmed by the results of other studies that use somewhat different methods and sources of data.[9] Pechman (1983) estimates that U.S. federal corporate taxes as a percentage of corpo-

Table 8.3
Corporate Taxes as a Share of Corporate
Operating Surplus, United States and
Japan, 1971–1983 (in Percentages)

Year	United States	Japan
1971	38.15	28.92
1972	37.18	26.85
1973	39.19	32.69
1974	42.97	51.78
1975	36.55	47.61
1976	38.91	40.38
1977	36.69	43.33
1978	36.32	40.96
1979	36.00	43.13
1980	35.32	42.15
1981	29.27	46.02
1982	24.94	47.91
1983	25.53	51.20

Source: Adapted from Organization for Economic Cooperation and Development, *National Accounts, 1971–1983, Detailed Tables* (Paris: OECD, 1985), pp. 41 and 67.

rate profits were greater than 40 percent for each year between 1951 and 1961, greater than 30 percent but less than 40 percent for each year between 1962 and 1973, greater than 20 percent but less than 30 percent for each year between 1974 and 1981, and only 13 percent in 1982.

In contrast, revenue losses from tax breaks benefiting corporations in relation to corporate taxes paid in Japan are estimated to have been 28.6 percent in 1955,[10] 9.0 percent in 1972, 4.9 percent in 1976, 2.2 percent in 1980, and 3.2 percent in 1985.[11] There were several reasons for the reduction in the number and revenue effect of these tax breaks. First, large government budget deficits developed after 1973, and reductions in tax breaks were part of the general efforts to reduce the deficits. Second, a number of the policy goals used to legitimize certain of the tax breaks were achieved, so that opposition to their repeal was weakened. For instance, by the early 1970s it was evident that the tax breaks for exporting were no longer needed, and in this case foreign governments also pressured Japan to end the breaks. Studies by

Noguchi (1985) and by others conclude that tax breaks toward corporations are now relatively unimportant at the aggregate level—the effective rate of corporate taxation is very close to the statutory rate.

A number of studies of the variations of effective corporate taxation across industries exist for the United States and for Japan. The various U.S. studies find noticeable differences across industries and types of assets, especially after the 1981 tax cut. This variation results from the large and largely arbitrary shortening of depreciation periods in relation to useful asset lives incorporated in ACRS, and from the interaction of ACRS with the ITC. The 1981 tax cut thus provided a large tax bias in favor of investment in equipment in comparison with buildings, and favored some kinds of equipment much more than others. In fact, investments in certain assets incurred negative tax rates—an economically profitable investment would also result in a lowering of taxes paid on the return to a corporation's other profitable investments.

A major study by Fullerton and Henderson (1985) calculated the effective long-run corporate tax rates on marginal investments for eighteen broad industries.[12] Under 1980 law the average effective tax rate for these industries was 42.0 percent, with a high rate of 48.4 percent, a low rate of 28.4 percent, and a standard deviation of 4.2 percentage points. Under the 1981 law the average fell to 33.7 percent, with a high of 43.3 percent, a low of 13.2 percent, and a larger standard deviation of 7.7 percentage points. The tax increase enacted in 1982, especially the reduction of the asset value used for depreciation by half of the ITC, reduced some of this variation, but differences across specific assets and industries continue to exist. Under the 1982 law the average effective tax rate for the eighteen industries was 37.2 percent, with a high of 44.0 percent, a low of 25.4 percent, and a standard deviation of 4.8 percentage points.

Studies of variations in corporate taxation across Japanese industries, although not fully comparable to U.S. studies, conclude that by the late 1970s differences across industries were very small.[13] Depreciation periods in Japan are rather closely related to an asset's useful life, and many tax breaks had been curtailed or ended by the late 1970s.

In conclusion, the studies summarized above suggest that corporate tax policy may once have been a major instrument of industrial policy in Japan, but that its importance has declined substantially. By the early 1980s corporations in Japan were subject to relatively high effective rates of corporate taxation, and these rates were relatively uniform across industries. Tax breaks continue to act as incentives to certain activities and investments, but the scope of this promotion is closely circumscribed and its intensity generally mild.

In contrast, in the United States effective corporate tax rates fell in the early 1980s, and important variations arose across assets and industries. Some of this variation is intended, in that certain tax breaks apply only to specific industries or assets, and in that general tax rules that create tax breaks, such as ACRS, are written to benefit certain industries or assets more than others. However, these general rules also create unintended, and sometimes unexpected, benefits for other industries and assets.

2. OVERVIEW OF THE PROCESSES OF TAX REFORM

Taxation is by its nature controversial. The tax system has different impacts on different groups, including different industries. It influences individual behavior and decision making as well as the performance of the national economy. Various groups may desire changes in the country's tax system, and they attempt to enact revisions.

Tax revision follows a typical process in both the United States and Japan, and the discussion of the current tax-reform efforts in these countries is best understood within the framework of each country's typical process. This section of the chapter briefly describes the typical process of revision in each country. The discussion makes clear the considerable amount of open debate that occurs in the United States, with important roles played by the President and by Congress. Informal discussions used to achieve some consensus on desirable changes are of major importance in Japan, and the formal role of the Diet is relatively unimportant.

2.1. The Typical Process of Tax Revision in the United States

Revisions to the tax code have been made regularly in the United States. Pechman (1983) identifies twenty-two major tax bills enacted between 1948 and 1982, as well as many lesser bills. Most major bills follow a similar process toward becoming enacted.[14]

The President and his administration usually initiate a tax-revision bill, although occasionally Congress does so. The President may decide to pursue such a bill for any of a number of reasons—the state of the economy or some of its sectors, requests from various constituents, or his broad philosophical beliefs, among others. The Treasury Department has the major responsibility for the work of preparing a recommendation to Congress. Preparation work often begins months before a recommendation is sent to Congress.

The staffs of various agencies contribute to the preparation. These agencies include the Office of Tax Analysis, Office of Tax Legislative Counsel, Office of International Tax Counsel, and the Internal Revenue Service within the Treasury, and the Council of Economic Advisors and the Congressional Budget Office. The Treasury may also call upon consultants from outside the government, and it receives input from various groups that might be affected by the changes. The Secretary of the Treasury keeps informed of the progress of the work and makes the final decision on the program given to the President.

The President makes the final decisions on the content of the recommendations and discloses them to Congress and the public. Disclosure of a major tax revision sets off a public debate. Various groups examine the recommendations and discuss their desirability, from the point of view of their own interests or the "public interest." The forces of support and opposition are rather clearly defined by the time that Congress begins to discuss the proposals formally.

The U.S. Constitution states that "[a]ll bills for raising revenue shall originate in the House of Representatives." Although this formal requirement can be satisfied even though the Senate actually leads the process, the House usually does begin the congressional consideration of a tax bill.

The House Ways and Means Committee has jurisdiction over all tax bills, as well as bills regarding the national debt, foreign trade, social security, and various other social programs. Ways and Means thus is regarded as the most powerful House committee. It consists of thirty-five members, split between Democrats and Republicans according to their overall numbers in the House.

The Ways and Means Committee begins its formal consideration of a tax bill by holding public hearings. The first witness is the Secretary of the Treasury, and the next witnesses often come from other executive agencies, including the Office of Management and the Budget, the Council of Economic Advisors, and the Federal Reserve Board. The committee then hears witnesses from various private groups who request the opportunity to testify. These witnesses usually discuss the bill from the point of view of their own "special" interest, objecting to some provisions, suggesting modifications to others, or proposing additional provisions. The length of these hearings varies, but may take several months. At the same time, various groups are pursuing less formal contacts (lobbying) with the committee members and their staffs to try to influence the bill reported by the committee.

After the hearings are concluded, the committee moves to a mark-up session to draft the actual bill to be considered by the House. Technical assistance comes from the staffs of the committee members and often from the Treasury. Once decisions on the contents of the bill are made, the legislative counsel of the House supervises turning these into legislative language, a painstaking effort because the bill must be explicit, unambiguous, and administrable. The committee also prepares a detailed report providing an analysis of the bill's provisions, their rationale, and estimates of the bill's impact on tax revenues. Minority views may also be contained in this report.

The entire House usually considers the tax bill under the "modified closed rule," under which the allowable amendments and alternatives to be considered are only those approved beforehand by the Ways and Means Committee. Given these restrictions, debate of the bill is usually brief. At the end of the debate, a motion is usually made to send the bill back to the Ways and Means Committee for further consideration. If this fails, the House votes on any amendments and then conducts a vote on the bill. If approved, the bill is sent to the Senate.

In the Senate the Committee on Finance has jurisdiction over tax bills, in addition to bills concerning foreign trade, health, social security, veterans affairs, revenue sharing, and other finance matters. The committee is composed of twenty Senators with a party balance similar to that of the entire Senate. The committee begins its formal consideration of the tax bill with public hearings. The committee hears many of the same witnesses, including the Secretary of the Treasury. These witnesses may focus on the House bill, suggesting certain modifications, deletions, or additions. At the same time, lobbying by various groups attempts to influence the committee members. After the hearings, the commitee moves into a mark-up session. The committee usually drafts a bill that is different from the House bill. The committee sends its draft bill and detailed report to the full Senate.

In Senate debate of the committee bill there is no limit on discussion or amendments. Many amendments are usually offered, and the debate is often long. Administration officials and Senate leaders are active in attempting to defeat unacceptable amendments, many of which are obviously responsive to special interests, and otherwise to modify the bill to their liking. The Senate votes on the various amendments, some of which pass, and votes on the entire bill. If the vote fails, the bill is sent back to the Finance Committee or abandoned.

If the bill passes, the Senate version is usually different from the House version. The House usually adopts a motion not to accept the Senate version. A Conference Committee is then appointed by the Speaker of the House and the President of the Senate. Based on the recommendations of the chairman of the Tax Committee of the chamber, each typically appoints seven to nine people, mostly senior members from this committee, with four or five people from the majority party in the chamber. Each chamber has one vote on the committee, with each vote determined by the majority of the Conference Committee members from that chamber.

The Conference Committee is formally charged with eliminating the differences in the two versions, but may go beyond this in seeking a version acceptable to both chambers. The committee members use their own staffs and Treasury staff. The formal sessions are open to the public, but much occurs informally in an effort to shield decisions from interest-group pressure. Among those attempting to influence the outcome are the President and his administration. Agreement is usually achieved, and a Conference Report is issued showing and explaining the changes accepted. After some discussion, both chambers almost always approve the Conference Report and send the bill to the President.

Various executive agencies and departments analyze the bill and submit statements to the Office of Management and Budget, which summarizes the major issues for the President. The President considers and discusses these issues. He usually signs the tax bill into law and issues a statement about the bill. The date of effect varies and can be retroactive. The executive branch then prepares new regulations, forms, and related materials to administer the new law.

A veto of a tax bill is rare, because the administration has been continuously involved in the legislative process. If the President does veto the bill, he issues a statement explaining his reasons for doing so. Congress then may attempt to override the veto, a vote requiring a two-thirds majority, or Congress may attempt to revise the bill and send it again to the President, or it may abandon the tax-revision effort for the time being.

2.2. The Typical Process of Tax Revision in Japan

Revisions to the tax code have occurred almost annually in Japan, as part of the process of enacting a budget for the next fiscal year. The enacting of the tax revisions follows a regular process.[15] The major participants in this process include the Ministry of Finance (MOF), especially its Tax Bureau, the Government's Tax Commission (GTC), the Tax Commission of the Liberal Democratic Party (LDPTC), the Prime Minister and the Cabinet, and the Diet.

During the summer the various ministries of the government consider possibilities for changes in the tax code that they will recommend to the MOF. The ministries focus on tax issues of direct interest to the groups that fall within their purview, and they also examine the implications and indirect effects of other possible changes on these groups. For instance, in the Ministry of International Trade and Industry (MITI), industry bureau chiefs receive suggestions from the representatives of business federations and trade associations, and obtain comments from these groups on possible tax changes being considered by MITI or other government bodies. The bureau chiefs decide which recommendations to send to the Business Activity Division, the coordinating office for tax (and other) matters in MITI. This office conducts further study and discussion in order to reach decisions on which proposals to send to the MOF.

By September the various ministries have sent their suggestions and proposals to the Tax Bureau of the MOF. The career officials of the Tax Bureau discuss these proposals with the ministries and various interest groups. In the fall the Tax Bureau presents a report to the GTC. The report includes various points of view and opinions, but it also makes clear the preferences of the MOF as to desirable tax revisions. For instance, the MOF recently has succesfully opposed most MITI suggestions for new special-taxation measures.

The GTC, established in 1955, is composed of about 30 regular members appointed by the Prime Minister. It may also have ad hoc members and economist members, also appointed by the Prime Minister. The ad hoc members can attend all meetings and express opinions—they are thus nearly equal to the regular members. The regular and ad hoc members include journalists, academics (especially authorities on public finance), former national and local government officials, labor unionists, representatives of large corporations, of small and medium-sized enterprises, and of agriculture, and others. The diversity of occupations and interest groups is deliberate. The GTC attempts to act as an arbiter among interest groups and a developer of a viable political consensus on desirable tax revisions.

The GTC takes up discussion of the recommendations and options presented by the Tax Bureau. The GTC uses the Tax Bureau for staff work such as data and analysis, and it occasionally uses ad hoc committees or panels of experts as well. The level of discussion is often not technical, and there appears to be at most a minor impact of rigorous quantitative economic studies of tax issues. The Tax Bureau actively promotes the positions favored by the MOF, but the GTC also discusses the proposals with other government ministries and agencies or receives their views through one of the members of the commission. For instance, the views of MITI may be transmitted through the business representatives. The GTC also receives input from other groups, again often through its members and the opinions they express. The GTC occasionally holds public hearings, but these are not frequent or wide-ranging. By December the GTC sends to the Prime Minister its recommendations for tax revisions to be included in the budget for the next fiscal year. Its recommendations are usually similar to those advocated by the Tax Bureau.

At the same time that the GTC is discussing the annual tax revisions, the LDPTC is also doing so. The LDPTC receives the Tax Bureau report on recommendations, options, and opinions. It has no independent staff, but uses the Tax Bureau as an informal staff. It receives input from various constituents and interest groups. This lobbying is qualitatively different from the lobbying that occurs in the United States. In Japan lobbying is not usually done by professionals. It is more informal and based on old acquaintances and long-term relationships. In addition, there may be a larger role played in Japan by money contributions in gaining attention and influence—at the least, it is unlikely that the importance of money is less significant. In its decisions the LDPTC is apparently more responsive to interest groups that are closely allied to the LDP than is the GTC, even though the GTC is appointed by the LDP Prime Minister.

By December the Prime Minister receives the recommendations of the GTC and the LDPTC. The Prime Minister and the Cabinet discuss these recommendations. By January 1 they must reach a final decision on the tax revisions to be included in the budget for the next fiscal year, which starts April 1. This process forces the tax revisions to be considered as part of the overall budget. The tax revisions usually include some changes in special taxation measures. Increasingly in the last decade, the LDPTC recommendations have been chosen over those of the GTC when the two differ. This seems to reflect the failure of the GTC to forge a viable political consensus, so that the LDPTC has been successfully defending its proposals as politically necessary. For instance, the LDPTC in recent years has successfully opposed the curtailment of the tax exemption on physicans' earnings from the national health insurance system, a revision that has been proposed several times by the GTC.

The budget is then submitted to the Diet, which must enact a new budget, including any tax revisions, by April 1.[16] The House of Representatives is the first to consider the budget bill. Most debate takes place in the Budget Committee, composed of fifty members distributed by party in proportion to the overall composition of the house. Visitors and observers attend only with the permission of the committee. The Management Committee sets the date and time at which the entire house considers the bill, as well as the order in which speakers take the floor to discuss the bill. If the bill passes the House of Representatives, it is sent to the House of Councilors, where a similar procedure is followed. The Budget Committee of this house is composed of forty-five members distributed according to the party composition of the house.

If the House of Councilors passes a bill different from that passed by the House of Representatives, or if it fails to pass a bill, a joint committee is set up to work out a compromise, or a second vote of two-thirds by the House of Representatives can be used to enact the bill. Because the LDP has had working control of both houses since its formation in 1955, such procedures have not been used since the 1950s. More importantly, a budget bill becomes law if passed by the House of Representatives, regardless of the action taken by the House of Councilors.

Although the LDP has working control of both houses, the opposition parties can resort to a variety of delaying tactics to register opposition to a bill. In response to such delaying tactics, the LDP can use "railroading" tactics, to move from termination of deliberations and a vote in the relevant committee, or to unilaterally call the bill before the full house, attend the session alone, and pass the bill. The LDP can also call for an interim report on the bill by the relevant committee to the full house, and then force a vote on the bill. The opposition usually boycotts not only the session at which the bill is considered, but also all subsequent sessions for the remainder of the Diet term.

Such forcing of a vote by the LDP generates some negative public opinion, as it represents a departure from the practice of reaching a consensus through discussion and compromise. Consequently, the LDP usually fashions bills to obtain at least informal acceptance by most of the opposition parties, or amends controversial bills to gain this acceptance.

Given these practices, the real work in designing the budget is done before the budget bill is formally submitted to the Diet. The LDP settles any differences with the opposition parties in informal discussions. Even if the opposition parties publicly oppose the provisions of the budget, the LDP designs provisions that the opposition parties quietly or implicitly accept.

After being enacted by the Diet, the new budget and the tax revisions it contains go into effect on April 1, the beginning of the new fiscal year.

3. TAX REFORM EFFORTS IN THE MID-1980s

The United States and Japan were both in the process of enacting major tax reforms during the mid-1980s. This section describes these efforts.

3.1. The United States

Politicians in the United States regularly announce that they favor tax reform to simplify the federal tax system and to increase its fairness. In August 1982 two Democrats, Senator Bradley and Representative Gephardt, introduced a bill calling for the elimination of many tax breaks and a large reduction in general tax rates. Although this bill had little chance of passing, by late 1983 strategists for the Republican party began to worry that the Democrats might make taxation and tax simplification major issues in the 1984 election. In his State of the Union address in January 1984, President Reagan called for a study by the Treasury Department of major tax reform, with the report due after the election. This effectively neutralized the issue during the election, but over the year Reagan became more committed to seeking a major reform.

Following his landslide reelection, President Reagan made tax reform the top domestic priority of his second administration. Reagan thus took on a major challenge, to enact a full-scale revision of the U.S. tax code, the first since 1954, to create a simpler and fairer system. He imposed two major constraints on this revision. First, the changes had to be revenue-neutral, given the large and continuing government budget deficits. Second, the changes should not be anti-growth or anti-business. It may be noted that a serious political danger confronts any politician who seeks meaningful tax reform in the United States. The public favors a simpler and fairer tax system in general, but also opposes losing any specific tax breaks that benefit them directly.

In late November 1984 the Reagan administration unveiled the Treasury report, known as "Treasury I," containing a plan for a major tax reform. The plan apparently was drafted by technical tax experts in Treasury with little political guidance from the President or his close advisors. Some of the major features of this reform plan, as well as the corresponding information for the then-existing law and for subsequent versions of reform, are shown in Table 8.4.

Table 8.4
Selected Features of the U.S. Taxation System: Previous Law, Various Reform Plans and Bills, and New Law

Item	Previous Law	Treasury I	Treasury II	House Version	Senate Version	New Law
Top personal tax rate	50%	35%	35%	38%	27%[a]	28%[b]
Top capital gains tax rate:						
Long-term	20%	35% with inflation indexing	17.5%	22%	27%[a]	28%[b]
Short-term	50%	35%	35%	38%	27%[a]	28%[b]
Top corporate tax rate	46%	33%	33%	36%	33%	34%
Equipment depreciation:						
Acceleration	ACRS	Almost none	Moderate	Somewhat	More than ACRS	Somewhat less than ACRS
Inflation indexation	None	Full	Full	Partial	None	None
Investment tax credit	6–10%	None	None	None	None	None[c]
Incremental R&D tax credit	25%	25%	25%	20%	25%	20%
Special treatment of dividends	Personal exclusion $100–$200	Corporate deduction 50%	Corporate deduction 10%	Corporate deduction 10%	None	None
Corporate minimum tax	15%, applies to few companies	None	20%, tougher	25%, tougher	20%, tougher	20%, tougher
Crude oil and natural gas	Major tax breaks	Substantially reduced	Reduced	Reduced	Largely maintained	Largely maintained

[a] In the income range in which phaseouts of lower rate and personal exemptions apply, effective marginal rate can be 32 percent or more.
[b] In the income range in which phaseouts of lower rate and personal exemptions apply, effective marginal rate is 33 percent.
[c] Repealed retroactive to January 1, 1986.

Almost immediately after the plan was made public, a variety of groups and individuals attacked it. Included among those announcing publicly their opposition to the plan were a number of groups that generally support the Republican Party, especially a number of business organizations. Reagan admitted that the plan was flawed and promised to revise it. Public discussion became quiet but lobbying to influence the revision intensified.

In early 1985 James A. Baker III succeeded Donald T. Regan as Secretary of the Treasury and took charge of the revision. Deputy Treasury Secretary Richard G. Darman assumed responsibility for redesigning the reform, in the process becoming an expert on the U.S. tax system. Baker and Darman used extensive consultations with leaders in Congress and with various interest groups to line up political support. However, the revision process took longer than expected.

During the week before the revised plan was issued, a number of last-minute concessions were made to several interest groups. To make up the resulting large loss of revenue, the Treasury rather quickly designed a tax to recapture the "windfall" benefits to business from the combination of depreciation previously taken under ACRS and the subsequent higher profits that would be taxed at the lower corporate tax rates included in the reform. This scheme was rather complex, and subsequent analysis indicated that it was not well designed. On certain investments it would recapture far more than the amounts intended.

The revised plan, known as "Treasury II," was released to the public on May 28, 1985, and some of its major features are shown in Table 8.4. The revised plan offered lower tax rates for the corporate tax, including a decline in the top rate paid by the larger corporations from 46 percent to 33 percent. In many other ways the revised plan raised corporation taxes.

In comparing the two plans, it seems that Treasury I was fairly good economics and a substantial reform, but poor politics. Treasury II was more responsive to political concerns, but it was not a major simplification of the tax system. Nonetheless, as a reform it did have some economic value, in that it would create a corporate tax system that was more nearly neutral across classes of investments, thus reducing the rather arbitrary variations introduced by the 1981 tax changes, especially ACRS.

By this time it was becoming clear that Reagan faced major political problems in his effort to enact tax reform. The Republicans controlled the Senate, but many senators appeared uninterested in tax reform, largely because they viewed reducing the budget deficit as the top priority facing the country.

The Republican members of the House of Representatives also were largely uninterested in Reagan's tax-reform efforts, and the House in any case was controlled by the Democrats. Thus, Reagan was forced to rely on the House Democrats to begin the process of enacting a tax reform. Directly, this implied that Reagan had to rely on Dan Rostenkowski, the chairman of the House Ways and Means Committee. These are strange allies. The Reagan tax cut of 1981 was enacted in place of the tax bill that Rostenkowski and his committee reported that year, and in 1982 the Republican Senate completely rewrote the next House tax bill, forcing a tax increase that Rostenkowski opposed.

In June and July 1985 Treasury II served as the basis for public hearings in the Ways and Means Committee. The committee heard over 350 witnesses testifying about tax reform, and most (following Baker, the first witness) were opposed to Treasury II in some way. Furthermore, in July the Congressional Budget Office issued a report concluding that Treasury II would result in a net loss of tax revenue. To reestablish a revenue-neutral reform, Baker was forced to propose three additional changes in the Treasury plan.

By August the administration essentially had abandoned Treasury II, and instead began to rely on Rostenkowski to produce some bill from his committee. However, many committee members were not convinced that reform was a good idea.

Following a two-day retreat to hear seminars on tax reform, the members of the Ways and Means Committee began drafting the tax reform legislation on September 17. The drafting was done mainly in closed sessions in an attempt to shield the process from direct pressure by various interest groups. Lobbying nonetheless continued outside the sessions. The administration also actively lobbied to prevent too much deviation from its plan.

The drafting proceeded slowly. In an effort to speed up the process, Rostenkowski released his version of the outline of a tax-reform bill in October. No other committee member endorsed this version. Furthermore, the outline suggested reducing several tax breaks for business, and business lobbying in favor of reform declined. The committee finally approved the specific content of a bill on November 23. The tedious process of actually drafting the legal language of the bill was completed in early December.

Some of the major features of the House bill are shown in Table 8.4. The top tax rate for the personal income tax would fall from 50 percent to 38 percent. High-income individuals thus may benefit, but many would end up paying higher taxes, because a toughened minimum tax would limit their ability to use tax shelters and other tax breaks, and because the top tax rate on long-term capital gains would rise slightly to 22 percent from 20 percent.

The bill would lower the corporate tax rate from 46 percent to 36 percent. At the same time the bill would end the ITC, provide acceleration of depreciation much less generous than ACRS, lower the tax credit for increases in R&D spending from 25 percent to 20 percent, introduce a tough minimum tax at a rate of 25 percent, and alter many accounting rules to increase taxes payable. In general, the bill would lower the taxes paid by high-technology and service industries, and raise the taxes paid by heavy and capital-intensive industries. In large part these shifts represent an equalization of tax rates across different types of investments, reversing some of the distortions of the 1981–1982 tax changes. The bill also would reduce tax breaks benefiting the oil and gas industry, timber, commercial banking, and defense contractors.

The bill retained many of the basic features of Treasury II, but in a number of ways provided even less simplification. Although it eliminated or curtailed many tax preferences, it retained a number of tax breaks benefiting particular interest groups that were reduced or eliminated in Treasury II. As another indication of its complexity, the House bill was 1357 pages long.

It is estimated that the House bill would result in an increase in corporate taxes and a tax cut for individuals of about $140 billion over the first five years. The estimated shift under Treasury II would be somewhat smaller, $118 billion.

Business lobbying against the House bill began, with strong opposition by most business organizations, including the U.S. Chamber of Commerce, the National Association of Manufacturers, and the Business Roundtable. The business groups stressed that the tax reform diverted attention from the major issue confronting the nation, the fiscal budget deficit. The groups also indicated that the changes would reduce the incentives for investment and reduce economic growth. However, some other business organizations supported the bill because they would benefit from the general lowering of the tax rates.

On December 4 Reagan rather weakly asked Republican representatives to vote for a tax-reform bill, either the committee bill or a Republican alternative, calling both a good start in the reform process. Then on December 7 Reagan clearly urged the Republican representatives to vote for the committee bill so that it could be sent to the Senate. On December 11 the House voted on procedures to be used for considering the bill. The vote was to adopt the standard procedure of limiting debate and ruling out any amendments offered from the floor. The motion failed to pass, 223 no to 202 yes. Only fourteen Republicans voted yes, while 168 voted no.

Reagan intensified his lobbying of the Republican House members. He urged approval so that the Senate could consider the bill and rewrite it. If the House failed to act in 1985, there would not be enough time for the Senate to act before the pressure of the 1986 elections took hold.

On Monday December 16 Reagan went to the Capitol to meet with Republican House leaders. Reagan also sent a letter to Republican representatives, urging them to vote for the House bill, and promising to veto any reform bill eventually sent to him if it did not meet six conditions. Included in these six conditions were a reduction in the top tax rates to 35 percent for individuals and 33 percent for corporations and the maintenance of "basic tax incentives for American industries." Simplification was not one of the conditions. In essence, Reagan in the letter was asking the Republican representatives to vote for a bill that he himself promised to veto if it ever reached his desk.

On Monday evening the Reagan administration informed the House Democratic leaders that at least fifty Republican members would vote yes on the procedural vote. On the next day, December 17, the House voted again and approved the procedures for considering the tax-reform bill by a vote of 258 to 168. The majority of Republicans still voted no (70 yes, 110 no). Later on Tuesday, after the Republican alternative failed to pass, the Republicans offered the standard motion to send the bill back to committee, but this was defeated 256 no to 171 yes. The House then approved the tax-reform bill by voice vote, and the bill was sent to the Senate.

In January 1986 the Senate Finance Committee began its consideration of a tax-reform bill. Many committee members remained unconvinced of the need for reform. The chairman, Robert Packwood, had previously stated that he liked the tax code as it was. He believed in using tax breaks to advance various social and economic goals, and he had sponsored or supported enactment of many of the existing breaks.

On January 24–25 eighteen of the twenty members of the committee attended a retreat, along with officials from the Treasury Department, to develop a plan of action. The discussions failed to resolve a number of differences or to reach a clear agreement on goals and procedures. The group rejected using the House bill or Treasury II as a basis for their deliberation, and instead instructed Chairman Packwood to draft a new plan.

The committee held public hearings in late January and in February. Most witnesses opposed or expressed concern about various aspects of the House bill.

In March Packwood issued a reform plan to the rest of the committee members and made it public. Among its features was a new category of depreciable assets called "productivity property," which would permit more accelerated depreciation for certain equipment used in certain industries. The stated objective of this change was to enhance the international competitiveness of various industries, but some observers suggested that some of the equipment or industries were included for political reasons.

In drafting sessions in early April the committee voted to retain many tax breaks for industry and individuals. Committee discipline had apparently broken down in the absence of commitment to reform, and a substantial need for additional revenue developed. Packwood devised a plan to increase revenues by disallowing business deductions for excise taxes and import tariffs paid. A number of major corporations and industry groups that had been supporting tax reform would experience large increases in their tax bills under this change. It thus threatened to reverse their support and the support of such business-lobbying groups as the CEO Tax Group and the Tax Reform Action Coalition.

By April 18 the bill had become so loaded with tax breaks that Packwood was compelled to withdraw it and suspend public deliberations. The efforts toward tax reform were in danger of coming to a halt, and Packwood decided that something drastic had to be done. On April 24 Packwood unveiled a new plan to reduce the maximum personal rate to 25 percent and to eliminate almost all tax breaks for personal taxpayers. Other committee members viewed the plan as too radical, and Packwood withdrew it the next day.

On April 29 Packwood presented a third plan that lowered the top personal tax rate to 27 percent, eliminated a number of personal tax breaks, but maintained certain others that had strong political support. A core group of six other committee members, three Republicans and three Democrats, endorsed the plan. A key member of this group was Democrat Bill Bradley—the plan was very similar to the bill that he and Gephardt first introduced in 1982.

The committee began to meet behind closed doors, violating Senate rules requiring public hearings. The shift away from the first version of the bill was so sudden that many lobbyists were not able to react effectively to protect their interests. The committee adopted a rule that any revenue-losing amendments to the bill must specify how the revenue would be regained.

Based on this strategy, on May 7 the committee voted 20 to 0 to adopt the plan as the reform bill to be reported to the full Senate. It survived largely intact, although concessions to maintain certain tax breaks for oil and gas drilling were accepted to gain the support of several senators from oil-producing states. Although the committee vote was unanimous, several members had serious reservations about some features of the bill.

The full Senate began its debate of the tax-reform bill on June 4. An informal rule was accepted that any amendment that proposed a change that reduced revenue must indicate the source of additional revenue to offset the loss. A small number of minor amendments were passed, but many others were defeated or withdrawn. On June 24 the Senate passed the bill, 97 yes to 3 no, with the no votes cast by three Democrats.

As shown in Table 8.4, the Senate version of the reform, essentially the same as that reported by the Finance Committee, would lower the top personal tax rate to 27 percent, although for some high-income taxpayers the phasing out of the lower rate of 15 percent and the personal exemptions creates effective marginal rates of 32 percent or more. Capital gains are taxed as ordinary income. The bill would eliminate deductions for most sales taxes, for interest on consumer loans, and for contributions to IRAs by those already covered by a pension plan. The bill would end most tax shelters and tighten the 20 percent minimum tax.

The top corporate tax rate would fall to 33 percent. The ITC would be eliminated, but depreciation on equipment would be accelerated even more than under ACRS, in order to make up for the loss of the ITC. A variety of changes in accounting rules would raise taxes. A large number of specific tax breaks for business would be maintained, including many of those for the oil and gas industries, timber, and other natural resource industries, as well as the special deduction for bad-debt and similar reserves for financial institutions. A tougher minimum tax at a rate of 20 percent would be imposed on corporations.

The Senate version would increase corporate taxes and lower personal taxes by about $100 billion over its first five years, an amount less than that implied by the House version. Whereas the House version would make minor changes in personal income taxation and major changes in corporate taxation, the Senate version would do the opposite. Neither version is a simplification of the tax code. The Senate version of the bill is almost 3000 pages long, and the taxation of corporate income would become noticeably more complicated.

Under the Senate version industries such as computers, consumer goods, financial services, retailers and wholesalers, software, the media, and advertising were likely to benefit, while industries such as machinery, metals, real estate, restaurants, aerospace, airlines, some utilities, and venture capital were likely to be harmed. A number of corporations and business organizations, including the U.S. Chamber of Commerce and the National Association of Manufacturers, supported adoption of the Senate bill, because it would not be as adverse to business as would the House version.

The Conference Committee to reconcile the two versions of the tax-reform bill began its deliberations on July 17. Each chamber had eleven conferees, with seven from the respective majority parties of the two chambers. At first the Conference Committee made no progress in reconciling the two versions. Rostenkowski and Packwood then met alone for four days and nights to complete a reconciled version. On August 16 the Conference Committee approved the basic tax-reform bill, but various transition rules were not completed until September 18. The bill was about 2000 pages long. As shown in Table 8.4, in many of its features the new law is based more on the Senate version than on the House version. The bill is expected during its first five years to reduce personal income taxes and increase corporate taxes by about $120 billion.

On September 25, with little debate, the House approved the conference bill, 292 yes to 136 no, with a majority of both Democrats and Republicans voting yes. On September 27, also with little debate, the Senate approved the bill, 74 yes to 23 no. Efforts to draft corrections and additional transition rules continued but eventually failed. On October 21 President Reagan signed the tax-reform bill into law. Most of its provisions became effective on January 1, 1987, and some have gradual phase-in periods.

3.2. Japan

The need for a major tax reform, the first since 1950, has been under discussion in Japan for several years. An important aspect of the discussion has been the belief that the tax system is no longer equitable, because wage earners are treated rather differently from those who run their own businesses, and because there is widespread tax evasion by certain groups. This belief in relation to the individual income tax is evident in the expression "nine–six–four"—employed workers pay taxes on 90 percent of their income, the self-employed and the owners of small businesses on 60 percent of their income, and farmers on 40 percent of their income. With respect to corporate taxation, there is widespread concern that businesses inflate expenses or understate revenues in order to show losses, or at least little or no profit.

Progress toward tax reform has been slow though there has been some agreement that the tax reform probably would include four major elements. These four elements are cuts in the rates of individual income taxation, an end to (or at least a tightening of the rules concerning the use of) the exclusion from taxation of interest earned on small savings deposits, reductions in corporate income taxation, and the introduction of a broad-based indirect tax. The reductions in individual and corporate income taxation are generally acceptable, but the other two changes are controversial, as are possible elimination or curtailment in a number of special taxation measures.

Consensus to curtail the tax exemption for small savings has been slow to develop, and major interest groups have been resisting any change at all. The Ministry of Posts and Telecommunications (MOPT) has been successful in deflecting past efforts by the MOF and the GTC to reform the tax-exempt-savings system to reduce widespread illegal holding of multiple accounts. In addition, the end of the exemption is a politically unattractive change, because most voters would experience a highly visible tax increase.

As in the United States, a major constraint imposed on the tax-reform effort in Japan was that the package should be revenue-neutral, so that the government budget deficit does not become larger. However, the size of the reductions in individual and corporate income taxation would be much larger than any revenue increases resulting from the end of the small-savings exemption and curtailment of certain other tax breaks. Thus, another source of revenue is needed, and this could take the form of the introduction of a broad-based indirect tax. Discussion of such a tax has occurred in the past. Prime Minister Ohira suggested early in the 1979 election campaign for the House of Representatives that an indirect tax should be introduced to reduce the government budget deficit. The LDP then suffered a setback at the polls and failed to win a majority of the seats in the House. The Diet subsequently passed a resolution registering its opposition to a general consumption tax.

Because of these various controversial items, progress toward tax reform has been slow, even though a variety of meetings have taken place and groups formed to seek a consensus. For instance, Prime Minister Nakasone and several other LDP leaders met with leaders of the business community in late 1984 to discuss tax reform. The business leaders included the chairman and the vice president of the *Keidanren,* the president of the Japan Chamber of Commerce and Industry, the chairman of the Japan Committee for Economic Development, and the president of the Japan Federation of Employers Association. Some shift in the positions of the business leaders seemed to occur. The *Keidanren* and the Japan Chamber of Commerce and Industry had been maintaining a policy opposed to any new taxes and supporting further restraint on government spending. *Keidanren* Chairman Inayama cited the need to bring about a fairer distribution of the tax burden, which was interpreted to mean that business would be willing to accept a broad-based indirect tax if other taxes were lowered. Chairman Gotoh of the Chamber stated more clearly a willingness to accept the introduction of a broad-based indirect tax. However, by March 1985 both organizations had reverted to their opposition to any new tax or tax increase.

In September 1985 Nakasone, after almost three years as Prime Minister, during which time he often discussed the need for a major tax reform, formally charged the GTC to study tax reform. He requested that the GTC submit an interim report in spring 1986 on the tax reductions to be included in the reform, and a full report by fall 1986 outlining both tax reductions and tax increases. Nakasone announced that the major reform should be adopted as part of the budget for fiscal year 1987 (beginning in April 1987).

Nakasone was concerned about the manner in which the GTC would study and promote tax reform, so much so that he considered setting up a separate tax-reform committee. Instead, he decided to alter the GTC by adding ten more ad hoc members. The composition of the GTC in early 1986 is shown in Table 8.5. The distribution of newly appointed ad hoc members is particularly interesting. Rather than adding expertise to the Commission, Nakasone apparently was interested in adding business representatives who could work toward a business consensus, and in adding media representatives who might influence public opinion in favor of the tax-reform package that would eventually emerge from the commission. A peculiar omission is the lack of any representative on the GTC from the distribution industries, even though these industries are probably the clearest business opponents to any broad-based indirect tax.

Other groups were also studying tax reform and preparing reports and position statements. In October 1985 the MOF submitted a report to the GTC prepared with the assistance of the National Institute for Research Advancement. The report suggested a reduction of individual and corporate income taxes and the introduction of a broad-based indirect tax. The advantages of the indirect tax would be not only the revenue generated but also the more equitable spreading of the tax burden because the tax would be difficult to evade. The disadvantages would be not only the obvious political opposition to a new tax, but also the cost and complexity of administering the tax. Several other considerations were considered neutral or unimportant. The tax would be applied to almost all products, including food. Any concerns about the possible

Table 8.5
Composition of Japan's Government Tax Commission, Early 1986

Group Represented	Ordinary Members	Ad Hoc Members	
		Previously Appointed	Newly Appointed[a]
News media	7	4	5
Former national government officials	4 ⎫		
	⎬	4	1
Local government officials	3 ⎭		
Large corporations	5 ⎫		
	⎬	1	3
Small and medium-sized enterprises	1 ⎭		
Labor unions	2	0	0
Academics[b]	5	5	1
Other	3	4	0

[a]*New appointments made in fall 1985.*
[b]*There are also twelve economist members who are all professors at various universities.*

regressiveness of such a tax were considered rather minor. The effect on savings—that is, the possibility that a consumption-based tax might further increase the high personal savings rate—was also not considered of much importance, partly because of the other tax changes, including the reduction in or end to the tax exemption on small savings. Nonetheless, there has been some ongoing discussion of the possible effects of saving behavior.

Also in October a panel of tax experts appointed in March 1985 and chaired by former Finance Minister Tatsuo Murayama presented its interim report on tax reform to the LDP, for use by the LDPTC. The panel's recommendations were very similar to those in the MOF report.

In December decisions were made on the budget for fiscal year 1986. As had happened in the previous several years, the expectation of a major tax reform in the near future was used as a basis for resisting major changes in the tax system for the next fiscal year. Instead, only a few minor changes were included in the new budget.

In March 1986 a MITI advisory panel, in a report submitted to the GTC, stated the need to lower corporate taxes, because the tax burden on Japanese corporate income is high in relation to that in other industrial countries. The report called not only for an end to the surtax, but also for a lowering of statutory rates. The report recommended an acceleration of the depreciation periods through a shortening of the useful lives recognized for tax purposes, and the restoration of full use of carryforward and carryback privileges by corporations showing losses. Abuse of these provisions would be prevented by auditing by the MOF. The report also called for the introduction, retention, or strengthening of a number of tax breaks, including incentives for investment, technology development, imports, and overseas investment. The report also recommended the end of tax-exempt savings, but did not take a position on the indirect tax. Some industries supervised by MITI opposed the tax, and this opposition prevented MITI from stating any position publicly.

Also in March the *Keidanren* issued its position in support of a review of the entire existing tax system. The *Keidanren* was seeking a number of changes in corporate taxes, including general reductions similar to those contained in the MITI report, but not any new special tax measures or incentives. The report also called for a reduction of individual income taxes on wage earnings and the end to tax-exempt savings and other unfair tax breaks. Although the *Keidanren* formally maintained its position favoring fiscal restraint without any tax increases, the report also stated that the system must accomplish a fairer distribution of the tax burden. The *Keidanren* seemed again to be giving implicit support to the introduction of a broad-based indirect tax, although it could not say so directly because no consensus existed among its members. Indeed, some industry associations, especially those from the wholesale and retail distribution industries, were actively opposing the indirect tax, and no industry association was actively supporting this tax.

In late April the GTC submitted its interim report on tax reform, supporting the expected four basic elements. The LDPTC also adopted an interim report similar to that of the GTC. As interim reports, most details of the changes were not spelled out.

A double election for the Diet was held in early July 1986. Nakasone and the other LDP leaders hoped to avoid discussion of the indirect tax and other possible tax increases—this was presumably the major purpose for requesting the full report from the GTC in fall 1986. However, in the election campaign the opposition parties pressed the LDP on tax issues. Nakasone and other LDP leaders responded by issuing carefully worded statements that the LDP would not attempt to introduce any large-scale indirect tax opposed by the public. Several LDP leaders also indicated that the exemption for small savings would not be abolished. In the election the LDP won a major victory. Subsequently, Nakasone received a one-year extension of his term as Prime Minister, in order to allow him to complete the process of adopting the major tax reform and the other economic reforms that he had supported.

In late October the GTC submitted its final recommendations for the major tax reform, including almost Y3 trillion per year in individual income tax reductions, almost Y2 trillion per year in corporate tax reductions, an end to tax-exempt small savings (to raise about Y1 trillion per year), and a new broad-based indirect tax (to raise about Y4 trillion per year). However, the GTC did not recommend a specific type of indirect tax, but instead outlined eight alternative forms. In December the LDPTC approved its plan for the major tax reform, similar in outline to that of the GTC, with the differences that the new tax on small savings was to raise almost Y2 trillion per year, and the new indirect tax about Y3 trillion per year.

Controversy over the proposed new indirect tax was severe. Some LDP Diet members, several local LDP chapters, and many business groups expressed opposition. Tens of thousands of people attended anti-tax rallies, and polls showed that four-fifths of the Japanese people opposed the indirect tax. In late January 1987 the opposition parties boycotted the Diet soon after it opened, shutting it down for five days.

Nonetheless, on February 4 the government submitted two packages of tax-reform bills, including a complex new indirect tax. The complexity developed as the MOF sought to enhance support for the tax by exempting small firms and fifty-one categories of items. The exemption for small firms was apparently poorly designed, in that a larger total tax would be collected if a small, tax-exempt firm was in the middle of a chain of transactions. Nakasone argued that he had not broken his campaign promise, because the indirect tax would be "medium-scale" with the various exemptions, rather than "large-scale."

After the LDP opened the Budget Committee of the House of Representatives to consider tax reform without the attendance of the opposition parties, they effectively closed the Diet for several weeks by boycotting all deliberations. With the beginning of the new fiscal year approaching, the LDP announced that it would hold hearings on the budget proposal, but the opposition parties renewed their boycott. Hearings finally began in late March, but the opposition parties delayed the budget bill, demanding the withdrawal of the indirect tax proposal. The government began the new fiscal year operating on a fifty-day provisional budget.

On April 15 the LDP "railroaded" the fiscal 1987 budget through the Budget Committee. The opposition then used various delaying tactics, including long speeches, no-confidence motions, and slow-motion voting, to prevent a vote on the budget in the full House. On April 23 Nakasone agreed to send the tax reform plan to an LDP-opposition committee for further study. The Diet then quickly approved the rest of the budget without debate.

In September the Diet approved a tax bill that included reductions in individual income taxes of Y1.5 trillion per year and an end to the tax-exempt-savings system. This bill did not include any major changes in corporate taxation or the introduction of a broad-based indirect tax. In October Noboru Takeshita became the new Prime Minister. He stated that tax reform, including a broad-based indirect tax, remained a major objective of the government.

4. DISCUSSION AND CONCLUSIONS

The process of designing and enacting a major tax reform has been difficult and lengthy in both the United States and Japan. In the United States the initial motivating objectives for pursuing tax reform were simplification and fairness. In Japan these were evasion-reduction and fairness. In each country changes in the tax laws produce immediate gainers and immediate losers. In addition, even those who benefit overall from the package of changes have an incentive to attempt to influence specific aspects of the package in their favor. Thus, different interest groups take different positions on the desirability and desirable form of the tax changes. Both countries are constrained by their large fiscal deficits, so that both have been attempting to implement reform packages that are revenue-neutral. In Japan tax changes are considered as part of the general process of defining the budget, whereas in the United States tax changes are debated as an item separate from the budget. This creates certain pressures in the United States. On the one hand, the two issues compete for the time and attention of congressmen, their staffs, and the public. On the other hand, there were some efforts to merge the two, or at least to use the tax-reform effort to increase tax revenues and thereby reduce the budget deficit.

This chapter has presented an examination of taxation, tax revision, and efforts toward tax reform in the mid-1980s in the United States and Japan. Comparing and contrasting the experiences in the two countries shed light on a number of issues in the formation and implementation of industrial and other economic policies.

4.1. Industrial Policy

The discussion of corporate taxation and tax reform makes it clear that both Japan and the United States have an "industrial policy," although the U.S. government does not usually use that term. In both countries tax policy has been used at times to influence the development, growth, competitiveness, or rationalization of various industries. In both countries decisions about the use of industrial policy intended to have differential effects across industries or sectors are influenced both by economic ideology and concepts of the national interest and by special-interest politics.

In Japan a conceptual framework for pursuing an activist industrial policy exists and has some coherence. Currently there is broad agreement that industrial policy should promote the development and growth of various high-technology (or knowledge-intensive) industries and assist the adjustment of declining industries.

However, a confluence of factors has reduced the effectiveness of industrial policy in Japan. Not only is business willing and able to be more independent of government guidance, but policies directed toward increasingly important goals other than economic growth and industrial restructuring compete for available government resources. Furthermore, the continuing government budget deficits in Japan have placed a severe limit on the growth of available government resources and have resulted in the reduction of many tax breaks in order to raise additional tax revenue without increases in general tax rates. Certain tax breaks and other aspects of the tax system are directed toward the two major current objectives of Japan's industrial policy. However, the tax system provides only a small amount of implicit subsidy to activities supported by industrial policy, and much of this is in the form of special depreciation, deferrals, and temporary reserves that provide the equivalent of interest-free loans rather than outright grants. Many other tax breaks exist, some directed toward national objectives other than those of industrial policy, and others that were created and are maintained largely in response to politically powerful special-interest groups.

In the United States there is no clear conceptual framework for the conduct of an activist industrial policy, beyond broad macroeconomic policies intended to promote aggregate business investment or international competitiveness. Rather, the prevailing economic philosophy stresses the role of market forces in guiding economic developments and growth. Government intervention, especially into the activities of specific industries, generally is viewed with skepticism, both about its motivation and about its possible effectiveness. Lacking any clear framework, industrial policy in the United States is developed largely as an ad hoc response to specific problems and issues that arise. It is shaped largely by the pressures of special-interest politics, in competition with the prevailing philosophy of nonintervention.

Many of the industries that receive specific tax breaks in the United States maintain their benefits largely through the support of Congressmen whose home districts or states are the locations of major production activities by these industries. In these cases industrial policy is determined by regional special-interest politics. For instance, various tax breaks for oil and gas development can be related to U.S. energy policy, but they remain controversial nonetheless. They were reduced very little in the U.S. tax reform, largely because of the political power of Senators from the producing states.

One potential new instrument of an active U.S. industrial policy surfaced in the discussion about tax reform. This was the concept of "productivity assets," certain equipment used in certain industries that would receive additional depreciation benefits. Charges that the concept was largely special-interest politics in disguise arose quickly, however, and the idea was dropped. Such charges are difficult to refute without a framework for industrial policy that implies criteria for choosing who should benefit.

In addition, the discussion of corporate taxation and tax reform indicates that policy toward industry is continuously shifting and changing in both countries. In Japan the change generally is gradual, as industrial and other economic policies are adjusted to such factors as the emergence of a larger number of important policy goals and the continuing budget deficits. The annual tax revisions impart a continual flexibility to the Japanese tax system and allow its ongoing adjustment to changing economic circumstances. Although this adjustment is often pursued effectively, some changes can be blocked by political considerations. Incremental change in corporate taxation has resulted not only in the decline in the use of business tax breaks aimed at achieving particular industrial-policy objectives, but also in the rising and now high levels of the corporate tax burden. The portion of the tax reform enacted in Japan in 1987 included no reduction in corporate taxation.

In the United States policy toward industry in tax and other areas is subject to rapid, large changes. Not only did the 1981 tax changes bring a large decline in corporate taxes, but changes such as ACRS also created large changes in the relative tax positions of different industries. The incentives for investment in different industries were dramatically altered. Although some bias toward mature, capital-intensive manufacturing industries—the "smokestack industries"—was probably intended, benefits to other industries were largely unintended. Tax reform in the mid-1980s has resulted in a substantial increase in corporate taxation. The repeal of the ITC (which had been suspended several times in the past two decades but was supposedly made "permanent" in 1981) and the alteration of depreciation rules reduce the distortions in the incentives to invest in different assets and industries. This can be viewed as a return toward the position that the government should not in general pursue policies that alter the structure of the economy, but rather should allow competition in the capital and product markets to determine this structure.

The claim of close business-government cooperation often made about Japan is not supported by the examination of recent tax revisions and the tax-reform effort in Japan. In the various tax revisions enacted over the last decade the government has slowly been raising the tax burden on corporations to levels that are high by international standards. Business itself has not been effective in taking a clear stand on tax issues. For instance, the inability to achieve a consensus on the acceptability of a broad-based indirect tax has reduced lobbying by the major business organizations to statements that the burden of corporate taxes in Japan is too high and should be reduced. This position has been inadequate to have a major influence on the reform package. In another case, there is broad agreement that depreciation should be accelerated through a general shortening of useful lifetimes. But some industries could be harmed by a full-scale review, if the useful lives of their plant and equipment are lengthened. These industries have apparently offered some resistance to such a review. Given this, MITI has been having difficulty in formulating an acceptable proposal regarding the general acceleration of depreciation.

In the United States the last six years have seen wide swings in the business-government relationship with respect to the tax system, and this has occurred under a Republican President who has not obviously shifted his ideology. The 1981 tax changes provided a large reduction in corporate taxation, so much so that there was discussion of the disappearance of the corporate tax, de facto if not de jure. Reagan has stated that he is in favor of abolishing the corporate income tax, calling it illogical and the equivalent of double taxation. Nonetheless, the tax-reform proposals issued by his administration in 1984 and 1985, and the tax reform eventually enacted in 1986, reduce many of the tax benefits provided by the earlier changes and on net result in a large increase in corporate tax collections.

Lobbying by business in the United States is generally strong. However, business was split on the recent tax reform, with some supporting it and others opposing it in general or in some of its specifics. Indirectly, this split may have promoted the achievement of reform, especially one that raised corporate taxes in general.

4.2. Power and Conflict

The loci of power in economic policy making differ between Japan and the United States. In Japan the administrative bureaucracy has substantial power. This is evident in the primary role of the

MOF in tax revision and reform efforts. The MOF is the collector and organizer of various tax proposals, as well as an effective advocate for the changes that it views as desirable. The MOF provides major reports to the two important tax commissions, the GTC and the LDPTC. The MOF also provides ongoing staff work for these two commissions.

However, a rising complexity in the loci of power is also apparent in Japan. The LDP politicians, including the LDP Diet members, are more vocal and active in fashioning tax proposals that are politically acceptable to interest groups allied to the LDP. Individual LDP members and groups openly opposed aspects of the tax-reform proposal submitted by the LDP government in February 1987. At the same time, the Diet itself is generally not an initiator or drafter of important legislation, and Diet members have very small staffs, so they must rely on the ministries for staff work. Nonetheless, opposition parties, although in the minority, can block or slow down legislative change. The boycotts and slowdowns initiated by the opposition parties forced the withdrawal of the reform package in April 1987, based on adamant opposition to the broad-based indirect tax. The tax bill passed later in the year did not include this indirect tax.

In the United States power is more diffused, and Congress is stronger and more independent than is the Diet. Based on work by the Treasury Department, the President usually provides the initial proposal for a tax revision or reform. Congress then drafts and redrafts the proposal, usually at least three times, once in the House of Representatives, once in the Senate, and once in the Conference Committee formed to reconcile the House and Senate versions. The members of Congress utilize their own relatively large staffs, as well as obtaining staff work from Treasury and from other agencies and organizations.

The power of the administrative bureaucracy in the United States is limited by turnover in personnel. Not only do responsibilities change, but people move in and out of government service rather frequently. Such changes also bring shifts in policy emphasis, not only as the result of shifting election results, but also as the philosophy and personality of the specific people in charge change. In the tax area, even such a seemingly minor shift as the change of Treasury Secretary to Baker from Regan in early 1985 brought a change in emphasis. Regan apparently took the objective of simplification seriously, while Baker was more willing to shape the tax change proposal to fit political imperatives.

The types of conflict within the government and the ways they are manifested and resolved also differ between Japan and the United States. In Japan much intragovernment conflict is interministerial. MITI is searching for a new approach to implementing industrial policy. In the tax area, MITI continues to propose new special taxation measures and to defend existing ones. The MOF has adopted the position that in principle there should be no new government spending programs or new tax breaks, because the budget deficit has been too large. The MOF has been very successful in recent years in limiting new initiatives by MITI. The MOF has also apparently used the prospect of an imminent tax reform to resist any major changes being incorporated into the annual tax revisions in recent years.

In the United States much of the intragovernment conflict is manifested in Congress. In the tax area various interest groups focus their efforts on influencing the congressional process. In the face of these pressures, broader economic considerations and national policy goals are often overwhelmed. The tax-reform package was written and rewritten at least five times. In the process a major goal such as simplification was sacrificed.

Unusual alliances and compromises may appear as the conflict evolves. In order to keep the process of tax reform going, Reagan first had to rely on Dan Rostenkowski, a Democrat, to draft a tax bill in the House of Representatives. Then, when the Ways and Means Committee had predictably produced a bill that was not acceptable to most Republican representatives (and some Democratic representatives), Reagan had to pressure the Republicans to vote for the bill. In order to gain enough support, he had to promise to veto the bill he was asking them to vote for, if it was eventually sent to him in anything close to that version. In the Senate the key event was the conversion of Robert Packwood from a defender of tax breaks to the sponsor of a tax-reform bill that would greatly reduce tax breaks for individual taxpayers (although not for corporations) in exchange for dramatically lower tax rates. Essentially, Republican Senator Packwood adopted the approach to tax reform that had been advocated for several years by Democratic Senator Bill Bradley, and the two became close allies in guiding the bill through committee and the full Senate. In the case of Packwood's conversion, it may be that the broader national interest prevailed over the collection of various special interests. The completion of the compromise bill by the Conference Committee then depended on the personal cooperation of the Democrat Rostenkowski and the Republican Packwood. It may also be noted that the Department of Commerce appears to have little influence or even visibility in the process of tax reform, in contrast to the role played by MITI in Japan in attempting to influence tax changes.

The discussion of tax reform also shows differences in the processes of conflict resolution in the two countries, which differences have implications for the ability to achieve controversial policy changes. In Japan, meetings, councils, committees, and commissions are used to slowly build a consensus about desirable changes. Although conflicts do arise, various groups are often circumspect in stating their positions. A lack of internal consensus may also force an organization to remain silent, at least in public statements, about certain issues. This is seen in the lack of clear statements by MITI and the *Keidanren* about the possible imposition of a broad-based indirect tax. In another forum, the LDP usually obtains the implicit acceptance by the opposition of any bills that are passed in the Diet. Although there may be public debate, true conflict has been minimized by prior informal discussion and compromise. Thus, in Japan efforts are made to resolve conflicts without contention and confrontation. At times this can result in an inability to address and resolve conflicts.

In the United States conflict is much more open, with substantial, real public debate and majority voting over truly contentious issues occurring in Congress. Lobbying is rather open, and lobbying groups may change their positions as the outline of a bill changes as it proceeds through Congress. For instance, various business organizations changed their position from support for tax reform to opposition as alterations were made in the proposed changes in corporate taxation in the House version of the reform bill. Many of these organizations then became supporters of the Senate version, because it was less harmful to their interests, once it became clear that some version of tax reform was likely to be enacted.

Such different manners of dealing with conflict have an impact on the likely outcome and its predictability. In both countries the process of tax reform has been a lengthy one, because the conflicts are important and broad. In the United States the acceptance of open conflict led to several large shifts in the outline of the reform package. At the same time, the willingness to accept open conflict permitted a movement toward a reform that was acceptable to a majority in Congress and to the President. In situations where conflict is inevitable and serious, open, constructive confrontation can lead to successful resolution.

In Japan the approach of minimizing conflict can work well if various groups can agree to objectives and acceptable trade-offs. This approach, however, is likely to be increasingly unsuccessful as the number of objectives increases or the differential effects on various groups becomes more severe. The ability of the Japanese approach to effect changes in fundamental policies such as taxation that have such differential effects is limited. Instead, certain groups can refuse to accept changes, forcing a continuation of the status quo, even though the status quo is not necessarily in the national interest.

Thus, in Japan the general outline of the proposed tax reform had been known for some time. The government attempted and failed to build a consensus for the package, especially because one element, the broad-based indirect tax, was unacceptable to certain groups (and also was not popular with the general public). The inability to achieve consensus in the face of this conflict prevented the enactment of a comprehensive tax reform in Japan. Although tax reform, including a broad-based indirect tax, remains a stated major goal of the government, it is not clear how the necessary consensus can be forged to permit this to become a reality.

NOTES

1. A detailed discussion of the tax systems and corporate taxation can be found in Pechman (1983) for the United States, and in Pechman and Kaizuka (1976) or *Outline of Japanese Taxes 1985* for Japan.

2. See the discussion in Lincoln (1984) or Pepper et al. (1985).

3. Pepper et al. (1985) discuss a rough and probably overly generous analysis done by the Japan Science and Technology Agency of the effects of this credit.

4. Eisner et al. (1984) provide a more skeptical analysis of the effects of this type of tax credit. See also the discussion by Mansfield (1986) and the references cited therein.

5. See the discussion in Pepper et al. (1985).

6. See Ikemoto et al. (1984) or Ishi (1985).

7. For an analysis of the effects of these incentives, see Okita (1975).

8. See Horst and Pugel (1977) for an analysis of the effects of DISC on U.S. exports. See Lee and Bloom (1985) for a comparison of DISC and the Foreign Sales Corporation.

9. For two comparative studies, see Kubouchi (1984) and Gravelle (1983).

10. Japan–U.S. Businessmen's Conference (1984), p. 99.

11. Data from Japan Ministry of Finance.

12. Another important study is Auerbach (1983).

13. See Ikemoto et al. (1984) and Ishi (1985).

14. See Pechman (1983), chapter 3, for additional discussion.

15. See Pechman and Kaizuka (1976) for a discussion of this process.

16. The role of the Diet and the process of enacting a bill are described in Matsui et al. (1985).

BIBLIOGRAPHY

Auerbach, Alan J. "Corporate Taxation in the United States." *Brookings Papers on Economic Activity,* no. 2 (1983):451–505.

Eisner, Robert; Albert, Steven H.; and Sullivan, Martin A. "The New Incremental Tax Credit for R&D: Incentive or Disincentive?" *National Tax Journal* 37, no. 2 (1984):171–183.

Fullerton, Don, and Henderson, Yolandra Kodrzycki. "Long-Run Effects of the Accelerated Cost Recovery System." *Review of Economics and Statistics* 67, no. 3 (1985):363–372.

Gravelle, Jane G. *Comparative Corporate Tax Burdens in the United States and Japan and Implications for Relative Economic Growth.* Congressional Research Service Report No. 83-177E. Washington, D.C.: Library of Congress, 1983.

Horst, Thomas, and Pugel, Thomas A. "The Impact of DISC on the Prices and Profitability of U.S. Exports." *Journal of Public Economics* 7, no. 1 (February 1977):73–87.

Ikemoto, Yukio; Tajika, Eiji; and Yui, Yuji. "On the Fiscal Incentives to Investment: The Case of Postwar Japan." *Developing Economies* 22, no. 4 (December 1984):372–395.

Ishi, Hiromitsu. "Corporate Tax Burdens and Tax Incentives in Japan." Manuscript, May 1985.

Japan–U.S. Businessmen's Conference. *Understanding the Industrial Policies and Practices of Japan and the United States: A Business Perspective.* Washington, D.C.: Advisory Council on Japan–U.S. Economic Relations, 1984.

Kubouchi, Yoshimasa. "Tax Burden on Corporate Income: An International Comparison." *Keidanren Review,* no. 87 (June 1984):9–12.

Lee, B. E., and Bloom, Donald R. "Deficit Reduction Act of 1984: Changes in Export Incentives." *Columbia Journal of World Business* 20, no. 2 (1985):63–70.

Lincoln, Edward J. *Japan's Industrial Policies.* Washington, D.C.: Japan Economic Institute of America, 1984.

Mansfield, Edwin. "The R&D Tax Credit and Other Technology Policy Issues." *American Economic Review* 76, no. 2 (May 1986):190–194.

Matsui, Akira; Sakuma, Yoshio; and Sato, Yuichi. *The Diet, Elections, and Political Parties.* About Japan Series No. 13. Tokyo: Foreign Press Center, 1985.

Noguchi, Yukio. "Tax Structure and Saving-Investment Balance." *Hitotsubashi Journal of Economics* 26, no. 1 (June 1985):45–58.

Okita, Yoichi. "Japan's Fiscal Incentives for Exports." In *Japanese Economy in Perspective,* edited by Isaiah Frank, pp. 207–230, Baltimore: Johns Hopkins University Press, 1975.

Outline of Japanese Taxes 1985. Tokyo: Ministry of Finance, 1985.

Pechman, Joseph A. *Federal Tax Policy.* 4th ed. Washington, D.C.: Brookings Institution, 1983.

Pechman, Joseph A., and Kaizuka, Keimei. "Taxation." In *Asia's New Giant,* edited by Hugh Patrick and Henry Rosovsky. pp. 317–382, Washington, D.C.: Brookings Institution, 1976.

Pepper, Thomas; Janow, Merit E.; and Wheeler, Jimmy W. *The Competition: Dealing with Japan.* New York: Praeger, 1985.

9
ASSUMPTIONS ON DECISIONS, DECISIONS ON ASSUMPTIONS— SOME FUTURE PERSPECTIVES

KICHIRO HAYASHI
Aoyama Gakuin University

INTRODUCTION

THERE ARE three problems at the base of the eight studies included in this book. The first is that United States–Japan economic relations are not as productive as they could or should be. The relations involve (1) intraorganizational relations between the U.S. and Japanese managers within the Japanese subsidiary in the United States or the U.S. subsidiary in Japan; (2) interorganizational relations between the core firm and its subcontractors in their respective countries, resulting in differential competitiveness and trade imbalance; and (3) macroeconomic policy coordination between the two countries.

The second problem is that economic conflict, real and perceived, has developed between the two nations. A transition from conflict to new, beneficial relations has been delayed by a mutual lack of understanding. Each country has felt that the other has engaged in unfair competition and practices, which might potentially develop into an economic war. This would be a counterproductive use of resources for the world economy as a whole.

The third problem is deficiency in analysis on the communications level regarding this misunderstanding between the two nations. The communicational deficiency is conspicuous particularly for the differences between the two nations in the management of cross-cultural interface, subcontracting, and formation and implementation of economic policies.

In section 1 of this summary chapter, we identify some of the basic conceptual differences between Japan and the United States relevant to these three problems, based on a questionnaire survey conducted by this author. The basic question addressed in the questionnaire is: What barriers are being produced by the conceptual differences? From the findings, we also infer some of the underlying assumptions of the two cultures.

In section 2 we examine how much of the structural and behavioral differences causing economic conflict and misunderstanding between Japan and the United States can be explained by such underlying assumptions.

In section 3 we set out to inquire what can and/or should be done about the differences for better performance and/or economic relations. The basic questions are what third-culture concepts need to be developed and what new structures and types of behavior can be expected from the third-culture concepts. This discussion of problem-solving strategies is focused on examining whether there is anything to be hybridized and/or internationalized for successful transplantation.

1. WHAT ARE SOME OF THE BASIC CONCEPTUAL AND PRECONCEPTUAL DIFFERENCES BETWEEN JAPAN AND THE UNITED STATES RELEVANT TO OUR CONSIDERATION?

1.1. Methods

A questionnaire survey was conducted both in Japanese and in English. The English version was produced first, then the substance and point of each question were expressed in Japanese by the author himself, rather than by the usual translation procedure of going back and forth between the two versions. This was based on the judgment that the author knows best what it is he wishes to ask and that his near-bilingual skills should be utilized. Finally, some adjustments were made for each pair of questions.

The English version was distributed to eighty-nine non-Japanese managers (mostly Americans) as well as twenty-four MBA students at UCLA. There were fifty-two effective respondents. Fourteen of the fifty-two had had the experience of living overseas for three years or more. The age distribution of respondents was bimodal, with concentrations in the twenties and forties.

The Japanese version was sent to 241 Japanese managers living in Japan and 131 managers living overseas, a total of 372. Effective responses were collected from 143, 75 of whom lived overseas for three years or more. Most of the Japanese respondents were in their forties and fifties, in middle to top management.

The questionnaire had about sixty questions. It dealt with eleven hypotheses indicating differences in basic concepts between the United States and Japan making cross-cultural-interface management difficult. The eleven hypothesized concepts were uncertainties, future, conflict/confrontation, interpersonal relations, groupism, decision making, planning, organizational community, corporate culture as a means of control, perspective, and root problems.

SPSS (Statistical Package for Social Sciences) analyses have been conducted for the 195 responses to the sixty-odd questions.

1.2. Some Preliminary Findings

We present below the results for nine of the eleven hypotheses. Uncertainties and perspectives are not included for they need further research, i.e., the results were not conclusive.

The concept of the future

We have some understanding and feeling for the future, though some of us may not be well aware of it. For instance, we have some feeling regarding whether we should create our future or whether this is impossible. If you feel you should/can create your future, do you have a clear vision and plan for your future? Without necessarily denying the idea of having a clear vision and plan for the future, you may still feel that the future will basically result from factors not under your control.

The hypothesis was that Americans feel that one's future is something one should create, while the Japanese tend to feel that the future will emerge from factors well beyond their control. A study conducted by Donald Harnett and Larry Cummings (1980) supported this hypothesis.

The result of the questionnaire, however, was that the Japanese, like Americans, apparently believe that one should create one's own future. Does this imply that the Japanese have now grown away from the Buddhist perspective? The basic difference, however, between the American and the Japanese is that the future is to be created by the individual for the American and by the group for the Japanese. This difference is very important, because this Japanese concept of the future has to do with the communal Japanese concept of the firm discussed in Chapter 2.

However, those Americans who have lived overseas three years or more are inclined to believe that the future occurs and cannot be created by ourselves. It is conjectured that they experienced situations they could not control overseas, but which they could have controlled in their home country. There was no difference between the Japanese with and without overseas experiences.

Conflict and confrontation

The question here is how respondents feel about contention and confrontation as a means of resolving interpersonal conflict. When conflicts of interest and/or opinion occur, would one include contention, which might eventually lead the way to confrontation, among the viable methods to solution?

If someone should feel the need to avoid confrontation, it might be because of some inherent discomfort associated with confrontation or because of a harmful influence upon his interpersonal relations in general in the long run.

On the other hand, someone else may feel that conflict is part of human life, so that it would be best to place it in the open and face it squarely for a fair solution. If you try to ignore it or hide it, it would result in other, worse problems.

The hypothesis that the former is a Japanese approach and the latter American has been supported by the questionnaire results. This difference has created problems in cross-cultural organizations. From the Japanese point of view, American managers express themselves too aggressively on matters of self-interest, while Americans feel that the Japanese do not face problems fairly and squarely but try to avoid them through under-the-table transactions.

Among the Japanese respondents, those with cross-cultural experience go further in avoiding conflict/confrontation. This implies that a belief of this type would not change easily even in an adversarial environment.

However, it was also clear from the Japanese responses that they would confront one another more in the work environment than in the residential environment.

The concept of interpersonal relations

Interpersonal relations at work or in business are based on functional collaboration for work or business purposes. This means that interpersonal relations at work or in business are formed not for their intrinsic value but as a means for work or business. It is known, however, that work and business are intrinsically influenced by the nature of the interpersonal relations that are formed. The question here is how the intrinsic side of interpersonal relations at work or in business—their private side in a way—should be treated.

The Japanese generally think Americans believe in a "business is business" sort of thinking—a "businesslike" approach—so that Americans wish to distinguish business relations from private ones. Not that Americans appear to deny warm friendship in work or business, but they keep work and business separate from the friendly side of relationships. This impression of the Japanese about Americans was turned into a working hypothesis.

In Japan, on the other hand, it appears to be impossible to separate semifamilial, friendly relations from work or business relations. There is a strong orientation in favor of personal relations, or the general belief that cultivating close interpersonal relations is good either for business or for personal friendships. This is another hypothesis for the Japanese side.

The questionnaire responses supported neither hypothesis. The responses indicated that the Japanese tend to believe that business and private relations had better be separate, confirming that "familial relations" at work tend to be pseudofamilial ones. Americans also recognized the need to separate work and private relations, but they indicated in higher proportions than the Japanese respondents that some of the friends they today appreciate most have come from their work or business relations. This finding is worthy of note, and the Japanese should revise their common misunderstanding about Americans in light of this.

Groupism

It is a common cliché today that the Japanese are inclined toward groupism and Americans toward individualism. Japanese groupism is defined as a set of values placing the interest of the group above that of the individual and based on the belief that the two are in accord.

The question was "Suppose you need to prioritize Plans A and B for which you expect to spend a great deal of time and energy during the coming twelve months. You wish to choose Plan A, for the plan is better for your personal growth and benefit than Plan B, but the latter appears to be better for the organization you work for. Which would you prioritize?"

The finding was again worthy of note. Americans declined to place self-interest above group interest. Further, they denied it relatively more strongly than the Japanese if one assumes that the American and Japanese results are comparable, though this may be questioned. Japanese responses were bimodal: that is, 42.8 percent voted for self-interest above group interest and 41.3 percent against it. This implies that Japanese groupism is far more complex, or perhaps in transition, than is usually assumed, and that American individualism is qualified more than is generally believed in Japan.

Decision making

The point of the question on decision making was whether organizational choice of critical courses of action should be made by a participative process of consensus. Associated with this was the issue of giving some consideration and/or compensation to those who might be placed at a disadvantage as a result of such critical choices.

There is a general understanding in this area that Japanese decision making works by consensus and U.S. decision making by individual authority and responsibility. This general understanding was used as a hypothesis.

The responses did not support either the U.S. or the Japanese part of the hypothesis. In fact, the results were more extreme than that. Americans supported the participative process in greater proportion than the Japanese. This may reflect the Americans' reaction to their present experience, because the question did not inquire into what was but what should be. On the Japanese side, 48.6 percent supported decision making by individual authority and responsibility. This also may reflect their reactions to their current experience, or the Japanese system may be in transition.

The concept of planning

The concept of planning varies considerably. The focus here is placed on long-range planning. The question is whether long-range planning for a corporation is considered merely a process of informational exchange among participating individuals with a view to developing a common vision for the future. Alternatively, the concept could go a step further, suggesting a continuous process of developing strategic programs of action that could serve as a basis for monitoring and controlling strategic actions.

The hypothesis that the Japanese conceive long-range planning as a process of developing a common vision derived from the findings of research in the mid-seventies (covering twenty-odd Japanese firms)—suggesting that long-range planning was merely a vehicle for informational exchange and not for monitoring or control (Hayashi 1978). U.S. research has indicated that U.S. firms were not engaged in long-range planning in textbook fashion either, but planning was used for purposes of monitoring and control.

The questionnaire responses were quite contrary to these hypotheses. Americans believed that long-range planning should be mainly a vehicle for informational exchange, while the Japanese believed it should go further as a means of controlling action. This implies that the concept of planning has changed over the years in Japan. Those Americans who had lived overseas and had experience in cross-cultural organizations showed a stronger tendency to deem long-range planning a simple vehicle for informational exchange. This suggests that overseas experience made people prefer looser arrangements.

The second, interrelated hypothesis was that the Japanese stressed the formulation of outlines, leaving details to case-by-case decision making, while Americans preferred formulating detailed programs of action that are most likely to achieve the objective. The questionnaire results were opposite to these hypothesized preferences.

Our final hypothesis was on the rigidity of planning. Our presumption was that Americans felt that plans should always be subject to change if the environment changed, while Japanese felt that one should stick to the plan as rigidly as possible once it had been formulated. Both the American and Japanese respondents felt that plans were always subject to change.

Thus, most of the planning hypotheses have been contradicted. It has been conjectured that Americans have shifted toward a more flexible planning process, while the Japanese are interested in creating their own futures with advanced planning techniques unimaginable from their planning in the seventies.

The concept of organization as a community

Members of some organizations have built a familial community within the organization far beyond the level and range of contact expected from the usual interpersonal business relations. How should one consider the building of an intimate community within the average organization vis-a-vis other organizational objectives? The hypothesis here is that the Japanese would consider the community-building objective as important as any other organizational objectives, while Americans would deem it secondary to some other organizational objectives.

The survey results showed that Japanese, like Americans, consider the community-building objective secondary to other organizational objectives. This result, when considered together with the finding on the nature of interpersonal relations at work, implies rapid changes in Japanese society. Does this mean that the Japanese company is rapidly transforming itself from a *Gemeinschaft* into a *Gesellschaft?*

Corporate culture and control

It was hypothesized that the Japanese significantly depend upon corporate culture for the control of managers, while Americans depend upon job descriptions. In the Japanese approach, it then becomes important to assimilate managers into certain favorable orientations, values, and concepts based on the history and culture of the firm. The assumption here is that managers, once assimilated, would make effective decisions and behave appropriately without close direction and control. For this, managers are expected to keep up with continuous, dynamic changes in the organization in order to form appropriate judgments as a base for their decisions and behavior.

According to the hypothesized U.S. approach, clear and detailed job descriptions were necessary for each manager to be thoroughly familiar with his authority and responsibilities. Each manager is expected to possess complete freedom in judgment and action within his authority and responsibilities for the fulfillment of his job.

The questionnaire results indicated that control through job description was supported by Americans but not by the Japanese, as expected. However, control through corporate culture was supported by Americans as well as by the Japanese. It goes without saying that the image of corporate culture may differ considerably between the two countries. For instance, the author is reminded of a remark made by an American marketing director of a U.S. firm in Japan to the effect that his problem in Japan was that his Japanese managers would not grow out of their production orientation into a marketing orientation and that marketing orientation was the culture of his corporation.

Problem definition

How we define a problem depends very much upon our basic attribution of its cause, i.e., whether one attributes the cause of the problem to oneself or to the environment.

It was hypothesized that Japanese believe that they get a better result by attributing the cause to self and seeking a solution from that point of view, while Americans attribute the cause to environment and try to solve the problem by working on the environment.

The questionnaire results confirmed the hypothesis on the Japanese part but indicated a split attitude on the American side. The author was impressed by the 46.2 percent of the American respondents that supported the attitude of attributing the cause to oneself. This inclination was particularly strong among the Americans with long overseas experience.

A considerable number of Americans and an even greater number of Japanese object to attributing the cause to the environment. Does this imply that Americans as well as the Japanese "know" that the United States–Japan economic conflict is attributable to self?

1.3. Differences in Assumptions Behind the Differences in Concept

Both Japanese and Americans appear to think that the future is something you create. However, there is a critical difference between the two nations in the way the future is to be created—whether it is to be created by the individual or by collaboration.

This point may be clarified to a great extent by the different concepts of planning, because planning refers to the way the future is to be created. Americans conceive of long-range planning mainly in terms of informational exchange, as contrasted with the Japanese concept of it as formulating strategic action programs.

While strategic action programs indicate the design of coordinated joint action, informational exchange implies a much looser arrangement and control over the coordination of individual actions. Thus, informational exchange presents a context in which action takers are relatively more independent, loosely linked individuals who move in a common direction under a general framework. On the other hand, strategic action programs imply a much tighter coordination of individual actions.

This contrast is further clarified by the different preferences regarding the content of a plan. Americans believe that a plan should simply be an outline, while Japanese wish to see details in a plan. Both nationalities, however, believe that plans should be modifiable.

More generally, the future is created by choice or some form of decision making—i.e., the future is the consequence of today's decisions. In the context of organizational decision making and the future, Americans insist that individuals should be able to participate in the strategic (i.e., important) decision making of their organizations, while half of the Japanese are willing to accept the choice made by their organization's leaders, thus showing a bimodal distribution.

This contrast, again, implies that Americans think that action takers are individuals, so they prefer not to be controlled by one-way orders emanating from above. Japanese, on the other hand, believe that their leaders take subordinates into consideration when making choices because of the conviction that their future is produced only through close collaboration. If the subordinates are taken into account, they have reasons to believe that the choices made must also be good for them.

It should be clear in this discussion that organizational decisions are influenced by the concept of human relations in the organization. Thus, we now need to discuss the differences between the Japanese and the U.S. concepts of human relations. One dimension of the concept is interpersonal conflict.

The concept of conflict represents the most distinct contrast between the Japanese and Americans identified among the questionnaire's eleven hypotheses. When a conflict takes place, Japanese try to solve it without contention or confrontation while Americans would rather face it, argue it out, and try to find a fair solution. The Japanese consider conflict undesirable and unnecessary in itself, while Americans consider conflict inevitable and natural, so that any solution arranged behind the curtain is suspect.

This contrast corresponds to the homogenistic, hierarchical view vs. the heterogenistic, interactive view of the world in Maruyama's Mindscape model (Maruyama 1978, 1980, 1982). Maruyama argues that a significant proportion of the U.S. population holds the former view, while most of the Japanese population holds a mixture of those views. The homogenistic, hierarchical view essentially considers people homogeneous—having similar desires and outlooks that are bound to compete against one another. The heterogenistic, interactive view perceives people as having heterogeneous attributes that are interdependent and complementary.

Thus, in the homogenistic, hierarchical view, relations are basically counterproductive, competitive, instrumental (rather than intrinsic), and unnatural, with zero-sum game connotations, while in the heterogenistic, hierarchical view, relations are productive, complementary, interdependent, and natural, with positive-sum game connotations.

Francis Hsu (1971), an American psychologist, has said that for Americans relations are means, while for the Japanese they are ends. I believe that the Japanese find value in relations because of their preconception that individuals are heterogeneously complementary with one another.

Under this preconception, one would look for proper ways of forming relations. When these relations are right, they should be beneficial. While not all relations work, this would not change the basic presumption.

A mechanistic approach to forming relations—i.e., a mechanistically designed organization—puts heterogeneous viewers off, because such relations do not appear to take advantage of people's potential.

Once relations are set right, they work quite organically. Westerners may view the Japanese as prone to groupism or particularistic principles of organizing. Given the organic way Japanese relations work, the Japanese may appear easily organized and administered, and may not seem independent. Such views are not wrong, but reflect an intercultural bias. These Japanese relations are discussed by Shumpei Kumon (1978) as "contextualism," which provides the context within which "right relations" emerge. Like the "frame" as defined by Chie Nakane (1970), the Kumon context provides a motivation to form "right" relations.

Though relations in the organization are perceived differently by Japanese and Americans, both agree that work relations should promote organizational objectives and not private objectives, and therefore should be separated from private relations. If the two kinds of relations were mixed, the organization would be unable to survive.

Similarly, action takers in U.S. organizations are individuals, but individual independence is allowed only within the frame of achieving organizational objectives. Individual actions that would interfere with organizational objectives are denied, since Americans place organizational interest above individual self-interest when they work for an organization. In contrast, one-half of the Japanese respondents believe that individual self-interest can be placed above organizational interest.

However, the Japanese concept of self-interest appears different from the American concept. The Japanese concept of self-interest, within the context provided by the questionnaire, involves the development of individual attributes that are complementary to the rest of the organization under the heterogenistic, hierarchical view; the concept of the workplace as a place for personal growth justifies self-interest in personal growth. In the U.S. context, on the other hand, the pursuit of self-interest would be perceived as interfering with organizational objectives. Also, the cost of personal growth should be borne by the individual, not by the firm, in the U.S scheme of things. Not so in Japan.

Similarly, concepts of community building within an organization have been rejected by both Japanese and Americans as objectives superior or equal to business objectives, e.g., profit making. This clearly indicates that interpersonal relations are limited by the situation. Both nationals apparently realize the importance of business objectives for the survival of their organization.

The assumption that action takers are individuals, not groups, supports a mechanistic organization controlled by job descriptions because the mechanistic frame is less binding than organic frames and forms of control. On the other hand, the Japanese assumption that action takers are groups suggests an organic approach to organization.

Americans also realize that job descriptions are not enough for effective coordination. They also support the development of corporate culture as a necessary ingredient of effective organizations. However, the U.S. concept of corporate culture appears to be more narrowly conceived within the frame of business, as exemplified by the marketing concept which an executive of a U.S. subsidiary in Japan insisted to be his company's corporate culture. The marketing concept would have been considered a business tool, not a culture in Japanese firms. This contrasts with the Japanese counterpart, which is more comprehensive, implying, for example, society-serving organizations, internationalized organizations, etc.

In conclusion, the difference between the Japanese concept of relations within the organization and that of Americans is not a matter of degree but of kind. Recognition of this difference is essential in explaining other differences between the two nations.

2. HOW THE DIFFERENCES IN ASSUMPTION AND CONCEPT CAN EXPLAIN THE DIFFERENCES IN STRUCTURE AND BEHAVIOR BETWEEN JAPAN AND THE UNITED STATES

Evident throughout the chapters in this book is the conspicuous difference in the concept of relation between Japan and the United States. Japanese find inherent value in forming relations, while Americans do not. This has a bearing upon the different concepts of the firm. And this concept is central to the differences in cross-cultural-interface management between Japan and the United States. The Japanese concept of "communal ownership" puts employee relations at the base of the firm. Had relations not been conceived as intrinsically complementary and permanent, the concept of communal ownership would not have been developed. This contrasts with the U.S. contractual concept of relations in the firm as basically a means to achieve corporate objectives. In Japan, the firm is socio-psychologically "owned" by the employees communally and collectively. As a result, the United States has produced relatively mechanistic organizations based on a set of job descriptions, while Japan has produced organic organizations.

These differences have prevented Americans working for Japanese subsidiaries in the United States from becoming part of the Japanese network of communal ownership. Chapter 2 made it clear that the most salient source of frustration for American managers in the organic Japanese subsidiary was the decision-making process. This stemmed primarily from the difference in the basic assumptions regarding who action takers are. Americans wished to have their responsibilities specified and their authority clarified so that individuals could take actions, while Japanese did not believe that such clarifications would contribute to better decisions. The Japanese believe that decisions should emerge from interpersonal relations.

As a result, top-notch local managers were hard to find, and a sense of distrust prevailed, as a relatively large number of Japanese expatriate managers were needed for important functions in Japanese subsidiaries. As a result, the organizational typology of Japanese subsidiaries is predominantly autonomous (Japanese autonomy) on the policy/strategy level and mixed (between Japanese and locals) on the administrative level.

On the industry level, Roehl argues that subcontracting in the Japanese style is a long-term relationship, requiring various adjustments over time under changing economic conditions. Adjustments mean costs, and these costs need to be reasonable. This point of Roehl's is well taken in economic terms; but economics alone misses the point. The basic Japanese premise of relations is that right relations are essentially beneficial. The opportunity costs of breaking off the subcontracting relationship is considered to be too high. When expected future benefits are included, net-cost calculations are also different.

Roehl also discusses whether technology transfer is a one-way or two-way process between the core firm and the subcontractors. If it is one way, Roehl states, "the key issues then become the ability of the partner to absorb important technology from the parent, and the ability of the core firm to price the transfer of technology appropriately to maintain its competitive position." The fact is that it is two-way because of the division of labor within technology—each side acquiescing to the development of technology it is not capable of duplicating easily. Roehl argues that this technological link is made feasible by the resultant expected growth and profits for both firms. The core firm and subcontractors are heterogeneous and complementary to one another.

While this economic, contractual interpretation of Japanese subcontracting makes some sense, particularly for American readers, the firms' economic conditions alone may or may not lead to subcontracting. The key factor is the core firm's ability to internalize the division of labor in technological innovations in expectation of growth and profits. It is thoughts about the future that come sharply into the picture here. Feelings that one would be better off standing together rather than alone in creating the future must enter the mind of the decision maker. In the Japanese mind, contractual bonds have much less meaning than for Americans, because contractually bound individuals would not be able to create their future

together, in the Japanese view, unless they also are bound culturally.

Roehl's analysis of economic conditions is a useful complement
to Minato's argument, particularly as it applies to the transfer of
Japanese management systems to the United States. Most of the
Japanese concepts and premises would not be helpful in considering such transfers, so economic analyses need to play an important
role in understanding the U.S. case.

In general, economy and culture are not separate. Cultural concepts and values penetrate economic systems, while economic conditions provide the base for any systems designed to achieve cultural goals. Economy and culture are thus two sides of the same coin in
all human affairs.

On the national level, the U.S. concept of free enterprise under
minimal government regulation provides a justification for neglect-
ing industrial policy in most Americans' minds. This is linked with
the belief in competition and the "invisible hand" that labels industrial policy as "market-distorting." The common American concept of industrial policy is that of government officials choosing
industries to be given subsidies, special loans, and privileged tax
treatment. This concept suggests that corporate executives rather
than government officials have not only the ability but the right to
make decisions that affect business activities. Thus, the basic conceptual frame in the United States has created a political climate
hostile to intentionally designed industrial policy.

If the basic difference between the Japanese and U.S. approach to
industrial policy is characterized by a nationally directed focus on
certain industries in Japan (notably "knowledge-intensive" industries) in order to create comparative advantage, as contrasted with a
market-oriented approach in the United States, the economic conflict currently in question would be ideological at its base.

A widespread view in the United States is that industrial policy
will not achieve results superior to those of the free market. The
presumption behind this view, Ishiyama says, is that discriminatory
government policies are distortionary, leading to misallocation of
resources (see page 232 of this book).

The effectiveness of tax policy and industrial policy in Japan has
been gradually declining, but remains continuous and consistent, as

compared to the United States, where it is subject to "abrupt, rather substantial changes." This may stem, at least in part, from basic conceptual differences manifest in the greater acceptance of open conflict and the use of more explicit rules in the United States and the opposite conceptual inclination in Japan.

Pugel believes that the Japanese attempt to minimize outright conflict and the U.S. openness about conflict are evidenced by the processes of tax reform in the two countries. Various groups in Japan are often circumspect in stating their positions before an internal consensus is reached. This was seen in the lack of clear statements by MITI and *Keidanren* about the large-scale indirect tax. In the United States, conflict is much more open, with substantial, real public debate and majority voting over truly contentious issues occurring in Congress. Even Republican senators and representatives openly disagree with the Republican president.

On the legal level, the main players in the formative process of industrial policy are the central bureaucracy, e.g., economic ministries in Japan and Congress in the United States. One of the conspicuous differences between Japan's central bureaucracy and the U.S. Congress is fluidity of personnel. Politicians may be out of office next term either in the United States or in Japan, but Japanese bureaucrats are permanent. Japanese bureaucrats are recruited from among top-notch graduates by the severely competitive examination for superior offices. The successful "career" officials stay in office permanently. They form steady, continuous relations with industry and all other institutions in and out of the country. Given these permanent relations, no politicians can compete with the central bureaucracy in terms of information accumulation and effective action.

The difference, on the legal level, in the concept of relations between Japan and the United States is evident also in the legal cultures of the two nations. According to the list of differences in legal culture presented by Sakurai (see page 184 of this book), the basic legal principle in the United States is the claim of individual rights, while it is harmony within community in Japan. If individuals have homogeneous perspectives and desires, zero-sum games tend to prevail, so that each needs to claim his own rights to secure his share in the given pie. But under the assumption of complementary perspectives and desires, problems are solved more satisfactorily by improving relations or harmony between individuals.

Thus, the base of conscience is harmony within the community in Japan, while it is universal righteousness in the United States. Law is a tool to claim individual rights in the United States because it provides a frame or a set of rules within which free activity is guaranteed. However, law is the last resort in Japan. Within a set of rules, competition is encouraged between individuals in the United States, while it is disruptive if it is encouraged carelessly within the community in Japan. Competition is therefore typically encouraged between communities or groups in Japan.

Another difference is in how conflicts of interest are dealt with. In the United States, individuals and firms resort to court decisions, while mutual consultation is the means of solution in Japan. Under the assumption of zero-sum games, a conflict of interest is best solved by the courts, but it is "corrected" by mutual consultation in positive-sum games.

3. WHAT CAN AND/OR SHOULD BE DONE ABOUT THE DIFFERENCES? IS THERE ANYTHING TO BE LOCALIZED, HYBRIDIZED, INTERNATIONALIZED?

What needs to be done at present depends upon what one wishes to see in the future. In this final section the desired future, as the author sees it, is discussed in relation to the probable future as an extention of the present.

Japan's international enterprises are currently managed chiefly by Japanese, both at the head office and on the local scenes. Given an expected rate of growth in the proportion of foreign production in Japan's global production from the present 2–3 percent to 20–30 percent by the end of the century, Japanese enterprises would not survive unless entrepreneurs and managers are nativized and internationalized for Japan's international enterprises. If the current proportion of expatriate Japanese in foreign subsidiaries is extended in the future, corporate costs as well as social costs would be too great. Not only that, but it is also possible that the current trade conflict will slide into an investment conflict in the future, given the present state of Japanese management.

The essential point of this argument is that for the survival of the Japanese enterprises the real *shutai,* or subjects, of the enterprises must be localized and internationalized, so that creative initiatives are autonomously taken by nationals of host countries to design and implement effective changes in the structures of the enterprises under changing local and international conditions.

There are several necessary conditions for the nativization of entrepreneurs and managers. The first condition is the indigenization of capital of both parent and local subsidiaries. Without this, there would be no basic motivation for local nationals to contribute to the enterprise. As a practical approach to this goal, stock options need to be more seriously considered by Japanese corporations. Too little serious consideration has so far been given to this approach. Also relevant is the public offering of parent and subsidiary stocks on the local stock market. This approach is not yet mature in many of the developing host countries, but it should be realized rapidly in developed-country markets.

The second condition is the localization of management in terms of approaches, concepts, methods, etc. The process of management in Japanese enterprises must be hybridized so that local entrepreneurs and managers can participate effectively and their brain power and energy are truly utilized.

However, the localization of management brings forth two types of fear for Japanese enterprises. One is the possibility that the international transfer of know-how to and from the subsidiary may not take place effectively when management is localized. Specifically, any advantages stemming from certain know-how of the parent enterprise need to be capitalized in the local subsidiary. This involves cross-cultural-interface management because the cross-cultural transfer of know-how requires conceptual translation. In order for the transferred know-how to be effective in the new environment it needs to be hybridized. This is achieved by cultural interrelators. Such interrelators are not yet available in sufficient numbers.

The other fear is the possible loss of control by the parent entrepreneur. There are perhaps two conditions for effective relations. The first necessary condition is that the parent receives a return appropriate to its input and the risk it takes. Return may be cash flow, know-how flow or experience of value to the entrepreneur. The second condition is that the relations between the local enterprise and the parent enterprise are well coordinated from some point of view. In order for these necessary conditions to prevail, the parent needs to participate in the process of strategic decision making for the local enterprise. I emphasize participation, not control. We need a system in which this process is a participatory one, not parental control beyond the necessary level.

Excessive control may prevail for one or more of the following reasons.

1. Some individuals in the parent enterprise possess a desire to control.

2. "Owner" behavior stems from the Japanese concept of collective ownership of the firm. Collective owners may feel that they need to know what is going on in the enterprise they "own."

3. A high level of control may be attributable to a fear of uncertainties stemming from the lack of understanding of local culture, including behavioral patterns, common sense, standards, meaning, etc.

4. Ethnocentricity creates the need of control.

In the case of Japanese enterprises one needs to guard against the possibility of excessive control stemming from (2) and/or (3) above. Some U.S. enterprises also may fall into excessive control stemming from (3) and (4). Reasons (2) and (3) are often mixed with (4). Japanese enterprises particularly may be characterized as still in their ethnocentric stage of development before they enter the polycentric or geocentric stages of development.

Under these circumstances, what needs to be done is to hybridize the *shutai* of the parent enterprise. In this context, hybridization means that corporate identity, ideals, concepts, and methods of management are changed into those that are acceptable and workable/functional in the international community.

Hybridization may have the following substantive effects. First, the standard of behavior of the parent enterprise is not biased against any specific set of countries or cultures. The unbiased nature of the global view is particularly critical in order to develop and maintain a set of policies to help foreign subsidiaries develop into leading positions within the global system of the parent enterprise. At the present time, the know-how necessary to develop such policies is conspicuously lacking in both U.S. and Japanese enterprises, but particularly in the Japanese ones.

Second, one of the most important functions of the parent enterprise is the coordination of various foreign subsidiaries in terms of the long-term well being of the enterprise as a whole. The point of view in setting priorities in the process of coordination must be flexible, not ethnocentric. Particularly relevant are adjustments between polycentric (local) and geocentric priorities.

A word of caution is necessary here. We have such concepts as ethnocentrism, polycentrism, and geocentrism in the literature of international business. Polycentrism means an emphasis is placed on the independence of each of the local subsystems or subsidiaries, while geocentrism emphasizes a central point of view for the optimization of the global system. In the present discussion, the point is that polycentrism and geocentrism are currently pursued from an ethnocentric point of view. We are trying to argue that a good balance of priorities between polycentric and geocentric strategies must be pursued from some unbiased point of view. We need to develop "de-ethnotized" coordinates of view. This is possible only as a result of a great deal of culturally blended experiences, perspectives, and interests. It may be achieved by a group of individuals who have had a great deal of multicultural experience and realize they have a stake in the exercise of a truly international perspective. A group with such a responsibility must consist of individuals who complement one another, so that as a whole they have a wide range of experiences and perspectives. This group is, by definition, third-cultural.

On the industry level, the concept of hybridization applies to the discussion of the possibility of transferring Japanese-style subcontracting to either indigenous U.S. firms or to Japanese subsidiaries in the United States. Japanese can only explain how subcontracting works in Japan, and Americans can judge if it can be transplanted to the United States. Even when Americans feel there is a real possibility of transplantation, they still need to work with Japanese to translate it conceptually into a set of U.S. concepts so that it would be acceptable and workable in the U.S. environment.

Minato says, in a nutshell, that under rapid environmental changes involving increasingly diversified consumer tastes, ever-shortened product life cycles, and a constant flux of technological innovations, the Japanese subcontracting arrangements have created the flexibility essential for international competitiveness better than the U.S. model of highly integrated production systems. The Japanese advantage thus created in international competition caused the trade imbalance and economic conflict between the two countries. Thus, Minato argues that the concept of Japanese subcontracting should be transferred to and hybridized in the United States.

Minato has observed that U.S. firms were in fact beginning to feel that a solution should be sought through the adoption of some aspects of the Japanese subcontracting systems, and that some U.S. firms had already started to introduce some of the Japanese concepts of interfirm relations in their production systems. For instance, as discussed in Chapter 3, GM announced that the Saturn Corporation would adopt procurement systems that would be similar to Japanese subcontracting systems. But not all is transferrable to the U.S. environment."

A substantive question needs to be asked before discussing the transplanting of one country's system into another country. It pertains to the understanding of the existing economic system in the host country. For instance, the existing U.S. approaches have been to respond to underlying U.S. needs and concepts such as avoiding dependence and preferring arm's length negotiation, so that the way these U.S. needs and concepts have been satisfied must be clarified—since the new solutions also must satisfy the same needs and concepts.

To cite Minato's examples, GM announced it would reduce suppliers by half, but this has not proceeded well because suppliers wish to avoid excessive dependence on one customer, just as assemblers wish to keep maximum dependence on one supplier under 20–30 percent. This relates to the U.S. presumption that interfirm relations are not necessarily dependable. For any newly introduced system to be successful, certain structural conditions are also necessary, as Roehl argues. Expectations of growth, for instance, assume a certain stable level of orders, technological innovations (and their transfer), risk sharing, etc. Without such expectations supported by objective data or circumstances, U.S. entrepreneurs have no reason to believe that the interfirm relations will work and be dependable.

Minato's discussion of U.S. automobile manufacturers trying to computerize their transactions is an interesting example of a more successful direction of development in the United States. This represents a hybridized solution, in that they are trying to achieve paperless transactions with much lower documentation costs (currently $200 per car) by forming an interfirm group. For this, they have formed the Automotive Industry Action Group (AIAG) as discussed by Minato. The relational premise usually serves as a basic concept of forming an interfirm group. In the United States relations do not have the inherent positive connotation that they do in Japan. Still, in this instance, cost reduction through the use of computer networks produced positive results. This experience will be unlikely to change their concept of relation, but their concept does not deny the existing experience.

Minato also cited other instances of interfirm relations. A U.S. manufacturer of electronic measuring instruments, which dealt with as many as 11,000 suppliers, chose forty-five key suppliers and is reaping benefits by working closely with them on quality control and delivery scheduling. A new-venture firm in the field of computer peripherals has also adopted the Japanese system on a large scale. This firm was formed in 1981 and has a Japanese-style no-layoff policy. To help reduce the risk of poor performance from fluctuations in its sales, it subcontracts as much as 75 percent of the value of its output. The firm deals with 272 suppliers, and has formed close ties with seventeen of them. The firm guarantees certain levels of orders for four of these suppliers that produce exclusively for it. This demonstrates that the adoption of Japanese management practices necessitates that a Japanese concept of supplier relations be translated into local contractual terms.

Yet another example is Panasonic's Chicago color-television plant, discussed in Chapter 3, purchased from the troubled Quasar. The plant's quality level and profit performance rose markedly as a result of the partial adoption of Japanese-style production control and procurement methods. The number of suppliers has been reduced from 1000 under Quasar to 200, thirty of which are key suppliers doing 20 percent or more of their business with

Panasonic. The purchasing staff has also been cut in half, to twenty-five, and close working relations have reduced transaction costs. One of the thirty is a firm supplying molded plastic parts doing nearly 50 percent of its business with one core firm, Panasonic—a rare example in the United States. A representative of the firm cited three advantages of its relations with Panasonic: good working relations, geographical proximity, and scale economies resulting from large, stable orders unlike the widely fluctuating orders received from U.S. automakers. These cases of interfirm relations indicate that some of the necessary economic conditions suggested by Roehl are being satisfied.

When an interfirm subcontracting group is formed in the United States, the relations may need to be fixed and controlled contractually, unlike in the Japanese system. There is nothing wrong with this, as long as interfirm collaboration and flexibility can be produced. This may still be possible within the legalistic U.S. relations, but it will take time and experience before full effective relations are realized.

Barriers to suppliers' participation in the process of new-product development in its early stage include the need to determine detailed product design prior to bidding; contracts disallowing later price adjustments; and problems relating to product confidentiality. Long-term relations based on mutual trust, which would circumvent some of these problems, could not be established under the short-term purchase policies of U.S. firms, due partly to purchasing officers trying to be promoted by short-term performance or trying to be transferred to a better position in another firm.

In actuality, Minato argues, Japanese subcontractors have accumulated considerable management resources, and no longer depend upon specific core firms as exclusively as before. These firms have turned from the pursuit of economies of scale to the pursuit of economies of scope, for which their need for certain information is mounting. A purchasing manager at Sony says that core firms could now effectively control subcontractors even if only a few percent of the subcontractors' business were dependent on the core firm —if the core firms had the ability to successively churn out new market-leading products. This has interesting implications for the United States.

On the national level, the polycentric and geocentric development of multinational enterprises may produce circumstances unfavorable to home-country needs. These include industrial "hollowing," ethnocentric exploitation by foreign multinationals, and a reduction of national security.

Industrial hollowing is particularly problematic because, first, it usually involves a painful process of industrial adjustments through pressures for lower wages (lower standards of living) from the unemployed. Second, competent managers (managerial know-how) and engineers (technological know-how) disappear if the hollowing continues for a long period. The latter requires investment from foreign multinationals to stimulate the recovery of the "hollow" industrial sectors. Issues relating to national security inevitably arise, given the current political system based on national sovereignty.

Under these circumstances, a decision is eventually required on the proper balance between short-term resource allocation and long-term resource allocation. This judgment must come from a long-term perspective on national and global industrial structures. A critical question is whether this perspective is an ethnocentric one or balanced between polycentric and geocentric views. For instance, the Japanese vision is said to be that of creating a knowledge-intensive industry. The question is how this vision includes the rest of the world in relation to the Japanese knowledge-intensive industry.

This leads us to propose the establishment of a committee in charge of international industrial structure, whose job it is to envision for the world an ideal industrial/postindustrial global structure. The job of the committee should not contradict the U.S. premise against any government being involved directly in developing certain industries, nor should it keep its hands entirely off industrial policy. When a vision is inspiring, it can do wonders, as we know from Japanese experience.

The differences in orientation between Japan and the United States stem in part from the differences in presumptions about action takers *(shutai)* and their relations. It may not be practical to try to change these premises. Rather, we should accumulate our experience and know-how to work with the differences.

In writing this concluding section, I have tried to describe the ideal future while taking into account the differences in premise and concept between Japan and the United States. Because of this, the ideas expressed here are different from ideas in general at least in the following points:

1. The main path of development is localization or a polycentric path. This idea comes from respecting the local premises and cultural orientations of the host nation. Along the path of localization, hybridization is proposed. This is of critical importance, but hybridization can only be pursued from a local perspective.

2. We must build a new corporate system in which contributions to results are rewarded in the form of value to the contributor. There are two difficult terms here: *results* and *value to the contributor.* Results must be evaluated from both polycentric and geocentric points of view. Value to the contributor is determined by the culture of the contributor. The common, practical denominator in the present world is pecuniary. However, the position of money in the total value function, and the relationship of money with other values in particular, depends upon the culture of the contributor. Cross-cultural interface must be managed with these constraints taken into consideration.

3. The main idea centers around vision building. The vision must be a workable mosaic of different premises. The United States built a new culture out of a melting pot of cultures, but at the sacrifice of minorities. We should look for a mosaic harmony of world cultures.

BIBLIOGRAPHY

Drucker, Peter. "What We Can Learn from Japanese Management." *Harvard Business Review* (March–April 1971).

Hamaguchi, Eshun, ed. *Gendai no Esupuri: Shudanshugi* [Present-Day Esprit: Groupism]. Tokyo: Shibundo, 1980.

Hamaguchi, Eshun, and Kumon, Shumpei, eds. *Nipponteki Shudanshugi: Sono Shika o Tou* [Japanese Groupism: Questioning Its Value]. Tokyo: Yuhikaku, 1982.

Harnett, D. L., and Cummings, L. L. *Bargaining Behavior: An International Study.* Houston, Texas: Dame Publications, 1980.

Hayashi, Kichiro. *Ibunka Intahfeisu Kanri* [Cross-Cultural Interface Management]. Tokyo: Yuhikaku, 1985.

————. "Corporate Planning Practices in Japanese Multinationals." *Academy of Management Journals* 21, no. 2 (1978):211–226. Also Research Roundup in *The International Executive* 20, no. 3 (1978):7–9.

Hsu, Francis. "Psycho-Social Homeostasis and Jen," *American Anthropology*, 1971.

————. *Postulates of United States Culture; The Study of Literate Civilizations.* New York: Holt, Rinehart and Winston, 1968.

Kumon, Shumpei. *Shakai Sisutemuron* [Theory of Social Systems]. Tokyo: Nippon Keizai Shimbun, 1978.

Maruyama, Magoroh. "Heterogenistics and Morphogenetics: Toward a New Concept of the Scientific." *Theory and Society* 5, no. 1 (1978):75–96.

————. "Mindscapes: How to Understand Specific Situations in Multicultural Management." Mimeographed, 1986.

————. "Mindscapes and Science Theories." *Current Anthropology* 21, no. 5 (1980):589–599.

————. "Mindscapes, Management, Business Policy, and Public Policy." *Academy of Management Review* 7, no. 4 (1982):612–619.

McDonough, Culbert. *The Invisible War: Pursuing Self-Interest at Work.* New York: Wiley, 1980.

Nakane, Chie. *Japanese Society.* Berkeley: University of California Press, 1970.

Appendix

QUESTIONNAIRE ON EPISTEMOLOGICAL DIFFERENCES BETWEEN CULTURES

INSTRUCTIONS

Here are 28 statements that describe attitudes, beliefs, assumptions and inclinations in thoughts, etc.

Would you read each statement together with its introductory remark, and ask yourself how agreeable it reads to you personally. Please consider this in terms of how you view it at the moment, say, in your work circumstances. Please take it as an exercise and not as expressions of your absolute or permanent attitudes or beliefs in any way. Also, each of the 28 statements needs to be responded to separately and independently even if some statements under the same introductory remark may appear to be pairs reverse to one another.

Then would you place one of 0, 1, 2, 3, 4 and 5 in the space provided on the separate response sheet, based on the following:

0—The statement is not too meaningful or is too uncomfortable to respond to adequately.
1—You feel very disagreeable to the statement.
2—You feel disagreeable to the statement.
3—You cannot determine your feelings one way or the other about the statement.
4—You feel agreeable to the statement.
5—You feel very agreeable to the statement.

Please do not analyze the statements. Respond to them quickly, inserting the number that first feels right to you. Try not to be influenced by exceptional incidents. Please write your comment on the separate response/comment sheet to complement your response including your choice of 0 if you will.

It is important that your response is not your observation of what is going on currently in the organization you are familiar with. Instead, it should be your own feelings and personal preference from your own perspective and position in the organization.

Thank you for your time and consideration.

STATEMENTS

[A] People take varied attitudes toward uncertainties. Suppose the organization you are a part of currently faces important legislative uncertainties which will affect your organization's business. In facing such uncertainties, you may think that you should collect as much information as possible to predict what in fact will most likely happen to the legislation, while you may also think that it will be important to better prepare the organization to meet any possible outcome of the legislation through some restructuring such as better interpersonal relations, more flexible policies, etc.

(1) In facing uncertainties, flexibility on your part naturally is important, but even more important is predictability, so that you should analyze the elements of uncertainties to know them better and to control, if possible, some of the important elements.

(2) When you face uncertainties, usually it is more likely that you can neither predict nor control the elements of uncertainties. Thus we should allocate our limited resources to developing programs to create flexibility as well as preparedness for facing any unexpected outcome.

[B] Each of us holds some concept and feelings about the future. We may or may not be conscious of such concept and feelings, however. Please think about it a moment and react to the following concepts and feelings of the future.

(3) The future is what we create. We should develop clear visions and plans to bring about our future by ourselves.

(4) I do not deny visions and plans necessarily, but I still feel that the future basically occurs by itself. There simply are too many things to control to create our own future.

[C] Let us think for the moment of interpersonal conflict and its resolution. Specifically, we have a question of contention and eventual confrontation as a method of conflict resolution. Assuming you disagree with your friendly colleague in the task force on the priority of the action plan which involves your beliefs and values, think of the tendency of your general attitude regarding the method of resolution.

(5) I would try to resolve the disagreement under these circumstances in all the possible ways other than the contention which may eventually lead to confrontation, because contention or confrontation would be in itself an embarrassment and harmful to not only this relationship but also my general interpersonal relations one way or another eventually.

If this statement is in reference to my workplace, my feelings are

_____

If this statement is in reference to my residential community, my feelings are _____

(6) Interpersonal conflict is part of our life. Efforts to ignore it and/or to keep it from surfacing could develop other even worse problems. It would be better to put it on the table and face it openly to look for a fair solution.

If this statement is in reference to my workplace, my feelings are

_____

If this statement is in reference to my residential community, my feelings are _____

[D] Interpersonal relations at the workplace are based on work relations designed to fulfill business objectives. Thus, they are basically meant to be instrumental to some business ends rather than to be intrinsic objectives by themselves. However, such work relations are known to be painted or influenced by the closeness, or lack thereof, of intrinsic personal relations developed over time.

(7) As a principle, one should try to have work or business relations separated from personal relations. This does not mean to deny friendship developed out of work or business relations, so far as you keep it separate from work and business.

(8) It is not always possible to separate work or business relations from friendly relations. Business may result from some good friendship. One should positively cultivate closer personal relations in work or business either for friendship or for business.

(9) Some of the most gratifying friendships I have experienced came originally out of my work or business relations.

[E] Suppose you face the need to prioritize the two courses of action, A and B, to which you will devote a great deal of your time and effort for the coming 12 months. You prefer to do Project A to B because Project A provides definitely better experience for your personal growth and career, but you have a feeling that the organization you work for would benefit somewhat more if you chose Project B.

(10) I would give priority to Project A unless I clearly needed to do otherwise.

(11) I believe that it would be my duty to place my organization's interest above my personal interest in this case.

[F] This section is to ask about your views on the organizational choice-making processes, particularly important choices to be made for the organization. In responding to the following, assume that you are the executive officer in a position to make such choices as you wish.

(12) Important choices need to be made through some participative process of consensus formation within the organization.

This is because important choices made are bound to influence some people in the organization adversely, and these people need to be given some special concession or consideration in one way or another. _____

(13) Given the organizational structure, there must be someone in the organization who is supposed to know most about the choices in question which fall within the realm of his authority and responsibility. He should be the one making such choices, but if he did not have the answer, he should hire an expert consultant on the matter.

[G] The concept and meaning of planning differ substantially among people. Respond to the following within the context of the organization you work for or are familiar with. However, please do not answer in terms of what is presently in the organization. Instead, please answer in terms of what you feel should be. Please try to respond to each of the following independently of other seemingly related statements.

(14) Long-range planning should be a vehicle for informational exchange to form a common vision for the future to be shared by the participants. It is not so much of developing a strategic program of action to be used as a tool of control.

(15) Long-range planning should provide a continuous process of forums to develop strategic programs of action. Thus, such programs should be used as tools by which strategic actions are to be monitored and controlled.

(16) In project planning it would be better if you set a clearly defined skeleton but not too detailed a program. It would be preferable if you dealt with details case by case as they occur.

(17) Planning is to maximize the feasibility of attaining the optimally set goals. It is only logical to produce carefully detailed programs of action that are most likely to achieve the goals.

(18) We can always change or modify our plans if necessitated by environmental or circumstantial change.

(19) Once we developed good plans, we should stick to them to the best possible extent even under environmental or circumstantial change.

[H] A good balance between the organizational objectives, e.g. profit, etc., and the objectives of the individuals comprising the organization, e.g. satisfaction, personal growth, pay, etc., more often than not promotes organizational objectives. Under certain organizational culture the members of the organization may build a familial community well beyond the level of limited contact and of business-like relationships. In this context, how agreeable would you be to each of the following?

(20) I believe that community building in the organization should have in itself as much value as any organizational objectives.

(21) The development of such an internal community need not be denied or, in some cases, should be even encouraged so far as it would serve for the achievement of organizational objectives. But it would be secondary to original organizational objectives.

[I] You need to administer and organize managers on the jobs one way or another to attain organizational objectives. This much is agreed widely, but beyond this, there is a variation in the principles employed. The following are just a few examples of such principles. How agreeable would you be, given your perspective and position, with each of the following statements?

(22) One approach is through enculturating and assimilating the managers into certain desired orientations, values and attitudes based on the history, culture and other essential characteristics of the organization. Once enculturated and assimilated, the managers need not be regulated too tightly because they would decide and act properly and effectively within an expected range of standards and behavior. _____

In this approach, it is reasonable to expect that the managers are aware of what is going on in the reality of the organization and to be alert to form good judgment for action in their jobs since any organization is alive, dynamic and constantly changing. _____

(23) It would be essential to provide each person on the job with a clear and detailed job description and to let him know well his functions and responsibilities if you should wish to control people on the jobs together as an effective group. _____

In this approach, however, he should be allowed to exercise complete freedom and judgment to fulfill his expected responsibilities within his assigned authorities and responsibilities. _____

[J] Social or organizational issues arise almost by definition when people disagree with one another in their views over the issues. Why do you think these interpersonal differences in views occur and how should such differences be dealt with? Please evaluate the following two approaches.

(24) Interpersonal differences in views over social or organizational issues often consist of errors in information or judgment held by the persons involved. Thus, primary efforts should be directed to collecting additional objective information relevant to the solution of the issues.

(25) Interpersonal differences in views over social or organizational issues comprise vital information in themselves. Thus, different views, including minor views, should be carefully synthesized to reveal new dimensions of the issues.

[K] Problems may develop in our family, workplace, etc. Our attitude toward problems depends upon the circumstances under which they have occurred mostly, but it is also true that people take different attitudes to similar problems under similar circumstances. What is your reaction to the following attitudes?

(26) The root causes of the problem may exist either in yourself, in the environment, or in both. But it would be better if you emphasized the possibility of the problem originating in you one way or another, and solved the problem primarily from that point of view.

(27) When problems occur, they are most likely to have come from unfavorable environmental occurrences. _____

Thus, we would be better off if we either tried to influence our environment the best we could, or solved such problems through at least working on the environmental circumstances. _____

(28) A problem is a problem only if you make it so. You should not easily accept the problem and own it.

Thank you indeed for your patience and cooperation!

February 26, 1986

Dear

It was very good indeed to meet you a few months ago. Your participation and assistance made my part of the program certainly more enjoyable and fruitful for me, which I appreciated.

I am wondering if you could give me an additional help by responding to the questionnaire enclosed which might take half an hour or a little more. This is a major part of my ongoing research, and your participation would be appreciated much more than you might imagine.

In this research, I am trying to identify some basic epistemological differences, if any, between peoples in different cultures in the way they make decisions in the organizational setting. I believe that such differences, if any, should be considered in designing and managing cross-cultural interface in a culturally mixed organization, be it the United Nations, a foreign business subsidiary, or even in business negotiation. I would be delighted to send you my findings if you indicated your interest on your response sheet. It would be helpful if your response reached me in March, but I still would like to receive it even at a later date.

Thank you indeed for your time and kind consideration, and with warmest regards,

Sincerely yours,

Kichiro Hayashi, Ph.D.
Professor of International Management

PERSONAL DATA SHEET

Your name: _____ Age:_____

Home address: _____

Home telephone number:_____

Your affiliation:_____

Position:_____

Office address:_____

_____

Office telephone number:_____

Your work experience:_____years

Main country in which you were brought up:_____

Length of time living outside your main country:_____years

in_____(country), _____years in_____

_____, _____years in_____,

_____years in_____

Work experience (training included) in cross-cultural organizations:_____years

Student experience outside your main country:_____ years

(ages from _____ to _____)

Your major area of study in the last school you graduated from:

_____

Any information relevant to your cultural identity (optional):____

_____

RESPONSE/COMMENT SHEET

(1)_____   (2)_____   (3)_____   (4)_____   (5)_____

_____ (6)_____ _____ (7)_____   (8)_____   (9)_____

(10)_____   (11)_____   (12)_____ _____ (13)_____

(14)_____   (15)_____   (16)_____   (17)_____   (18)_____

(19)_____   (20)_____   (21)_____   (22)_____   (23)_____

_____ (24)_____   (25)_____   (26)_____   (27)_____

_____ (28)_____

Please write any comment below with relevant statement numbers in the parenthesis:

(   )_____

_____

(   )_____

_____

(   )_____

_____

(   )_____

_____

(   )_____

_____

(   )_____

_____

(   )_____

_____

(   )_____

_____

(   )_____

_____

(   )_____

_____

Please write on the back if you run out of space.

Please mail your response/comment sheet and personal data sheet to:

        Dr. Kichiro Hayashi
        Professor of International Management
        Aoyama Gakuin University
        4-4-25 Shibuya, Shibuya-Ku, Tokyo
        Japan   150

INDEX